Jennifer,

I think you may
get more out of from
these writings than I
will.

If you ever decide to
enter the "helping"
profession - counseling,
social work, family
therapy give one
a call if you'd
like of [signature]

The Structure of Sociological Theory

The Dorsey Series in Sociology
Editor
ROBIN M. WILLIAMS, JR.   *Cornell University*

The Structure of Sociological Theory

JONATHAN H. TURNER
University of California, Riverside

Revised Edition

1978

 The Dorsey Press Homewood, Illinois 60430
Irwin-Dorsey Limited Georgetown, Ontario L7G 4B3

ISBN 0-256-02061-2
Library of Congress Catalog Card No. 77–085782
Printed in the United States of America

1 2 3 4 5 6 7 8 9 0 K 5 4 3 2 1 0 9 8

To my wife, Sandy

PREFACE

In this revised edition, I have sought to correct earlier shortcomings and to expand the coverage of scholars and topics. I have done this in several ways: First, the discussion of the historical antecedents of each theoretical orientation is greatly expanded. My goal is not to seek to improve upon the brilliant analyses of Robert Nisbet in his *The Sociological Tradition* or Lewis Coser in his *Masters of Sociological Thought*, but I have included discussion of all the major historical figures in sociology. As before, these figures are analyzed with an eye to what they have contributed to the emergence of the four major theoretical perspectives in sociology—functionalism, conflict theorizing, the exchange perspective, interactionism, phenomenology, and ethnomethodology.

Second, I have included discussion of more contemporary scholars. For example, the work of Richard Emerson in the exchange perspective and of Ralph H. Turner in the interactionist orientation are given detailed analyses.

Third, each of the four major perspectives is given similar treatment: The emergence of the perspective in question is first analyzed; then two or more variants of this perspective and prominent proponents of these variants are discussed; and finally, an assessment of the future of a perspective is discussed. Each section thus contains four chapters—one on the emergence, two on contemporary variants, and one on a perspective's future.

Fourth, I have reorganized the sections. This organization seeks to move from macro to micro theorizing in sociology. Thus, the book opens with a discussion of functionalism, moves through an analysis of conflict and exchange theory, and ends with chapters on interactionism, phenomenology, and ethnomethodology.

Fifth, I have made an effort to strengthen weak chapters and to make amends for obvious omissions in the first edition. I have totally rewritten the chapters on symbolic interactionism and ethnomethodology. I have added four completely new chapters on the future of each perspective, a new chapter on phenomenology, and a new introductory chapter on theory. All other chapters have been extensively revised. And as I mentioned, new scholars are discussed, but in particular I should note that Max Weber's ideas are to be found throughout the book. I had omitted discussion of this intellectual giant in the first edition, because his work did not inspire any one particular perspective. This was a mistake, for Weber influenced virtually all theoretical perspectives. I have thus discussed his ideas when they appear to have influenced the course of sociological theorizing.

And finally, I should emphasize that the intent of the book remains the same as before—to explore the question: In what diverse ways have sociologists attempted to understand how patterns of social organization are created, maintained, and changed?

Acknowledgments

I would like to thank Ira E. Robinson, John Scanzoni, Barbara A. Goodnight, and John R. De Martini, who provided the critical reviews of the first edition which served me well in revising this book. I should acknowledge once again the special efforts of Robin M. Williams, Jr., my former teacher and Dorsey Series editor. His insistence upon clear, balanced, and fair exposition is appreciated. Finally, let me thank again my typist of eight years, Clara Dean, who has finally mastered my handwriting and who knows how to spell, punctuate, and achieve subject-verb agreement better than I.

December 1977   J. H. TURNER

PREFACE TO
FIRST EDITION

In this volume I have sought to analyze the historical roots and contemporary profile of the four dominant paradigms of sociological theorizing: functionalism, conflict theory, interactionism, and exchange theory. I have also attempted, in the last chapter, to introduce the reader to the ethnomethodological alternative to these dominant paradigms.

There are several points of emphasis running through my analysis. Appreciation of these can perhaps make each chapter more readable. First, social theory must ultimately address the Hobbesian "problem of order": How and why is society possible? Phrased more scientifically this problem becomes one of discerning the conditions under which different social processes and patterns of social organization are likely to occur.

Second, in addressing this fundamental problem all social theory reveals—sometimes only implicitly—certain characteristics. All theories present a substantive "image" of society, of what the world is "really" like. All theories consider certain causal relations more important than others. All theories imply certain methodological strategies. And all theories reveal key propositions. In reviewing sociology's dominant paradigms, I have attempted to highlight these characteristics.

Third, I have sought to analyze social theory from the criteria of science. This analysis has not involved a mechanical comparison of each theory with the canons of scientific protocol. Such an exercise is sterile and futile, since all social theory can be found deficient in these terms. Rather, I have addressed a more meaningful set of questions: What *potential* does a theory offer for eventual conversion into scientific theory? What must be done to realize this potential?

And fourth, in Chapter 16, I outline some of the basic issues that social theory has ignored. Only after the detailed exposition and analysis of sociology's dominant paradigms can these issues be exposed. I offer my assessment of these issues with the hope that they will stimulate conceptual effort in some long neglected, and yet critical, areas.

Acknowledgments

The particular form of theoretical analysis in this book is the result of my fortunate exposure to a few distinguished scholars. Each might consider my analysis of social theory to violate his preferences; and yet, the pages to follow represent a mixture of learning experiences with a diverse group of teachers. While each will be horrified with some aspects of my analysis, I would nevertheless like to acknowledge my long-standing debt to them. Tomatsu Shibutani taught me the importance of phrasing arguments propositionally, but I am afraid he will be somewhat dismayed by my analysis of interactionism. Walter Buckley first exposed me to the broad range of sociological theory, but will disagree with my portrayal of functional theory. Donald R. Cressey first emphasized that in "science" one should state arguments succinctly and not waste time pontificating on issues; I have always tried to follow this dictum, but I suspect I will always have a tendency to embellish discussion. Robin M. Williams, Jr., reaffirmed Professor Shibutani's earlier concern with stating arguments propositionally, while expanding the conceptual base first laid by Professor Buckley. To William Friedland, who reinforced Professor Cressey's dictum, I owe a no-nonsense desire to get to the guts of a conceptual perspective.

I would also like to thank Robin Williams—the Sociology Series editor for The Dorsey Press—for engaging in two separate line by line reviews of the manuscript during its various stages of development. Supplementing these two reviews have been the perceptive and face-saving comments of Professors Everett K. Wilson and Jerald T. Hage. I appreciate their critical remarks.

In preparing a manuscript, many embarrassing details are overlooked by the author. I would like to thank my typist and editor, Clara Dean, who despite all my efforts to the contrary produced an intelligible manuscript.

J.H.T.

CONTENTS

The Social System. Elaboration of System Requisites. The Informational Hierarchy of Control. Generalized Media of Exchange. Parsons on Social Change. Persistent Criticisms of Parsonian Functionalism: *Criticisms of Parsons' Image of Society. The Logical Criticisms of Requisite Functionalism.* Talcott Parsons: An Overview.

Theories of the Middle Range. Merton's "Paradigm" for Functional Analysis. A Protocol for Executing Functional Analysis: *An Illustration of Merton's Protocol: Political Machines in America. Another Illustration of Merton's Protocol: "Social Structure and Anomie."* Merton's Functional Strategy: An Overview.

Is Functional Analysis a Myth? The Functional Approach. Problems and Prospects of Functional Analysis: *Logical Problems of Functionalism. Substantive Problems of Functionalism.* Summary and Conclusion.

PART II
CONFLICT THEORIZING

Marx's and Simmel's Legacy: *Contrasting Intellectual Purposes and Goals. Contrasting Visions about the Nature of Social Conflict. Contrasting Conceptualization of Variables. Contrasting Theoretical Propositions.* The Emergence of Conflict Theory: An Overview.

Dahrendorf's Image of the Social Order. Criticisms of the Dialectical Conflict Model: *Problems in the Causal Analysis. Methodological Problems.* From Utopia to Where? A Concluding Comment.

Images of Social Organization. Propositions on Conflict Processes: *The Causes of Conflict. The Intensity of Conflict. The Violence of Conflict. The Duration of Conflict. The Functions of Social Conflict.* Strategies for Reformulating Coser's Scheme.

PART IV
INTERACTIONIST THEORIZING

PART V
PHENOMENOLOGICAL AND
ETHNOMETHODOLOGICAL
THEORIZING

1

SOCIOLOGICAL
THEORIZING

THE BASIC QUESTION

In the 17th century Thomas Hobbes proclaimed the natural state of human society to be one of "continual fear, and danger of violent death; and the life of man, solitary, poor, nasty, brutish, and short."[1] Left to themselves, humans were viewed by Hobbes as continually in pursuit of power and profit and as governed primarily by motives of self-interest. In light of this situation and its potential for generating a social world of perpetual war and strife, Hobbes was led to ask: How can some semblance of social order and organization be created and maintained?

While few contemporary sociologists would accept his assumptions about the natural state of humans, Hobbes can be given credit for touching upon the most fundamental question facing sociological theorizing: How and why is society possible? To phrase this question, or "the problem of order" as it has become known, it is not necessary to impute motives to humans in their natural state, nor is it essential to view the natural social order as an incessant war. Rather, it is only necessary to display a curiosity about how patterns of social organization are created, maintained, and changed.

This curiosity about the "problem of order" has been translated into a large number of specific theoretical questions concerning how and

---

[1] Thomas Hobbes, *Leviathan* (New York: Macmillan Co., 1947); originally published in 1651.

1

why various types of social structure, in all their diverse forms are built up, maintained, changed, and broken down. Whether investigation focuses on a small face-to-face group, a restless crowd or mob, a large and complex organization, or an entire society, sociological theory is concerned with developing principles that will allow increased understanding of social events.

The vehicle of all understanding in science is theory. Theory is a way of answering the question, "Why?" Why is this process operative? Why is one structure prevalent and not another? Why do humans act in certain ways? The goal of all science, then, is to develop plausible theory. For only through theory can Hobbes' basic question about the "problem of order" be given an answer. And thus, before exploring the structure of sociological theory, it is essential that the general features of theory be examined.

WHAT IS THEORY?

Theory is a mental activity. It is a process of developing ideas that can allow scientists to explain why events should occur. Theory is constructed with several basic elements or building blocks:[2] (1) concepts, (2) variables, (3) statements, and (4) formats. While there are many divergent claims about what theory is, or should be, these four elements are common to all of them. An understanding of what each represents is thus the first step in the analysis of social theory.

Concepts: The Basic Building Blocks of Theory

Theories are built from concepts. Most generally, concepts denote or point to phenomena; in so doing they isolate features of the world

---

[2] Among several fine introductory works on the nature of scientific theory, the discussion in this chapter draws heavily upon Paul Davidson Reynolds' excellent, *A Primer in Theory Construction* (New York: Bobbs-Merrill Co., 1971). For excellent introductory works, see Arthur L. Stinchcombe, *Constructing Social Theories* (New York: Harcourt, Brace, & World, 1968), pp. 3–56; Karl R. Popper, *The Logic of Scientific Discovery* (New York: Harper & Row, 1959); David Willer and Murray Webster, Jr., "Theoretical Concepts and Observables," *American Sociological Review* 35 (August 1970): 748–57; Hans Zetterberg, *On Theory and Verification in Sociology*, 3d ed. (Totowa, N.J.: Bedminister Press, 1965); Gerald Hage, *Techniques and Problems of Theory Construction in Sociology* (New York: John Wiley, 1972); Walter L. Wallace, *The Logic of Science in Sociology* (Chicago: Aldine, 1971); Robert Dubin, *Theory Building* (New York: Free Press, 1969); Jack Gibbs, *Sociological Theory Construction* (Hinsdale, Ill.: Dryden Press, 1972); Herbert M. Blalock, Jr., *Theory Construction: From Verbal to Mathematical Formulations* (Englewood Cliffs, N.J.: Prentice-Hall, 1969); Nicholas C. Mullins, *The Art of Theory: Construction and Use* (New York: Harper & Row, 1971).

which are considered, for the moment at hand, important. For example, notions of atoms, protons, neutrons, and the like are concepts, pointing to and isolating phenomena for certain analytical purposes. Familiar sociological concepts would include group, formal organization, power, stratification, interaction, norm, role, status, and socialization. Each term is a concept that embraces aspects of the social world which are considered essential for a particular purpose.

Concepts are constructed from definitions. A definition is a system of terms, such as the sentences of a language, the symbols of logic, or the notation of mathematics, that inform investigators as to the phenomenon denoted by a concept. For example, the concept, "conflict," only has meaning when it is defined. One possible definition might be:[3] "Conflict equals interactions among social units in which one unit seeks to prevent the other from realizing its goals." Such a definition allows scientists to visualize the phenomena that is denoted by the concept. It allows them, they hope, to "see the same thing" and to understand what it is that is being studied.

Thus, concepts that are useful in building theory have a special characteristic: They strive to communicate a uniform meaning to all those who use them. However, since concepts are frequently expressed with the words of everyday language, it is difficult to avoid words that connote varied meanings—and hence point to different phenomena—for different groups of scientists. It is for this reason that many concepts in science are expressed in technical or more "neutral" languages, such as the symbols of mathematics. In sociology, expression of concepts in such special languages is sometimes not only impossible, but also undesirable. Hence, the verbal symbols used to develop a concept must be defined as precisely as is possible in order that they point to the same phenomena for all investigators.[4] While perfect consensus may never be attained with conventional language, a body of theory rests on the premise that scientists will do their best to define concepts unambiguously. Not to do so, or to give up because the task is difficult, is to invite conceptual chaos and thereby to preclude the accumulation of theoretical knowledge.

The concepts of theory reveal a special characteristic: *abstractness.*[5]

---

[3] This definition is only for illustrative purposes and should not be considered as wholly adequate.

[4] For more detailed work on concept formation, see Carl G. Hempel, *Fundamentals of Concept Formation in Empirical Science* (Chicago: University of Chicago Press, 1952).

[5] For a useful and insightful critique of sociology's inability to generate abstract concepts and theory, see David and Judith Willer, *Systematic Empiricism: Critique of a Pseudoscience* (Englewood Cliffs, N.J.: Prentice-Hall, 1973).

Some concepts pertain to concrete phenomena at specific times and locations. Other more abstract concepts point to phenomena that are not related to concrete times or locations. For example, in the context of small-group research, *concrete concepts* would refer to the persistent interactions of particular individuals, whereas an *abstract* conceptualization of such phenomena might refer to those general properties of face-to-face groups which are not tied to particular individuals interacting at a specified time and location. Abstract concepts are thus not tied to a specific context, whereas concrete concepts are. In building theory, abstract concepts are crucial. They transcend particular events or situations and point to the common properties of similar events and situations. The importance of abstractness can perhaps be illustrated by the fact that people watched apples fall from trees for centuries, but real understanding of this phenomenon came only with the more abstract concept of gravity, which allowed for many similar occurrences to be visualized and incorporated into a theoretical statement that explained much more than why apples should fall from trees.

Abstractness poses a problem: How is it possible to attach abstract concepts to the ongoing, everyday world of events? While it is essential that many of the concepts of theory transcend specific times and places, it is equally critical that there be procedures for making these abstract concepts relevant to observable situations and occurrences. After all, the utility of an abstract concept can only be demonstrated when the concept is brought to bear on some specific empirical problem encountered by investigators; otherwise, concepts remain detached from the very processes they are supposed to help investigators understand. For this reason, abstract concepts should be accompanied by a series of statements known as *operational definitions*, which are sets of procedural instructions telling investigators how to go about discerning phenomena in the real world which are denoted by an abstract concept. It is thus through these kinds of definitions that the problem of how to relate abstract concepts to empirical events is resolved. For highly abstract concepts embracing a wide spectrum of empirical phenomena, it is usually necessary to have a large number of operational definitions—each one describing procedures for discerning a particular situation or event encompassed by the concept. In fact, the more operational definitions attached to an abstract concept, the more likely is the concept to serve many different investigators seeking to comprehend the complex operation of events in the empirical world.

In sum, then, concepts are the building blocks of theory. In turn, concepts are constructed from systems of definitions. Of particular importance for theory are the more abstract concepts that are not tied to particular temporal and spatial settings. Yet such concepts must specify procedures, through the vehicle of operational definitions, for their application to concrete events in the world.

Variables as an Important Type of Concept

When used to build theory, two general types of concepts can be distinguished:[6] (1) those that simply label phenomena and (2) those that refer to phenomena that differ in degree. Concepts that merely label phenomena would include such commonly employed abstractions as "dog," "cat," "group," "social class," "star," and the like. When stated in this way, none of these concepts reveal the ways in which the phenomena they denote vary in terms of properties such as size, weight, density, velocity, cohesiveness, or any of the many criteria used to inform investigators about differences in degree among phenomena. It is for this reason that scientific theory typically utilizes concepts that refer to the *variable properties* of such phenomena as dogs, cats, groups, social classes, and stars. These kinds of concepts allow investigators to distinguish different events and situations from each other in terms of the degree to which they reveal some important property, such as size, weight, density, cohesiveness, and the like. For example, to note that an aggregate of people is a "group" does not indicate what type of group it is or how it compares with other groups in terms of such criteria as size, differentiation, and cohesiveness. Thus, the concepts of scientific theory should denote the *variable* features of the world. For, indeed, to understand events requires that scientists visualize how variation in one phenomenon is related to variation in another. However, this transformation of concepts into full-blown theory requires their incorporation into theoretical statements.

Theoretical Statements

Concepts are related to each other with theoretical statements. By itself, a concept simply points to the existence of a phenomenon. A variable concept does somewhat better in that it allows investigators

---

[6] Reynolds, *Primer in Theory Construction*, p. 57; see also Stinchcombe, *Constructing Social Theories*, pp. 38–47 for a discussion of how concepts not only point to variable properties of phenomena, but to the interaction effects of interrelated phenomena. For an interesting discussion of the importance of variable concepts and for guidelines on how to use them, see Hage, *Techniques and Problems of Theory Construction*.

to see and appreciate variations in the phenomenon. But science must do more than point out and describe variations in the world. The ultimate goal is to understand how phenomena or events are *related to each other.* For example, Einstein's famous formula, $E = mc^2$, allowed physicists to see and understand the relationship between energy, light, and matter. This formula was a theoretical statement. It linked concepts to each other and informed scientists of their relationship. The concept of energy simply said: Energy exists. The concept of matter (m) asserted: Matter exists. The concept of light (c) did the same thing: Light exists. The statement, $E = mc^2$, linked these together and provided new insights into the nature of matter, light, and energy.

To take a more sociological example, the concept of "conflict" asserts that varying forms of hostile interactions exist in the social world. The concept of "social unit" reveals that individuals are organized into different types of collective patterns. The concept of "solidarity" denotes the fact that social units evidence different degrees of internal cohesion and unity. The following theoretical statement allows scientists to see the *relation* among these concepts: "The greater the degree of conflict among social units, the greater the degree of solidarity in each unit." Several features of this statement should be emphasized. It is abstract, because it does not talk about a specific conflict among particular units in a given time and place. It transcends time and space. And it is a theoretical statement, because it asserts a relationship among three social phenomena: "conflict," "social units," and "solidarity."[7]

Of course, the statement may not be true or valid. With operational definitions, however, an indicator of each concept in the real world can be found. The relationship can be tested, and if confirmed, then the theoretical statement has increased plausibility.

Rarely do theoretical statements stand alone, as in this example. They are usually organized into systems of statements. Thus, just as concepts are related to each other, so statements are often interrelated. This has led to a concern with the form of theoretical statements.

The Forms of Theory

Theoretical statements may be organized into a number of different formats.[8] While many arguments for and against different formats can

---

[7] This example borrowed from Georg Simmel, whose work will be examined in a later chapter.

[8] For readable discussions of these various formats, see Reynolds, *Primer in Theory Construction,* pp. 83–114; Zetterberg, *On Theory and Verification in Sociology,* pp. 87–113; Blalock, *Theory Construction.*

be made, it is more appropriate here simply to argue that theoretical statements should be *systematically organized* in accordance with logical rules of the theorist's choosing. There is, however, no more difficult task in the building of theories than providing for the systematic organization of statements. In sociology there are a great many important abstract statements, as well as empirical generalizations capable of being converted into theoretical statements, but their organization into logically rigorous formats has proven very difficult. At this juncture, it is too time consuming to list the reasons why these difficulties exist, and it is not helpful to indict the discipline for failing to be more systematic. Rather, it is more useful simply to note how the challenge of the task may be met. As the substantive perspectives of subsequent chapters unfold, an effort will be made to assess the extent to which the theoretical statements are amenable to incorporation into more systematic formats and, equally important, some general and tentative suggestions for how such systematic formats should be constructed will be offered.

Unless theoretical statements can be ordered systematically, they cannot be efficiently tested. Without some sense of the interrelationships among statements, each and every statement would have to be tested independently. But when statements are organized, bearing clear-cut relations with one another, the testing of a few crucial statements can shed light on the plausibility of other statements. There are two major formats for ordering theoretical statements in the social sciences: (1) axiomatic and (2) causal process.[9]

Axiomatic formats. The axiomatic organization of theoretical statements takes, in general, this form: First, it contains a set of concepts. Some of the concepts are highly abstract; others, more concrete. Second, there is always a set of existence statements that describe those situations in which concepts and relational statements apply. These existence statements make up what is usually called the *scope conditions* of the theory. Third, and most nearly unique to the axiomatic format, relational statements are stated in a hierarchical order. At the top of the hierarchy are *axioms*, or highly abstract statements, from which *all* other theoretical statements are derived. These latter statements are usually called

---

[9] These labels have had fairly standard meaning among those concerned with the forms of theory construction. The utility of the axiomatic form in sociology has been urged by many, including Zetterberg (*Theory and Verification in Sociology*) and George C. Homans, "Sociological Theory" in *Handbook of Sociology*, ed. E. Faris (Chicago: Rand McNally, 1964), and *The Nature of Social Science* (New York: Harcourt, Brace & World, 1967). The causal process form has been recently urged by Reynolds (*Primer in Theory Construction*) and W. Buckley, *Sociology and Modern Systems Theory* (Englewood Cliffs, N.J.: Prentice-Hall, Inc., 1967), particularly pp. 62–81.

propositions and are logically derived in accordance with varying rules from the more abstract axioms. The selection of axioms is, in reality, a somewhat arbitrary matter, but usually they are selected with these criteria in mind: (a) The axioms should be consistent with one another, although they do not have to be logically interrelated; (b) axioms should be highly abstract; (c) they should state relationships among abstract concepts; (d) these relationships should be "law-like" in that the more concrete propositions derived from them have not been disproved by empirical investigation, and (e) the axioms should have an "intuitive" plausibility in that their truth appears "self-evident."

The end result of tight conformity to axiomatic principles is an inventory or set of interrelated propositions, each derivable from at least one axiom and usually more abstract propositions. There are several advantages to this form of theory construction: First, highly abstract concepts, encompassing a broad range of related phenomena, can be employed. These abstract concepts do not have to be *directly* measurable, since they are logically tied to more specific and measurable propositions, which, when empirically tested, can *indirectly* subject the more abstract propositions and the axioms to empirical tests. Thus, by virtue of this logical interrelatedness of the propositions and axioms, research can be more efficient, since the failure to refute a particular proposition lends credence to other propositions and to the axioms. Second, the use of a logical system to derive propositions from abstract axioms can generate many interesting propositions that point to previously unknown or unanticipated relationships among social phenomena.

Causal process formats. The *causal process* form of theory construction takes a somewhat different tack: First, like axiomatic theory, it contains both abstract and concrete concepts, with appropriate operational definitions. Second, and again much like axiomatic theory, it reveals a set of existence statements that establish the scope conditions of the causal statements. Third, and *unlike* axiomatic theory, the causal process form presents a set of causal statements describing the effect of one variable on another without establishing a strict hierarchical ordering of the statements. Rather, causal processes are considered of equal importance, although, clearly, some independent variables are recognized to have more impact on dependent variables than others. Thus, while axiomatic formats will resemble hierarchies of statements emanating from the axioms, the causal process format will resemble a flow diagram that charts the interactions among selected variables.

In Figure 1–1, these two types of formats are compared. The axiomatic format moves from abstract axioms, through logical derivations, to a

FIGURE 1–1
The Axiomatic and Causal Process Formats

A. Axiomatic

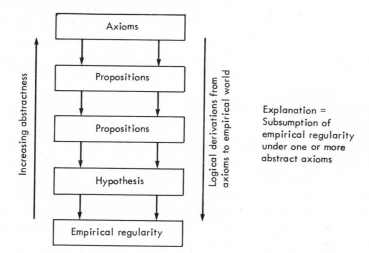

Explanation =
Subsumption of
empirical regularity
under one or more
abstract axioms

B. Causal Process

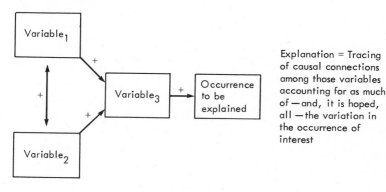

Explanation = Tracing
of causal connections
among those variables
accounting for as much
of —and, it is hoped,
all —the variation in
the occurrence of
interest

specific proposition, or a hypothesis, that predicts how events in a concrete empirical situation should occur. If the logical derivations are correct, then confirmation of the hypothesis makes the axioms more plausible. In this form of theory, moreover, the empirical event is presumed to be *explained* when it is seen as a specific empirical instance of the more abstract relationships stated in the axioms.

In contrast, a causal process explanation involves an effort to trace the causal sequence of events that influence a particular occurrence. Explanation does not involve logical deductions, but rather statements of causal connections among variables in a sequence which account for the variation in the particular occurrence of interest to an investigator.

Which of these formats is superior? An answer to this question varies with investigators and with their theoretical purpose. At present, the causal process format is preferred in sociology, primarily because it lends itself to multiple-regression statistical techniques. The more developed sciences, however, more typically use axiomatic theory.

Axiomatic theory will tend to be more abstract than causal process theory, and hence it will allow for explanation of more diverse phenomena. Moreover, it lends itself, through the proliferation of logical derivations, to creating new hypotheses and propositions which might otherwise have been ignored. Causal process theorizing enables investigators to see causal connections, something that axiomatic theorizing obscures. Yet, because it seeks to map or model causal connections among specific variables, it rarely becomes highly abstract. In fact, much supposed causal process theorizing is little more than descriptions of causal connections among empirical events.[10] Thus, causal process theorizing is less likely than axiomatic theorizing to yield abstract statements of relationships, such as $E = mc^2$, but it is much more likely to provide a sense of how events causally affect each other.

The Elements of Theory: A Summary

Theory is a type of thought that seeks to explain events. It attempts to answer the question, "Why?" Theory is not idle thinking or speculation, however. Speculation is often involved, of course, as are other creative mental processes. But to be useful, theory must be constructed from clearly defined concepts. These concepts are created through the vehicle of abstract and operational definitions. But by themselves, concepts only denote and classify. They point to events but do not help in understanding their relations. Theoretical statements connect concepts to each other. Statements enable scientists to visualize the relationships among phenomena in the world. Statements are organized into formats in order that many complex relations can be understood. Two formats are most prominent: (1) axiomatic and (2) causal process. The relations among these elements of theory are summarized in Figure 1–2.

What distinguishes theoretical statements in science is that they are *created to be proven wrong*. A theory which, in principle, cannot be

---

[10] For a forceful presentation and elaboration of this argument, see: Willer and Willer, *Systematic Empiricism.*

FIGURE 1–2
The Elements of Theory

	Theory	= Formats of interrelated theoretical statements
	↑	
Arrows show the way theory is built	Theoretical statements	= Asserted relationships among concepts
	↑	
	Concepts	= Systems of abstract and operational definitions
	↑	
	Definitions	= Systems of terms that denote a property of the world

---

proven wrong is not very useful. It becomes a self-sustaining dogma which is accepted on faith. A theory must allow for understanding of events, and hence, it must be tested against the facts of the world. If a theoretical statement is proven wrong by empirical tests, science has advanced.[11] When a theory is rejected, then one less possible line of inquiry will be required in search of an answer to the question, "Why?" By successively eliminating incorrect statements, those that survive attempts at refutation offer, for the present at least, the most accurate picture of the real world. Although having one's theory refuted may cause professional stigma, refutations are crucial to theory building. It is somewhat disheartening, therefore, that some scientists appear to live in fear of such refutation. For, in the ideal scientific process, just the opposite should be the case, as Karl Popper has emphasized:

---

[11] There is a growing conviction among some sociologists that "science" is much like any other thought system in that it is devoted to sustaining a particular vision, among a community of individuals called scientists, of what is "really real." "Science" simply provides one interesting way of constructing and maintaining a vision of reality, but there are other, equally "valid" views among different communities of individuals. Obviously, this book does not accept this argument, but will close with a chapter on the "ethnomethodological" alternative to current varieties of sociological theory. For some interesting explorations of the issues, see Edward A. Tiryakian, "Existential Phenomenology and the Sociological Tradition," *American Sociological Review* 30 (October 1965):674–88; J. C. McKinney, "Typification, Typologies, and Sociological Theory," *Social Forces* 48 (September 1969):1–11; Alfred Schutz, "Concept and Theory Formation in the Social Sciences," *Journal of Philosophy* 51 (April 1954):257–73; Harold Garfinkel, *Studies in Ethnomethodology* (Englewood Cliffs, N.J.: Prentice-Hall, Inc., 1967); George Psathas, "Ethnomethods and Phenomenology," *Social Research* 35 (September 1968):500–520; Don H. Zimmerman and Melvin Pollner, "The Everyday World as a Phenomenon," in *Understanding Everyday Life*, ed. J. D. Douglas (Chicago: Aldine Publishing Co., 1970), pp. 80–103; and Don H. Zimmerman and D. Lawrence Wieder, "Ethnomethodology and the Problem of Order," in *Understanding Everyday Life*, ed. J. D. Douglas, pp. 285–95.

Refutations have often been regarded as establishing the failure of a scientist, or at least of his theory. It should be stressed that this is an inductive error. Every refutation should be regarded as a great success; not merely as a success of the scientist who refuted the theory, but also of the scientist who created the refuted theory and who thus in the first instance suggested, if only indirectly, the refuting experiment.[12]

Even statements that survive refutation, and hence bring professional prestige to their framers, are never fully "proven." It is always possible that the next empirical test could disprove them. Yet, if statements consistently survive empirical tests, they have high credibility and are likely to be at the core of a theoretical body of knowledge. In social science, it is these highly credible statements that will offer the best comprehension of why patterns of social organization emerge, persist, change, and break down. Thus, the testing and interrelating of such statements constitutes a strategy for answering scientifically the question that Thomas Hobbes in the 17th century so forcefully asked.

SOCIOLOGICAL THEORY

One of the simplest, but most fruitless, enterprises in sociology is to play a game called *criticize-the-discipline*. One variant of this game is to list the general features of proper scientific theory, as done briefly above, and then to examine critically a particular theoretical perspective in sociology. A certain result is to find the perspective in question sadly deficient, which is what the *critic-of-the-discipline* usually wants anyway. This game takes little skill and always produces the same results. Yet, it continues as a favorite sport among sociologists.

Any analysis of sociological theory should begin with a blunt admission: From the perspective of ideal scientific theory, sociological theorizing has a long way to go. Such a confession is not meant to imply that *all* theory in sociology is so lacking. Indeed, some of the specific theoretical perspectives of sociology can be converted rather easily into proper theoretical formats. Still, the most general theoretical orientations that have guided sociological theorizing and research will be found wanting by those playing *criticize-the-discipline*.

An important and appropriate concern in an analysis of dominant theoretical perspectives is: In what ways do these perspectives deviate from scientific formulations? But this obvious question should be followed

---

[12] Karl R. Popper, *Conjectures and Refutations* (New York: Basic Books, 1962), p. 243.

quickly by more important ones, infrequently asked: What can be done about these inadequacies? Potentially, can they be corrected? What should be the general direction of remedies? Assuming that current theoretical perspectives are not going to be converted immediately into ideal theory—and this indeed is a safe assumption—what strategies are possible for making such conversions in the long run?

As soon as the question becomes one of *potential* for theory building, critical analysis must move beyond the mechanical comparison of a particular theoretical perspective with the canons of scientific theory. While such comparisons cannot be ignored, their polemical intent often gets in the way of the productive analysis of a particular conceptual perspective.

THEORETICAL PERSPECTIVES IN SOCIOLOGY

Much of what is labeled sociological theory is, in reality, only a loose clustering of implicit assumptions, inadequately defined concepts, and a few vague and logically disconnected propositions. Sometimes assumptions are stated explicitly and serve to inspire abstract theoretical statements containing well-defined concepts, but most sociological theory constitutes a verbal "image of society" rather than a rigorously constructed set of theoretical statements organized into a logically coherent format. Thus, a great deal of so-called theory is really a general "perspective" or "orientation" for looking at various features of the social world which, if all goes well, can be eventually translated into true scientific theory.

The fact that there are many such perspectives in sociology poses problems of exposition. These problems, in turn, are compounded by the fact that the perspectives blend one into another, sometimes rendering it difficult to analyze them separately. The initial solution to this dilemma is to limit arbitrarily the number of perspectives covered and, at the same time, to act as if they were separable. Accordingly, only four general sociological perspectives or orientations are covered in the sections to follow: (1) functional "theory," (2) conflict "theory," (3) exchange "theory," and (4) interactionism and role "theory."

The quotations around the word "theory" above do not represent an indictment, but again, a recognition of current inadequacies of sociological theory. These four perspectives have been selected for a number of reasons: (1) They are the most general perspectives in sociology, and underlie most specific perspectives in the field. (2) These perspectives are also the most widespread and influential—the subjects of much analytical elaboration and, of course, inevitable scrutiny by both constructive critics and those playing *criticize-the-discipline*. (3) Each of these perspectives, at various times, has been proclaimed by its more exuberant proponents as the only one that could take sociology out of its theoretical difficulties. Therefore, each must be considered in a book attempting to assess the structure of sociological theorizing.

These four theoretical orientations might be termed theoretical paradigms. Yet, the term, "paradigm," connotes more fundamental divisions within sociology than exist among functional, conflict, exchange, and interactionist orientations.[13] While there are sharp disagreements among advocates of these four orientations, these are not so great as to constitute partitioning of sociology into distinctive paradigms.[14] There is too much overlap and convergence among sociology's major orientations for this to be true.

Recently, however, a true paradigmatic split has occurred in sociology. Emerging out of interactionism and German phenomenology, a school of thought termed "ethnomethodology" appears close to constituting a distinctive paradigm. At present, ethnomethodology constitutes a new definition of reality which, despite the claims of its advocates, has yet to replace other theoretical orientations. This paradigm will, however, be briefly examined near the end of the book. It represents an alternative paradigm to the four conventional orientations in sociology.

PREVIEW OF THE BOOK

In the chapters to follow, the functional, conflict, exchange, and interactionist theoretical orientations will be explored. None of these orientations closely approximates a true body of theory, as has been outlined. Concepts are often vaguely defined; statements are frequently implicit and loosely organized into either causal process or axiomatic formats. Thus, concern will not be on how these orientations fail to live up to the canons of good theory but on the potential that they reveal for developing theory.

While each chapter will reveal a unique organization, certain common

---

[13] Many commentators would disagree with my failure to view a number of orientations in sociology as separate paradigms. George Ritzer's insightful analysis in his *Sociology: A Multiple Paradigm Science* (Boston: Allyn & Bacon, 1975) makes use of the notion of paradigms. He defines paradigm in a way similar to what I call orientation or perspective.

[14] I visualize separate paradigms as truly different visions about the nature of the world. The four perspectives to be covered in this book are different, but they all hold a similar view of the basic nature of the social world. Hence, they all constitute one paradigm.

elements in the analysis to follow are evident. Each major section of chapters on a particular theoretical orientation will focus on: (1) the historical emergence of each perspective, (2) the thought of its dominant contemporary practitioners, and (3) its future as a part of sociological theorizing.

Within each chapter, a number of key topics will be given emphasis: (1) the assumptions about the nature of the social world that a perspective, and its advocates, hold; (2) the theory building strategy typically advocated by those working with a perspective; (3) the image of causal processes that a perspective reveals; (4) the key concepts and propositions developed within the perspective; and (5) the existence, if any, of formats of theoretical statements within a perspective.

In sum, it can be said that sociological theorizing is in its intellectual infancy. Yet, the analysis of its major orientations will demonstrate that theory in sociology has great potential. The chapters which follow will, it is hoped, challenge and direct theorizing in sociology to realize this potential.

PART I

Functional Theorizing

THE EMERGENCE OF FUNCTIONALISM

FUNCTIONALISM AND THE ORGANISMIC ANALOGY

During the 19th century, the utilitarian doctrines of British classical economics were increasingly being called into question by social thinkers on the European continent. No longer were humans viewed as rational and calculating entrepreneurs in a free, open, unregulated, and competitive marketplace. Nor was the doctrine of the "invisible hand of order" considered a very adequate explanation of how social organization could emerge out of free and unbridled competition among individuals. Although utilitarianism remained a prominent social doctrine for the entire 19th century, the first generation of French sociologists had ceased to accept the assumption that social order would automatically be forthcoming if only free competition among individuals was left intact.

The disenchantment with utilitarianism was aided in France, and to a lesser extent in all of continental Europe, by the disruptive social changes wrought by industrialization and urbanization. Coupled with the political instability of the late 18th century, as revealed most dramatically by the violent French Revolution, early-19th–century social thinkers in France displayed a profound concern with the problems of maintaining the social order. While each was to phrase the question somewhat differently, social thinkers began to ask seriously: Why and how is society possible? What holds society together? What makes it change?

Whether in France or elsewhere in Europe, the answer to this fundamental question was to be shaped by events occurring in the biological sciences. It was in the 19th century that biological discoveries were to alter significantly the social and intellectual climate of the times. For example, as many of the mysteries of the human body were being unfolded, the last vestiges of mysticism surrounding the body's functioning were being laid to rest. The diversity of the animal species was finally being systematically recorded under the long-standing classification procedures outlined by the Swedish biologist Carolus Linnaeus. And most important, conceptions of evolution, culminating in the theories of Wallace and Darwin, were stimulating great intellectual and social controversy. Since it was in this social and intellectual milieu that sociology as a self-conscious discipline was born, it is not surprising that conceptions of social order were influenced by a preoccupation with biology.

The Organicism of Auguste Comte (1798–1857)

Auguste Comte is usually given credit for being the "founder of sociology." While philosophizing about humans and society had long been a preoccupation of lay people and scholars alike, it was Comte who advocated a "science of society" and coined the term "sociology." And although Comte's work was soon to fall into neglect and obscurity and he was to live out his later years in frustration and bitterness, his work profoundly influenced social thought. Few recognize this influence, even today. But the emergence of the functionalist perspective began with Comte's work and was carried forward by other thinkers in the latter half of the 19th century.[1]

Like most French thinkers of his time, Comte was preoccupied with propagating order and harmony out of the chaos created by the French Revolution. He attacked the individualism of utilitarian doctrines so prominent in England and carried forward Rousseau's and Saint-Simon's desire to develop a "collective philosophy"—one which would provide the principles for creating social consensus. In so doing, however, he was to articulate the principles of science as they should be applied to society.

Comte felt that human evolution in the 19th century had reached the "positive" stage in which empirical knowledge about the social world could be used to understand this world and to create a "better society."

---

[1] Comte's first organic doctrines can be found in *Philosophie positive*, vol. 10, pp. 430–98. For a summary of Comte's organicism, see Howard Becker and Harry Elmer Barnes, *Social Thought from Lore to Science* (New York: Dover Publications, 1952), vol. 2, pp. 572–75. It should be emphasized that Comte was not the first social thinker to view society in organic terms. On the contrary, organic analogizing goes at least as far back as Aristotle and Plato, as Comte was quick to point out.

Comte thus became an advocate of the application of the scientific method to the study of society—a strategy which, in deference to Comte, is still termed "positivism" in the social sciences. This application of the scientific method was to give birth to a new science, sociology.

Comte's entire intellectual life represented an attempt to legitimate sociology. His efforts on this score went so far as to construct a "hierarchy of the sciences," with sociology as the "queen" of the sciences. While this hierarchy allowed Comte to assert the importance of sociology, and thereby separate it from social philosophy, his most important tactic for legitimating sociology was to borrow terms and concepts from the highly respected biological sciences. Sociology was thus initiated and justified by appeals to the biological sciences—a fact which will help explain why functionalism was sociology's first, and until recently, most nearly dominant theoretical orientation.

Comte saw the affinity between sociology and biology to reside in their common concern with "organic bodies." This affinity led him to divide sociology into social "statics," or morphology, and "dynamics," or social growth and progress. But Comte was convinced that while "Biology has hitherto been the guide and preparation for Sociology . . . Sociology will in the future . . . [provide] the ultimate systematization of Biology."

Comte visualized an initial borrowing of concepts from biology, and later with the development of positivism in the social sciences, the principles of sociology would inform biology. Thus, sociology must first recognize the correspondence between the individual organism in biology and the social organism in sociology:

> We have thus established a true correspondence between the Statical Analysis of the Social Organism in Sociology, and that of the Individual Organism in Biology. . . . If we take the best ascertained points in Biology, we may decompose structure anatomically into *elements, tissues,* and *organs.* We have the same things in the Social Organism; and may even use the same names.[2]

Comte then began to make clear analogies between specific types of social structures and the biological concepts:

> . . . I shall treat the Social Organism as definitely composed of the Families which are the true elements or cells, next the Classes or Castes which are its proper tissues, and lastly of the Cities and Communes which are its real organs.[3]

---

[2] Auguste Comte, *System of Positive Polity or Treatise on Sociology* (London: Burt Franklin, 1875), pp. 239–40.

[3] Ibid., 241–42.

Sociology thus emerged as discipline with two points of emphasis: (1) the "positivistic" concern with the use of the scientific method to gather empirical facts about the world; and (2) the preoccupation with analogizing between the individual organism and society. In Comte's scheme, these themes were not seen as incompatible, nor were they by subsequent scholars until much later. But to the modern critics of what this organicism was eventually to create—that is, functionalism— positivism was to be one of the main weapons in attacks aimed at discrediting modern functionalism. For in the present era, functionalism is often defined as nonempirical and nontestable, thereby violating the dictates of positivism. Implicit in Comte's work, then, was a contradiction which more than 125 years later was to become a full-blown intellectual controversy.

The Organicism of Herbert Spencer (1820–1903)

While Comte founded sociology, Herbert Spencer carried its banner forward during the mid-decades of the last century. Working in England under more stable political conditions than Comte, and enjoying enormous intellectual popularity, Spencer rejected the collectivism of Comte and became a staunch ideological defender of early industrial capitalism. Like Comte, he emphasized positivism, and borrowing from Comte, he stressed the similarity between sociological and biological principles.

Spencer developed two explicit lines of analogizing with the biological sciences. These, as he recognized, paralleled Comte's distinction between statics and dynamics.[4] The first type of analogy was to the process of evolution from simple to complex forms. This analogy was both to the species—they evolved through adaptations—and to individual organisms—they grow and mature. The second line of analogy involved comparisons between the individual and the social organism:

1. Both society and organisms can be distinguished from inorganic matter, for both grow and develop.
2. In both society and organisms an increase in size means an increase in complexity and differentiation.
3. In both, a progressive differentiation in structure is accompanied by a differentiation in function.

---

[4] Spencer acknowledged his debt to Comte in a number of places: "To [Comte] I believe, I am indebted for the conception of social consensus." And he gave Comte credit for the ideas that "the principles of organization are common to societies and animals . . . and . . . that the evolution of structures advances from the general to the special."

4. In both, parts of the whole are interdependent with a change in one part affecting other parts.
5. In both, each part of the whole is also a micro society or organism in and of itself.
6. And in both organisms and societies, the life of the whole can be destroyed but the parts will live on for a while.[5]

Perhaps the two most critical points in this analogy are (2) and (3) above. For it is these which Spencer was to elaborate upon and which were to become the cornerstone of modern functionalism.

Unlike Comte, and anticipating Durkheim's famous analysis of the division of labor, Spencer emphasized that a change in the profile of a structure represented a change in its function for the social organism:

> Changes of structure cannot occur without changes of functions. . . . If organization consists in such a construction of the whole that its parts can carry on mutually-dependent actions, then in proportion as organization is high there must go a dependence of each part upon the rest so great that separation is fatal; and conversely. This truth is equally well shown in the individual organism and in the social organism.[6]

Thus, structure and function are distinguished in Spencer's work, a division which was to become more thoroughly developed by Émile Durkheim, but which provided the basis for functionalism as a unique orientation in the social sciences. In addition to this critical distinction, Spencer introduced another concept from biological terminology into sociology: the concept of functional "needs":

> There can be no true conception of a structure without a true conception of its function. To understand how an organization originated and developed, it is requisite to understand the *need* subserved at the outset and afterwards [emphasis added].[7]

Sociological analysis must therefore recognize that "needs" of the social organism are critical in determining why a structure should exist and persist. This concept was to become, as will be evident throughout

---

[5] Herbert Spencer, *The Social Organism* (1860) Herbert Spencer, *Principles of Sociology*, vol. 1, pt. 2, chap. 2. As Spencer clearly notes, "the permanent relations among the parts of a society *are analogous* to the permanent relations among parts of a living body" (Spencer's emphasis); see also, Becker and Barnes, *Social Thought from Lore to Science* (New York: Dover Publications, 1952), p. 680.

[6] Herbert Spencer, *The Works of Herbert Spencer, Volume 1: Essays Scientific, Political and Speculative* (Osnabrück: Otto Zeller, 1966), p. 473; originally published in 1885.

[7] Herbert Spencer, *The Works of Herbert Spencer, Volume 8: Principles of Sociology* (Osnabrück: Otto Zeller, 1966); originally published in 1896.

these chapters on functionalism, one of the most problematic for the functional orientation, since it easily could be taken to imply that events are caused by the social needs they meet.

While Spencer was initially cautious in emphasizing that such statements were *analogies*, his followers, such as Paul von Lilienfield and René Worms, moved from mere analogies to visualizing society not as just *like* an organism, but as an actual living organism. Apparently carried away by such assertions, these followers of Spencer were inspired to view society as the highest form of organism on a somewhat contrived phylogenetic "scale." This extreme organicism was perhaps inevitable in light of the mood of the times, but an equally important influence was Spencer's unfortunate inclination to forget the distinction he had made between analogy and reality.

While many of the extremes of the organismic analogy had been rejected by the latter part of the 19th century, the conception of society as an organism introduced three assumptions that began to typify sociological functionalism: First, social reality is visualized as a *system*. Second, the processes of a system can only be understood in terms of the *interrelatedness* of its parts. And third, like an organism, a system is *bounded*, with certain processes operating to maintain both its integrity and its boundaries. Stated in this minimal form, these assumptions would appear necessary for a proper understanding of social structures and processes. However, because these basic functionalist tenets were inspired by the organismic analogy, many additional and questionable biological concepts "slipped in the back door" as sociologists developed theoretical schemes. In fact, much of the century-old debate over functionalism stems from the implicit organicism accompanying this conceptual perspective. Depending on whose schema is under scrutiny, the number of implicit organismic assumptions has varied.

In the most *extreme* form, functional theorizing began to include the following conceptions: (1) Society as a bounded system is self-regulating, tending toward homeostasis and equilibrium. (2) As a self-maintaining system, similar to an organism, society perhaps has certain basic needs or requisites, which must be met if survival is to ensue, if homeostasis is to be preserved, or if equilibrium is to be maintained. (3) Sociological analysis of a self-maintaining system with needs and requisites should therefore focus on the function of parts in meeting system needs and hence maintaining equilibrium and homeostasis. (4) In systems with needs, it is probable that certain types of structures *must* exist to ensure survival/homeostasis/equilibrium. While perhaps several alternative structures can exist to fulfill the same need, a delimited range of necessary alternative structures exists to fulfill any system need.

These assumptions have often persisted and have been the subject of much of the debate over functionalism.[8] Organisms display homeostatic tendencies, but do societies? Organisms might reveal stable sets of survival requisites or needs, but do societies? Organisms may display interrelated parts that must exist to meet system needs, but is this a viable assumption for societies? These questions have persisted for close to a century, as can be seen from the more self-conscious formulations of functionalism by Émile Durkheim, Bronislaw Malinowski, and A. R. Radcliffe-Brown—the titular founders of functionalism.

FUNCTIONALISM AND ÉMILE DURKHEIM

As the inheritor of a long French tradition of social thought, especially Comte's organicism, it is not surprising that Émile Durkheim's early works were heavily infused with organismic terminology. While his major work, *The Division of Labor in Society*, was sharply critical of Herbert Spencer,[9] many of Durkheim's formulations were clearly influenced by the 19th-century intellectual preoccupation with biology. Aside from the extensive use of biologically inspired terms, Durkheim's basis assumptions reflected those of the organicists: (1) Society was to be viewed as an entity in itself that could be distinguished from, and was not reducible to, its constituent parts. In conceiving of society as a reality, *sui generis*, Durkheim in effect gave analytical priority to the social whole. (2) While such an emphasis by itself did not necessarily reflect organismic inclinations, Durkheim, in giving causal priority to the whole, viewed system parts as fulfilling basic functions, needs, or requisites of that whole. (3) The frequent use of the notion "functional needs" is buttressed by Durkheim's conceptualization of social systems in terms of "normal"

---

[8] It should be emphasized that many of the critics of functional analysis have assumed that the concepts of "equilibrium" and "homeostasis" *necessarily* connote a vision of the social world as unchanging and static. This interpretation is incorrect, for notions of equilibrium can also provide an analytical reference point for observing instances of change and disequilibrium. Thus, there is no logical reason for assuming that the concept of equilibrium allows only a static image of the social world. Critics sometimes appear to talk as if there were such a logical compulsion.

[9] Émile Durkheim, *The Division of Labor in Society* (New York: Macmillan Co., 1933), bk. 1; originally published in 1893. Durkheim tended to ignore the fact that Spencer wore several "intellectual hats." He reacted to Spencer's advocacy of utilitarianism, seemingly ignoring the similarity between Spencer's organismic analogy and his own organic formulations.

and "pathological" states. Such formulations, at the very least, connote the view that social systems have needs that must be fulfilled if "abnormal" states are to be avoided. (4) In viewing systems as normal and pathological, as well as in terms of functions, there is the additional implication that systems have equilibrium points around which normal functioning occurs.

Durkheim recognized all of these dangers so evident in Spencer's formulations. And thus he explicitly tried to deal with several of them. First, he was clearly aware of the dangers of teleological analysis—of implying that some future consequence of an event causes that very event to occur. Thus, he warns that the causes of a phenomenon must be distinguished from the ends it serves:

> When, then, the explanation of a social phenomenon is undertaken, we must seek separately the efficient cause which produces it and the function it fulfills. We use the word "function" in preference to "end" or "purpose," precisely because social phenomena do not generally exist for the useful results they produce.[10]

Thus, despite giving analytical priority to the whole, and in viewing parts as having consequences for certain "normal" states, and hence meeting system requisites, Durkheim remained aware of the dangers of asserting that all systems have "purpose" and that the need to maintain the whole causes the existence of its constituent parts. Yet, Durkheim's insistence that the function of a part for the social whole always be examined sometimes led him, and certainly many of his followers, into questionable teleological reasoning. For example, even when distinguishing "cause" and "function" in his major methodological statement, he leaves room for an illegitimate teleological interpretation: "Consequently, to explain a social fact it is not enough to show the cause on which it depends; we must also, at least in most cases, show its function *in the establishment of* social order" (emphasis added).[11] In this summary phrase, the words "in the establishment of" could connote that the existence of system parts can be explained only by the whole, or "social order," which they function to maintain. From this view, it is only a short step to outright teleology: The social fact is caused by the needs of the social order that the fact fulfills. Such theoretical statements do not necessarily have to be illegitimate, for it is conceivable that a social system could be "programmed" to meet certain "needs" or designated

---

[10] Émile Durkheim, *The Rules of Sociological Method* (Glencoe, Ill.: Free Press, 1938), p. 96.

[11] Ibid., p. 97.

"ends" and thereby have the capacity to cause variations in cultural items or "social facts" in order to meet these needs or ends. But if such a system is being described by an analyst, it is necessary to document how the system is programmed and how it operates to cause variations in "social facts" to meet needs or ends. As the above quotation illustrates, Durkheim did not have this kind of system in mind when he formulated his particular brand of functional analysis; thus, he did not wish to state his arguments teleologically.

Despite his warnings to the contrary, Durkheim appears to have taken this short step into teleological reasoning in his substantive works. In his first major work on the division of labor, Durkheim went to great lengths to distinguish between cause (increased moral density) and function (integration of society).

However, as Cohen indicates,[12] the causal statements often become fused with functional statements. The argument runs, very generally, something like this: Moral density leads to competition, which threatens the social order, which, in turn, leads to the specialization of tasks, mutual interdependence, and increased willingness to accept the morality of mutual obligation. This transition to a new social order is not made consciously, or by "unconscious wisdom," but because division of labor is necessary to restore the order that "unbridled competition might otherwise destroy."[13] Hence, the impression is left that the "threat" or the need for social order "causes" the division of labor. Such reasoning can be construed as an illegitimate teleology, since the consequence of the division of labor—the social order—is the implied cause of the division of labor. At the very least, then, cause and function are not kept as analytically separate as Durkheim so often insisted.[14]

Similarly, Cohen argues further,[15] Durkheim's analysis of the origins and nature of religion slips into teleological reasoning: Society constrains

---

[12] *Modern Social Theory* by Percy S. Cohen, © 1968 by Percy S. Cohen, Basic Books, Inc., Publishers, New York, pp. 35–37. Whether the line of argument presented here is "true" is debatable. But the very fact that it is a "debatable topic" would indicate that perhaps there was some disparity between what Durkheim said and what he did when actually analyzing social facts.

[13] Ibid., p. 35.

[14] There are ways out of this causal analysis, if one can impute some additional assumptions to Durkheim's analysis. First, competition must occur under conditions of scarcity of resources (perhaps caused by increased moral density). Second, a law of economic utility must be invoked. Third, it must be assumed that actors are motivated to avoid "unbridled competition" (an "individualistic" assumption, which, at this point in his writing, Durkheim might not accept). With these assumptions, the division of labor can be "explained," for now the explanation involves a legitimate teleology (the assumption that actors are motivated to avoid competition).

[15] Cohen, *Modern Social Theory*, p. 36.

its members, while providing them with the cultural resources necessary to be creative; primitive men are vaguely aware of the constraining force of society, but are incapable of stating such dependency despite a *need* to do so; therefore, they choose some object to represent society and their collective attitudes toward it. By virtue of representing the social (moral) order, these symbols became sacred; and, as they become the central focus of ritual activity, they arouse and sustain group sentiments and hence social solidarity. Such a "theory" thus relies on the notion of "need" in men to express their vague awareness of the social constraints on them and on the assumption that such a need has beneficial consequences for "normal" social functioning, that is, social solidarity. The teleology occurs at the individual level, a need to express; or if this imputation of purpose is not accepted, then a social need for solidarity causes religion. Thus, the emergence of religion, and its maintenance, is not explained by prior antecedent conditions, or carefully documented causal chains, but by the purpose of the activity for meeting either individual and/or group "needs."

In sum, then, despite Durkheim's warnings about illegitimate teleology, he often appears to waver on the brink of the very traps he wished to avoid. The reason for this failing can probably be traced to the organismic assumptions built into his form of sociological analysis. In taking a strong sociologistic position on the question of emergent properties— that is, on the irreducibility of the whole to its individual parts—Durkheim saved sociology from the naïve psychology and anthropology of his day.[16] However, in supplementing this emphasis on the social whole with organismic assumptions of "function," "requisite," "need," and "normality/pathology," Durkheim helped weld organismic principles to sociological theory for nearly three quarters of a century. The brilliance of his analysis of substantive topics, as well as the suggestive features of his analytical work, made a "functional" mode of analysis highly appealing to subsequent generations of sociologists and anthropologists.

FUNCTIONALISM AND THE ANTHROPOLOGICAL TRADITION

Functionalism as a well-articulated conceptual perspective emerged in the 20th century with the writings of two anthropologists, Bronislaw

---

[16] Robert N. Nisbet, *Émile Durkheim* (Englewood Cliffs, N.J.: Prentice-Hall, Inc., 1965), pp. 9–102.

Malinowski and A. R. Radcliffe-Brown.[17,18] Each of these thinkers was heavily influenced by the organicism of Durkheim, as well as by their own field studies among primitive societies. Despite the similarities in their intellectual backgrounds, however, the conceptual perspectives developed by Malinowski and Radcliffe-Brown reveal a considerable number of dissimilarities.

The Functionalism of A. R. Radcliffe-Brown (1881–1955)

While Radcliffe-Brown disavowed the label *functionalism* in favor of *structuralism*, his perspective was more thorough than Malinowski's and was therefore to guide a generation of functional analysis in anthropology. Recognizing that "the concept of function applied to human societies is based on an analogy between social life and organic life" and that "the first systematic formulation of the concept as applying to the strictly scientific study of society was performed by Durkheim,"[19] Radcliffe-Brown tried to indicate how some of the problems of organismic analogizing might be overcome.

For Radcliffe-Brown, the most serious problem with functionalism was the tendency for analysis to appear teleological. Noting that Durkheim's definition of function pertained to the way in which a part fulfills system "needs," he emphasized that, in order to avoid the teleological implications of such analysis, it would be necessary to "substitute for the term 'needs' the term 'necessary condition of existence.'" In doing so, he felt that no universal human or societal needs would be postulated; rather, the question of which conditions were necessary for survival would be an empirical one, an issue that would have to be discovered for each given social system. Furthermore, in recognizing the diversity of conditions necessary for the survival of different systems, analysis would avoid asserting that every item of a culture must have a function and that items in different cultures must have the same function.

---

[17] For basic references on Malinowski's functionalism, see his "Anthropology," *Encyclopedia Britannica*, supp., vol. 1 (London and New York, 1936); Malinowski, supp., vol. 1 *A Scientific Theory of Culture* (Chapel Hill: University of North Carolina Press, 1944); Malinowski, *Magic, Science, and Religion and Other Essays* (Glencoe, Ill.: Free Press, 1948).

[18] For basic references on Radcliffe-Brown's functionalism, see his "Structure and Function in Primitive Society," *American Anthropologist 37* (July–September 1935); 58–72; *Structure and Function in Primitive Society* (Glencoe, Ill.: Free Press, 1952); and *The Andaman Islanders* (Glencoe, Ill.: Free Press, 1948).

[19] Radcliffe-Brown, "Structure and Function in Primitive Society," p. 68.

Once the dangers of illegitimate teleology were recognized, functional—or, to use his term, *structural*—analysis could legitimately proceed from several assumptions: (1) One necessary condition for survival of a society is minimal integration of its parts; (2) the term *function* refers to those processes that maintain this necessary integration or solidarity; (3) thus, in each society structural features can be shown to contribute to the maintenance of necessary solidarity. In such an analytical approach, social structure and the conditions necessary for its survival are irreducible. In a vein similar to that of Durkheim, Radcliffe-Brown saw society as a reality in and of itself. For this reason he was usually led to visualize cultural items, such as kinship rules and religious rituals, as explicable in terms of social structure—particularly its "need" for solidarity and integration. For example, in analyzing a lineage system, Radcliffe-Brown would first assume that some minimal degree of solidarity must exist in the system. Processes associated with lineage systems would then be assessed in terms of their consequences for maintaining this solidarity. The conclusion to be reached was that lineage systems provided a systematic way of adjudicating conflict in societies where families owned land, because such a system specified who had the right to land and through which side of the family it would always pass. In doing so, the integration of the economic system—landed estates owned by families—is explained.[20]

This form of analysis poses a number of problems that have continued to haunt functional theorists. While Radcliffe-Brown admits that "functional unity [integration] of a social system is, of course, a hypothesis," he fails to specify the analytical criteria for assessing just how much or how little functional unity is necessary for system survival, to say nothing of specifying the operations necessary for testing this hypothesis. As subsequent commentators were to discover, without some analytical criteria for determining what is and what is not minimal functional integration and societal survival, the hypothesis cannot be tested, even in principle. Thus, what is typically done is to assume that the existing system encountered by the investigator at a particular point in time is minimally integrated and surviving, because it exists and persists. Without carefully documenting how various cultural items promote instances both of integration and malintegration of the social whole, such a strategy can reduce the hypothesis of functional unity to a tautology: If one can find a

---

[20] Radcliffe-Brown, *Structure and Function in Primitive Society*, pp. 31–50. For a secondary analysis of this example, see Arthur L. Stinchcombe, "Specious Generality and Functional Theory," *American Sociological Review* 26 (December 1961): 929–30.

system to study, then it must be minimally integrated; therefore, lineages that are a part of that system must promote this integration. To discover the contrary would be difficult, since the system, by virtue of being a system, is already composed of integrated parts, such as a lineage system. There is a non sequitur in this reasoning, since it is quite possible to view a cultural item like a lineage system as having both integrative and malintegrative (and other) consequences for the social whole. In his actual ethnographic descriptions, Radcliffe-Brown often slips inadvertently into a pattern of circular reasoning in which the fact of a system's existence requires that its existing parts, such as a lineage system, be viewed as contributing to the system's existence.

Assuming integration and then assessing the contribution of individual parts to the integrated whole leads to an additional analytical problem. Such a mode of analysis implies that the causes of a particular structure, for example lineages, lie in the system's needs for integration (most likely an illegitimate teleology).

Radcliffe-Brown would, of course, have denied these conclusions. His awareness of the dangers of illegitimate teleology would have seemingly eliminated the implication that the needs of a system cause the emergence of its parts, while his repeated assertions that the notion of function "does not require the dogmatic assertion that everything in the life of every community has a function"[21] should have led to a rejection of tautological reasoning. However, much like Durkheim, what Radcliffe-Brown asserted analytically was frequently not practiced in the concrete analysis of substantive systems. Such lapses were not intended, but appeared to be difficult to avoid when functional "needs," functional integration, and "equilibrium" were his operating assumptions.[22]

Thus, while Radcliffe-Brown displayed an admirable awareness of the dangers of organicism[23]—especially of the problem of illegitimate teleology and the hypothetical nature of notions of solidarity—he all too often slipped into a pattern of questionable teleological reasoning. Forgetting that integration was only a "working hypothesis," he opened his analysis to problems of tautology. Such problems were persistent in Durkheim's

---

[21] See, for example, Radcliffe-Brown, "Structure and Function in Primitive Society."

[22] A perceptive critic of an early draft of this manuscript provided an interesting way to visualize the problems of tautology:

> When do you have a surviving social system?
> When certain survival requisites are met.
> How do you know when certain survival requisites are met?
> When you have a surviving social system.

[23] Don Martindale, *The Nature and Types of Sociological Theory* (Boston: Houghton-Mifflin Co., 1960), p. 459.

analysis; and despite his attempts to the contrary, their spectre haunted even Radcliffe-Brown's insightful essays and ethnographies.

The Functionalism of Bronislaw Malinowski (1884–1942)

Many of Radcliffe-Brown's reasoned theoretical statements were responses to the assertions of Malinowski—the first to apply the title *functionalism* to organismic forms of analysis. While Radcliffe-Brown was prone to fall unintentionally into the pitfalls of organicism, Malinowski appeared to plunge headlong into them. Malinowski's conceptual perspective was built around the dogmatic assertion that cultural items exist to fulfill basic human and cultural needs: "The functional view of culture insists therefore upon the principle that in every type of civilization, every custom, material object, idea and belief fulfills some vital function, has some task to accomplish, represents an indispensable part within a working whole."[24] Such a position can easily become teleological, for the impression is left that cultural items exist (that is, are caused) by the needs of the system and/or its members.

Probably the most distinctive aspect of Malinowski's functionalism was its reductionistic tendencies. His analytical scheme starts with an emphasis on such individual human needs as food, shelter, and reproduction. To meet these needs, organization of human populations into groups and communities is necessary, as is the creation of cultural symbols to regulate such organization. In turn, the creation of patterns of social organization and culture gives rise to additional needs, which must be met by other, more elaborate forms of social organization. By such reasoning, it is possible to visualize several types of requisites shaping culture: (1) those that are biologically based; (2) acquired psychological needs; and (3) derivative needs that are necessary to maintain the culture and patterns of social organization which originally met basic biological and acquired psychological needs. Thus, the impression is left that structures arise in response to a number of different types of needs: biological, psychological, and cultural. By visualizing culture as meeting several "layers" of such requisites, Malinowski could employ reductionist argument to explain the existence and persistence of any strucure in a society. If such a structure does not meet cultural requisites, it may be said to meet psychological ones; and, if it cannot be linked to either of these types, it may be said to meet biological needs. It was perhaps this ability to shift levels of requisites that allowed Malinowski to proclaim so confi-

---

24 Malinowski, "Anthropology," p. 132.

dently that any cultural item *must* have some "task to accomplish . . . within a working whole."

Malinowski's work thus represented an attempt to cross-tabulate different levels of needs with different types of structures which these needs met. Typically, Malinowski would postulate a list of "basic needs" and then enumerate the "cultural reactions" to meet these needs. One example of his efforts is presented in Table 2–1.[25]

TABLE 2–1
Basic Needs and Response

Basic Needs	Cultural Reaction to Need
Food, nutrition $\longrightarrow$	Nutritive structures
Reproduction $\longrightarrow$	Kinship, schools
Bodily comfort $\longrightarrow$	Shelters, houses
Safety $\longrightarrow$	Weapons, fortifications, armies
Movement $\longrightarrow$	Activities, sports
Health $\longrightarrow$	Hygiene, therapy

TABLE 2–2
Derived Needs and Response

Derived Needs	Cultural Reaction to Need
Production $\longrightarrow$	Economic system
Organization of collective activities $\longrightarrow$	Political organization
Regulation of actions $\longrightarrow$	Social control structures
Transmission of cultural heritage $\longrightarrow$	Educational system

Malinowski did not stop here, however. Once created, cultural (social) systems generate their own "derived needs" which require further "cultural (social) reactions" in order to be met. Thus, his analysis would typically involve a cross-tabulation of "derived needs" and "cultural reactions," such as the one in Table 2–2.

The arrows in these tables are intended to emphasize Malinowski's implication that needs—through processes never clearly documented—cause the existence and persistence of the structures which meet them. Such reasoning is not only teleological—the cultural item emerges to

---

[25] Bronislaw Malinowski, *A Scientific Theory of Culture and Other Essays* (London: Oxford University Press, 1964), pp. 71–125.

meet the end it fulfills—it is also tautological in that any cultural item exists to meet a need of the cultural whole, while the cultural whole exists to meet biological and psychological needs. Such circular reasoning appears inevitable once teleological reasoning is compounded by reductionist assumptions. As will be evident, it is to the credit of modern functionalists that such teleological reductionism was not adopted.

FUNCTIONALISM AND THE GHOST OF MAX WEBER

It is difficult to address contemporary theory in sociology without recognizing the impact of Max Weber. During the latter 19th century and into the early part of this century, Max Weber developed a particular approach for sociological analysis. Weber's approach in a wide range of substantive areas in sociology—economic sociology, stratification, complex organizations, sociology of religion, authority and social change, for example—still guides modern research and theory in these areas. In the development of general theoretical orientations, however, Weber's influence has been less direct. While his impact on some perspectives, such as phenomenological theorizing (to be examined in Part V of this book) is clear, Weber's influence on functionalism is less evident. And yet, because several contemporary functionalists were so important in initially exposing American scholars to Weber's thought, it would seem unlikely that these functionalists' theorizing was not influenced by the power of Weber's approach.

What, then, has been Weber's impact on the emergence of functionalism? Generally, two aspects of Weber's work appear to have had important influences on the development of functionalism: (1) his substantive vision of "social action," and (2) his strategy for analyzing social structures. Weber argued that sociology must understand social phenomena on two levels, at the "level of meaning" of the actors themselves and at the level of collective action among groupings of actors. Weber's substantive view of the world and his strategy for analyzing its features were thus influenced by these dual concerns. In many ways, Weber viewed two realities—that of the subjective meanings of actions and that of the emergent regularities of collective action.[26] Much functionalism similarly addresses this dualism: How do the subjective states of

---

[26] For basic references on Weber, see his *The Theory of Social and Economic Organization* (New York: The Free Press, 1947); "Social Action and its Types" in Talcott Parsons et al., eds., *Theories of Society* (New York: The Free Press, 1961); Hans Gerth and C. Wright Mills, eds., *From Max Weber: Essays in Sociology* (New York: Oxford Univesity Press, 1958).

actors influence emergent patterns of social organization and vice versa?

As will be evident shortly, Talcott Parsons, in particular, labels his functionalism, "action theory," and his early theoretical scheme was devoted to analyzing the basic components and processes of the subjective processes of individual actors. But, much like Weber himself, Parsons and other functionalists were to move to a more macroscopic concern with emergent patterns of collective action.

This shift from the micro to macro represents only part of the Weberian analytical strategy. One of the most enduring analytical legacies of Weber is his strategy for constructing "ideal types." For Weber, an ideal type represented a category system for "analytically accentuating" the important features of social phenomena. Ideal types were thus abstractions from empirical reality and their purpose was to highlight certain common features of similar processes and structures. Moreover, they could be used to compare and contrast empirical events in different contexts by providing a common analytical yardstick. For by noting the respective deviations of two or more concrete, empirical situations from the ideal type, it would be possible to compare these two situations and thus better understand them. And thus, for virtually all phenomena studied by Weber—religion, organizations, power, and the like—he constructed an ideal type in order to visualize its structure and functioning.

In many ways, the ideal type strategy corresponds to taxonomic procedures for categorizing species and for describing somatic structures and processes in the biological science. While Weber's work is devoid of the extensive organismic imagery of Durkheim's and other early functional thinkers, his concern with categorization of different social structures was highly compatible with the organismic reasoning of early functionalism. Thus, it is not surprising that contemporary functionalists borrowed both the substantive vision of the world implied by the concepts of structure and function as well as Weber's use of the taxonomic approach for studying structures and processes.

For functionalists in general, and Talcott Parson in particular, the construction of ideal types remain an important activity. Functionalists elaborately categorize the social world, or organism, in order to emphasize the importance of some structures and processes for maintaining the social system. For example, much like Weber before him, Parsons first developed a category system for individual social action and then elaborated this initial system of categories into an incredibly complex analytical edifice of concepts. What is important to recognize is that this strategy of developing category systems *first* and only then propositions about the relationships among categorized phenomena lies at the heart of contemporary functionalism. This emphasis on category systems is, no doubt, one of the subtle ways that Weber's "ideal type strategy" continues to influence functional theorizing in sociology.

THE EMERGENCE OF FUNCTIONALISM:
AN OVERVIEW

With its roots in the organicism of the early 19th century, functionalism is the oldest and, until recently, the dominant conceptual perspective in sociology. The organicism of Comte and later that of Spencer and Durkheim clearly influenced the first functional anthropologists—Malinowski and Radcliffe-Brown—who, in turn, with Durkheim's timeless analysis, helped shape the more modern functional perspectives. Coupled with Weber's emphasis on social taxonomies—or ideal types—of both subjective meaning and social structure, a strategy for studying the properties of the "social organism" similarly began to shape contemporary functionalism.

In emphasizing the contribution of sociocultural items to the maintenance of a more inclusive systemic whole, early functional theorists often conceptualized social "needs" or "requisites." The most extreme formulation of this position was that of Malinowski, in which all cultural items were viewed as meeting one of various levels of needs or requisites: biological, psychological, and sociocultural. More tempered in their statements and more aware of the problems in postulating social "needs" were Émile Durkheim and A. R. Radcliffe-Brown, who implicitly "hypothesized" the requisite for social integration, but who also recognized that needs for integration do not necessarily cause the processes and structures leading to such integration. For them, it was important to analyze separately the causes and functions of a sociocultural item, since the causes of an item could be unrelated to its function in the systemic whole. However, despite their awareness of this fact, in their analyses of actual phenomena both Durkheim and Radcliffe-Brown lapsed into assertions that the need for integration caused a particular event—say, for example, the emergence of a particular type of lineage system or the division of labor.

This tendency for their theoretical statements to blur the distinction between cause and function created two related problems in the analyses of Durkheim and Radcliffe-Brown: those of tautology and illegitimate teleology. To say that a structural item, such as the division of labor, emerges because of the need for social integration is a teleological assertion, for an end state—social integration—is presumed to cause the event—the division of labor—which brings about this very end state.

Such a statement is not necessarily illegitimate, since, indeed, the social world is rife with systemic wholes that initiate and regulate the very structures and processes maintaining them. However, to assert that the need for integration is the cause of the division of labor is probably an illegitimate teleology, since to make the teleology legitimate would require some documentation of the causal chain of events through which needs for integration operate to produce a division of labor. Without such documentation, the statement is vague and theoretically vacuous. Assumptions about, and taxonomies of, system "needs" and "requisites" also create problems of tautology, for, unless clear-cut and independent criteria can be established to determine when a system requisite is fulfilled, or not fulfilled, theoretical statements become circular: A surviving system is meeting its survival needs; the system under study is surviving; a sociocultural item is a part of this system; therefore, it is likely that this item is meeting the system's needs. Such statements are true by definition, since no independent criteria exist for assessing when a requisite is met and whether a given item meets these criteria. To stretch Durkheim's analysis for purposes of illustration, without clear criteria for determining what constitutes "integration" and what levels of "integration" denote a "surviving" system, the statement that the division of labor meets an existing system's needs for integration must be true by definition, since the system exists and is therefore surviving and the division of labor is its most conspicuous integrative structure.

In looking back on the theoretical efforts of early functionalists, then, the legacy of their analytical work can be summarized as follows:

1. The social world was viewed in systemic terms. For the most part, such systems were considered to have needs and requisites that had to be met to assure survival.

2. Despite their concern with evolution, thinkers tended to view systems with needs and requisites as having "normal" and "pathological" states—thus connoting system equilibrium and homeostasis.

3. When viewed as a system, the social world was seen as composed of mutually interrelated parts; the analysis of these interrelated parts focused on how they fulfilled requisites of systemic wholes and, hence, maintained system normality or equilibrium.

4. By typically viewing interrelated parts in relation to the maintenance of a systemic whole, causal analysis frequently became vague, lapsing into tautologies and illegitimate teleologies.[27]

---

[27] For a more thorough analysis of the historical legacy of functionalism, see Don Martindale's *The Nature and Types of Sociological Theory* and his "Limits of and Alternatives to Functionalism in Sociology," in *Functionalism in the Social Sciences*, American

Much of contemporary functionalism has attempted to incorporate the suggestiveness of early functional analysis—especially the conception of "system" as composed of interrelated parts. At the same time, current forms of functional theorizing have tried to cope with the analytical problem of teleology and tautology, which Durkheim and Radcliffe-Brown so unsuccessfully tried to avoid. In borrowing the organicism of the 19th century and in attempting to exploit conceptually the utility of viewing system parts as having implications for the operation of systemic wholes, modern functionalism provided early sociological theorizing with a unified conceptual perspective.

Moreover, in developing a concern with categorizations, as opposed to propositions, functional theory often appeared to "make sense" of the complexities of social structures and processes. However, the adequacy of this perspective has increasingly been called into question in recent decades, for as will be discovered throughout this book, such questioning has often led to excessively polemical and counterproductive debates in sociology. On the positive side, however, the controversy over functional theorizing has also stimulated attempts to expand upon old conceptual perspectives and to develop new perspectives as alternatives to what are perceived to be the inadequacies of functionalism.

Without this sometimes heated dialogue, a book on theory in sociology might be short, since there would be little diversity among perspectives. The intensity of the debate over functionalism has divided the field into various "theoretical camps," which, while overlapping to some extent, do allow demarcation of several major theoretical perspectives and their respective proponents. Two figures have emerged to expound the utility of the functionalist perspective: Talcott Parsons and Robert K. Merton, who are discussed in Chapters 3 and 4, respectively. Thinkers who question the functionalist approach are treated in subsequent sections.

Academy of Political and Social Science Monograph, no. 5 (Philadelphia, 1965), pp. 144–62; see also in this monograph, Ivan Whitaker, "The Nature and Value of Functionalism in Sociology," ibid., pp. 127–43.

3

REQUISITE FUNCTIONALISM: TALCOTT PARSONS

In 1937, Talcott Parsons published his first major work, *The Structure of Social Action*.[1] With exhaustive and detailed scholarship seldom equaled in sociological works, Parsons delineated the strengths and weaknesses of prominent thinkers in three main intellectual traditions: utilitarianism, positivism, and idealism. In this review, Parsons indicated how key assumptions and concepts from these three traditions could be synthesized to form a more adequate conceptual base for subsequent sociological theorizing. Emerging from this effort was not only a substantive vision of social phenomena, which was to become the subject of heated controversy, but also a unique strategy for building sociological theory.[2]

In reviewing Parsons' contribution to sociological theorizing, it is necessary to remain attuned to the interplay between Parsons' initial substantive vision of social life and the strategy he advocated for conceptualizing this vision. Out of this interplay has proliferated a "general theory of action." While constantly supplemented over the last four decades, the general theory of action has never become conceptually disassociated from the analytical base first laid in *The Structure of Social Action*.

---

[1] Talcott Parsons, *The Structure of Social Action* (New York: McGraw-Hill Book Co., 1937); the most recent paperback edition (New York: Free Press, 1968) will be used in subsequent footnotes.

[2] While few appear to agree with all aspects of "Parsonian theory," rarely has anyone quarreled with the assertion that he has been the dominant sociological figure of this century. For documentation of Parsons' influence, see Robert W. Friedrichs, *A Sociology of Sociology* (New York: Free Press, 1970); and Alvin W. Gouldner, *The Coming Crisis of Western Sociology* (New York: Basic Books, 1970).

The developmental continuity in action theory over several decades is perhaps one of its most distinguishing features.[3] To appreciate how such an intellectual feat has been possible requires an understanding of Parsons' faithful adherence to a somewhat unique conception of how to build sociological theory.

THE PARSONIAN STRATEGY FOR BUILDING SOCIOLOGICAL THEORY

In *The Structure of Social Action*, Parsons advocated an "analytical realism" in building sociological theory. Theory in sociology must utilize a limited number of important concepts that "adequately 'grasp' aspects of the objective external world. . . . These concepts correspond not to concrete phenomena, but to elements in them which are analytically separable from other elements."[4] Thus, theory must, first of all, involve the development of concepts that abstract from empirical reality, in all its diversity and confusion, common analytical elements. In this way, concepts will isolate phenomena from their imbeddedness in the complex relations that go to make up social reality.

The unique feature of Parsons' "analytical realism" was his insistence on how these abstract concepts are to be employed in sociological analysis. Parsons did not advocate the immediate incorporation of these concepts into theoretical statements, but rather, their use to develop a "generalized system of concepts." This use of abstract concepts would involve the ordering of concepts into a coherent whole that would reflect the important features of the "real world." What is sought is an ordering of concepts into analytical systems that grasp the salient and systemic features of the universe without being overwhelmed by empirical details. This emphasis upon systems of categories represents Parsons' application of Weber's "ideal type strategy" for analytically accentuating salient features of the world. Thus, much like Weber's work, Parsons' view is that theory should initially resemble an elaborate classification and cate-

---

[3] It has been emphasized again and again that such continuity does not exist in Parsons' work. For the most often quoted source of this position, see Joseph F. Scott, "The Changing Foundations of the Parsonian Action Scheme," *American Sociological Review* 28 (October 1969): 716–35. This position is held to be incorrect in the analysis to follow. In addition to the present discussion, see also Jonathan H. Turner and Leonard Beeghley, "Current Folklore in the Criticisms of Parsonian Action Theory," *Sociological Inquiry*, 44 (Winter, 1974). See also, Parsons' reply and comments on this article, ibid. For a more recent comment on this issue, see: Dean Robert Gerstein, "a note on the continuity of Parsonian Action Theory," *Sociological Inquiry*, 46 (Winter, 1976).

[4] Parsons, *Structure of Social Action*, p. 730.

gorization of social phenomena which reflects significant features in the organization of these social phenomena.

However, Parsons had more than mere classification in mind, for he was advocating the priority of developing systems of concepts over systems of propositions. Concepts in theory should not be incorporated into propositions prematurely. They must first be ordered into analytical systems that are isomorphic with the systemic coherence of reality; then, if one is so inclined, operational definitions can be devised and the concepts can be incorporated into true theoretical statements.

Thus, only after systemic coherence among abstract concepts has been achieved is it fruitful to begin the job of constructing true theory. Propositional inventories of existence, associational, and causal statements cannot hope to capture the "realness" of the social world until conceptual classification of the systemic nature of the universe is performed. Extending Weber's methodology, then, Parsons has thus advocated a particular *strategy* for theory building in sociology. It is only after this strategy is comprehended that Parsons' subsequent theoretical and substantive work makes sense. For indeed, throughout his intellectual career—from *Structure of Social Action* to the present—Parsons has adhered to this *strategy* for building sociological theory.[5]

THE PARSONIAN IMAGE OF SOCIAL ORGANIZATION

Parsons' strategy for theory building maintains a clear-cut ontological position: The social universe displays systemic features that must be captured by a parallel ordering of abstract concepts. Curiously, the substantive implications of this strategy for viewing the world as composed of systems were recessive in *The Structure of Social Action*. Much more conspicuous were assumptions about the "voluntaristic" nature of the social world.

The "voluntaristic theory of action" represented for Parsons a synthesis of the useful assumptions and concepts of utilitarianism, positivism, and idealism. In reviewing the thought of classical economists, Parsons noted the excessivenesses of their utilitarian conceptualization of unregulated and atomistic actors in a free and competitive marketplace rationally attempting to choose those actions that would maximize their profits in their transactions with others. Such a formulation of the social order

---

[5] See Parsons, ibid., especially pp. 3–43, 727–76. For an excellent secondary analysis of Parsons' position and why it does not appeal to the critics, see Enno Schwanenberg, "The Two Problems of Order in Parsons' Theory: An Analysis from Within," *Social Forces* 49 (June 1971): 569–81.

presented for Parsons a number of critical problems: Did humans always behave rationally? Were they indeed free and unregulated? How was order possible in an unregulated and competitive system? Yet, Parsons saw as fruitful several features of utilitarian thought, especially the concern with actors as seeking goals (or profits) and the emphasis on the choice-making capacities of human beings who weighed alternative lines of action. Stated in this minimal form, Parsons felt that the utilitarian heritage could indeed continue to inform sociological theorizing. In a similar critical stance, Parsons rejected the extreme formulations of radical positivists, who tended to view the social world in terms of observable cause-and-effect relationships among physical phenomena. In so doing, he felt, they ignored the complex symbolic functionings of the human mind. Furthermore, Parsons saw the emphasis on observable cause-and-effect relationships as too easily encouraging a sequence of infinite reductionism: groups were reduced to the causal relationships of their individual members; individuals were reducible to the cause-and-effect relationships of their physiological processes; these were reducible to physicochemical relationships, and so on, down to the most basic cause-and-effect connections among particles of physical matter. Nevertheless, despite these extremes, radical positivism did draw attention to the physical parameters of social life and to the deterministic impact of these parameters on much—but, of course, not all—social organization. Finally, in assessing idealism, Parsons saw as useful their conceptions of "ideas" as also circumscribing both individual and social processes, although all too frequently these "ideas" were seen as detached from the ongoing social life they were supposed to regulate.

The scholarship in Parsons' analysis of these traditions cannot be recaptured, but perhaps more important than the details of his analysis is the weaving of selected concepts from each of these traditions into a "voluntaristic theory of action."[6] For it is at this starting point that, in accordance with his theory-building strategy, Parsons began to con-

---

[6] Recently, there has been considerable debate, and acrimony, over "de-Parsonizing" Weber and Durkheim. The presumption is that Parsons gave a distorted portrayal of these and other figures and it is necessary to reexamine their works in an effort to remove Parsons' interpretation from them. This plea ignores two facts: (1) Parsons never maintained that he was summarizing works; he was using works and selectively borrowing concepts to build a theory of action; (2) all sociologists can read these classic thinkers for themselves and derive their own interpretation; there is no reason that they should be overly influenced by Parsons. For the relevant articles, see Jere Cohen, Lawrence E. Hazelrigg, and Whitney Pope, "De-Parsonizing Weber: a Critique of Parsons' interpretation of Weber's Sociology," *American Sociological Review*, 40 (April 1975): 229–41; and Whitney Pope, Jere Cohen, and Lawrence Hazelrigg, "On the Divergence of Weber and Durkheim: A Critique of Parsons' Convergence Thesis," *American Sociological Review*, 40 (August 1975): 417–27.

struct a functional theory of social organization. In this initial formulation, he conceptualizes voluntarism as the subjective decision-making processes of individual actors, but he views such decisions as the partial outcome of certain kinds of constraints, both normative and situational. Voluntaristic action therefore involves these basic elements: (1) *actors* who, at this point in Parsons' thinking, are individual persons; (2) actors are viewed as *goal seeking;* (3) actors are also in possession of alternative *means* to achieve the goals; (4) actors are confronted with a variety of *situational conditions,* such as their own biological makeup and heredity as well as various external ecological constraints, which influence the selection of goals and means; (5) actors are seen to be governed by values, norms, and other ideas in that these ideas influence what is considered a goal and what means are selected to achieve it; thus, (6) action involves *actors making subjective decisions about the means to achieve goals,* all of which are *constrained by ideas* and *situational conditions.* This conceptualization of "voluntarism" is represented diagrammatically in Figure 3–1.

FIGURE 3–1
The Units of Voluntaristic Action

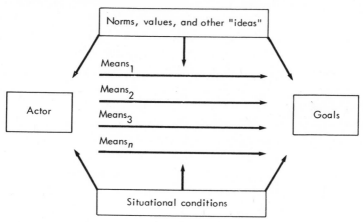

The processes diagrammed in Figure 3–1 are often termed the *unit act,* with social action involving a succession of such unit acts by one or more actors. Parsons appears to have chosen to focus on such basic units of action for at least two reasons: (1) He felt it necessary to synthesize the historical legacy of social thought—from social philosophy and classical economics to early sociological theory—concerning the most basic social process, especially when dissected into its most elementary components. (2) Given his position on what theory should be, it is clear that the first analytical task in the development of sociological theory was to isolate conceptually the systemic features of the most basic unit from which more complex processes and structures were built.

Once these basic tasks were completed, Parsons appears to have asked: How are unit acts connected to each other and how can this connectedness be conceptually represented? Indeed, near the end of *The Structure of Social Action*, he recognized that "any atomistic system that deals only with properties identifiable in the unit act . . . will of necessity fail to treat these latter elements adequately and be indeterminate as applied to complex systems."[7] However, only the barest hints of what was to come were evident in those closing pages.

Yet, perhaps only through the wisdom of hindsight, Parsons did offer several clues about the features of these "more complex" systems. Most notable, near the close of this first work, he emphasized that "the concept of action points again to the *organic* property of action systems" [emphasis added].[8] Buttressed by the ontology of his strategy for building theory—that is, the development of systems of concepts that mirror reality—it is clear what he intended to do: develop a conceptual scheme that captured the systemic essence of social reality.

By 1945, eight years after he published *The Structure of Social Action*, Parsons became more explicit about the form this analysis should take: "The structure of social systems cannot be derived directly from the actor-situation frame of reference. It requires *functional* analysis of the complications introduced by the interaction of a plurality of actors" [emphasis added].[9] More significantly, this functional analysis should allow notions of "needs" to enter: "The functional needs of social integration and the conditions necessary for the functioning of a plurality of actors as a 'unit' system sufficiently well integrated to exist as such impose others."[10] Starting from these assumptions, which bear a close resemblance to those of Spencer, Durkheim, Radcliffe-Brown, and Malinowski, Parsons began to develop a complex functional scheme.

THE EARLY SYSTEMS OF ACTION

The transition from the analysis of discrete unit acts to systems of action appears to have occurred in a series of conceptual elaborations:

---

[7] Parsons, *Structure of Social Action*, pp. 748–49.

[8] Ibid., p. 745.

[9] Talcott Parsons, "The Present Position and Prospect of Systemic Theory in Sociology," *Essays in Sociological Theory* (New York: Free Press, 1949), p. 229.

[10] Ibid.

(1) Unit acts are not emitted in a social vacuum—as was clearly recognized in *The Structure of Social Action*. (2) Rather, unit acts occur in a social context, a context in which an actor occupies a status and enacts normatively prescribed role behaviors. (3) Status-roles are not unrelated, but, in fact, are connected to each other in various types of systems. (4) Unit acts must therefore be viewed from the perspective of *systems of interaction*, in which action is now seen as patterns of role enactments by actors. (5) These interaction systems comprised of a plurality of actors occupying statuses and enacting normatively prescribed roles are viewed as comprising a *social* system.

However, as can be recalled from *The Structure of Social Action*, the "structure of action" involves more than normatively prescribed behaviors. First, action involves individual decision making in the pursuit of goals. Second, values and other ideas circumscribe the actor's decision making in the pursuit of goals. Third, situational conditions, such as heredity and features of the physical environment, further constrain action.

These components of action also began to be viewed in a systemic context, leading Parsons at first to postulate one additional system of action, the *personality*, which would encompass the systemic interrelations among needs and decision-making capacities of actors enacting roles in the social system. At this early stage in the transition from the analysis of unit acts to systems of action, neither culture nor the organic and physical features of action were viewed as systems. However, *cultural patterns* figured prominently in the analysis in that they were seen as underlying both the normative structure of the social system and the need dispositions and decision-making processes of the personality system.[11] But given Parsons' commitment to developing analytical schemes that captured the connected coherence of reality and given this new commitment to analytically separating the components of the unit act into discrete systems of action, he soon began to visualize culture in systemic terms. And somewhat later the physical features of organisms, such as heredity and other biological processes, were also seen as a separable system of action.

As a sociologist, Parsons recognized that his main theoretical concern involved the analysis of social systems. Thus, his second book, appearing

---

[11] However, even at this early stage Parsons frequently talked as if culture were a system, anticipating the later conceptualization of culture as a true system. For a comparison of the different emphases, see, first, Talcott Parsons, *Toward a General Theory of Action* (New York: Harper & Row, 1951), pp. 20–23, and then, Talcott Parsons, *Societies: Evolutionary and Comparative Perspectives* (Englewood Cliffs, N.J.: Prentice-Hall, Inc., 1966.

some 14 years after *The Structure of Social Action*, was appropriately entitled *The Social System*.[12] It was in this book that the analytical distinctions among social and personality systems, as well as cultural patterns, were first analyzed in detail. Since much of the subsequent development of "action theory" is an elaboration of this analysis, it is perhaps wise to pause and examine this work in detail.

Parsons' *The Social System*

Analyzing social systems involves developing a system of concepts that, first of all, captures the systemic features of society at all its diverse levels and, second, points to the modes of articulation among personality systems, social systems, and cultural patterns.

To capture conceptually the systemic features of culture, society, and personality, Parsons wastes little time in introducing notions of functional requisites for each of these basic components of action. Such requisites pertain not only to the internal problems of the action components, but also to their articulation with one another. Following both Durkheim's and Radcliffe-Brown's lead, he views *integration* within and among the two action systems and the cultural patterns as a basic survival requisite. Since the social system is his major topic, Parsons is concerned with the integration within the social system itself and between the social system and the cultural patterns, on the one hand, and between the social system and the personality system, on the other. In order for such integration to occur, at least two functional requisites must be met:

1. A social system must have "a sufficient proportion of its component actors adequately motivated to act in accordance with the requirements of its role system."[13]
2. Social systems must avoid "commitment to cultural patterns which either fail to define a minimum of order or which place impossible demands on people and thereby generate deviance and conflict."[14]

Having made explicit the incorporation of requisites, which in later works are expanded and made even more prominent, Parsons then attempts to develop a conceptual scheme that reflects the systemic interconnectedness of social systems, although he later returns to the integrative

---

[12] Talcott Parsons, *The Social System* (New York: Free Press, 1951).
[13] Ibid., p. 27.
[14] Ibid., pp. 27–28.

problems posed by the articulation of culture and the personality system with the social system. Crucial to this conceptualization of the social system is the concept of *institutionalization*, which refers to relatively stable patterns of interaction among actors in statuses. Such patterns are normatively regulated and infused with cultural patterns. This infusing of values can occur in two ways: First, norms regulating role behaviors can reflect the general values and beliefs of culture. Second, cultural values and other patterns can become internalized in the personality system and, hence, affect that system's need structure, which, in turn, determines an actor's willingness to enact roles in the social system.

Parsons views institutionalization as both a process and a structure. It is significant that he initially discusses the *process of institutionalization* and only then refers to it as a structure—a fact that is often ignored by critics who contend that action theory is overly structural. As a process, institutionalization can be typified in this way: (1) Actors who are variously oriented enter into situations where they must interact. (2) The way actors are oriented is a reflection of their need structure and how this need structure has been altered by the internalization of cultural patterns. (3) Through specific interaction processes—which are not clearly indicated, but which by implication include role taking, role bargaining, and exchange—norms emerge as actors adjust their orientations to each other. (4) Such norms emerge as a way of adjusting the orientations of actors to each other, but, at the same time, they are circumscribed by general cultural patterns. (5) In turn, these norms regulate subsequent interaction, giving it stability. It is through such a process that institutionalized patterns are created, maintained, and altered.

As interactions become institutionalized, a "social system" can be said to exist. While Parsons has typically been concerned with whole societies, a social system is not necessarily a whole society, for indeed any organized pattern of interaction, whether a micro or macro form, is termed a "social system." When focusing on total societies, or large parts of them that are composed of several of these interrelated clusters of institutionalized roles, Parsons frequently refers to the constituent social systems as *subsystems*.

In sum, then, institutionalization is the process through which social structure is built up and maintained. Institutionalized clusters of roles—or, to phrase it differently, stabilized patterns of interaction—comprise a social system. When the given social system is large and is composed of many interrelated institutions, these institutions are typically viewed as subsystems. A total society may be defined as one large system composed of interrelated institutions. At all times, for analytical purposes, it is necessary to remember that a social system is circumscribed by cultural patterns and infused with personality systems.

In his commitment to the development of concepts that reflected the properties of all action systems, Parsons was led to a set of concepts denoting some of the variable properties of these systems. Termed "pattern variables," they allowed for the categorization of the modes of orientation in personality systems, the value patterns of culture, and the normative requirements in social systems. The variables were phrased in terms of polar dichotomies, which, depending upon the system under analysis, would allow for a rough categorization of decisions by actors, the value orientations of culture, or the normative demands on status roles.

1. *Affectivity–affective neutrality* concerns the amount of emotion or affect that is appropriate in a given interaction situation. Should a great deal or little affect be expressed?

2. *Diffuseness-specificity* denotes the issue of how far reaching obligations in an interaction situation are to be. Should the obligations be narrow and specific or should they be extensive and diffuse?

3. *Universalism-particularism* points to the problem of whether evaluation and judgment of others in an interaction situation is to apply to all actors or should all actors be assessed in terms of the same standards?

4. *Achievement-ascription* deals with the issue of how to assess an actor, whether in terms of performance or on the basis of inborn qualities, such as sex, age, race, and family status. Should an actor treat another on the basis of achievements or ascriptive qualities that are unrelated to performance?

5. *Self-collectivity* denotes the extent to which action is to be oriented to self-interest and individual goals or to group interests and goals. Should actors consider their personal or self-related goals over those of the group or large collectivity in which they are involved.[15]

Some of these concepts, such as self-collectivity, have been dropped from the action scheme, while others, such as universalism-particularism have assumed greater importance. But the intent of the pattern variables has remained the same: to categorize dichotomies of decisions, normative demands, and value orientations. However, in *The Social System*, Parsons

---

[15] These pattern variables were developed in collaboration with Edward Shils and were elaborated upon in *Toward a General Theory of Action*, pp, 76–98, 203–4, 183–89. Again, Parsons' debt to Max Weber's concern with constructing "ideal types" can be seen in his presentation of the pattern variables.

is inclined to view them as value orientations that circumscribe the norms of the social system and the decisions of the personality system. Thus, the patterns of the two true systems of action—personality and social—are a reflection of the dominant patterns of value orientations in culture. This implicit emphasis on the impact of cultural patterns on regulating and controlling other systems of action was to become more explicit in later work—as will be discussed shortly.

However, for the present, it is evident that Parsons has woven a complex conceptual system that emphasizes the process of institutionalization of interaction into stabilized patterns called social systems, which are penetrated by personality and circumscribed by culture. The profile of institutionalized norms, of decisions by actors in roles, and of cultural value orientations can be typified in terms of concepts—the pattern variables—that capture the variable properties in each of these components of action.

Having built this analytical edifice, Parsons returns to a question first raised in *The Structure of Social Action*, which has guided all his subsequent theoretical formulations: How do social systems survive? More specifically, why do institutionalized patterns of interaction persist? This question again raises the issue of system imperatives or requisites, for Parsons is asking how systems resolve their integrative problems. The "answer" to this question is provided by the elaboration of additional concepts that point to the ways personality systems and culture are integrated into the social system, thereby providing assurance of some degree of normative coherence and a minimal amount of commitment by actors to conform to norms and play roles. In developing concepts of this kind, Parsons begins to weigh his analysis in the direction of an ontology that stresses the equilibrating tendencies of social systems.

Just how are personality systems integrated into the social system, thereby promoting equilibrium? At the most abstract level, Parsons conceptualizes two "mechanisms" that integrate the personality into the social system, mechanisms of socialization and mechanisms of social control. It is through the operation of these mechanisms that personality systems become structured such that they are compatible with the structure of social systems.

In abstract terms, *socialization mechanisms* are seen by Parsons as the means through which cultural patterns—values, beliefs, language, and other symbols—are internalized into the personality system, thereby circumscribing the latter's need structure. It is through this process that actors are made willing to deposit motivational energy in roles (thereby willing to conform to norms) and are given the interpersonal and other skills necessary for playing roles. Another function of socialization mechanisms is to provide stable and secure interpersonal ties that alleviate much of the strain, anxiety, and tension associated with acquiring "proper" motives and skills.

Mechanisms of social control involve those ways in which status roles are organized in social systems to reduce strain and deviance. There are numerous specific control mechanisms, including (*a*) institutionalization, which makes role expectations clear and unambiguous, while segregating in time and space contradictory expectations; (*b*) interpersonal sanctions and gestures, which actors subtly employ to mutually sanction conformity; (*c*) ritual activities, in which actors act out symbolically sources of strain that could prove disruptive, and which at the same time reinforce dominant cultural patterns; (*d*) safety-valve structures, in which pervasive "deviant" propensities are segregated in time and space from "normal" institutional patterns; (*e*) reintegration structures, which are specifically charged with coping with and bringing back into line deviant tendencies; and, finally, (*f*) the institutionalization into some sectors of a system which has the capacity to use force and coercion.

These two mechanisms are thus viewed as resolving one of the most persistent integrative problems (read *requisites*) facing social systems. The other major integrative problem facing social systems concerns how cultural patterns contribute to the maintenance of social order and equilibrium. Again at the most abstract level, Parsons visualizes two ways in which this occurs: (*a*) Some components of culture, such as language, are basic "resources" necessary for interaction to occur. Without symbolic resources, communication and hence interaction would not be possible. Thus, by providing common "resources" for all actors, interaction is made possible by culture. (*b*) A related but still separable influence of culture on interaction is exerted through the substance of "ideas" contained in cultural patterns (values, beliefs, ideology, and so forth). These ideas can provide actors with common viewpoints, personal ontologies, or, to borrow from W. I. Thomas, a common "definition of the situation." These "common meanings" (to use G. H. Mead's term) allow interaction to proceed smoothly with minimal disruption.

Naturally, Parsons acknowledges that the mechanisms of socialization and social control are not always successful, hence allowing deviance and social change to occur. But it is clear that the concepts developed here in *The Social System* weight analysis in the direction of looking for processes that maintain the integration and, by implication, the equilibrium of social systems. The subsequent developments of "action theory" represent an attempt to expand upon the basic analytical scheme of *The Social System*, while trying to accommodate some of the critics' charges of a static and conservative conceptual bias (see later section). The critics of action theory have not been silenced, but some interesting elaborations of the scheme have occurred in the quarter century following Parsons' first explicitly functional work.

ELABORATION OF SYSTEM REQUISITES

Shortly after the publication of *The Social System*, Parsons, in collaboration with Robert Bales and Edward Shils, published *Working Papers in the Theory of Action*.[16] It was in this work that conceptions of functional imperatives came to dominate the general theory of action; and by 1956, with Parsons and Neil Smelser's publication of *Economy and Society*,[17] the functions of structures for meeting system requisites were well "institutionalized" into action theory.

During this period, systems of action were conceptualized to have four survival problems, or requisites: adaptation, goal attainment, integration, and latency. *Adaptation* involves the problem of securing from the environment sufficient facilities and then distributing these facilities throughout the system. *Goal attainment* refers to the problem of establishing priorities among system goals and mobilizing system resources for their attainment. *Integration* denotes the problem of coordinating and maintaining viable interrelationships among system units. *Latency* embraces two related problems: pattern maintenance and tension management. Pattern maintenance pertains to the problem of how to insure that actors in the social system display the "appropriate" characteristics (motives, needs, role-playing skills, and so forth). Tension management concerns the problem of dealing with the internal tensions and strains of actors in the social system.

All of these requisites were implicit in *The Social System*, but they tended to be viewed under the general problem of integration. Yet, in the discussion of integration within and between action systems in *The Social System*, "problems" of securing facilities (adaptation), allocation and goal seeking (goal attainment), socialization and social control (latency) were conspicuous. The development of the four functional requisites—abbreviated A, G, I, and L—is thus not so much a radical departure

---

16 Talcott Parsons, Robert F. Bales, and Edward A. Shils, *Working Papers in the Theory of Action* (Glencoe, Ill.: Free Press, 1953).

17 Talcott Parsons and Neil J. Smelser, *Economy and Society* (New York: Free Press, 1956).

from earlier works, but an elaboration of concepts implicit in *The Social System.*

However, with the introduction of A, G, I, L, there is a subtle shift away from the analysis of structures to the analysis of functions. Structures are now viewed *explicitly* in terms of their functional consequences for resolving the four problems. Interrelationships among specific structures are now analyzed in terms of how their interchanges affect the requisites that each must meet. In fact, Parsons now views every system and subsystem as having to resolve the problems of A, G, I, and L. Diagrammatically, this view of the social system is represented in Figure 3–2.

FIGURE 3–2
The Functional View of Social Systems

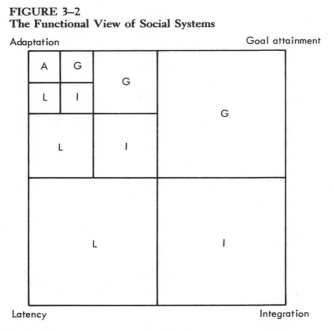

As is evident from Figure 3–2, any system or subsystem can be divided into four sectors, each denoting a survival problem—whether A, G, I, or L. Thus, a total society has to resolve the problems of A, G, I, L; but so does each of its constituent subsystems, as is illustrated for the adaptation sector in Figure 3–2. Thus, as is depicted in the adaptation sector of Figure 3–2, all systems at any system level, whether large or small, must resolve the four system requisites of A, G, I, L.

Of critical analytical importance in this scheme are the interchanges among systems and subsystems. It is difficult to comprehend the functioning of a designated social system without examining the interchanges among its A, G, I, and L sectors, especially as these interchanges are affected by exchanges among constituent subsystems and other systems in the environment. In turn, the functioning of a designated subsystem cannot be understood without examining internal interchanges among its adaptive, goal attainment, integrative, and latency sectors, especially as these interchanges are influenced by exchanges with other subsystems and the more inclusive system of which it is a subsystem. Thus at this juncture, as important interchanges among the functional sectors of systems and subsystems are outlined, the Parsonian scheme now begins to resemble an elaborate mapping operation.

THE INFORMATIONAL HIERARCHY OF CONTROL

Toward the end of the 1950s, Parsons turned attention toward interrelationships *among* (rather than within) what were then four distinct action systems: culture, social structure, personality, and organism. In many ways, this concern represented an odyssey back to the analysis of the basic components of the "unit act" outlined in *The Structure of Social Action*. But now, each element of the unit act was a full-fledged action system, each confronting four functional problems to resolve: adaptation, goal attainment, integration, and latency. Furthermore, while individual decision making was still a part of action as personalities adjusted to the normative demands of status-roles in the social system, the analytical emphasis had shifted to the input-output connections among the four action systems.

It is at this juncture that Parsons begins to visualize an overall action system, with culture, social structure, personality, and organism comprising its constituent subsystems.[18] Each of these subsystems is seen as fulfilling one of the four system requisites—A, G, I, L—of the overall action system. The organism is considered to be the subsystem having the most consequences for resolving adaptive problems, since it is ultimately through this system that environmental resources are made available to the other action subsystems. As the goal-seeking and decision-making system, personality is considered to have primary consequences for resolving goal-attainment problems. As an organized network of status-

---

[18] Talcott Parsons, "An Approach to Psychological Theory in Terms of the Theory of Action," in *Psychology: A Science*, ed. S. Koch, vol. 3 (New York: McGraw-Hill Book Co., 1958), pp. 612–711. By 1961, these ideas were even more clearly formulated; see Talcott Parsons, "An Outline of the Social System," in *Theories of Society*, ed. T. Parsons, E. Shils, K. D. Naegele, and J. R. Pitts (New York: Free Press, 1961), pp. 30–38. See also Jackson Toby, "Parsons' Theory of Social Evolution," *Contemporary Sociology* 1 (September 1972): 395–401.

norms integrating the patterns of the cultural system and the needs of personality systems, the social system is viewed as the major integrative subsystem of the general action system. As the repository of symbolic content of interaction, the cultural system is considered to have primary consequences for managing tensions of actors and assuring that the proper symbolic resources are available to assure the maintenance of institutional patterns (latency).

After viewing each action system as a subsystem of a more inclusive, overall action system, Parsons begins to explore the interrelations among the four subsystems. What emerges is a hierarchy of informational controls, with culture informationally circumscribing the social system, social structure informationally regulating the personality system, and personality informationally regulating the organismic system. For example, cultural value orientations would be seen as circumscribing or limiting the range of variation in the norms of the social system; in turn, these norms, as translated into expectations for actors playing roles, would be viewed as limiting the kinds of motives and decision-making processes in personality systems; these features of the personality system would then be seen as circumscribing biochemical processes in the organism. Conversely, each system in the hierarchy is also viewed as providing the "energic conditions" necessary for action at the next higher system. That is, the organism provides the energy necessary for the personality system, the personality system provides the energic conditions for the social system, and the organization of personality systems into a social system provides the conditions necessary for a cultural system. Thus, the input-output relations among action systems are reciprocal, with systems exchanging information and energy. Systems high in information circumscribe the utilization of energy at the next lower system level,

FIGURE 3–3
The Cybernetic Hierarchy of Control

Function	System	Interrelations
Latency	Cultural system control energy	Informational controls
Integration	Social system control energy	
Goal attainment	Personality system control energy	
Adaptation	Organismic system	Energic conditions

while each lower system provides the conditions and facilities necessary for action in the next higher system. This scheme has been termed a "cybernetic hierarchy" and is diagrammatically represented in Figure 3–3.

GENERALIZED MEDIA OF EXCHANGE

In the last two decades, Parsons has maintained his interest in the intra- and inter-systemic relationships of the four action systems. Although he has yet to develop the concepts fully, he has begun to view these inter- and intra-systemic relationships in terms of "generalized symbolic media of exchange."[19] In any interchange, generalized media are employed—for example, money is used in the economy to facilitate the buying and selling of goods. What typifies these generalized media, such as money, is that they are really symbolic modes of communication. The money is not worth much by itself; its "value" is evident only in terms of what it "says" symbolically in an exchange relationship.

Thus, what Parsons proposes is that the links among action components are ultimately informational. This means that transactions are mediated by symbols. Parsons' emphasis on information is consistent with the development of the idea of a cybernetic hierarchy of control. Informational exchanges, or cybernetic controls, are seen as operating in at least three ways: First, the interchanges or exchanges *among* the four subsystems of the overall action system are carried out by means of different types of symbolic media, that is, money, power, influence, or commitments. Second, the interchanges *within* any of the four action systems are also carried out by means of distinctive symbolic media. This determination of media by functional requisites will hold equally whether within a particular action system or among the four general systems of action. Finally, the system requisites of adaptation (A), goal attainment (G), integration (I), and latency (L) are thought to determine the type of generalized symbolic media used in an inter- or intra-systemic exchange.

Within the social system, the adaptive sector utilizes money as the medium of exchange with the other three sectors; the goal-attainment

---

[19] Parsons' writings on this topic are incomplete, but see Talcott Parsons, "On the Concept of Political Power," *Proceedings of the American Philosophical Society* 107 (June 1963): 232–62; Talcott Parsons, "On the Concept of Influence," *Public Opinion Quarterly* 27 (Spring 1963): 37–62; and Talcott Parsons, "Some Problems of General Theory," in *Theoretical Sociology: Perspectives and Developments*, eds. J. C. McKinney and E. A. Tiryakian (New York: Appleton-Century-Crofts, 1970), pp. 28–68. See also Talcott Parsons and Gerald M. Platt, *The American University* (Cambridge: Harvard University Press, 1975).

sector employs power—the capacity to induce conformity—as its principal medium of exchange; the integrative sector of a social system relies upon influence—the capacity to persuade; and the latency sector uses commitments—especially the capacity to be loyal. The analysis of interchanges of specific structures within social systems should thus focus on the input-output exchanges utilizing different symbolic media.

Among the subsystems of the overall action system, a similar analysis of the symbolic media used in exchanges should be undertaken, but, as yet, Parsons has not clearly described the nature of these media.[20] What he appears to be approaching is a conceptual scheme for analyzing the basic types of symbolic media, or information, linking systems in the cybernetic hierarchy of control (see Figure 3–3).[21]

PARSONS ON SOCIAL CHANGE

In the last decade Parsons has become increasingly concerned with social change. Built into the cybernetic hierarchy of control is a conceptual scheme for classifying the locus of such social change. What Parsons visualizes is that the information-energic interchanges among action systems provide the potential for change within or between the action systems. One source of change may be excesses in either information or energy in the exchange among action systems, which, in turn, alter the informational or energic outputs across systems and within any system. For example, excesses of motivation (energy) would have consequences for the enactment of roles, and perhaps ultimately for the reorganization of these roles, of the normative structure, and eventually of cultural value orientations.[22] Another source of change comes from an insufficient supply of either energy or information, again causing external and internal readjustments in the structure of action systems. For example, value (informational) conflict would cause normative conflict (or anomie), which, in turn, would have consequences for the personality and organismic systems. Thus, inherent in the cybernetic hierarchy

---

[20] For his first attempt at a statement, see Parsons, "Some Problems of General Theory," pp. 61–68.

[21] For a more readable discussion of these "generalized media," see T. S. Turner, "Parsons' Concept of Generalized Media of Social Interaction and its Relevance for Social Anthropology," *Sociological Inquiry* 38 (Spring 1968): 121–34.

[22] There are several bodies of empirical literature that bear on this example. McClelland's work on the achievement motive as initiating economic development in modernizing societies is perhaps the most conspicuous example; see David C. McClelland, *The Achieving Society* (New York: Free Press, 1961).

of control are concepts that point to the sources of both stasis and change.[23]

To augment this new macro emphasis on change, Parsons has become interested in utilizing the action scheme to analyze social evolution in historical societies. In this context, it is of some importance that the first line of *The Structure of Social Action* posed a simple question: "Who now reads Spencer?" Parsons then answered the question by delineating some of the reasons why Spencer's evolutionary doctrine had been so thoroughly rejected by 1937. Now, after some 40 years, Parsons has chosen to reexamine the issue of societal evolution which he so easily dismissed in the beginning.

Drawing heavily not only from Spencer,[24] but also from Durkheim's insights into societal development,[25] Parsons proposes that the processes of evolution display the following elements:

1. Increasing differentiation of system units into patterns of functional interdependence,
2. Establishment of new principles and mechanisms of integration in differentiating systems, and
3. Increasing survival capacity of differentiated systems in relation to the environment.

From the perspective of action theory, evolution therefore involves: (*a*) increasing differentiation of the personality, social, cultural, and organismic systems from one another; (*b*) increasing differentiation within each of these four action subsystems; (*c*) escalating problems of integration and the emergence of new integrative structures; and (*d*) the upgrading of the survival capacity of each action subsystem, as well as of the overall action system, to its environment.[26]

Parsons then embarks on an ambitious effort in two short volumes to outline the pattern of evolution in historical systems through primitive, intermediate, and modern stages.[27,28] In contrast with *The Social System,*

[23] For a fuller discussion, see Alvin L. Jacobson, "Talcott Parsons: A Theoretical and Empirical Analysis of Social Change and Conflict," in *Institutions and Social Exchange: The Sociologies of Talcott Parsons and George C. Homans*, ed. H. Turk and R. L. Simpson (Indianapolis: Bobbs-Merrill Co., 1970).

[24] Herbert Spencer, *First Principles*, vol. 1, 5th ed. (New York: A. L. Burt, 1880), pp. 107–483.

[25] Émile Durkheim, *The Division of Labor in Society* (New York: Free Press, 1933) (first published in 1893).

[26] Parsons, *Societies.*

[27] Ibid., and Talcott Parsons, *The System of Modern Societies* (Englewood Cliffs, N.J.: Prentice-Hall, Inc., 1971).

[28] The general stages of development were first outlined in Talcott Parsons, "Evolutionary Universals in Society," *American Sociological Review* 29 (June 1964): 339–57.

where he stressed the problem of integration between social systems and personality, Parsons draws attention in his evolutionary model to the *inter-* and *intra-* differentiation of the cultural and social systems and to the resulting integrative problems. In fact, each stage of evolution is seen as reflecting a new set of integrative problems between society and culture as each of these systems has become both more internally differentiated and increasingly differentiated from the other. Thus, the concern with the issues of integration within and among action systems, so evident in earlier works, has not been abandoned, but has been applied to the analysis of specific historical processes.

While Parsons is vague about the causes of evolutionary change, he apparently views evolution as guided by the cybernetic hierarchy of controls, especially the informational component. In his concern for documenting how integrative problems of the differentiating social and cultural systems have been resolved in the evolution of historical systems, the informational hierarchy is regarded as crucial, because the regulation of societal processes of differentiation must be accompanied by legitimation from cultural patterns (information). Without such informational control, movement to the next stage of development in an evolutionary sequence will be inhibited.[29]

Thus, the analysis of social change represents an attempt to use the analytical tools of the "general theory of action." What is of interest in this effort is that Parsons develops many propositions about the sequences of change and the processes that will inhibit or accelerate the unfolding of these evolutionary sequences. It is of more than passing interest that preliminary tests of these propositions indicate that, on the whole, they have a great deal of empirical support.[30]

It might be argued from such preliminary "success" that vindication of the strategy for developing sociological theory as first expounded in *The Structure of Social Action* has occurred. As will be recalled, Parsons has steadfastly urged that sociological theory first develop systems of concepts for classifying the social world, and only then attempt to construct bodies of propositions. Perhaps, after many years of developing a system of concepts for depicting social action, Parsons felt it was time to employ that system to develop an inventory of propositions.

---

[29] It should be emphasized that Parsons does not advocate a strict unilineal pattern of evolution. Rather, he is attempting to point to *continuities* in patterns of social change—a tactic that left him open to criticism by those who would point to the discontinuities in social change.

[30] See Gary L. Buck and Alvin L. Jacobson, "Social Evolution and Structural-Functional Analysis: An Empirical Test," *American Sociological Review* 33 (June 1968): 343–55; A. L. Jacobson, "Talcott Parsons: Theoretical and Empirical Analysis."

However, the recent emphasis on social change and the ability of Parsons to use his "theory of action" to generate testable propositions have not silenced his critics. In fact, functionalism has consistently provoked controversy, primarily because the very utility of any form of functional theorizing has been increasingly called into question. It is not surprising, then, that the critics periodically resurrect the same analytical problems first raised by Durkheim and Radcliffe-Brown to indict Parsons' scheme in particular and all forms of functionalism in general.

PERSISTENT CRITICISMS OF PARSONIAN FUNCTIONALISM

Criticisms of Parsons' Image of Society

By the early 1960s a number of critics had begun to question whether Parsons' emerging "system of concepts" corresponded to events in the "real" world. Such a line of criticism is significant because the Parsonian strategy assumes that it is necessary to elaborate a system of concepts that "adequately grasp" salient features of the social world, from which propositions can eventually be derived. Assertions that the maturing system of concepts inadequately mirrors features of actual social systems represent a fundamental challenge to the strategy and substance of Parsons' form of functional theorizing.

Ralf Dahrendorf—the subject of a later chapter—codified this growing body of criticism when he likened functionalism to a "utopia." [31] Much like prominent portrayals of social utopias of the past, Dahrendorf asserted, Parsons' concepts point to a world that (a) reveals no developmental history, (b) evidences only consensus over values and norms, (c) displays a high degree of integration among its components, and (d) reveals only mechanisms that preserve the "status quo." Such an image of society is utopian, because there appears little possibility that ubiquitous phenomena like deviance, conflict, and change could occur.

While the evidence marshaled to support these assertions is minimal, it is not difficult to visualize the source of the critics' dismay. With the publication of *The Social System*, the critics seem to charge, Parsons

---

[31] Ralf Dahrendorf, "Out of Utopia: Toward a Reorientation of Sociological Analysis," *American Journal of Sociology* 64 (September 1958): 115–27. This polemic echoed the earlier assessments by others, including David Lockwood ("Some Remarks on 'The Social System,' " *British Journal of Sociology* 7 [June 1950]: 134–46), C. Wright Mills (*The Sociological Imagination* [New York: Oxford University Press, 1959], pp. 44–49), and Lewis Coser (*The Functions of Social Conflict* [New York: Free Press, 1956], pp. 1–10).

becomes overly concerned with the integration of social systems. In a vein similar to Radcliffe-Brown and Durkheim, the emphasis on the "need" or "requisite" for integration in social systems leads, in the critics' eyes, to a disproportionate concern with those processes in social systems that meet this need for integration. In *The Social System*, this concern with integration is evidenced by the tendency to assume, for analytical purposes, a system that is in "equilibrium." From this starting point, analysis "must" then focus on the elaboration of concepts promoting integration and equilibrium. For example, the extended discussion of institutionalization describes the processes whereby structure is built up, with relatively scant mention of concepts denoting the breakdown and change of institutionalized patterns. To compound this omission, a discussion of how institutionalized patterns are maintained by the "mechanisms" of socialization and social control is launched. For the critics, too much emphasis is placed upon how socialization assures the internalization of values and the alleviation of strains among actors and how mechanisms of social control reduce the potential for malintegration and deviance. When deviance and change are discussed, the critics contend, they are viewed as residual or, in a way reminiscent of Durkheim, as "pathological." In fact, deviance, conflict, and change are so "alien" to the scheme that the social equilibrium is considered to constitute, in Parsons' words, a "first law of social inertia."

The subsequent expansion of concepts denoting four system requisites—adaptation, goal attainment, integration, and latency—has further horrified the critics. For now system processes become almost exclusively viewed in terms of their consequences for meeting an extended list of system needs. In all this concern for the consequences of processes for meeting needs, how is it, the critics ask, that deviance, conflict, and change are to be conceptualized?[32] Are they merely "pathological" events that occur on those rare occasions when system needs are not met? Or, in reality, are not these phenomena pervasive features of social systems, which are "inadequately grasped" by the proliferating system of concepts?

The elaboration of the informational hierarchy of control among the overall systems of action and its use to analyze social *change* has still not silenced the critics, for the only type of change that is conceptualized is "evolution," as opposed to "revolution" and other forms of violent disruption social systems. Much like that of Durkheim and Spencer,

---

[32] Leslie Sklair, "The Fate of the Functional Requisites in Parsonian Sociology," *British Journal of Sociology* 21 (March 1970): 30–42.

Parsons' view of change involves a "progressive" differentiation and integration, with the inexorable progress of societal development delayed from time to time by a failure to integrate the differentiating cultural and social systems.[33]

The Logical Criticisms of Requisite Functionalism

The problems of illegitimate teleology and tautology have consumed a considerable amount of the literature on functionalism.[34] For the most part, this literature holds that since assumptions of needs and requisites are so prominent in functional theorizing, theoretical statements will too frequently lapse into illegitimate teleologies and tautologies. Typically, conspicuous examples of the functional works of Durkheim, Radcliffe-Brown, and Malinowski are cited to confirm the truth of this assertion, but, by implication, the efforts of contemporary functionalists are similarly indicted—otherwise, the criticisms would not be worth the considerable efforts devoted to making them. To the extent that this indirect indictment of Parsons' requisite functionalism can be sustained, it can

---

[33] Perhaps the most recent and scholarly attempt to document the reasons behind these "problems" in Parsonian action theory is provided by Alvin Gouldner in *The Coming Crisis of Western Sociology* (New York: Basic Books, 1970). However, John K. Rhoads in "On Gouldner's Crisis of Western Sociology," *American Journal of Sociology* 78 (July 1972): 136–54, emphasizes that Gouldner has perceived what he wants to perceive in Parsons' work, ignoring those passages that would connote just the opposite of stasis, control, consensus, and order. See also Rhoads, "Reply to Gouldner," *American Journal of Sociology* 78 (May 1973): 1493–96, which was written in response to Gouldner's defense of his position (Alvin Gouldner, "For Sociology: 'Varieties of Political Expression' Revisited," *American Journal of Sociology* 78 [March 1973]: 1063–93, particularly pp. 1083–93).

[34] For analyses of the logic of functionalist inquiry, see R. B. Braithwaite, *Scientific Explanation* (New York: Harper Bros., 1953), chaps. 9 and 10; Carl G. Hempel, "The Logic of Functional Analysis" in *Symposium on Sociological Theory*, ed. L. Gross (New York: Harper & Row, 1959), pp. 271–307; Percy S. Cohen, *Modern Social Theory* (New York: Basic Books, 1968), pp. 58–64; Francesca Cancian, "Functional Analysis of Change," *American Sociological Review* 25 (December 1960): 818–27; S. F. Nadel, *Foundations of Social Anthropology* (Glencoe, Ill.: The Free Press, 1951), pp. 373–78; Ernest Nagel, "Teleological Explanation and Teleological Systems," in *Readings in the Philosophy of Science*, ed. H. Feigl and M. Broadbeck (New York: Harper & Bros., 1953), pp. 537–58; Phillip Ronald Dore, "Function and Cause," *American Sociological Review* 26 (December 1961): 843–53; Charles J. Erasmus, "Obviating the Functions of Functionalism," *Social Forces* 45 (March 1967): 319–28; Harry C. Bredemeier, "The Methodology of Functionalism," *American Sociological Review* 20 (April 1955): 173–80; Bernard Barber, "Structural-Functional Analysis: Some Problems and Misunderstandings," *American Sociological Review* 21 (April 1956): 129–35; Robert K. Merton, *Social Theory and Social Structure* (Glencoe, Ill.: Free Press, 1957), pp. 44–61; Arthur L. Stinchcombe, *Constructing Social Theories* (New York: Harcourt, Brace & World, 1968), pp. 80–116; Hans Zetterberg, *On Theory and Verification in Sociology* (Totowa, N.J.: Bedminister Press, 1965), pp. 74–79.

be considered to represent a serious criticism. For Parsons' strategy for theory building has revolved around the assumption that his system of concepts can generate testable systems of propositions that account for events in the empirical world. But if such a conceptual system inspires illegitimate teleologies and tautologous propositions, then its utility as a strategy for building sociological theory can be called into question.

The Issue of Teleology. Parsons has always considered "action" to be goal-directed—whether it is a single "unit act" or the complex informational and energic interchanges among the organismic, personality, social, and cultural systems. Thus, Parsons' conceptualization of "goal attainment" as a basic system requisite would make inevitable teleological propositions, since for Parsons much social action can only be understood in terms of the ends it is designed to serve. Such propositions, however, are often considered to be vague, for to assess the goal-attainment consequences of a particular process can frequently be used as a way to obscure the specific causal chains whereby goal-attainment sectors in a system activate processes to meet specified end states. Yet, when looking closely at the Parsonian legacy, it is clear that in his many essays and formal theoretical statements he has been vitally concerned with just how, and through what processes, system processes are activated to meet goal states. For example, Parsons' various works on how political systems strive to legitimate themselves are filled with both analytical and descriptive accounts of how the processes—such as patterns of socialization in educational and kinship institutions—are activated to meet goal-attainment requisites.[35,36] While the empirical adequacy of this discussion can be questioned, Parsons' analysis does not present illegitimate teleologies, for his work reveals a clear concern for documenting the causal chains involved in activating processes designed to meet various end states.

---

[35] See, for example, Talcott Parsons, *Family, Socialization and Interaction Process* (New York: Free Press, 1955); Talcott Parsons, "Social Structure and the Development of Personality," *Psychiatry* 34 (November 1958): 321–40; Talcott Parsons, "The School Class as a Social System," *Harvard Educational Review*, vol. 54 (Fall 1959): 487–99; Talcott Parsons, "The Link between Character and Society," in *Culture and Social Character*, ed. S. M. Lipset and L. Lowenthal (New York: Free Press, 1961); Talcott Parsons, "Youth in the Context of American Society," *Daedalus*, vol. 28 (Winter 1961); Talcott Parsons, "Comment on Dennis Wrong's 'The Over-socialized Conception of Man,'" *Psychoanalysis and Psychoanalytic Review*, vol. 10 (Summer 1962): 322–34; and Talcott Parsons, *Social Structure and Personality* (New York: Free Press, 1964).

[36] For example, see Talcott Parsons "Authority, Legitimation and Political Action" in *Authority*, ed. C. J. Friedrich (Cambridge, Mass.: Harvard University Press, 1958); Parsons, "On the Concept of Power"; and Talcott Parsons, "The Political Aspect of Structure and Process," in *Varieties of Political Theory*, ed. David Easton (Englewood Cliffs, N.J.: Prentice-Hall, Inc., 1966).

It is perhaps the other three requisites—adaptation, integration, and latency—which would seemingly pose a more serious problem of illegitimate teleology. Critics would argue that to analyze structures and processes in terms of their functions for these three system needs compels analysts to state their propositions teleologically, when in fact the processes so described may not be goal-directed or teleological. Logically, as several commentators have pointed out, teleological phrasing of propositions in the absence of clear-cut goal-attainment processes does not necessarily make the proposition illegitimate, for at least two reasons.

1. Nagel has argued that phrasing statements in a teleological fashion is merely a shorthand way of stating the same causal relationship nonteleologically.[37] For example, to argue that the relief of anxiety (an end state) is the "latency function" of religion (a present phenomenon) can be rephrased nonteleologically without loss of asserted content: under conditions C_1, C_2, C_3, . . . , C_n, religion (concept x) causes reduction of group anxiety (concept y). Such a form is quite acceptable in that it involves existence and relational statements: Under C_1, C_2, . . . , C_n, variations in x cause variations in y. However, other authors have contended that such transposition is not always possible, because the existence statements so necessary to such conversion are absent from the statements of functionalists such as Parsons. Without necessary existence statements, to assert that the function of religion is to reduce group anxiety can be interpreted to mean that the latency needs of the group for low levels of anxiety cause the emergence of religion. This most likely constitutes an illegitimate teleology, since little information is provided about the nature of the "latency purposes" of the given system and the specific causal chains involved in keeping the system in pursuit of its latency goals. Or, if teleology is not intended, then the statement is simply vague, offering none of the necessary information that would allow its conversion to a nonteleological form. As Nadel was led to conclude: "To pronounce at once upon the ultimate functions subserved by social facts is to short-circuit explanation and reduce it to generalities which, so prematurely stated, have little significance."[38]

However, a careful review of Parsons's work reveals many insightful essays on the processes and mechanisms whereby various system requisites are maintained. This fact mitigates the severity of the critics' charges, for such descriptions do specify conditions under which requisites are met by specific parts of the more inclusive system. However, the fact

---

[37] Nagel, "Teleological Explanation and Teleological Systems."
[38] Nadel, *Foundations of Social Anthropology*, p. 375.

that Parsons frequently describes these processes in essays that are not
systematically tied to his more formal conceptualizations of action theory
makes the conversion of teleological statements into nonteleological form
somewhat difficult. Such conversion would require considerable synthesis
of the conceptual scheme with Parsons' more discursive essays on a
wide variety of system processes. Despite the fact that Parsons has
neglected this important task, such synthesis is possible—thus throwing
into doubt the assertion that Parsons has, in principle, "short-circuited
explanation." Rather, Parsons has merely failed to realize the full explanatory power of a more rigorous attempt to link his formal theory of action
to his more discursive essays on a wide range of empirical events. For
example, Parsons'[39] analytical discussion of how inputs from the latency
sector of appropriately skilled (socialized) labor into the adaptive sector,
or economy, of a social system would be greatly supplemented by a
more systematic linking of his numerous essays on socialization to these
analytical statements.[40] If such a task were more seriously undertaken,
even critics such as Nadel would have difficulty asserting that Parsons'
use of system requisites such as adaptation had allowed him to "short
circuit" a full causal explanation.

2. Perhaps the most significant defense of Parsons' tendency to phrase
propositions teleologically comes from the fact that such propositions
point to *reverse causal chains* that are typical of many social phenomena.[41]
By emphasizing that the function served by a structure in maintaining
the needs of the whole could *cause* the emergence of that structure,
Parsons' functional imperativism forces analysis to be attuned to those
causal processes involved in the *initial selection,* from the infinite variety
of possible social structures, of only certain types of structures. The
persistence over time of these selected structures can also be explained
by the needs and/or equilibrium states of the whole: Those structures
having consequences for meeting needs and/or maintaining an equilibrium have a "selective advantage" over those that do not. Such statements
need *not* be illegitimate teleologies, for it is quite possible for the systemic
whole to exist *prior in time* to the structures that emerge and persist
to maintain that whole.

For example, Parsons' analysis of the evolution of legal systems and
their impact on the transition to a "modern" system of societies represents

---

[39] See, for example, Parsons and Smelser, *Economy and Society;* Talcott Parsons,
"Some Reflections on the Institutional Framework of Economic Development," *The
Challenge of Development: A Symposium* (Jerusalem: The Hebrew University, 1958).

[40] See n. 44.

[41] Stinchcombe, *Constructing Social Theories,* pp. 87–93.

the use of such a reverse causal chain. Legal residues (codified, secular codes) of previous cultures—most notably Greece—came to have a "selective advantage" in subsequent societies, because they allowed for the secular legitimation of the political system, while at the same time regulating diverse institutional spheres, such as the economy, family, and religion.[42]

Furthermore, it is not even necessary to impute purpose to the systemic whole. Just as in the biophysical world ecological and population balances are maintained by nonpurposive selective processes (for example, predators increase until they eat themselves out of food, and then decrease until the food supply regenerates itself), so social wholes can maintain themselves in a state of equilibrium or meet the imperatives necessary for survival.

This line of argument has led Stinchcombe to summarize:

> Functional explanations are thus complex forms of causal theories. They involve causal connections among . . . variables as with a special causal priority of the consequences of activity in total explanation. There has been a good deal of philosophical confusion about such explanations, mainly due to the theorist's lack of imagination in realizing the variety of reverse causal processes which can select behavior or structures according to their consequences.[43]

The above considerations would lead to some tentative conclusion about Parsons' scheme and the issue of teleology: (1) The scheme has always been teleological, from the initial conceptualization of unit acts to the four-function paradigm embracing the concept of goal attainment. (2) Contrary to the opinion of his detractors, most of Parsons' theoretical statements can be converted into nonteleological form, such that relevant statements about the conditions under which x varies with y can be discerned. (3) Parsons' work is filled with discussions on the mechanisms and processes through which specific end states or requisites of a system are met. (4) Parsons' work is replete with reverse causal chains in which a systemic whole existing prior in time to the emergence of subsystems causes the perpetuation of a subsystem because of its selective advantages in meeting problems faced by the systemic whole.

Most of the criticisms outlining the dangers of illegitimate teleology in functional theorizing have drawn examples from early functional anthropology, where it is relatively easy to expose the questionable teleolo-

---

[42] For the details of what is obviously a more complex argument, see Parsons, *Societies*, pp. 95–115, and *System of Modern Societies*.

[43] Stinchcombe, *Constructing Social Theories*, p. 100.

gies of thinkers such as Malinowski and Radcliffe-Brown. But it is difficult to see how Parsons' notion of system requisites has led him to this same trap, thus allowing the defenders of the action-theoretic strategy to challenge the critics to find conspicuous instances in Parsons' work where there is an illegitimate teleology.

The Issue of Tautology. Parsons' conceptualization of four system requisites—adaptation, goal attainment, integration, and latency—is based on the assumption that if these requisites are not met "survival" of the system is threatened. However, when employing this assumption, it is necessary to know what level of failure in meeting each of these requisites is necessary to pronounce a crisis of survival. How does one determine when adaptive needs are not being met? Goal attainment needs? Integrative requisites? And latency needs? Unless there is some way to determine what constitutes the survival and nonsurvival of a system, propositions documenting the contribution of items for meeting survival requisites become tautologous: The item meets survival needs of the system because the system exists and, therefore, must be surviving. Thus, to phrase propositions with regard to system requisites of adaptation, goal attainment, integration, and latency, Parsons would have to provide either of two types of information: (1) evidence on a "nonsurviving" system where a particular item did not exist; or (2) specific criteria as to what constitutes survival and nonsurvival in various types and classes of social systems. Without this kind of information, propositions employing notions of requisites are likely to be untestable, even in principle; therefore, they are not likely to be very useful in building sociological theory.

Parsons' solution to this problem has not been elegant, for he has been unable to provide clear criteria specifying the minimal levels of adaptation, goal attainment, integration, and latency necessary for system survival. At times, however, Parsons has accumulated "evidence" of systems that did not meet certain requisites and therefore did not "survive." For example, in his recent analysis of social evolution, he is able to discern, at least to his satisfaction, when certain requisites for evolutionary development were not met, since it is relatively "easy" to establish that in a given historical period a system ceased to evolve. For instance, in his discussion of why Greece and Israel failed to move beyond what he termed the "advanced intermediate" stage of evolution, he postulated that certain integrative requisites had not been met—namely, the codification of universalistic norms (legal codes) that legitimated the political (goal attainment) system, while insulating other institutional spheres (such as family, religion, economy) from each other.[44] This kind of analysis would seemingly denote some of the important structural and cultural components necessary for meeting various requisites for adaptation, goal attainment, integration, and latency in historical and, by inference, contemporary societies at different levels of development. The absence of these components, Parsons implies, would indicate that these systems are not meeting requisites for further development. However, requisites for further development are not quite the same as those for survival, although a failure to meet requisites for the next stage of evolution gives some indication of what is minimally necessary for survival of systems at this next stage. Thus, while Parsons has obviated at least some of the problems of tautology in his extensive use of system requisites, his "solution" is not likely to silence the critics—perhaps with some justification.

The Theoretical Utility of Survival Imperatives. Considering the problems of tautology created by using the concept of requisites, it may be asked: What do requisites add to Parsons' theoretical scheme and to the analysis of specific events? And why does he continue to use the concept? For the detractors of imperativism, it would appear possible to document the conditions under which events influence each other in systemic wholes without dragging in notions of survival requisites. In fact, as the critics might observe, Parsons often appears to abandon reference to system requisites when discussing concrete empirical events, causing one to ponder why the requisites are retained in his more formal conceptual edifice.

An answer to such queries can only be tentative, but Parsons appears to retain the requisites for strategic reasons: to provide crude and rough criteria for distinguishing "important" from "unimportant" social processes. Parsons' entire intellectual career has been spent elaborating the complex systems of interrelationships among the basic "unit acts" he first described in *The Structure of Social Action.* The more the system of concepts has been brought to bear on increasingly complex patterns of organization among unit acts, the more Parsons has relied upon the requisites to sort out what processes in these complex patterns of interaction will help explain the most "variance." Thus, Parsons' imperatives constitute not so much a metaphysical entity, but a yardstick for distinguishing what is "crucial" from "not crucial" among the vast number of potential processes in social systems. Despite the fact that Parsons

---

[44] Parsons, *Societies,* pp. 69–115.

is unable to specify exact criteria for assessing whether adaptive, goal-attainment, integrative, and latency needs are being met, he appears to be able to use these somewhat vaguely conceptualized requisites to assess the theoretical significance of concrete social phenomena. To the extent that Parsons has employed the requisites in his many essays, the widely acknowledged insightfulness of these essays, which even the critics do not deny, can perhaps justify his continued use of the requisites to assess social phenomena.

Furthermore, as Parsons would seemingly argue, the requisites can be particularly useful in studying complex empirical systems, since for empirical systems it may be possible to specify more precisely criteria necessary for their survival. With these criteria, it is then possible to distinguish significant from less significant social processes in these systems, thereby assuring more insightful explanations. It appears, then, that despite some of the logical problems created by their retention, Parsons feels that the strategic value of the requisites in explaining social processes in social systems will more than compensate for the logical difficulties so frequently stressed by the critics.

TALCOTT PARSONS: AN OVERVIEW

The "theory of action" as it has unfolded over the last decades reveals an enormous amount of continuity—starting with the basic unit act and proliferating into the cybernetic hierarchy of control among the systems of action. Such continuity is the outgrowth of Parsons' particular view of how theory in sociology should be constructed, for he has consistently advocated the priority of systems of concepts over systems of propositions. The latter can only be useful when the former task is sufficiently completed.

Both the substantive vision of the world connoted by Parsons' concepts and the logical problems imputed to the scheme have stimulated widespread criticism of his functional perspective. In fact, it is unlikely that other forms of sociological theorizing can be understood unless the revulsion of many critics for the perspective is appreciated. As will become evident in subsequent chapters, other theoretical perspectives in sociology typically begin with a rejection of Parsonian functionalism and then proceed to build what is considered a more desirable alternative. In fact, Parsons appears to have become "the straw man" of sociological theorizing, for no "theory" is now considered adequate unless it has performed the necessary ritual of rejecting functional imperativism.

4

THE BALANCE OF
FUNCTIONS APPROACH:
ROBERT K. MERTON

THEORIES OF THE MIDDLE RANGE

Just as Talcott Parsons was beginning to embrace a form of requisite functionalism,[1] Robert K. Merton launched a critique of Parsons' functional strategy for building sociological theory.[2] At the heart of this criticism was Merton's contention that Parsons' concern for developing an all-encompassing system of concepts would prove both futile and sterile: To search for "a total system of sociological theory, in which observations about every aspect of social behavior, organization, and change promptly find their preordained place, has the same exhilarating challenge and the same small promise as those many all-encompassing philosophical systems which have fallen into deserved disuse."[3]

For Merton, such grand theoretical schemes are premature, since the theoretical and empirical groundwork necessary for their completion has not been performed. Just as Einsteinian theory did not emerge with-

---

[1] As will be recalled, Parsons in 1945 began to conceptualize unit acts in systemic terms and began to visualize such systems in terms of requisites. See Talcott Parsons, "The Present Position and Prospects of Systemic Theory in Sociology," *Essays in Sociological Theory* (New York: Free Press, 1949).

[2] Robert K. Merton, "Discussion of Parsons' 'The Position of Sociological Theory'," *American Sociological Reveiw* 13 (April 1948): 164–68.

[3] Ibid. Most of Merton's significant essays on functionalism have been included, and frequently expanded upon, in Robert K. Merton, *Social Theory and Social Structure* (New York: Free Press, 1949). Quotation taken from page 45 of the 1968 edition of this classic work. Most subsequent references will be made to the articles incorporated into this book. For more recent essays on Merton's work, see Lewis A. Coser, ed., *The Idea of Social Structure* (New York: The Free Press, 1975).

out a long cumulative research foundation and theoretical legacy, so sociological theory will have to wait for its Einstein, primarily because "it has not yet found its Kepler—to say nothing of its Newton, Laplace, Gibbs, Maxwell or Planck."[4]

In the absence of this foundation, what passes for sociological theory, in Merton's critical eye, consists of "general orientations toward data, suggesting types of variables which theorists must somehow take into account, rather than clearly formulated, verifiable statements of relationships between specified variables."[5] Strategies advocated by those such as Parsons are not really "theory," but "philosophical systems," with "their varied suggestiveness, their architectonic splendor, and their sterility."[6] However, to pursue the opposite strategy of constructing inventories of low-level empirical propositions will prove equally sterile, thus suggesting to Merton the need for "theories of the middle range" in sociology.

Theories of the middle range offer more theoretical promise than grand theory, because they are couched at a lower level of abstraction, revealing clearly defined and operationalized concepts that are incorporated into statements of co-variance for a limited range of phenemena. While middle range theories are abstract, they are also connected to the empirical world, thus encouraging the research so necessary for the clarification of concepts and reformulation of theoretical generalizations. Without this interplay between theory and research, theoretical schemes will remain suggestive congeries of concepts, which are incapable of being refuted, while, on the other hand, empirical research will remain unsystematic, disjointed, and of little utility in expanding a body of sociological knowledge. Thus, by following a middle-range strategy, the concepts and propositions of sociological theory will become more tightly organized as theoretically focused empirical research forces clarification, elaboration, and reformulation of the concepts and propositions of each middle-range theory.

From this growing clarity in theories directed at a limited range of phenomena and supported by empirical research can eventually come the more encompassing theoretical schemes. In fact, for Merton, while it is necessary to concentrate energies on the construction of limited theories that inspire research, theorists must also be concerned with "consolidating the special theories into a more general set of concepts and mutually consistent propositions."[7] The special theories of sociology

---

[4] Merton, *Social Theory and Social Structure*, p. 47.

[5] Ibid., p. 42.

[6] Ibid., p. 51.

[7] Merton, *Social Theory and Social Structure* (1957), p. 10.

must therefore be formulated with an eye toward what they can offer more general sociological theorizing. However, just how these middle-range theories should be formulated to facilitate their eventual consolidation into a more general theory poses a difficult analytical problem, for which Merton has a ready solution: A form of functionalism should be utilized in formulating the theories of the middle range. Such functional theorizing is to take the form of a "paradigm" that would allow for both the easy specification and elaboration of relevant concepts, while encouraging systematic revision and reformulation as empirical findings would dictate. Conceived in this way, functionalism became for Merton a *method* for building not only theories of the middle range but also the grand theoretical schemes that would someday subsume such theories of the middle range.[8] Thus, in a vein similar to Parsons, functionalism for Merton represents a strategy for ordering concepts and for sorting out "significant" from "insignificant" social processes. But, unlike Parsons' strategy, Merton's functional strategy requires first the formulation of a body of middle-range theories. Only when this groundwork has been laid should a functional protocol be used to construct more abstract theoretical systems.

MERTON'S "PARADIGM" FOR FUNCTIONAL ANALYSIS

As with most commentators on functional analysis, Merton begins his discussion with a review of the mistakes of early functionalists, particularly the anthropologists Malinowski and Radcliffe-Brown.[9] Part of the reason for this assessment of the anthropological tradition stems from the fact that Merton's paradigm was first published in 1949,[10] when these anthropologists were still prominent figures in the social sciences. And yet, that this section of Merton's introduction to his paradigm has remained intact through two subsequent editions of his major theoretical work indicates his current view that contemporary functionalism faces the same problems that early anthropologists failed to resolve. Generally, Merton saw functional theorizing as potentially embracing three questionable postulates: (1) the functional unity of social systems, (2)

---

[8] M. J. Mulkay (*Functionalism, Exchange and Theoretical Strategy* [New York: Schocken Books, 1971], pp. 98–99) argues a similar position, although he places less emphasis on Merton's concern for eventually building grand theory with his functional protocol.

[9] Robert K. Merton, "Manifest and Latent Functions," in *Social Theory and Social Structure* (1968), pp. 74–91.

[10] See Robert K. Merton, *Social Theory and Social Structure* (Glencoe, Ill.: Free Press, 1949), pp. 45–61.

the functional universality of social items, and (3) the indispensibility of functional items for social systems.

The Functional Unity Postulate. As can be recalled from Chapter 2, Radcliffe-Brown in following Durkheim's lead frequently transformed the "hypothesis" that social systems reveal social integration into a necessary "requisite" or "need" for social survival. While it is difficult to argue that human societies do not possess some degree of integration—for otherwise they would not be systems—Merton views the degree of integration in a system as an issue to be empirically determined. To assume, however subtly, that a high degree of functional unity must exist in a social system is to define away the important theoretical and empirical questions: What levels of integration exist for different systems? What various types of integration can be discerned? Are varying degrees of integration evident for different segments of a system? And, most importantly, what variety of processes lead to different levels, forms, and types of integration for different spheres of social systems? For Merton, to begin analysis with the postulate of "functional unity" or integration of the social whole can divert attention away from not only these questions, but also the varied and "disparate consequences of a given social or cultural item (usage, belief, behavior pattern, institutions) for diverse social groups and for individual members of these groups."[11]

Underlying this discussion of the functional unity imputed to systemic wholes is an implicit criticism of Parsons' early concern with social integration. As will be recalled, Parsons first postulated only one requisite in his early functional work: the need for integration.[12] Later, this postulate was to be expanded into three additional functional requisites for adaptation, goal attainment, and latency. But Parsons' functionalism appears to have begun with the same concerns evident in Durkheim's and Radcliffe-Brown's work, leading Merton to question the "heuristic value" of an assumption that can divert attention away from important theoretical and empirical questions. Thus, in the place of the postulate of functional unity should be an emphasis on varying types, forms, levels, and spheres of social integration and the varying consequences of the existence of items for specified segments of social systems. In this way, Merton begins to direct functional analysis away from concern with total systems toward an emphasis on how different patterns of social organization within more inclusive social systems are created, maintained,

---

[11] Merton, *Social Theory and Social Structure* (1968), pp. 81–82.

[12] See Parsons, "Present Position and Prospects of Systemic Theory," and Talcott Parsons, *The Social System* (Glencoe, Ill.: Free Press, 1951).

and changed not only by the requisites of the total system but also by interaction among sociocultural items within systemic wholes.

The Issue of Functional Universality.   One result of an emphasis on functional unity was that some early anthropologists assumed that if a social item existed in an ongoing system, it must therefore have had positive consequences for the integration of the social system. This assumption tended to result in tautologous statements of the form: A system exists; an item is a part of the system; therefore, the item is positively functional for the maintenance of the system. In its most extreme form, Malinowski extended this form of reasoning to the point of asserting that "every custom, material object, idea and belief fulfills some vital function." To Merton, such an assumption was perhaps understandable in light of the fact that Malinowski was reacting to the view advanced by some anthropologists at the turn of the century that social "customs" could not be explained by their present utility, but rather, they could only be viewed as "survivals" of a culture's past history. Yet, Merton's analysis of Malinowski's excessive reaction to the now-discredited "historical reconstruction" school of anthropology has been retained to serve as a warning to contemporary functional theorizing, which might in more subtle form allow conceptions of "needs" and "requisites" to so skew analysis that only the positive functions of items for meeting these needs are analyzed.

For Merton, however, if an examination of empirical systems is undertaken, it is clear that there is a wider range of empirical possibilities. First, items may be not only positively functional for a system or another system item, but also dysfunctional for either particular items or the systemic whole. Second, some consequences, whether functional or dysfunctional, are intended and recognized by system incumbents and are thus "manifest," whereas other consequences are not intended or recognized and are therefore "latent." Thus, in contrast with the assertions of Malinowski and others such as Radcliffe-Brown who unwittingly fell into the same tautologous trap, Merton proposes the analysis of diverse consequences or functions of sociocultural items—whether positive or negative, manifest or latent—"for individuals, for sub-groups, and for the more inclusive social structure and culture."[13] In turn, the analysis of varied consequences requires the calculation of a "net balance of consequences" of items for each other and more inclusive systems. In this way, Merton visualizes contemporary functional thought as compensating for the excesses of earlier forms of analysis by focusing on the

---

[13] Merton, *Social Theory and Social Strucure* (1968), p. 84.

crucial types of consequences of sociocultural items for each other and, if the facts dictate, for the social whole.

The Issue of Indispensability. Merton views Malinowski's assertion that every cultural item "fulfills *some vital function*, has some task to accomplish, represents an *indispensable part* within a working whole" as simply an extreme statement of two interrelated issues in functional analysis: (*a*) Do social systems have functional requisites or needs that must be fulfilled? (*b*) Are there certain crucial structures that are indispensable for fulfilling these functions?

In response to the first question, Merton provides a tentative yes, but with an important qualification: The functional requisites must be established *empirically* for *specific systems*. For actual groups or whole societies it is possible to ascertain the "conditions necessary for their survival," and it is of theoretical importance to determine which structures, through what specific processes, have consequences for these conditions. But to assume a system of universal requisites—as Parsons does— adds little to theoretical analysis, since to stress that certain functions must be met in all systems simply leads observers to describe processes in social systems which meet these requisites. Such descriptions, Merton contends, can be done without the excess baggage of system requisites, for it is more desirable to describe cultural patterns and then assess their various consequences in meeting the specific needs of different segments of concete empirical systems.

Merton's answer to the second question is emphatic: Empirical evidence makes the assertion that only certain structures can fulfill system requisites obviously false. Examination of the empirical world reveals quite clearly that "alternative structures" can exist to fulfill basically the same requisites in both similar and diverse systems. This fact leads Merton to postulate the importance in functional analysis of concern with various types of "functional alternatives," or "functional equivalents," and "functional substitutes" within social systems. In this way, functional analysis would not view as indispensable the social items of a system and thereby would avoid the tautologous trap of assuming that items must exist to assure the continued existence of a system. Furthermore, in looking for "functional alternatives," analytical attention would be drawn to questions about the "range" of items that could serve as functional equivalents. If these questions are to be answered adequately, analysts should then determine why a particular item was selected from a range of possible alternatives, leading to questions about the "structural context" and "structural limits" that might circumscribe the range of alternatives and account for the emergence of one item over another. For Merton, examination of these interrelated questions would thus facilitate the separate analysis of the causes and consequences of structural items. By asking why one particular structure instead of various alternatives had emerged, analysts would not forget to document the specific processes leading to an item's emergence as separate from its functional consequences. In this way, the danger of assuming that items must exist to fulfill system needs would be avoided.

In looking back at Merton's criticisms of traditional anthropological reasoning, and by implication that of some contemporary functionalists, it is evident that much of his assessment of these three "functional postulates" involves the destruction of "straw men." The mistakes of Malinowski and Radcliffe-Brown were well understood even in 1949 when Merton's discussion was first published. Yet, in destroying his "straw men" Merton was led to formulate alternative postulates, which advocated a concern for the multiple consequences of sociocultural items for each other and for more inclusive social wholes, without a priori assumptions of functional needs or imperatives. Rather, functional analysis must specify (a) the social patterns under consideration, whether a systemic whole or some subpart; (b) the various types of consequences of these patterns for empirically established survival requisites; and (c) the processes whereby some patterns rather than others come to exist and have the various consequences for each other and for systemic wholes.[14]

With this form of functional analysis, Merton has sought to provide "the minimum set of concepts with which the sociologist must operate in order to carry through an adequate functional analysis."[15] In doing so, Merton hopes that this strategy will allow sociological analysis to avoid some of the mistaken postulates and assumptions of previous attempts to use a functional strategy. While the requisite functionalism of Parsons is only briefly assessed in Merton's proposals, it appears that he is stressing the need for an alternative form of functional analysis in which there is less concern with total systems and abstract statements of system requisites. Instead, to build "theories of the middle range," it is necessary to focus attention on the mutual and varied consequences of specified system parts for each other and for systemic wholes. While these parts and systemic wholes have conditions necessary for their survival, these conditions must be empirically established. For only through

---

[14] Merton's actual paradigm is more extensive than the above listing, but this description summarizes the thrust of his functional strategy. For the complete paradigm, see Merton, *Social Theory and Social Structure* (1968), pp. 104–9.

[15] Ibid., p. 109.

a clear understanding of the actual requisites of a concrete system can the "needs" of social structures provide a useful set of criteria for assessing the consequences, or functions, of social items. Furthermore, while the analysis of consequences of items is the unique feature of functional analysis, it is also necessary to discover the causal processes that have resulted in a particular item having a specified set of consequences for other items and systemic wholes. To assure adherence to this form of structural analysis, Merton went so far as to outline a set of procedures for executing the general guidelines of his functional orientation.

A PROTOCOL FOR EXECUTING FUNCTIONAL ANALYSIS

To ascertain the causes and consequences of particular structures and processes, Merton insists that functional analysis begin with "sheer description" of the activities of individuals and groups under study. In describing the patterns of interaction and activity among units under investigation, it will be possible to discern clearly the social items to be subjected to functional analysis. Such descriptions can also provide "a major clue to the functions performed" by such patterned activity. In order for these functions to become more evident, however, additional steps are necessary.

The first of these steps is for investigators to indicate the principal alternatives that are excluded by the dominance of a particular pattern. Such description of the excluded alternatives provides an indication of the "structural context" from which an observed patterned first emerged and is now maintained—thereby offering further clues about the functions, or consequences, the item might have for other items and perhaps for the systemic whole. The second analytical step beyond sheer description involves an assessment of the "meaning," or mental and emotional significance, of the activity for members of the group. Description of these meanings may offer some indication of the motives behind the activities of the individuals involved, and thereby shed some tentative light on the "manifest" functions of an activity. These descriptions require a third analytical step of discerning "some array of motives for conformity or for deviation" among participants, but these motives must not be confused with either the objective description of the pattern or the subsequent assessment of the functions served by the pattern. Yet, by understanding the configuration of motives for conformity and deviation among actors, an assessment of the psychological "needs" served (or not served) by a pattern can be understood—offering an additional clue to the various functions of the pattern under investigation.

But focusing on the meanings and motives of those involved in an activity can skew analysis away from unintended or latent consequences of the activity. Thus, a final analytical step involves the description of how the patterns under investigation reveal regularities not recognized by participants, but which appear to have consequences for both the individuals involved and other central patterns or regularities in the system. In this way, analysis will be attuned to the "latent" functions of an item.

By following each of these steps, Merton assumes that it will be possible to assess the "net balance of consequences" of the pattern under investigation, as well as to determine some of the independent causes of the item. These steps assure that a proper functional inquiry will ensue, because postulates of functional unity, assumptions of survival requisites, and convictions about indispensable parts do not precede the analysis of social structures and processes. On the contrary, attention is drawn only to observable patterns of activity, the structural context in which the focal pattern emerged and persists in the face of potential alternatives, the meaning of these patterns for actors involved, the actors' motives for conformity and deviation, and the implications of the particular pattern for unrecognized needs of individuals and other items in the social system. Thus, with this kind of preliminary work, functional analysis will avoid the logical and empirical problems of previous forms of functionalism. And, in this way, it can provide an understanding of the causes and consequences of system parts for each other and for more inclusive system units.[16]

An Illustration of Merton's Protocol:
Political Machines in America

Merton's paradigm and protocol for constructing functional theories of the middle range are remarkably free of statements about individual and system needs or requisites. In his protocol statements, Merton appears to prefer to approach the question of the needs and requisites fulfilled by a particular item only *after* description of (a) the item in question, (b) the structural context in which the item survives, and (c) its meaning for the individuals involved. With this information, it is then possible

---

[16] Ibid., p. 136.

to establish both the manifest and latent functions of an item, as well as the "net balance" of functions and dysfunctions of the item for varied segments of a social system. Unfortunately, the implied sequencing of functional analysis is not always performed by Merton, presumably for at least two reasons. First, in selecting an established structure in a system for analysis, the investigator usually assumes that the item persists because it is fulfilling some need. As will be evident, Merton *begins* (as opposed to concludes) with this assumption in his analysis of political machines—thus leaving him to conclude that "structure affects function and function affects structure." When description of items begins with an implicit assumption of their functions for fulfilling needs, then it is more likely that the description will be performed in a way assuring confirmation of the implicit assumption. Second, in analyzing the structural context of an item and assessing why it emerges and persists over alternative items, it is necessary to have some preconception of the functions served by an item in order to know why it fulfills a set of needs "better" than would various alternatives. Otherwise, it would be difficult to determine what potential alternatives could exist to "substitute" for the present item.

For at least these two reasons, then, execution of Merton's strategy is difficult. This fact becomes particularly evident in his analysis of American political machines. Much like that of his anthropological "straw men," such as Radcliffe-Brown and Malinowski, Merton's recognition of the necessity for analyzing separately the "causes" and "functions" of structural items is not as evident in his actual account of empirical events.

Merton begins his analysis of American political machines with the simple question: "How do they manage to continue in operation?"[17] Following this interesting question is an assumption reminiscent of Malinowski's functional analysis:

> Preceding from the functional view, therefore, that we should *ordinarily* (not invariably) expect persistent social patterns and social structures to perform positive functions *which are at the time not filfilled by other patterns and structures*, the thought occurs that perhaps this publicly maligned organization is, *under present conditions*, satisfying basic latent functions. [Merton's emphasis].[18]

In this passage, the fact that the word "ordinarily" is qualified by the parenthetical phrase "not invariably" is perhaps enough to allow

---

[17] Ibid., p. 125.
[18] Ibid., pp. 125–26.

Paul S. Weikel 2/8/79

Merton to escape the change of tautology: If an item persists in a surviving system, it must therefore have positive functions. Yet, Merton seems to be saying that if an enduring item does not fulfill "manifest" functions, then it fulfills "latent" functions, leading one to recall Malinowski's dictum that "every custom, material object, idea and belief fulfills some vital function, has some task to accomplish." For Merton, this assumption becomes translated into the dictum that social items that do not fulfill manifest functions must fulfill latent ones; and, as is added in a footnote, if the item has dysfunctions for some segments of the population, its persistence implies that it *ordinarily* must have positive functions for meeting the needs of other segments.

In fairness to Merton's suggestive analysis of political machines, it should be emphasized that he was offering this analysis only as an illustration of the usefulness of the distinction between "manifest" and "latent" functions. It was not intended as a full explication of his functional paradigm or protocol, but only as an example of how attention to "latent" functions can provide new insights into the operation of political machines. However, it would appear that Merton's commitment to a clear protocol was not enough to preclude an inadvertent lapse—so typical of earlier functionalists—into the postulates of "universality of functions" and "functional indispensability." Thus, Merton appears to begin his concrete analysis with a set of postulates that he earlier had gone to great lengths to discredit, resulting in this central assumption:

> The key structural function of the Boss is to organize, centralize and maintain in good working condition "the scattered fragments of power" which are at present dispersed through our political organization. By this centralization of political power, *the boss can satisfy the needs of diverse subgroups* in the larger community which are not adequately satisfied by legally devised and culturally approved social structures.[19]

For Merton, political machines emerge in the "structural context" of a system in which power is decentralized to the extent that it cannot be mobilized to meet the needs of significant segments of the population. The causal processes by which machines arise in this power vacuum to pick up the "scattered fragments of power" involve a sequence of events in which political machines are seen as able to satisfy the "needs" of diverse groups more effectively than "legally devised and culturally approved social structures." Logically, this form of analysis is not necessarily tautologous or an illegitimate teleology—as some critics might charge—

---

[19] Ibid., p. 126.

because Merton appears to be asserting that political machines at one time had a selective advantage over alternative structures in meeting *prior* needs of certain segments in a system. This kind of "reverse causal chain," to use Stinchcombe's term,[20] is a legitimate form of causal analysis, since the system needs are seen as existing *prior in time* to the events they cause—in this instance the emergence of political machines in the American social structure. Furthermore, it is not necessary to impute purposes—although at times purpose is certainly involved—to the segments of the system affected by the machines, since a political machine may be seen as a chance event that had a selective advantage over alternatives in a spiraling process similar to that which is typical of the expansions and contradictions of predator populations that grow rapidly until they eat themselves out of prey. Clearly, the emergence of a political machine is both a purposive and nonpurposive process in which the machine meets the prior needs of a population, which has signaled to the leaders or the "bosses" of the machine the efficacy of their expanded pursuits (purpose) in meeting its needs. Eventually, in a spiraling process of this nature, the original needs of the population which caused the emergence and expansion of political machines and big city bosses may recede in causal significance as the needs of the well-established political machine cause, in a reverse causal process, certain activities that have little consequence (or perhaps a dysfunctional consequence) for the needs of the population that initially caused the machine's emergence.

This kind of causal argument appears to be Merton's intent, but, unfortunately, his overriding concern with discerning the functions of the political machines obscures this necessary causal analysis, for, as he is prone to remark, "whatever its specific historical origins, the political machine persists as an apparatus for satisfying unfulfilled needs of diverse groups in the population."[21] By bypassing these specific causal chains involved in the emergence of the political machine in America, Merton is left with the relatively simple and ad hoc task of cross-tabulating the "needs" of a population and the activities of the political machine that fulfill them.

For example, the political machine fulfills the needs of deprived classes by providing vital services through the local neighborhood ward heeler, including "food baskets and jobs, legal and extra-legal advice, setting

---

[20] Arthur L. Stinchcombe, *Constructing Social Theories* (New York: Harcourt, Brace and World, 1968), p. 100.

[21] Merton, *Social Theory and Social Structure* (1968), p. 127.

to rights minor scrapes with the law, helping the bright poor boy to a political scholarship in a local college, looking after the bereaved," and so on. The political machine, according to Merton, can provide these services more effectively than various alternatives, such as welfare agencies, settlement houses, legal aid clinics, and the like, because it offers these services in a personal way through the neighborhood ward heeler with a minimum of questions, red tape, and abuse to people's self-respect. For other populations, such as the business community, the political machines provide another set of needed services—namely, political regulation and control of unbridled competition among corporations and businesses without undue governmental interference in the specific operations of economic enterprises. By virtue of controlling various public agencies and bureaus, the big city boss can rationalize and organize relations among economic organizations, while, at the same time, preventing too much governmental scrutiny into their various illegal activities. The political machine can perform this function more effectively than legal governmental alternatives because it recognizes the need of economic organizations for both regulation and noninterference in certain activities. In contrast, legally constituted government agencies would recognize only the former need—thus giving the political machine a selective advantage over legally constituted government. Similarly, the political machine can organize and rationalize illegal economic enterprises concerned with providing illicit services, including gambling, drugs, and prostitution, whereas legally constituted governmental agencies cannot condone, to say nothing of organizing, this kind of prevalent activity. Thus, for both legal and illegal businesses, the political machine provides "protection" by assuring a stable marketplace, high profits, and selective governmental regulation. Finally, for another population—notably the deprived—the political machine provides opportunities for social mobility in a society where monetary success is a strong cultural value, but where actual opportunities for such success are closed to many deprived groups. Thus, by opening the doors to social mobility for members of deprived groups who do not have "legitimate" opportunities, the political machine meets the needs of the deprived, while, at the same time, assuring itself of loyal, committed, and grateful personnel.

Merton's functional explanation of the persistence of political machines has considerable plausibility, for, indeed, the existence of political machines in America was correlated with a relatively ineffective federal establishment, deprived urban masses, high demand for illegal services, and high degrees of economic competition. But most of Merton's account is simply a statement of correlation, dressed in functional assumptions about how the needs of "diverse subgroups" led to the emergence and persistence of political machines in America. As is obvious, statements of correlation are not causal statements. To the extent that it simply notes the correlation between social "needs" and political machines, Merton's analysis will be of little utility in building theoretical statements of the form: under C_1, C_2, C_3, . . . , C_n, x causes variation in y. There are many *implied* causal chains in Metron's analysis, but his failure to make them explicit detracts from his analysis. As was emphasized in Chapter 2, Durkheim's concrete analysis of the division of labor lapsed into statements implying, at the very least, that the "need for social order" caused the division of labor.[22] Without explicit causal statements about how the need for order caused the division of labor, the analysis constituted an illegitimate teleology.

The difficulties that these "founders" of functionalism had in separating "cause" and "function" were clearly recognized by Merton and, presumably, served as the impetus to his insightful explication of a paradigm and protocol for functional analysis. Yet, much like his predecessors, Merton abandons the very protocol that would keep "cause" and "function" separated. Merton indicates that the emergence and persistence of political machines occur in response to needs, without documenting very precisely the causal chains through which "needs" cause the emergence and persistence of an event.

Merton also appears to fall into the problems of tautology so evident in Malinowski's functional analysis. By assuming that "ordinarily" persistent structures serve positive functions for meeting the needs of some segment of the population, Merton indicates that if an item persists in an existing system, then it is functional (perhaps only latent) for some groups. It is somewhat surprising that Merton falls back onto this postulate, since he went to such great lengths to sound the warning against just this assumption. Yet, Merton's analysis of political machines does not start with a description of the phenomenon, nor does he initially address the structural context in which it exists, but rather, Merton begins with the assumption that political machines exist to fulfill a function—if not a manifest function, then a latent one.

This criticism of Merton's analysis of a concrete phenomenon does not mean that, with more specification of causal processes, charges of tautology and illegitimate teleology could be avoided. Indeed, with more specification of the "historical origins" of the political machines and

---

[22] Émile Durkheim, *The Rules of the Sociological Method* (Glencoe, Ill.: Free Press, 1938), p. 96.

of the "feedback" processes between political machines, on the one hand, and the segments of the population they serve, on the other, Merton's account could be rephrased in less suspicious causal terms. This fact leads to an important question: Why did Merton fail to specify the causal chains that would make less suspicious his propositions? One answer to this question is simply that Merton offered this account of political machines only as an illustration of the utility in the concept of "latent" functions. As an illustration, the account would naturally be brief and not involve a thorough explication of the emergence of political machines in America. Merton's awareness of the problems inherent in previous functional analysis would lend credence to this argument, for how could he fall into the very traps that he sought to avoid?

However, Durkheim's and Radcliffe-Brown's similar failure to avoid completely the logical problems they clearly understood raises the more fundamental question: Is there something about functional analysis that encourages theorists to "short circuit" causal explanation?

Another Illustration of Merton's Protocol: "Social Structure and Anomie"

Probably the most widely read and influential theory developed by Merton is found in his essay, "Social Structure and Anomie." Perhaps no single theoretical essay of this century has prompted as much research and theoretical commentary as this. While the essay containing the initial formulation of the theory was written before Merton explicitly formulated his middle-range strategy and functional protocol, it has consistently reappeared in the various editions of his *Social Theory and Social Structure* after the discussion of his strategy and protocol. Moreover, his defense and elaboration of the theory in recent editions of *Social Theory and Social Structure* would argue to the point that he considers the theory of "social structure and anomie" to illustrate the functional protocol and middle-range strategy.[23]

Merton's theory of "anomie" seeks to answer the question: What causes deviance, its rate and type in a society? The way this question is formulated reveals Merton's debt to Durkheim who had asked much the same question about suicide.[24] Moreover, in seeking to maintain this continuity with Durkheim, he expands upon Durkheim's concept of "anomie." Deviance is to be seen as a response or "adaptation" of

---

[23] Merton, *Social Theory and Social Structure* (1968), pp. 185–248.
[24] Émile Durkheim, *Suicide* (New York: The Free Press, 1951).

populations in society to a state of anomie, while anomie is the result of malintegration within and between culture and structure. Thus, in approaching the question of deviance, Merton, like Durkheim before him, emphasizes that deviance is a result of malintegration and that the type of deviance is related to the nature of the malintegration. In this emphasis can be found several functionalist assumptions: (1) Social systems are composed of interrelated parts; (2) these parts must reveal some degree of integration or, as Merton phrases it, "equilibrium"; (3) malintegration or disequilibrium produces aberrant behavior; and (4) the nature and type of malintegration determines the nature and type of aberrant behavior.

In following, or as is actually the case, in anticipating, his functional protocol, Merton seeks to describe the item of concern in his analysis—the rate and type of deviant behavior and the structural context in which it appears. And while he rejects the view that deviance represents an expression of uncontrolled biological needs, he implicitly attempts to understand how culturally induced psychological needs operate to produce deviance in individuals. And in keeping with his concern over functions/dysfunctions and the "net balance of consequences," he implicitly analyzes the consequences of deviance for different social units: the social whole, the subgroup revealing high rates of deviance, and the individual deviants themselves. For the social whole, the implication is that deviance is dysfunctional, although he implies certain positive consequences of "innovative" deviance. For the subgroups involved, deviance represents an "adaptation" and hence appears to have some positive consequences for resolving their position in a malintegrated system. And for the needs of individuals, the deviance resolves many of the frustrations, anxieties, and motivational conflicts, with the result that it can sometimes be viewed as functional.

Merton's thesis can be stated simply, but this statement glosses over many of the profound problems in the theory. Basically, Merton argues that one crucial point of integration or "equilibrium" in social systems is between cultural goals and the structural paths for achieving these goals. Implicitly, he follows Durkheim's distinction between a system of ideas, or "collective conscience," and a system of structured relationships among actors. Parsons visualized this distinction in terms of a "cultural system" and a "social system." Merton follows this distinction, and like Durkheim and Parsons, recognizes that a major problem of integration exists between culture and structure. In particular, he emphasizes that cultural ideas dictate goals or ends toward which action is to be directed—an emphasis corresponding to Parsons' in the conceptualization of "the unit act" (see chapter 3). Realizing desired ends or goals occurs through actions in the status-role structure of the social system. And each social system will prescribe "legitimate means" or institutionalized paths through which actions in pursuit of ends are to be channeled. Thus, in all social systems culture dictates goals and ends which give action in society direction, while social systems provide means or avenues for achieving these ends. These avenues are defined as "legitimate" by cultural norms.

A system where cultural ends and structural means are integrated will be in equilibrium, because actors will all share, or have internalized, the goals and these will be a part of their psychological need structure. And, they will all accept as legitimate, and use, the means for realizing these ends. As Merton notes:

> An effective equilibrium between these two phases of the social structure is maintained so long as satisfactions accrue to individuals conforming to both cultural constraints, *viz.*, satisfactions from achievements of goals and satisfactions emerging directly from the institutionally canonized modes of striving to attain them.[25]

Malintegration or disequilibrium occurs when the implied balance between ends and means does not exist. In other words, when actors accept ends, but reject, remain ignorant of, or cannot use legitimate means or when they reject, are ignorant of, or develop alternative ends, "anomie" is said to exist. As is clear, Merton's use of Durkheim's concept is much broader, extending beyond a state of "normlessness." Yet, it is consistent with Durkheim's intent to communicate a "lack of regulation" by the "collective conscience," since for Merton anomie exists when dominant cultural goals and/or legitimate normative means do not regulate the conduct of actors within some designated population in a social system.

Merton's particular concern appears to be on (*a*) the conditions under which cultural goals are accepted by all segments of a population—that is, how they are internalized and become a part of their individual psychological needs—and (*b*) the conditions under which institutionalized means are unequally available to the members of a social system. This situation is anomic for some segments of the population and sets into motion efforts to adapt or cope with the disjunction between means and ends. It is this disequilibrium which causes deviance, with the rate and type of deviance reflecting the degree of disequilibrium, or anomie,

---

[25] Merton, *Social Theory and Social Structure* (1968), p. 188.

and the location of affected populations in the social structure of a system.

Merton's essay is highly discursive, with the result that terms used to label concepts vary, and hence, the connotative meanings of concepts often shift. Furthermore, Merton never states his argument propositionally, making it difficult to discern the relationships among concepts. Yet, if the theory is to prove useful and adhere to Merton's advocacy of the middle range strategy, it must be phrased more formally. Thus, the first proposition of Merton's theory can be phrased in the following manner:

Proposition 1: The more widespread and psychologically salient the culturally defined goals among the population of a system, and the less equally available to members of the system culturally legitimated structural means for realizing these goals, the greater the potential for anomie and the higher the rates of deviant behavior in that system.

The basic premises of Merton's theory are contained in this proposition. Merton emphasized that cultural goals must be "widespread"—that is, widely recognized—by a population and that they must have psychological meaning—or in the terms of the proposition, high "salience"—for the population. Means are those structures which are viewed as "appropriate" or, in the terms of the proposition, "culturally legitimate," for realizing culturally defined goals. The availability of means will determine which populations will be subject to anomic pressures and hence prone to deviate. As the proposition indicates, the unavailability of means in a system where goals are widely accepted and psychologically salient will create a situation of de-regulation, or anomie, for those who do not have access to legitimate means, thus increasing the rate of deviance.

Merton emphasizes that "success goals" are particularly likely to create disequilibrium between goals and means. Goals emphasizing "achievements" in particular spheres, such as job, income, and education, are likely to create strong psychological pressures in individuals to use and compete for means that enable them to realize these success goals. Thus, Merton's general proposition can be supplemented by an additional statement:

Proposition 2: The more cultural goals of a system dictate the pursuit of success in identifiable spheres, and the less equally available to members of the system are culturally legitimated structural means for realizing these success goals, the greater the potential for anomie and the higher the rates of deviant behavior in that system.

These two propositions state the causes of deviant behavior. Merton then turns to specifying the types of behavior likely to emerge under anomic conditions. Unfortunately, it is at this point in Merton's analysis that classification of different "modes of adaptation" to anomie takes precedence over causal statements about the conditions under which one type of adaptation is more likely to occur than another. This emphasis on classification—reminiscent of Weber's ideal type method and Parsons' penchant for typologies—is underscored by the typology of *individual* adaptations to disequilibrium, or anomie, that Merton develops at this point in his argument (see Figure 4–1):[26]

FIGURE 4–1
Adaptations to Anomie

Modes of Adaptation	Cultural Goals	Institutionalized Means
I. Conformity	+	+
II. Innovation	+	−
III. Ritualism	−	+
IV. Retreatism	−	−
V. Rebellion	±	±

In this typology, (+) signifies "acceptance," (−) "rejection," and (±) "rejection of prevailing values and substitution of new values." In discussing each adaptation, Merton provides what is essentially a *definition* of what he means by conformity, innovation, ritualism, retreatism, and rebellion. Intriguing examples of each mode of adaptation are offered, but few propositions of the form: Under C_1, C_2, C_3, . . . , C_n, anomie causes adaptation modes *I, II, III, IV*, or *V* to increase in frequency. However, some propositions can be inferred, and will be presented below. But it should be evident that they are vague, and if the theory is to be improved, it is in specifying the conditions under which one or another mode of adaptation is likely to increase in frequency within an anomic system.

Mode *I* of adaptation is not deviance, but its opposite, conformity. The individual accepts the cultural goals and uses the legitimate means for attempting to realize them. For Merton, then, the causes of conformity are simply the inverse of those causing anomie and deviance. This relationship is specified in proposition 3:

---

[26] Ibid., p. 194.

Proposition 3: The more widespread and psychologically salient are culturally defined success goals, and the more equally available to members of the system are culturally legitimated structural means for realizing them, the less the potential for anomie and the higher the rates of conforming behavior in that system.

Mode *II*, innovation, is the situation where cultural goals are accepted, but means are unavailable and rejected, with the result that new means are "invented" to realize success goals. In trying to explain why innovation should occur, Merton develops implicit propositions: First, Merton argues that the socialization experiences of individuals, particularly in the family, are especially important in determining their willingness to use nonlegitimate means and endure the psychological costs in abandoning the search for legitimate means. Second, in societies where cultural values emphasize *individual* achievements, as opposed to group or collective achievements, considerable stress is put upon individuals to realize success goals, even if this could involve the use of culturally nonlegitimate means. To not do so is to subject oneself to the personal stigma of failure, and thus, if the individual has fewer internal inhibitions against the use of nonlegitimate means, and success goals are highly salient, the likelihood of innovative deviance increases. And third, there is an implicit argument that, because illegitimate means have been used in the past by populations subject to anomic pressures, they will be more readily available to individuals who have needs to seek success and who are willing to violate culturally legitimated means. These implicit conditions fostering an innovative adaptation to anomie are more formally stated in proposition 4:

Proposition 4: The less available to members of a population are culturally legitimated structural means, and the fewer internal prohibitions against the use of culturally nonlegitimated means, the greater the incidence of innovative behavior in that populations, when: (4a) cultural values dictating individual achievement are widespread and salient; and (4b) illegitimate means are more readily available.

Merton then turns to ritualism, mode of adaptation *III* in his typology. Ritualism is a situation where individuals lose sight of, are ignorant of, are fearful of, or reject cultural success goals, but where legitimate means are accepted and become objects of slavish conformity. In discussing ritualism, Merton notes that it is the result of "status anxiety" experienced by people who have some degree of access to means but who, in a culture emphasizing individual achievement for success and personal stigma for failure, experience acute anxiety when using means for competitive efforts at success. However, since these individuals are located in positions where access to means exists, their socialization experiences are likely to have emphasized conformity to cultural norms. These individuals resolve their status anxiety by conforming to means and rejecting the success goals. These implicit, and admittedly vague propositions, are more formally stated in proposition 5:

Proposition 5: The greater the availability of culturally legitimated structural means to members of a population, and the greater the status anxiety experienced by members of this population in the pursuit of cultural success goals, the greater the incidence of ritualistic behavior among that population, when: (5a) cultural values dictating individual achievement are widespread and salient; and (5b) socialization experiences create strong psychological commitments to culturally legitimated means.

Adaptation *IV*, retreatism, involves rejecting both means and ends with the result that the individual apathetically exists within the social system. Retreatism, argues Merton, results from loss of, or limited access to, accepted means, coupled with strong internal inhibitions against the use of illegitimate means. The psychological frustrations inhering in this situation are particularly aggravated when cultural values dictating individual achievement are internalized. For individuals caught in this situation, withdrawal of commitment to cultural success goals and all means, both legitimate and illegitimate, is the most likely adaptation. This proposition is more formally stated as:

Proposition 6: The less available to members of a population are culturally legitimated structural means, and the greater the internal prohibitions against the use of culturally illegitimate means, the greater the incidence of retreatist behavior in that population, when: (6a) cultural values dictating individual achievement are widespread and salient; and (6b) socialization experiences create strong commitments to culturally legitimate means.

The last mode of adaptation discussed by Merton is rebellion. Merton views rebellion as distinct from resentment, because, in contrast to resentment, where goals are still held, rebellion involves the rejection of both means and ends as well as efforts to substitute new means and ends. Rebellious behavior is most likely, according to Merton, where frustration and perceived deprivations over the failure to realize goals through legitimate channels dramatically increase and where groups codifying an ideology capable of mobilizing deprivations exist. Implied in his discussion of rebellion is that deprivations do not need to be absolute, but *relative*, in that cultural success goals raise expectations and desires for success to a point where, regardless of limited success with legitimate means, frustrations and deprivations escalate. More formally, this last proposition in Merton's theory can be stated as:

Proposition 7: The more the members of a population experience a sense of frustration and deprivation over their involvement in culturally legitimated structural means for realizing success goals, and the more available to these members are groupings which ideologically criticize the structure of the system, the greater the incidence of rebellious behavior in that population.

In this illustration of Merton's theory of anomie, some of the problems with his strategy and protocol can be highlighted. This first problem is one usually reserved for attacks on Parsonian functionalism: the lack of propositions and overcategorization of the world.

In many ways, the ghost of Max Weber haunts Merton's analysis as much as it does Parsons'. Merton develops a typology, or ideal type, of adaptations—conformity, innovation, ritualism, retreatism, and rebellion—to means-ends integrative problems. But there is little theory of the nature: Under conditions C_1, C_2, C_3, . . . , C_n, a particular type of means-ends disequilibrium will cause a particular type of adaptation among a specific population located in a specific place in the social structure. Propositions 1 through 7 are far more explicit than the discursive prose of Merton's presentation and they can represent only approximations of Merton's argument, since the theory is never stated explicitly. This problem, and the criticism it implies, is particularly severe in light of Merton's advocacy of the middle-range strategy. For middle-range theory to be useful and represent an improvement over Parsons' alleged vagueness, it must reveal clear statements of co-variance among concepts. Merton never does this. Moreover, concepts are rarely defined formally, and the terms used to discuss each concept always vary from page to page, thus increasing the vagueness of concepts in the theory. And thus, it can be argued that Merton has fallen victim to the very tendency for which he criticized Parsons: the creation of an ill-defined system of categories.

In addition to this failure to follow the middle-range strategy revealing clear concepts and propositions about a limited range of phenomena, his analysis falls victim to some of the problems of functional analysis that he wished to avoid. Probably the most serious problem is the implicit acceptance of the "functional universality" argument in this theory. Deviance is functional for some system part: If not the social whole, then some population, or some individual, will be positively affected. His constant shifting from analysis of the social whole to social classes and then to individual modes of adaptation is reminiscent of Malinowski's approach of finding a need, at some level of social organization, served by a particular structure or process. Moreover, as Merton's protocol would seem to require, the "net balance" of functions is never assessed for any of the diverse units of analysis that he discusses.

Yet, Merton's "theory"—or congeries of concepts and implicit propositions—is suggestive. Otherwise, it would not have stimulated the sociological imagination as much as it has. The power of his "theory," however, lies not in its "functional trappings" or in its eloquence as middle-range theory. It is quite deficient as an exemplar of theory at any range or level of abstraction. Its appeal lies in the substantive imagery that it depicts and the "feeling" among many sociologists that it points to an important set of social processes. This is where Merton's genius lies, not in his faithful or even partially faithful adherence to his functional protocol or middle-range strategy.

MERTON'S FUNCTIONAL STRATEGY: AN OVERVIEW

Merton has occupied a unique position in sociological theorizing. His tempered and reasoned statements have typically resolved intellectually stagnating controversies in the field.[27] For example, his advocacy of theories of the "middle range" quelled a vigorous debate between theoretically and empirically inclined sociologists by reasserting the efficacy of empirically oriented theory and theoretically oriented research.

Similarly, Merton's functional paradigm and protocol were explicated to deal with the growing body of criticism of functional theorizing. By pointing to the logical problems inherent in certain functional postulates, Merton's paradigm was viewed as providing an alternative form of functional analysis which avoided these problems. The uncritical acceptance of this paradigm attests to Merton's seemingly charismatic capacity to "resolve" issues. However, as reasoned and as appealing as his argument appears, it does not obviate the very theoretical problems it was explicitly

---

[27] I would like to emphasize that, despite the highly critical tone that has been taken in analyzing Merton's functionalism, I hold his other works, in high admiration. It has always bothered me that the format of this book forces a review of Merton's weakest effort, his functionalism. This chapter does not communicate the power and insight of his many nonfunctional efforts.

designed to resolve. In fact, Merton's own analysis of political machines, for all its insight and intuitive appeal, does not conform to the dictates of his protocol, leading critics to wonder why it is that functional analysis keeps slipping back into certain long-standing problems. And despite the genius behind his theory of anomie, the theory, and its functional trappings, is vague, even when converted to explicit propositions.

On the surface, Merton's paradigm and protocol appear to guide investigators to the interconnections and mutual consequences of structures. Theoretical statements on the nature of these interconnections among diverse system units constitute one of the principal goals of sociological theory, but imperativist assumptions of individual and system needs often appear to have diverted analytical attention away from documentation of the precise causal connections among systemic phenomena. As Merton's analysis illustrates, the mere cross-tabulation of one item, such as the existence of political machines, with need states imputed to another item, such as the "needs" of new immigrants in the large city, is sometimes performed in lieu of more precise causal statements about the relations between the two phenomena.

This situation, however, need not automatically ensue from functional analysis, even one in which concepts of system and individual needs figure prominently. Cross-tabulation can suggest a further theoretical question: What causal linkages would account for the fact that phenomena are capable of being cross-tabulated? Unfortunately, Merton like Parsons before him does not take this "next step," suggesting again that perhaps functionalism encourages categorization in lieu of propositions.

5

THE FUTURE OF FUNCTIONALISM IN SOCIOLOGY

In this final chapter on functionalism, a review of the problems and prospects of functionalism in sociology will be undertaken. Questions which must be addressed include: What is distinctive about functionalism? How severe are the substantive and logical problems of functionalism? Can they be overcome? Are they worth overcoming? And can functional thought assist sociology in its search for true theory?

IS FUNCTIONAL ANALYSIS A MYTH?

A number of commentators have sought to minimize the distinction between functionalism and other approaches to building theory. Their argument can be expressed in the following manner:

1. All sociologists study humans not in isolation but as pluralities of interacting actors.
2. All sociologists tend to view pluralities of interacting humans as creating "structured" sets of relationships.
3. All sociologists seek to determine the properties of these emerging structures.
4. All sociologists, in seeking to understand social structures, attempt to discern the boundaries and patterns of integration among actors.
5. All sociologists thus implicitly employ the notion of "system" in studying the boundaries and nature of integration among pluralities of interacting actors.

6. All sociologists seek to understand how variations in the properties of human systems can be accounted for by variations in the parts of systems.
7. All general theories of human organization, in seeking to develop laws of human organization will, out of necessity, ask why certain social patterns appear almost universally in human societies.

For those who argue that functionalism is not a distinctive approach to theory, differences between practices (1) through (7) above and functionalism are mere "terminological misunderstandings." For example, as Kingsley Davis notes:

> If . . . the investigator uses phrases like "has the function of," "meets the need of," or simply "is for," the words have so many connotations and ambiguities that the effect is often to obstruct rather than to facilitate the conveyance of meaning. Part of the reason is that these are words borrowed from common discourse and hence are mainly used to indicate moral imperatives and volitional intent rather than sheer causal relationships.[1]

And while the language of functionalism does have this unfortunate consequence of misleading functionalisms' critics, functionalism is not a unique form of analysis or method:

> It thus appears that the most agreed-upon traits of functionalism are those broadly characterizing scientific analysis in general. Any distinction is not due to method per se, but to linguistic usage and the particular subject (society). Granted the linguistic matter is superficial, we find nothing to upset the view that it is another name for sociological analysis— the interpretation of phenomena in terms of their interconnections with societies as going concerns.[2]

Is this argument correct? Is a distinctive form of analysis called "functionalism" a linguistic myth? As this chapter argues, functionalism is more than "myth." It is a unique method of analysis which makes certain assumptions about the nature of reality and which employs a distinctive strategy for developing theories using these assumptions. The task of this chapter is thus to assess how useful these assumptions are for developing theory about how patterns of human organization are created, maintained, and changed.

---

[1] Kingsley Davis, "The Myth of Functional Analysis as a Special Method of Sociology and Anthropology," *American Sociological Review* 10 (December 1959): 759.

[2] Ibid., p. 760.

THE FUNCTIONAL APPROACH

As functionalism developed in the social sciences, it became increasingly distinctive. From the initial organicism of Comte and Spencer, functionalism became transformed in the work of Durkheim, Radcliffe-Brown, Malinowski, Merton, and Parsons, and many others into a particular mode of analysis.[3]

The first distinctively functional analysis was performed by Émile Durkheim. As noted in Chapter 2, it was Durkheim who made the critical distinction between "cause" and "function." Previously, thinkers had simply analogized between "organism" and "society" without recognizing that a particular method of inquiry was involved in making such analogies. Much like Spencer, Durkheim realized that organicism alerted investigators to the consequences of a system part for the maintenance of the social whole. But unlike Spencer, he also recognized, at least in his careful moments, that the existence of parts and their variations required a separate causal analysis. Several implicit assumptions can be found in Durkheim's work:

1. Social wholes—for him, society or the "body social"—require some pattern or means for integration of their constituent parts.
2. Certain processes or parts in social wholes—such as the division of labor, the collective conscience, law, or religion—operate to maintain the integration of the social whole.
3. The causes for the existence of parts and for their variations are distinguishable from the consequences they have for maintaining the integration of the social whole.

---

[3] The list of functional sociologists is long, but some of the important theoretical work using this orientation can be found in the following references: D. F. Aberle, A. Cohen, K. Davis, M. Levy, and F. X. Sutton, "The Functional Prerequisites of Society," *Ethics* 60 (1950)1:100–111; C. Ackerman and T. Parsons, "The Concept of System as a Theoretical Device" in C. J. Direnzo, ed., *Concepts, Theory and Explanation in the Behavioral Sciences* (New York: Random House, 1966):24–42; H. C. Bredemeier and R. M. Stephenson, *The Analysis of Social Systems* (New York: Holt, 1962); F. Cancian, "Functional Analysis of Change," *American Sociological Review* 25 (1960) 6:818–27; K. Davis, *Human Society* (New York: Macmillan, 1949); K. Davis and W. E. Moore, "Some Principles of Stratification," *American Sociological Review* 10 (1945) 2:242–49; D. Easton, *A Systems Analysis of Political Life* (New York: Wiley, 1965); R. Firth, "Function" in W. L. Thomas, ed., *Current Anthropology* (Chicago: University of Chicago Press, 1956); R. T. Holt, "A Proposed Structural-functional Framework for Political Science," in D. Martindale, ed. *Functionalism in Social Sciences* (Philadelphia: American Academy of Political and Social Science, 1965): 84–110; H. Kallen, "Functionalism," in E. R. A. Seligman, ed., *Encyclopaedia of the Social Sciences,* vol. 6 (New York: Macmillan, 1934): 523–35; and M. Levy, Jr., *The Structure of Society* (Princeton, N.J.: Princeton University Press, 1952).

4.   Therefore, functional analysis involves a two-fold method: (*a*) a search
     for those parts maintaining the integration of the social whole and
     (*b*) a separate search for the causes for the existence of, and variations
     in, the parts.

As was emphasized in Chapter 2, however, Durkheim sometimes
lapsed into a fifth assumption:

5.   The need for integration of the social whole can help explain the
     existence of, and variations in, those parts contributing to integration.

Thus, Durkheim's analysis subtly opened the door to an entirely new
form of teleological reasoning: End states of the social whole can cause
parts to emerge and can regulate their variation in ways which maintain
these states. Durkheim wished to avoid this kind of teleological analysis,
for he felt it to be illegitimate and not able to explain why a part should
exist and vary. Yet, this tendency to argue teologically is implicit in
Durkheim's work, and as will become evident shortly, it is one of the
weaknesses of the functional approach.

While Radcliffe-Brown's analysis represented the application of Durkheim's first four assumptions (and occasionally, to his dismay no doubt,
the fifth assumption) to ethnographic data on primitive tribes,
Malinowski radically departed from Durkheim's functionalism.[4] In so
doing, he began to address issues which Durkheim and Radcliffe-Brown
had ignored. The result was to extend the list of assumptions employed
in functional analysis.

In both Spencer's and Durkheim's formulations can be found the
concept of "needs" or "requisites." Radcliffe-Brown termed these "necessary conditions of existence." Among all of these theorists, however,
the concept of "functional needs," "functional requisites" or "functional
imperatives" revolves around one basic "need" of the "social organism":
the need for integration. In contrast to these early functionalists, Malinowski embraced and elaborated the concept of functional needs, thereby
explicitly adding an additional assumption to the functional orientation.
Furthermore, as will be emphasized, Malinowski addressed another issue
which Spencer, Durkheim, and Radcliffe-Brown had ignored: the relationship between "system needs" and "individual needs." Durkheim
had rejected psychologistic reasoning, and in many ways, his advocacy

---

[4] For basic references on Malinowski's functionalism, see "Culture" in E. R. A.
Seligman, ed., *Encyclopaedia of the Social Sciences*, vol. 4 (New York: Macmillan, 1934);
Coral Gardens and Their Magic (London: Allen and Unwin, 1935); "Anthropology,"
Encyclopaedia Britannica, supp. vol. 1, 1936, pp. 131–40; and *A Scientific Theory of
Culture and Other Essays* (London: Oxford University Press, 1969).

of the functional approach represented a way to examine social structures independently of the individuals who participate in them. While Malinowski's model presented many problems (see Chapter 2), he must be credited with raising an issue—the relationship between individual and social system (cultural) requisites or needs—that was to occupy the attention of modern functionalists such as Talcott Parsons and Robert K. Merton.

As was noted in Chapter 2, Malinowski's conceptualization of basic human needs for nutrition, reproduction, bodily comfort, safety, movement, and health led him to ask: What features of the cultural system (social system in sociological terms) evolved to meet these needs? [5] Similarly, his list of derived needs of cultural (social) systems for production, organization, codification of regulations, and cultural transmission led him to ask: What features of cultural (social) systems evolve to meet these derived needs? Thus, Malinowski's functional analysis directs inquiry toward an assessment of universal human and cultural ("derived" social system) needs or requisites and then toward an analysis of how specific types of social structures found in all societies meet these needs. For Malinowski, social structures exist for a reason: to meet individual or system needs. And it is this approach which enabled him to proclaim that "every type of civilization, every custom, material object, idea and belief fulfills some vital function, has some task to accomplish, represents an indispensable part within a working whole."[6] And as was emphasized in Chapter 2, the dangers of illegitimate teleology and tautology inherent in this kind of extreme requisite analysis are great. For present purposes, however, concern is with what Malinowski's approach added to the functional approach to building social theory. At least these additional assumptions were added:

1.   Social reality exists at different levels of organization—at a minimum, the individual and cultural (social).
2.   Basic needs for survival exist for individuals, and the creation of social organization (culture) represents a way of meeting these needs.
3.   Once elaborated, patterns of social organization have their own needs which are met by the further elaboration of social (cultural) patterns.
4.   Hence, in order to understand why a particular social (cultural) pattern exists, it is necessary to know the level or type of need or requisite that it meets.

---

[5] See, in particular, his *A Scientific Theory* (1969) and "The Group and the Individual in Functional Analysis," *American Journal of Sociology*, 44 (September 1938): 938–64.

[6] "Anthropology" (1936).

5. In studying social patterns, it is necessary to understand that social
    organization involves a complex adaptation to "derived" social (cul-
    tural) and "basic" individual needs.

While Malinowski's analysis was crude, often simplistic, and always
polemical, his work did represent a conceptual liberation from the extremes of Durkheim's strictly sociologistic emphasis on emergent realities
and on "social facts." And it explicitly interjected the concept of needs
and system levels to sociological analysis. And although Talcott Parsons
was to reach these same conclusions somewhat independently of Malinowski, he was to expand the concept of requisites and system levels
into one of the most distinctive features of the functional orientation.

Talcott Parsons' original "voluntaristic theory of action" represented
a system of categories for visualizing the components of individual decision-making and behavior. Parsons' early work thus focused on the individual, and only later, as he began to recognize that behavior is emitted
in a social context, did his scheme begin to capture the properties of
emergent system levels which Durkheim had emphasized. In making
the conceptual transition from individual "unit acts" to "systems of
action," Parsons was inevitably concerned with how individual actors
become integrated into social and cultural systems. That is, how are
actors made ready to participate in and conform to the normative requirements of the social system? To answer this question, Parsons began to
conceptualize the properties of personality systems, social systems, and
cultural systems and the problems of integration within and between
these systems. In so doing, he brought into further focus the distinctive
features of the functional orientation.

In *The Social System,* Parsons conceptualized the social system as
existing in "equilibrium"—a concept borrowed from economists, particularly the early Italian sociologist Vilfredo Pareto.[7] To maintain this equilibrium, integration of personality systems into the social and cultural
systems must occur. Parsons then postulated that two general mechanisms
could be isolated which perform this function: the mechanisms of "socialization" and "social control" discussed in Chapter 3. In this way, Parsons
began to shift subtly the nature of functional analysis away from Durkheim's and Radcliffe-Brown's concern with the functions of specific empirical structures for maintenance of the integration of the social whole
to an emphasis on general mechanisms which maintain equilibrium states

---

[7] Vilfredo Pareto, *Mind and Society,* vol. 1–4 (1936); and L. J. Henderson, *Pareto's General Sociology: A Physiologist's Interpretation.* (Cambridge: Harvard University Press, 1935).

of the social system. Concern with integration of the social whole was thereby transformed into a more comprehensive emphasis on the "equilibrium" of social systems, while analysis moved away from the functions of specific structures to a search for the more general functions of mechanisms. These mechanisms were, in turn, to assure the integration of actors into the status-role structure of the social system and the symbolic components—such as norms, values, and beliefs—of the cultural system. Through "socialization mechanisms," cultural symbols were viewed as becoming internalized as motives to participate in roles, while through "social control mechanisms" some minimal degree of order among status-roles, and conformity of actors to normative requirements, was assured. Specific social structures, then, were viewed by Parsons as an instance of a more general set of mechanisms for maintaining the social equilibrium.

Parsons' functionalism thus became a mechanism-equilibrium analysis, as opposed to the structure-function approach of Durkheim and Radcliffe-Brown. This shift in emphasis probably reflects the problem first addressed seriously by Malinowski: Social reality exists at different levels, and sociological analysis must be capable of conceptualizing these levels. For Parsons, this meant shifting the level of abstraction to general notions of social equilibrium (later to "moving equilibriums" and "homeostasis") and to mechanisms integrating different levels of social reality and thereby maintaining the equilibrium. The major "functional requisite" was thus the integration among personality, cultural, and social systems. At this stage of his work, then, Parsons had forged a distinctive form of functional analysis:

1. Reality is composed of different levels of systems.
2. Social systems tend toward equilibrium states.
3. Mechanisms in social systems operate to promote equilibrium states by integrating different levels of systems.
4. Therefore, sociological analysis must invoke an examination of social structures as instances of more general mechanisms of integration within and between system levels that, in turn, maintain equilibrium states of the social whole.

Later, as Parsons began to ponder the nature of action systems, the notion of functional requisites became more prominent. Unlike Malinowski, who constructed separate lists of requisites for different system levels (that is, "basic needs" and "derived needs"), Parsons postulated four universal requisites for all action systems: adaptation, goal attainment, integration, and latency. With these requisites, he began to analyze specific structures and processes in terms of how they operated to meet one of these requisites, and then, how the meeting of these requisites promoted the "survival" of the systemic whole. Thus, Parsons' functionalism shifted from a mechanism-equilibrium analysis to one involving structure, requisite, and system survival. In many ways, this later emphasis represents an odyssey back to the original functionalism of Herbert Spencer, who viewed society as an organism, with the "struggle for survival" involving the maintenance of requisites for integration. Parsons' theoretical development at this stage of his work thus created another form of functional analysis:

1. Social reality consists of different system levels.
2. All systems reveal universal requisites.
3. To survive and adapt, all systems must meet these requisites, to some minimal degree.
4. Functional analysis involves understanding how specific processes and structures operate to meet system requisites, and in turn, how varying degrees of meeting requisites fosters equilibrium (or dysequilibrium) of the social whole.[8]

A different form of functional analysis was developed by R. K. Merton in an effort to overcome the deficiencies in Malinowski's and Parsons' approaches. In questioning the "postulates" implicit in Malinowski's functionalism, and the "grand theoretical" style of Parsons' work (see Chapter 4), Merton sought to retain what is useful in functional analysis. For Merton, the unique feature of functional analysis is the concern with the consequences of a part for other social parts or a social whole. Notions of "survival requisites" are appropriate in assessing the consequences of system parts, but these survival requisites must be *empirically established* for *each* system under study. Moreover, it is necessary to follow Weber's lead and understand what the significance or meaning of involvement in a system is for the actors, and following Malinowski's emphasis, it is also necessary to discern the consequences of involvement of actors for their psychological needs. For such knowledge of the "meaning of action" and of the "psychological needs" it serves can provide additional clues as to the consequences of a part for other parts or a systemic whole. Thus, Merton might be said to have proposed a sociopsy-

---

[8] It should be emphasized that, at about this time, other authors were developing, or had developed, similar ideas, and catalogs of universal requisites. In addition to Malinowski's efforts can be found that of Levy, *The Structure of Society;* Davis, *Human Society;* and Aberle et al., "The Functional Prerequisites." Parsons' requisites became the best known and represent an exemplar of this form of functional analysis.

chological imperativism by assuming that a part or sociocultural item meets empirical established needs at the social-structural level, while also meeting needs at the individual psychological level. For Merton, then, functional analysis involves an attempt to assess the "net balance" of consequences of a specific structure for other structures and for individual needs. At times, a part may be "positively functional"—that is, meet the needs of—some parts, but not others, and for some individuals, and not others. For Merton, then, the task of functional analysis was to determine the "net balance" of positive and negative (dysfunctional) consequences of an item.

Naturally, Merton recognized, as did Durkheim before him, that the net balance of consequences does not reveal the cause of an item. This must be undertaken in a separate causal analysis, although Merton did not give great emphasis to this fact. Rather, his concern was with clarifying the problems in the concept of function—that is, of how to go about analyzing consequences of items for other items and the social whole. In so doing, Merton added several new dimensions to functional analysis:[9]

1. Empirical systems—not abstract analytical systems—must be the focus of functional analysis.
2. The task of functional analysis is to specify clearly the sociocultural item under investigation.
3. This item must be analyzed in terms of its consequences for meeting empirically established, as opposed to abstract a priori, survival requisites of the system in which it is implicated and for realizing empirically established psychological needs of the individual involved.
4. Attention must also focus on the positive, negative, and nonfunctional consequences of an item for individual needs and system requisites.
5. The goal of functional analysis thus becomes assessing the "net balance of consequences" of an item. With this assessment will come better understanding of social structures and processes.

In reviewing the nature of the functionalist approach to theory building, it is clear that functionalism involves several approaches. *Structural functionalism* was first espoused by Durkheim as an explicit method of inquiry. It involved the separation of causal and functional analysis, with

---

[9] For a somewhat different interpretation of Merton's functionalism, see: H. L. Lehman, "R. K. Merton's Concepts of Function and Functionalism," *Sociological Inquiry* 9 (1966)3:274–83.

specific attention to the isolation of structures, their causes, and then their functions or consequences for maintaining the integration of the social whole. This kind of analysis might be termed the most minimal type of functional inquiry. These features are schematically represented in Figure 5–1:

FIGURE 5–1
Minimal Functional Analysis: Structural Functionalism

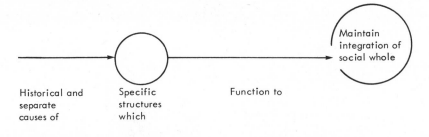

Historical and   Specific   Function to   Maintain
separate   structures   integration of
causes of   which   social whole

Malinowski, Parsons, and Merton all emphasized the problems of integration of system levels, particularly the individual and social system levels. Parsons' early functional analysis went beyond Malinowski's original insights and added additional assumptions. Parsons continually assumed a system to have equilibrium states and then attempted to assess how generalized mechanisms operated to reach and then to maintain these equilibrium states. This form of functional analysis might be termed *mechanism-equilibrium analysis.* Its major features are schematically represented in Figure 5–2:

FIGURE 5–2
Mechanism-Equilibrium Functional Analysis

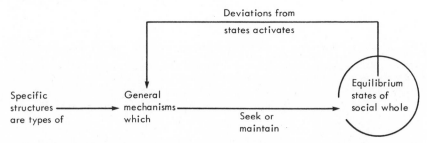

Deviations from
states activates

Specific   General   Equilibrium
structures   mechanisms   states of
are types of   which   Seek or   social whole
                                       maintain

In contrast to structural-functionalism, specific structures and their functions are analyzed as an instance of a more general mechanism which operates to maintain equilibrium states. Further, there is the recognition that, at times, the states of the equilibrium "activate" mechanisms which maintain the equilibrium—thus making this form of functional inquiry explicitly teleological.

Parsons' later emphasis on functional requisites, much like Malinowski's earlier efforts, reveals a third form of functional analysis: *functional imperativism* or *requisite functionalism*. In this form of functionalism, specific structures are viewed as meeting universal needs or requisites of systems, with the extent to which needs are met determining the survival of the system. This approach is represented in Figure 5–3:

FIGURE 5–3
Functional Imperativism or Requisite Functionalism

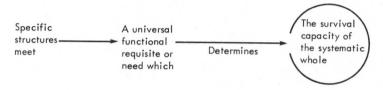

Functional imperativism is less explicitly teleological than mechanism-equilibrium analysis. Its emphasis is upon determining which requisite a structure operates to meet and on how the meeting of requisites determines the survival of the system. In turn, survival is defined rather ambiguously, but includes such notions as "adaptability" to the environment and "internal integration" of parts.

Merton's analysis also sought to understand the functions of items at different levels of social organization. In contrast to previous types of functionalism, however, dysfunctions are given particular emphasis, thus necessitating a concern for "net balances of functions" of parts for a social context. Diagrammatically this form of functionalism—termed *net functional balance*—is outlined in Figure 5–4.

FIGURE 5–4
Net Functional Balance Analysis

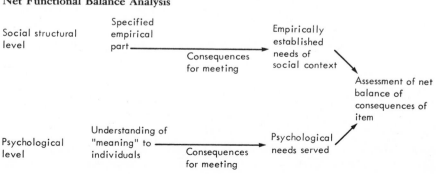

In this approach, only empirical units are to be analyzed, and the part and the social context of the part must be clearly specified. Then, the task becomes one of establishing the particular survival requisites of the empirical system—that is, what is necessary for *this particular empirical* system to survive. By assessing the functions, or consequences, of an item for meeting, or not meeting, these needs, insight into the nature of a part and its social contexts can be achieved. In addition to this structural analysis must come an analysis of the "meaning" of participation in a structural item for its participants, particularly as this analysis reveals the psychological needs served, or not served, by participation in an item. In this way, the net balance of consequences of an item at diverse levels of social organization can be assessed.

All of these forms of analysis share certain features in common which should be emphasized: (1) Functionalists are interested in the states of social wholes or larger social contexts. (2) They view the importance of a part within a more inclusive system or context in terms of what it does for the social whole. (3) They have various criterion—over-all contribution to integration, classes of equilibrium mechanisms, or survival requisites—for classifying structures and for isolating their effects upon the social whole. (4) Causal analysis is thus focused on how variations in parts, singularly or in combination with other parts, affect the states of the social whole. These are the common features of the functional analysis and they are what make it unique. It is in the utility of these features and the specifics of the forms outlined in the figures in this chapter that the future of functionalism resides. If these approaches obscure more than clarify, or distort more than sensitize, then there is little future in the functional orientation.

PROBLEMS AND PROSPECTS OF
FUNCTIONAL ANALYSIS

As has been noted, critics have viewed functionalism as revealing both logical and substantive problems. Any assessment of the future of functionalism must therefore address these two types of problems and determine if they close off the future development of this theoretical orientation.

Logical Problems of Functionalism

Rather consistently, two logical problems surface in discussions of functionalism: (1) the problem of illegitimate teleology, and (2) the problem of tautology. To the extent that either or both of these problems is endemic to functional analysis, the perspective will not be useful in the development of sociological theory. On the other hand, to the degree that these problems can be overcome, the four types of functionalism diagrammed in Figures 5–1 through 5–4 can perhaps have some utility in guiding the future of sociological theorizing.

The Problem of Illegitimate Teleology. The word "teleology" denotes purpose—processes and structures operate and exist to meet certain ends or goals. Much of the social world is teleological: People have goals toward which they organized their behaviors; organizations and groups also have ends for which members' activities are coordinated; and macro structures such as nation-states usually have goals—military superiority or full employment—toward which human and material resources are mobilized and allocated. At all levels of social organization, then, social processes and structures are frequently goal-directed. Teleological analysis is thus not necessarily illegitimate, for indeed, much of social reality is teleological.

Illegitimate teleologies exist when causal statements presume purposes or goals to cause the processes and structures realizing these goals or purposes, *without being able to document the causal sequences or mechanisms whereby purposes, end states, or goals create or regulate the structures and processes that are involved in their realization.*[10] For example, as was noted for Durkheim's analysis, there is a subtle implication that social solidarity—the end state or result—causes the organic division of labor to emerge out of social competition. If this is what Durkheim did indeed imply, then it is an illegitimate teleology since he does not document *how and through what causal processes* the need for solidarity, or the perception by some decision-making body of the need for solidarity,

---

[10] For basic references on this issue, see footnotes in Chapters 2, 3, and 4, as well as the following: G. Bergman, "Purpose, Function and Scientific Explanation," *Acta Sociologica* 5(1962):225–28; J. Canfield, "Teleological Explanation in Biology," *The British Journal for the Philosophy of Science*, 14 (1964):285–95; K. Deutsch, "Mechanism, Teleology and Mind," *Philosophy and Phenomenological Research* 12 (1951): 185–223; C. J. Ducasse, "Explanation, Mechanism, and Teleology," in H. Feigl and W. Sellars, eds., *Readings in Philosophical Analysis* (New York: Appleton, 1949); D. Emmet, *Function, Purpose and Powers* (London: Routledge-Kegan, 1958); L. S. Fever, "Causality in the Social Sciences," *Journal of Philosophy*, 51 (1954)1:191–208; W. W. Isajiw, *Causation and Functionalism in Sociology* (New York: Shocken, 1968); A. Kaplan, "Noncausal Explanation," in D. Lerner, *Cause and Effect* (New York: Free Press, 1965); C. A. Mace, "Mechanical and Teleological Causation," Feigl and Sellers, I. Scheffler, "Thoughts on Teleology," *The British Journal for the Philosophy of Science*, 9 (1958)6:265–284; P. Sztompka, "Teleological Language in Sociology," *The Polish Sociological Bulletin* (1969)2:56–69 and *System and Function: Toward a Theory of Society* (New York: Academic Press, 1974).

sets into motion a sequence of events leading to the organic division of labor. Similarly Merton's analysis of political machines appeared to lapse into an illegitimate teleology by assuming that the needs of immigrants for services or the needs to integrate immigrants into U.S. social structure (both end states) *caused* the emergence of the political machines which brought about these end states. Without specification of the causal mechanisms involved, these kinds of theoretical statements are illegitimate teleologies.

How readily, then, do the types of functional analysis represented in Figures 5–1, 5–2, 5–3, and 5–4 fall into illegitimate teleological reasoning? The minimal functional analysis of Durkheim and Radcliffe-Brown (Figure 5–1), or even the more extensive analysis of Merton (see Figure 5–4), appears to lapse into illegitimate teleological reasoning. Logically, there is no reason for this lapse to occur. Specific structures can be viewed as having separate causes, and then variations in the profile of the social whole can be viewed as caused by variations in specific structures. The problem emerges when analysis short-circuits this attention to causality and begins to view variations in the profile of the social whole as causing variations in specific structures, *without* specifying the causal chain of events involved. The second type of functional analysis— the mechanism equilibrium type (see Figure 5–2)—is explicitly teleological. General mechanisms are viewed as operating to maintain equilibrium states, and presumably these mechanisms are "activated" when deviations from these equilibrium states are too great. The approach, however, is rife with illegitimate teleologies, since just *how and through what causal processes* equilibrium states initiate the mechanisms is unspecified. Even when specific structures, such as the family, are viewed as a type of mechanism (socialization, for example, in the Parsons' scheme), just how the social equilibrium causes variations in the structure and socialization processes of the family is vague. In some cases, however, it might be possible to view a legitimate teleological process, as when the political elites repress deviations (and hence, operate as a "social control mechanism") to restore their conception of equilibrium. Yet, there is a clear bias for teleological reasoning in equilibrium-mechanism analysis—one which is fraught with logical problems when constructing causal statements.

Functional imperativism (see Figure 5–3) is not explicitly teleological. Specific structures are viewed in terms of their consequences for hypothetical system imperatives, and then the meeting of system imperatives is viewed as influencing variations in the social whole, particularly with respect to "survival" and "adaptation." However, this form of analysis can lapse into illegitimate teleologies with the simple implication that the need for meeting a system imperative causes the existence of, or variations in, a specific structure. Or the need of the systemic whole to adapt and survive creates specific pressures for meeting needs which, in turn, cause the emergence of, or variation in, specific structures. For example, the need for "adaptation" causes the economy to emerge, or the need to survive creates adaptive problems which are resolved by the economy. None of these kinds of statements specifies how and through what causal sequences an end state (the need for survival, or the need to meet an imperative) causes the events that realized this end state.

Most frequently, to avoid illegitimate teleologies an evolutionary mechanism is invoked:[11] Those systems in the past which did not meet certain imperatives perished, while those which did (through chance or experimentation) evolve structures to meet these needs, survived. The organic analogy is clearly evident in this kind of causal analysis, but it does avoid the problem of illegitimate teleology. But it also is a very limiting analysis, since one might want to know why present economic patterns reveal a particular profile and why they have the consequences that they do. The evolutionary "social selection" mechanism is not likely to be very useful for dealing with this problem.

Another way to avoid illegitimate teleologies in functional imperativism, and to some extent mechanism-equilibrium analysis, is through what was called in Chapter 3 "reverse causal chain analysis."[12] This is, in reality, a variant of the evolutionary "social selection" mechanism. The argument runs as follows: Survival and/or equilibrium states are often maintained without built-in purposes. Much biological and social life simply reflects natural selective mechanisms maintaining system balances. A certain trend—for example, a population increase, urban expansion, or bureaucratic growth—can occur until further movement in this direction decreases survival and thus sets into motion selection against the direction of the trend. For example, organizations can perhaps grow to a certain size, then find that they cannot make a profit, and resolve this problem by going out of business, divesting themselves of resources, or by differentiation into smaller corporate units. There is no grand purpose dictating organizational size, but rather a natural limit on how big corporations in certain environments can get until selective pressures

---

[11] For a thorough discussion see: Sztompka, "Teleological Language," pp. 138–52.

[12] See Arthur L. Stinchcombe, *Constructing Social Theories* (New York: Harcourt, Brace and World, 1968), p. 100.

operate to decrease size. To take another example, human populations can grow until their institutional structure can no longer support them, setting into motion selective pressures—starvation, political turmoil, and the like—which reduce the size through attrition and through selection for political elites who implement population control. There is no requirement to assume a state of optimal "population equilibrium" or a "need for a particular population size" in this kind of analysis but, rather, a natural set of negative feedback processes which select against further growth of the population. Thus, once a natural limit on survival is reached, selective pressures operate against further growth by forcing certain social developments.

There are, then, ways to avoid illegitimate teleological arguments in functional theorizing. The critical questions thus become: Can they always be avoided? And is it worth the effort?

Much of the problem of illegitimate teleologies in functional theorizing stems from the implicit organicism of this mode of analysis. In the body of an organism, it is possible to determine what equilibrium, homeostasis, or survival represent. Moreover, there exist clear mechanisms in the body which seek to maintain certain goal states, equilibriums, or homeostatic ranges. And because certain minimal bodily functions must be met, it is possible to offer an assessment of "survival requisites" which corresponds to what constitutes life or death for the system.

In turning to societies, however, life and death have no clear definition. It is not possible to determine an optimal equilibrium or range of homeostasis. And it is not always possible to isolate mechanisms maintaining what cannot be determined or defined. And yet social wholes do reveal integration; they often organize and regulate activities for end purposes; and they do indeed disappear or "die." Beyond these simple comparisons, however, organismic systems are much different than social systems. Furthermore such comparisons obscure the dramatic differences in actual causal processes.

The parts of human social systems are integrated by "interactions" which can change in content and form during the course of the interaction. The parts in interaction often reveal purposes, but these purposes often come into conflict. And thus, unlike an organism, the structure of a human system is not easily typified by an established type of structure. Rather, they are in a constant process of *structuring*. Processes sometimes operate as much to change, modify, or alter as to maintain the system. And unlike organisms, there are fewer "built-in" limits to change and restructure. This image of human organization does not deny that social wholes remain unchanged for periods of time, only that lack of change is not automatic. Human social systems are subject to complex interactive processes among system parts which can potentially alter their structure.

These considerations require a causal analysis that asks: In what ways do variations in one system part cause variations in another? And if one is interested in the relations of parts to more inclusive wholes, it is necessary to ask: To what degree do variations in a particular part cause variations, if any, in a more inclusive system? Moreover, if it is possible to establish a system with purpose or goals, then it must be asked: In what ways, through what specific processes, and with what demonstrable result do variations in system purpose affect variations in designated parts? And then, if one is interested in the part-to-whole issue, it is necessary to answer again the question: To what degree do variations in parts cause variations in the systemic whole? In answering these questions, it is essential, as Merton emphasized, to have a clear definition of "system part" and "system whole." Unless this kind of detailed attention to the units of analysis and the causal chains among them is emphasized in part-to-whole investigations, functional analysis can become illegitimately teleological. In fact, the label "functionalism" might be better replaced by the label "part-to-whole analysis," in which the causal chains between and among clearly designated parts and wholes are isolated.

The use of such concepts as "integration," "equilibrium," or "homeostasis" is probably ill-advised, because they assume (a) that the social scientists can determine by clear criteria what these mean for a particular system, and (b) that these states have causal significance in part-whole relations. Neither assumption is correct and each begins to distort analysis. With respect to "survival requisites," they can perhaps be useful in part-to-whole investigations if they are viewed not so much as necessary states of a system, but as criteria for sorting out critical part-to-part and part(s)-to-whole relations. For example, Parsons' concept of "adaptation" reveals little about system survival, except to say that systems take in, convert, and distribute resources and that, if some minimal level of this activity does not occur, the system will cease to exist. But just "what minimal level" means cannot be specified in the abstract; and contrary to Merton's belief, it usually cannot be specified when looking at a concrete, empirical system. What, for example, is minimally necessary to meet the adaptive problem of a school? Only when the school closes its doors would social scientists be able to answer the question. What a concept like adaptation provides is a sensitizing guidepost for discerning interesting structures and processes from less interesting ones. It indicates that, if an investigator desires to discern those parts accounting for the greatest variations in the social whole, then the investigator should examine those parts involved in extracting, converting, and distributing resources. The same holds true for other requisites. Any other usage of the concept of requisites is likely to begin obscuring causal analysis of relations between and among well-defined parts and wholes. Moreover, to postulate requisites as metaphysical entities which "must be met" to assure "survival" is to assume what cannot be assumed: (1) That one can draw the line between survival and nonsurvival of a system; (2) that one can measure degrees of surviving, or "social health"; and (3) that in attempting to measure these, one's assessment of what constitutes "survival" will not be a guise for what represents "the desirable."

Thus, to avoid the problems of illegitimate teleology, the word "function" should be abandoned. Analysis should focus on part-to-whole relationships and on the causal relationship among parts, on the one hand, and between parts and wholes, on the other hand. If one finds useful abstract criteria which denote important processes, then these can be stated not as "functional requisites" or "imperatives" but as criteria of importance in discovering those part-to-part relationships explaining the most variations in social wholes.

Such a mode of analysis is still unique. It still captures what Durkheim, Radcliffe-Brown, Malinowski, Merton, and Parsons found fascinating in the organismic analogy: How are variations in society accounted for by the nature of societal parts? But in abandoning the organismic trappings, the theoretical answers, involving clear causal statements, can be provided with less risk of illegitimate teleologies.

The Problem of Tautology. The problem of tautology revolves around circular causal statements. It is most likely to surface in functional analysis involving notions of "equilibrium" and "requisites." Thus, "mechanism-equilibrium" (Figure 5–2), "functional imperativism" (Figure 5–3), and "net balance analysis" (Figure 5–4) are most susceptible to circular kinds of statements. For example, in mechanism-equilibrium analysis (Figure 5–2), one might find statements like: The existing state of a system is its equilibrium point; because an item is a part of the existing system, it can be viewed as a specific manifestation of a more general mechanism maintaining the equilibrium. In such a statement, the implied cause of the part is its function to maintain the equilibrium, while the cause of the equilibrium is the existence of the part.

To repeat the example from Merton's "net balance of functions" (Figure 5–4) argument, it is all too tempting to assume implicitly that a persistent structure, such as a political machine, fulfills a need—for integration of ethnic populations into the city—and the cause of the structure is the need it fulfills—the need of immigrants for assistance. Or, to illustrate for functional imperativism (Figure 5–4), a statement such as the following is possible: a part, structure, or item meets the needs of the system because it is a part of a surviving system, while the existence of the part can be traced to the fact that the system exists. In all of these statements causality—what causes what—is obscured and potentially circular.

Many tautologies stated by functionalists are simply due to their failure to be more precise in explicating causal relationships, and often causality can be sorted out and made explicit. Thus, tautologies can often be avoided by following the guidelines outlined above for resolving problems of illegitimate teleologies. But the issue of tautology is perhaps more fundamental: The concepts of "equilibrium" and "needs" pose problems. It is all too simple to imply that equilibrium or survival needs cause parts, and the existence of parts maintains equilibrium or survival. The circularity of such statements can only be resolved by additional information on what constitutes survival or equilibrium. And if it can be demonstrated that without a part, equilibrium or survival would not exist, then the part can be said to cause the equilibrium or survival. But to ascertain this information, it would be necessary to demonstrate how an equivalent system, without the part in question, did not survive or revealed disequilibrium. Moreover, it would be critical to provide precise criteria of what "disequilibrium" or "nonsurvival" meant. Rarely are sociologists in a position to provide such needed information.

Thus, it may well be that assumptions of equilibrium or homeostasis, as well as conceptions of functional requisites or needs, should be abandoned (except perhaps as sensitizing guideposts for "important" social processes). They cannot be readily defined or measured and they tempt theorists to create circular causal statements. Rather, the critical question for functional, or preferably part-whole, analysis is: How are variations in social wholes caused by variations in critical parts, and vice versa? To presume that some equilibrium state or need is involved in this process is to insert an unmeasurable and vague concept into the causal analysis—thereby increasing the probabilities of tautologous statements.

Thus, to avoid the dangers of tautology in part-to-whole analysis, the concept of equilibrium should be abandoned, since the theoretical issue should not be what maintains, or causes deviations from, hypothesized equilibrium states, but how much variation in social wholes is caused by specified variations in parts, and vice versa. To impose a conception of equilibrium on this causal analysis invites substantive and logical problems. Conceptualizations of system requisites can be useful in providing criteria for finding significant parts for analysis, but once these parts are found, the concepts of requisites should be dropped and replaced by a causal analysis of the relationship between the part and the designated social whole. To invoke notions of system survival is, as with the concept of equilibrium, to invite logical and substantive problems.

Substantive Problems of Functionalism

The substantive criticisms of functionalism revolve around the "image of social reality" it presents. This image is assumed by critics to: (1) reveal an ahistorical bias, focusing only on existing social structures; (2) present a conservative bias, emphasizing only those structures and processes causing stability and order; and (3) offer a static bias, directing attention away from social change.[13] Considerable intellectual acrimony has occurred over these issues. It is necessary, therefore, to determine if indeed functional analysis reveals ahistorical, conservative, and static biases.

The Question of History. Logically, there is no reason why a minimal functional orientation cannot address historical questions. In fact, Durkheim's original distinction between cause and function was directed at separating the historical analysis of antecedent conditions causing a structure to exist and reveal a particular profile from the functions that the structure performed for the "body social." In contrast, however, functionalism in anthropology, especially that form advocated by Malinowski, was developed specifically as a reaction to evolutionary theorizing. As such, it was intended to be *ahistorical,* analyzing the relationship between different levels of needs and social structures. Early Parsonian functionalism—that is, mechanism-equilibrium analysis—was also ahistorical, since it emphasized mechanism-equilibrium processes rather than the historical events which had created a given equilibrium state. Parsons' more recent imperativism presents a more ambiguous picture. Early concern with the system imperatives for adaptation, goal attainment, integration, and latency tended to be ahistorical, focusing primarily upon the functions of structures, and their interrelations, for meeting system imperatives. More recent work, however, has been uniquely historical and involves an evolutionary history of modern, Western societies. In this analysis, stages of evolution are established in terms of how, or with what struc-

---

[13] See next chapter for specific formulations of these charges by conflict theorists. See also Piotr Sztompka's effort to deal with these charges in his *System and Function,* pp. 138–67.

tures, the four imperatives have historically been resolved. At each stage, Parsons argues, the requisites are resolved by particular structures, and unless particular types of new structures are created to deal with the four requisites, a society will remain at a given stage of development.

Merton's "net balance" approach does not preclude historical consideration of why a part or item should exist, but it does not encourage a concern for the historical antecedents of parts. In fact, concern with documenting the relationship between empirical needs and specific structures can inadvertently obscure the fact that the functions and dysfunctions of an item for meeting needs can have little to do with the causes of the item.

Thus, only the minimal analysis of Durkheim is free of the ahistorical bias. In general, it can be concluded that functionalism is not well-suited for isolating the past events which have caused the existence of, and variations in, parts. Its emphasis is upon part-to-whole causal relations and how, once they exist, a part and whole mutually affect variation in each other. Functional analysis thus suffers from a bias against determining the historical condition which causes the emergence of a part; and thus, its utility for developing theory is correspondingly limited.

The Question of Conservatism. In reviewing Figures 5–1 to 5–4, it is clear that all four types of functional analysis reveal a concern for integration, equilibrium, and needs of the social wholes. Durkheim was interested in those structures functioning to promote integration, Parsons with those operating as mechanisms of equilibrium or with those meeting survival requisites, and Merton's with items meeting empirical needs of systems and individuals. In all of these works, there is a noticeable lack of either theoretical or substantive analysis of tension, disorder, and conflict. Yet there is little in all these types of functional approaches which precludes addressing instability, disorder, and malintegration within social systems and between individuals and social systems.

In Durkheim's analysis, for example, the failure of the division of labor to provide an organic division of labor was examined and discussed extensively with the concept of "anomie." In Parsons' early mechanism-equilibrium model, there is nothing in this conceptualization that would not allow empirical investigators or theorists to recognize and study those occasions when the mechanisms do not operate and when equilibrium (assuming adequate criteria for its existence can be established) is not maintained. Or, in Parsons' later imperativism, the notion of four universal requisites provides a way to view different types of maladjustive processes in systems. For example, if adaptive problems exist, one type of disorder in a system could be expected; if integrative problems are intense, then another; and so on for the other requisites. And, finally, Merton's "net balance" of functions approach does not eliminate the possibility that the "net balance" is "negative." And in fact, Merton's approach might be seen as one way to assess the balance between integrative and malintegrative forces in a particular context.

Functional analysis thus does not preclude the analysis of malintegration, disequilibrium, maladaptation, or any other nonstasis state postulated by the critics of functionalism. In fact, it could be argued that functionalism, in focusing on what constitutes integration, equilibrium, and survival, provides criteria for assessing the degree of instability, tension, or conflict within a system. For only by comparison with what constitutes integration, stability, and survival do the notions of malintegration, instability, and nonsurvival become theoretically or empirically meaningful. Charges about the inherent conservatism of functionalism, therefore, do not consider its potential for the understanding of disorder, dissensus, and conflict.

The Question of Social Change. In many ways, the issue of social change is related to instability in social systems. Unstable systems are subject to change, sometimes radical changes. Yet, change can be "orderly," not involving instabilities or prolonged periods of malintegration. In assessing functionalism, then, it is necessary to ask: Does this perspective preclude or discourage the analysis of either sudden, disorderly change or slow, orderly change?

There can be little doubt that when those labeled "functionalists" have addressed the issue of change, they have preferred to discuss "evolutionary" alterations of social structure. Durkheim's analysis of the transition from mechanical to organic solidarity was decidedly evolutionary, focusing on the stages of transition from one form to the other. Parsons' recent work on change has, in significant respects, re-evoked Durkheim's method and substance for analyzing evolutionary changes by postulating stages of evolution in terms of how various survival requisites—primarily the requisite for "integration"—are met.[14] And Merton's essays on change, such as the emergence of science, are also more evolutionary than revolutionary in focus and tone.

Yet, what those labeled functionalists have preferred to study must be divorced from what their more general functional models preclude. Is the analysis of revolutionary, sudden, and violent change impossible within any or all of the functionalist frameworks summarized in Figures

---

[14] It should be noted that Parsons has also discussed revolutionary social change, as has Merton in his social structure and anomie.

5–1 to 5–4? The analysis of such change is not precluded, but neither is it encouraged. Violent, rapid, and pervasive change *could* be the outcome of anomie, a breakdown of equilibrium mechanisms, or a failure to meet needs, but functional models offer few concepts pointing to the conditions under which nonorderly change might occur. There is, of course, the clear possibility for developing such concepts within functional analysis, and, in fact, most change theorists assume a part-to-whole perspective (how a part or processes causes a change in the social whole). What is needed is the development of concepts and propositions which specify what types of malintegration, of anomie, of breakdowns in socialization and social control mechanisms, and of failures to meet individual and system needs will cause, under what additional conditions, different types—rapid, slow, pervasive, limited, violent, peaceful, and so forth—of social change. Functional theorists and those who have employed this perspective have yet to develop such concepts and propositions—thereby limiting the utility of their analysis of human organization.[15]

SUMMARY AND CONCLUSION

In reviewing the logical and substantive problems of functionalism, then, it is clear that the logical problems of teleology and tautology are more severe than the substantive problems. Some suggestions for eliminating these problems by focusing on causal relations between parts and wholes, while abandoning notions of functions, hypothetical states of integration and equilibrium, and revising the place of requisites and needs in part-whole analysis have been suggested. These suggestions can remove some of the logical traps to which functionalists, no matter how well-intentioned, appear to fall prey. The substantive criticisms of functionalism are less damaging than critics would contend. As presently formulated, functionalism is not well-suited for the analysis of history or nonorderly change. Few sociological perspectives deal well with historical antecedents, and functionalism is no more deficient than other perspectives on this score. Functionalism needs to develop additional concepts for incorporating more revolutionary forms of change into its form of part-whole analysis. As for the charge of conservatism, there is nothing inherently conservative in functionalism.

Finally, what is the future of functionalism in theory building? Even if it did not have a future, functionalism has made valuable contributions

---

[15] I should hasten to add that sociological theory in general has not been enormously productive in generating such concepts and propositions.

to theory in the social sciences. Without functionalism, sociology would not as readily have developed a number of important assumptions which can guide the development of theory:

1. Humans are organized into social systems.
2. Human behavior and society cannot be understood without attention to the emergent properties of social systems.
3. Social change, deviance, and other social processes develop in the context of relationships among parts in systems.
4. Social systems represent a focal point for integration between individuals, and their needs, and the necessity for group living among humans.
5. Human patterns of organization exist at different system levels, from micro units among individuals to macro forms of collective organization, and it is necessary to understand the properties of, and relations between, levels of organization.

Marxist sociologists, and other critics of functionalism, might claim that, if their orientation had initially dominated social theory, these facts of human social life would be more adequately understood today. While there might be some truth to this indictment, it is equally plausible that after decades of emphasis on conflict and change, a reaction to the "under-socialized conception of man and society"[16] would have emerged and that sociologists would seek to redress the onesidedness of conflict sociology with "stasis sociology." Much of the current appeal of conflict theory probably stems from the corrective it provides to a perspective which has tended toward ahistoricism and an evolutionary view of social change. As will become evident in the following group of chapters, this corrective provided by conflict theory was needed, but the deficiencies of functionalism should not negate its contributions to sociological thought.

But what of its future? Functionalism asks and addresses one of the most intriguing questions: What does a part "do for" or "contribute to" society? This question needs to be asked in social theory, but the implicit organicism in *the way it is asked* must be abandoned. "Part-to-whole analysis" is a better label, for it removes the word "function"— a word rife with organismic connotations. Moreover, the substance of organicism—hypothetical states of "normality" such as integration or

---

[16] To turn Dennis Wrong's criticism of Parsons' perspective around see: "The Oversocialized Conception of Man in Modern Sociology," *American Sociological Review* 26 (1961)2:183–93.

equilibrium—must also be abandoned. Notions of system requisites must be altered if they are to be useful. They can no longer be viewed as "survival requisites" (another organismic assumption), but instead they must be considered as criteria for preliminary isolation of important social structures and processes—that is, those likely to explain the most variance in social wholes. In this way, sociologists can concentrate their attention on causal analysis of the antecedents to parts and on the causal relations between parts and social wholes. Such a shift in emphasis can maintain what is intriguing about functionalism, while eliminating the logical and substantive problems of sociology's first, and until most recently, dominant theoretical orientation.

PART II

Conflict Theorizing

6

THE CONFLICT
HERITAGE

During the 1950s, as the essentials of the Parsonian scheme were unfolding, one body of criticism was taking on a clear focus. Functional theory in sociology, especially the Parsonian variety, was seen as underemphasizing the conflictual nature of social reality. Soon, attacks along these lines became ceremonial rituals for sociologists who sought theoretical redemption for past sins and who now held that conflict theory was to carry sociology out of its theoretical morass.

As David Lockwood argued in 1956, Parsons, in continually assuming for analytical purposes a system in equilibrium, had created a fictionalized conception of the social world.[1] From this world of fantasy, as Lockwood phrased the matter, it was inevitable that analysis would emphasize mechanisms that maintained social order rather than those that systematically generated disorder and change. Furthermore, by assuming order and equilibrium, the ubiquitous phenomena of instability, disorder, and conflict too easily became viewed as deviant, abnormal, and pathological. For, in reality, Lockwood insisted, there were "mechanisms" in societies that made conflict inevitable and inexorable. For example, power differentials assured that some groups would exploit others, and constituted a built-in source of tension and conflict in social systems. Additionally, the existence of scarce resources in societies would inevitably generate fights over the distribution of these resources. And finally, the fact that different interest groups in social systems pursue different goals, and

[1] David Lockwood, "Some Remarks on 'The Social System,' " *British Journal of Sociology* 7 (June 1956): 134–46.

hence often had to vie with one another, assured that conflict would erupt. These forces, Lockwood contended, represented "mechanisms" of social disorder that should be as analytically significant to the understanding of social systems as Parsons' mechanisms of socialization and social control.

As noted in Chapter 3, Ralf Dahrendorf crystallized this line of argument toward the end of the decade by comparing functional theory to a utopia.[2] Utopias usually have few historical antecedents—much like Parsons' hypothesized equilibrium; utopias display universal consensus on prevailing values and institutional arrangements—in a vein remarkably similar to Parsons' concept of institutionalization; and utopias always display processes that operate to maintain existing arrangements—much like the "mechanisms" of Parsons' "social system." Hence, utopias and the social world when viewed from a functional perspective do not change very much, since they do not concern themselves with history, dissensus over values, and conflict in institutional arrangements.

Conflict and change were thus rediscovered by the beginning of the last decade, moving some to proclaim the conflict perspective as the "new sociology."[3] But in fact, the conflict perspective is as old as functionalism, finding its inspiration in the works of two German sociologists, Karl Marx and Georg Simmel, who were approximate contemporaries of prominent organicists. And just as contemporary functionalism reflects the legacy of these organicists, so contemporary conflict theory is indebted to the thinking of Marx and Simmel.

MARX'S AND SIMMEL'S LEGACY

Marx's and Simmel's theories of conflict, and the current perspectives inspired by their genius, reveal many differences. These two scholars worked within different intellectual traditions, they held different assumptions about the nature of the social world, and thus, they were to develop contrasting theories of social conflict. Yet, as will become evident, these contrasts reveal a complementarity—what one author failed to emphasize, the other appears to have considered paramount. There is thus a balance in Marx's and Simmel's work and in the modern perspectives influenced by their formative efforts. These differences can be best understood by analyzing Marx's and Simmel's contrasting (1) intellectual purposes, (2)

---

[2] Ralf Dahrendorf, "Out of Utopia: Toward a Reorientation of Sociological Analysis," *American Journal of Sociology* 744 (September 1958): 115–27.

[3] For example, see Irving Louis Horowitz, *The New Sociology: Essays in Social Science and Social Theory* (New York: Oxford University Press, 1964).

assumptions about the nature of conflict, (3) conceptualization of variables, and (4) inventories of propositions.

Contrasting Intellectual Purposes and Goals

Marx and Simmel viewed their intellectual missions much differently.
Because Marx observed and was repulsed by the conditions of early
industrialization in Europe, he was concerned with initiating and legitimating social change. His intellectual life was committed to understanding how capitalism emerged, on what principles it operated, and in what
ways it could be eradicated.[4] Marx's theory of conflict is thus a theory
of how to change society, of how to eliminate capitalism. In contrast,
Simmel's intellectual goals were more in the traditional academic mold:
to reflect upon and to understand social life. Simmel was not politically
involved, nor does his work reveal any great passion for social change.

These diverging intellectual commitments are intimately connected
to Marx's and Simmel's view of social theory. Marx and Simmel both
sought to uncover the laws of social interaction and organization. Each
viewed the world as organized into patterns which could be described
and understood by developing abstract laws. But Marx viewed such laws
as temporary, as operative only during a particular historical period or
epoch. Hence, feudal society would reveal one set of laws, capitalist
society another. Marx's goal was thus to uncover the laws describing
the operation of capitalist modes of economic production in order that
capitalism could be eradicated. In contrast, Simmel sought to discover
universal laws which transcended space and time. For this reason he
distinguished between the substance and form of interaction, between
the diverse goals and contexts of interactions and the abstract properties
that they held in common. As he noted:

> The study of [society] may be called "pure sociology," which abstracts
> the mere elements of sociation. It isolates it . . . from the heterogeneity
> of its contents and purposes. . . . It thus proceeds like grammar, which
> isolates the pure forms of language from their contents through which
> these forms, nevertheless, come to life. In comparable manner, social
> groups which are the most diverse imaginable in purpose and general
> significance, may nevertheless show identical forms of behavior toward
> one another. . . .[5]

---

[4] For Marx's most powerful statement of the dynamics of capitalism, see *Das Capital*
(New York: Modern Library, 1946); originally published in 1867.

[5] See either: K. H. Wolff, ed., *The Sociology of Georg Simmel* (New York: Free
Press, 1950), p. 22 or D. N. Levine, ed., *Georg Simmel on Individuality and Social
Forms* (Chicago: University of Chicago Press, 1971), p. 26.

For Simmel, then, the goal of sociology was to search for the common features of diverse interactions, while for Marx, the purpose of theory was to uncover the unique laws of a period and then work for their suspension.

The approach that each took to developing theory reflects these diverging purposes and goals. Marx's concept of *praxis*—the supposed union of theory and practice—highlights these differences. Through confrontation with social reality, one comes to understand it better. By pushing, questioning, and observing reactions and defenses one can gain insight into the dynamics of a particular period. In contrast, Simmel was an unobtrusive observer of the social world around him. His concern was not to confront, but to passively observe. Moreover, unlike Marx, Simmel was dismayed by the lack of methodological tools available during his time and he felt that sociology would only develop when better methodologies were discovered and used to observe social processes without upsetting them. Until these methodologies were discovered, however, quiet observation of, and reflection about, the ongoing world was the key to understanding.

These differences in Marx's and Simmel's intellectual purposes and in the ways theory was to be used to achieve these purposes reflect differing personal commitments.[6] More fundamentally, however, they highlight different conceptions of social reality, particularly about the nature of social conflict.

Contrasting Visions about the Nature of Social Conflict

Both Marx and Simmel introduced the concept of "dialectics." For Marx, the concept of dialectics denotes the inherent contradiction in all social relationships. A given set of social relations contain their opposite. As Pitirum Sorokin once noted:

> Since any concept, and the reality that corresponds to it, contains in itself its own negation—is an identity of opposites—and in the process of its unfolding generates its antithesis, no change or movement can proceed forever continuously in the same direction and without turns and rhythms.[7]

---

[6] I would like to acknowledge the insights on Marx's thought that I have gained by reading Richard P. Appelbaum's "A Dialectical Alternative," presented at the Pacific Sociological Association meetings, April, 1976.

[7] Pitirim Sorokin, *Social and Cultural Dynamics* (Boston: Porter Sargent, 1957), p. 653. For additional references, see the chapters on Marx & Simmel in Lewis A. Coser's *Masters of Sociological Thought* (New York: Harcourt, Brace, Jovanovich, 1977). For a somewhat different view, see Dick Atkinson, *Orthodox Consensus and Radical Alternative* (London: Heineman, 1971).

Thus, "goodness" only takes on meaning in reference to its opposite, "badness." In social affairs, for example, "social order" is a concept that implicitly makes reference to its opposite, "social disorder." For Marx, then, all social relations inherently imply their opposite. Marx, however, went further than simply arguing, as had Hegel and other German idealists before him, that concepts imply their opposites. Rather, the reality denoted by concepts imply their opposites, and moreover, each social reality contains "contradictions" which will actually *generate* or "cause" their opposites. Thus, feudalism contained the contradictions which eventually "caused" capitalism, and capitalism reveals the contradictions that would result in its downfall and the emergence of communism. The dynamics of change, therefore, result from inherent contradictions in social relations. These contradictions make conflict inevitable, and hence, the goal of social analysis is to understand, and to encourage, the operation of these contradictions.

Simmel's notion of dialectics acknowledges the existence of tendencies for order and disorder.[8] All human relations reveal potential for order and conflict, stasis and change. As he noted:

> There probably exists no social unit in which convergent and divergent currents among its members are not inseparably interwoven. An absolutely centripetal and harmonious group . . . not only is unreal, it would show no real life process.[9]

Unlike Marx, however, Simmel does not view this as a "driving force of history." Rather, the notion of dialectics appears for Simmel to operate as a background assumption that underscores the ubiquity and inevitability of conflict processes. These contrasting points of emphasis reflect the differing purposes of Marx's and Simmel's analysis: Marx wanted to cause a certain direction of change and thus he required a concept like the dialectic to underscore the inevitability of the changes he desired, whereas Simmel wished to understand the forms of conflict and to assess, without any great personal commitments to outcomes, the consequences of changes. For this reason, then, Marx's assumptions about the nature of the social world focus on the unfolding of the dialectic, in ways

---

[8] Pierre van den Berghe has argued that a dialectical model of conflict is ultimately one where unification, albeit temporary, emerges out of conflict. But, as will be examined extensively in the next chapter, the ontological differences between Marx and Simmel have inspired vastly different theoretical perspectives in contemporary sociology. See Pierre van den Berghe, "Dialectic and Functionalism: Toward a Theoretical Synthesis," *American Sociological Review* 28 (October 1963): 695–705.

[9] George Simmel, *Conflict* trans. Kurt H. Wolff (Glencoe, Ill.: The Free Press, 1955), p. 15. Virtually all of Simmel's statements about conflict processes are contained in this essay.

causing conflict in social relations, while Simmel's merely acknowledges the existence of diverging forms of conflict.

Marx's theoretical analysis focused primarily on capitalist societies of the last century, a task consistent with his goal of uncovering the laws unique to a particular historical epoch. However, certain common assumptions endemic to all epochs are revealed in his analyses. Marx began with a simple—and in retrospect, simplistic—assumption: Economic organization, especially the ownership of property, determines the organization of the rest of a society. The class structure and institutional arrangements, as well as cultural values, beliefs, religious dogmas, and other idea systems, are ultimately a reflection of the economic base of a society. He then added an additional assumption: Inherent in the economic organization of any society—save the ultimate communist society—are forces inevitably generating revolutionary class conflict. In accordance with dialectical assumptions, such revolutionary class conflict would occur in epochs, with successive bases of economic organization sowing the seeds of their own destruction through the polarization of classes and subsequent overthrow of the dominant by the subjugated class. Hence, a third assumption: Conflict is bipolar, with exploited classes under conditions created by the economy becoming aware of their true "interests" and eventually forming a revolutionary political organization that stands against the dominant, property-holding class.

The criticisms leveled against these assumptions are perhaps self-evident:[10] (1) Societies are more than mere reflections of economic organization and patterns of property ownership; (2) social conflict is rarely bipolarized across an entire society; (3) interests in a society do not always cohere around social class; (4) power relations in a society are not always direct reflections of ownership of property; and (5) conflict does not always cause social change, dialectical or otherwise. In addition to a whole series of incorrect predictions—such as the formation of the modern proletariat into a revolutionary class during the present "capitalistic" epoch, the subsequent overthrow of capitalist economic systems, and the formation of a communist society—the wisdom of following Marx's lead can be questioned.

Abstracting above the specifics of Marx's economic determinism and excessive polemics, however, there emerges a set of assumptions in his work which directly challenge those imputed to functionalism and which

---

[10] C. Wright Mills, *The Marxists* (New York: Harcourt, Brace, 1948); Ralf Dahrendorf, *Class and Class Conflict in Industrial Society* (Stanford, Calif.: Stanford University Press, 1959), pp. 36–71.

serve as the intellectual springboard for the conflict alternative in sociological theorizing:

1. While social relationships display systemic features, these relationships are rife with conflicting interests.
2. This fact reveals that social systems systematically generate conflict.
3. Conflict is therefore an inevitable and pervasive feature of social systems.
4. Such conflict tends to be manifested in the bipolar opposition of interests.
5. Conflict most frequently occurs over the distribution of scarce resources, most notably power.
6. Conflict is the major source of change in social systems.

Unlike Marx, Simmel viewed social structure not so much as composed of domination and subjugation, but of various inseparable associative and dissociative processes, which are separable only in analysis:

> The structure may be *sui generis,* its motivation and form being wholly self-consistent, and only in order to be able to describe and understand it, do we put it together, *post factum,* out of two tendencies, one monistic, the other antagonistic.[11]

Part of the reason for this emphasis lies in Simmel's "organismic" view of the social world: In displaying formal properties, social processes evidence a systemic character—a notion apparently derived from his early exposure to the organismic doctrines dominating the sociology of his time. This subtle organicism led Simmel to seek out the consequences of conflict for social continuity rather than change:

> Conflict is thus designed to resolve dualisms; it is a way of *achieving some kind of unity,* even if it be through the annihilation of one of the conflicting parties. This is roughly parallel to the fact that it is the most violent *symptom of a disease* which represents the effort of the *organism* to free itself of disturbances and damages caused by them [emphasis added].[12]

In apparent contradiction to the harmony implied by this organicism, Simmel postulated an innate "hostile impulse" or a "need for *hating*

---

[11] Simmel, *Conflict,* p. 23 (All subsequent references to this work are to *Conflict and the Web of Group Affiliation* [1955].) However, with his typical caution, Simmel warns: "This fact should not lead us to overlook the numerous cases in which contradictory tendencies really co-exist in separation and can thus be recognized at any moment in the over-all situation" (pp. 23–24).

[12] Ibid., p. 13.

and *fighting*" among the units of organic wholes, although this instinct was mixed with others for love and affection and was circumscribed by the force of social relationships. Therefore, Simmel viewed conflict as a reflection of more than just conflicts of interest, but also of those arising from hostile instincts. Such instincts can be exacerbated by conflicts of interest, or mitigated by harmonious relations as well as by instincts for love. But in the end, Simmel still viewed one of the ultimate sources of conflict to lie in the innate biological makeup of human actors.

Perhaps in an effort to reconcile his assumptions about the nature of the social organism with notions of hating and fighting instincts, Simmel devoted considerable effort to analyzing the positive consequences of conflict for the maintenance of social wholes and their subunits. In this way, hostile impulses were seen not so much as a contradiction or cancer to the organic whole, but as one of many processes maintaining the body social. Thus, while Simmel recognizes that an overly cooperative, consensual, and integrated society would show "no life process," his analysis of conflict is still loaded in the direction of how conflict promotes solidarity and unification.

It is this aspect of Simmel's work on conflict which reveals an image of social organization decidedly different from that emphasized by Marx:

1. Social relationships occur within systemic contexts that can only be typified as an organic intermingling of associative and dissociative processes.
2. Such processes are a reflection of both the instinctual impulses of actors and the imperatives dictated by various types of social relationships.
3. Conflict processes are therefore a ubiquitous feature of social systems, but they do not necessarily, in all cases, lead to breakdown of the system and/or to social change.
4. In fact, conflict is one of the principal processes operating to preserve the social whole and/or some of its subparts.

Contrasting Conceptualization of Variables

The contrasting purposes of their analysis, coupled with their diverging assumptions about the nature of conflict, are reflected in Marx's and Simmel's diverging conceptualizations of the variables in their respective theoretical schemes. Since Simmel was looking for the basic *forms* of interaction, it is more likely that he would perceive the variable properties of conflict. On the other hand, by virtue of his political commitment to rapid social change, Marx would be more likely to focus on violent conflict processes that could initiate desired social changes. Thus, while Simmel did not follow his carefully drawn analytical distinctions, he formally conceptualized the variable properties of conflict phenomena in terms of (*a*) the degree of regulation, (*b*) the degree of direct confrontation, and (*c*) the degree of violence between conflict parties. The end states of the ensuing variable continuum were "competition" and the "fight," with competition involving the more regulated strivings of parties toward a mutually exclusive end and with the fight denoting the more violent and unregulated combative activities of parties directly toward one another. On the other hand, Marx paid little analytical attention to the variable properties of conflict processes and focused primarily upon its violent manifestations as social classes directly confront one another.[13]

Perhaps the most significant contrast between Marx's and Simmel's orientations as they bear on the development of conflict theory is the position of conflict variables in their respective causal schemes. For Simmel, conflict was considered to "cause" various outcomes for both the social whole and its subparts. The kind of outcome or "function" of conflict for the systemic whole or its parts was seen by Simmel to vary with the degree of violence and the nature of the social context. Marx was also concerned with how conflict causes certain outcomes for social wholes, but unlike Simmel, he fixed attention largely on the causes of the conflict itself. Thus, for Simmel, the sources of conflict remain unanalyzed, with emphasis being placed on conflict intensity and its outcomes for different social referents, while for Marx, the variables involved in the emergence of conflict groups are given considerably more analytical attention than the variables affecting its outcomes. These differences in the position of the variables in their schemes reflect Marx's and Simmel's contrasting assumptions and purposes. As has been noted, Simmel perceived the source of conflict to be buried in a constellation of "associative and dissociative" processes, as well as in human "instincts of hate." Apparently, the variability and complexity of these sources of conflict made analysis too formidable. Hence, Simmel considered it more prudent to focus on the consequences of conflict *once it was initiated.* For in the end, what was most important for Simmel was discovering the consequences of variations in social conflict on the basic forms of social interac-

---

[13] For a convenient summary concerning the ongoing debate over what is, and what is not, "conflict," see C. F. Fink, "Some Conceptual Difficulties in the Theory of Social Conflict," *Journal of Conflict Resolution* 12 (December 1968): 412–60.

tion—a task which he apparently felt could be accomplished without delving far into human instincts. On the other hand, Marx's commitment to dialectical assumptions about conflict and change made questions of the consequences of conflict on social forms easy to answer: radical alteration of the social order. The more important issue for Marx was documenting how such change-producing conflict could emerge in the first place, with the result that Marx's conceptualization of variables focused almost exclusively on *the causes of violent conflict.*

These contrasts in Marx's and Simmel's purposes of analysis, assumptions about the nature of conflict, and conceptualization of conflict variables are but necessary groundwork for what is theoretically most important: isolating, formalizing, and comparing their propositions on conflict processes. For in the end, a theory is only as good as the testable propositions it can generate. The analysis of theoretical orientations of scholars such as Marx and Simmel has been useful only to the extent that it provides information on *why* certain propositions are developed and *why* others are given little attention.

Contrasting Theoretical Propositions

Simmel's analysis is highly conducive to presentation of abstract propositions, since he was primarily concerned with discovering basic forms of relationships among abstractly stated variables. On the other hand, Marx might well object to presenting propositions which supposedly described processes beyond a particular temporal epoch. And yet, there is perhaps a "contradiction" or intellectual dialectic in Marx's own thought: His dialectical assumptions led him to formulate abstract propositions about the *universal* conditions under which inherent dialectical processes in *all* social systems would lead to conflict and structural change. And yet, much of his work concerns discerning the specific "laws of capitalism" and how the processes of capitalism would create conflict processes. Marx's work is thus couched at two levels of generality: At one level, he described how conflict is inevitable in *all* social systems, while at another, he delineated the laws and contradictions of capitalism. Many contemporary Marxian scholars would deny that Marx intended to create "universal laws" or abstract propositions, but it is clear that contemporary conflict theory has indeed been most influenced by Marx's more abstract principles. While his insights into the specific contradictions of capitalism have often proved penetrating and useful, it is his more abstract propositions which promise to yield the most enduring insights into conflict processes.

Thus, it is Marx's and Simmel's abstract propositions—that is, those which seek to transcend specific times, places, and social units—which continue to inform and inspire conflict theory. And therefore, it is necessary to omit the polemics and discursiveness, and hence, much of the flair and flavor, of each author's work in an effort to expose and highlight the theoretical core of their thought. Only in this way can the *theoretical* significance of their work be made explicit.[14] In this effort, Marx's basic propositions will be presented first, and then, Simmel's theory will be examined. Particular attention will be directed at the complementarity— what each theory adds to the other and a general theory of conflict— of their diverse approaches to the study of conflict. The first basic proposition in Marx's scheme can be briefly stated as follows:

1. The more unequal the distribution of scarce resources in a system, the greater will be the conflict of interest between dominant and subordinate segments in a system.

In this proposition, Marx viewed the degree of inequality in the distribution of scarce resources, most notably power, as determining the objective conflict of interests between those with, and those without, power. This proposition follows directly from Marx's assumption that in all social structures, the unequal distribution of power inevitably creates a conflict of interests between superordinates holding power and subordinates lacking power. Marx's next theoretical task was a documentation of conditions under which awareness of conflict of interests could cause subordinates to begin questioning the legitimacy of current patterns of resource distribution. The conditions translating awareness into a questioning of legitimacy are summarized in propositions 2, 2A, 2B, 2C, and 2D below:

2. The more subordinate segments become aware of their true collective interests, the more likely they are to question the legitimacy of the unequal distribution of scarce resources.
    A.   The more social changes wrought by dominant segments disrupt existing relations among subordinates, the more likely are the latter to become aware of their true collective interests.

---

[14] Probably more offensive to Marxian scholars is my firm conviction, after my own intense reading of Marx over a number of years, that Marx's theory is most explicit in his polemical essays. And further, *the best* statement of his theory came early in *The Communist Manifesto* (1848). Although Marx was to have second thoughts near the end of his career on some of the hypotheses contained in this work, these thoughts were never formulated into clear theoretical statements. For those who are dismayed at boiling down Marx's thought to a few propositions, I think that they can take solace in the fact that these few propositions have been sufficiently profound to shape the course of conflict theory in contemporary sociology.

B.   The more practices of dominant segments create alienative dispositions among subordinates, the more likely are the latter to become aware of their true collective interests.

C.   The more members of subordinate segments can communicate their grievances to each other, the more likely they are to become aware of their true collective interests.

   (1)   The more spatial concentration of members of subordinate groups, the more likely are they to communicate their grievances.

   (2)   The more subordinates have access to educational media, the more diverse the means of their communication, and the more likely are they to communicate their grievances.

D   The more subordinate segments can develop unifying systems of beliefs, the more likely they are to become aware of their true collective interests.

   (1)   The greater the capacity to recruit or generate ideological spokespersons, the more likely ideological unification.

   (2)   The less the ability of dominant groups to regulate the socialization processes and communication networks in a system, the more likely ideological unification.

In these basic propositions, Marx indicated that the more that dominant groups disrupt the existing relations of subordinates, thereby breaking down the very patterns of social organization which have limited the vision of subordinates, the more likely are subordinates to perceive objectively their actual situation and alternatives to their continued subordination. For as long as social relations remain stable, it is difficult for subordinates to see beyond the immediate exigencies of their existence. Disruption of life situations is likely to lead to increased awareness, especially when the activities of subordinates are highly alienating, allowing little emotional involvement and satisfaction. However, disruptive change of, and alienation from, current social relations are insufficient to cause widespread awareness of true interests; it is also necessary for subordinates to communicate, and mutually reinforce, their grievances. Such communication is more likely to occur when subordinates are in close proximity to each other and when they can become exposed to educational media, thereby liberating them from traditional means of socialization and communication. But in Marx's theory, mere communication of grievances is insufficient to cause intense questioning of legitimacy. It is also necessary for these grievances to become codified into a unifying belief system which can emphasize the *common* plight and interests of subordinates. The codification of such a belief system is most likely when ideological spokespersons, who present a consistent viewpoint in an appealing manner, can be recruited. These spokespersons, and the emerging belief system, can be most effective when dominant groups are unable to regulate and control completely socialization processes and communication networks.

With awareness of their common interests, Marx saw the next stage in the conflict process as involving political organization to pursue conflict. These organizational processes are summarized in propositions 3, 3A, 3B, 3C below:

3.   The more subordinate segments of a system are aware of their collective interests, the greater their questioning of the legitimacy of the distribution of scarce resources, and the more likely they are to organize and initiate overt conflict against dominant segments of a system.
   A.   The more the deprivations of subordinates move from an absolute to relative basis, the more likely they are to organize and initiate conflict.
   B.   The less the ability of dominant groups to make manifest their collective interests, the more likely are subordinate groups to organize and initiate conflict.
   C.   The greater the ability of subordinate groups to develop a leadership structure, the more likely they are to organize and initiate conflict.

In these propositions, Marx summarized some of the conditions leading to those forms of political organization which, in turn, will result in overt conflict. The first key question in addressing this issue is *why* an awareness of conflicting interests and a questioning of legitimacy of the system would lead to organization and the initiation of conflict. Seemingly, awareness would have to be accompanied by intense emotions if people are to run the risks of opposing those holding power. Presumably Marx's proposition on alienation would indicate one source of emotional arousal, since for Marx, alienation goes against human beings' basic needs. Further, ideological spokespersons would, as Marx's own career and works testify, arouse emotions through their prose and polemics. But the key variable in the Marxian scheme is "relative deprivation." The emotions aroused by alienation and ideological spokespersons are necessary but insufficient conditions for taking the risks of organizing and initiating conflict against those with power. Only when these conditions are accompanied by rapidly escalating perceptions of deprivation by subordinates is the level of emotional arousal sufficient to prompt political organization and open conflict with superordinates. Such organization, however, is not likely to be successful unless dominant groups fail to organize around their interests and unless political leaders among the subordinates can emerge to mobilize and channel aroused emotional energies.

Thus, while Marx assumed that conflict is inevitable, his theory of its causes was elaborate, setting down a series of necessary and sufficient conditions for the occurrence of conflict. It is in these propositions that Marx's great contribution to a theory of conflict resides, for his subsequent propositions appear to be simple translations of his dialectical assumptions into statements of co-variance, without the careful documentation of the necessary and sufficient conditions which would cause these conflict processes to occur.

In his next propositions, Marx attempted to account for the degree of violence in the conflict between politically organized subordinates. The key variable here was polarization, a somewhat vague concept denoting the increasing partitioning of a system into two conflict organizations:

4. The more subordinate segments are unified by a common belief and the more developed their political leadership structure, the more the dominant and subjugated segments of a system will become polarized.
5. The more polarized the dominant and subjugated, the more violent will be the ensuing conflict.

In contrast to his previous propositions, propositions 4 and 5 do not specify any conditions under which polarization will occur, nor do they indicate when polarized groups will engage in violent conflict. Marx just assumed that such would be the case as the dialectic mechanically unfolds. Presumably, highly organized subordinates in a state of emotional arousal will engage in violent conflict. But as only a cursory review of actual events underscores, such a state often results in just the opposite: less violent conflicts with a considerable degree of negotiation and compromise. This fact points to the Marxian scheme's failure to specify the conditions under which polarization first occurs and then leads to violent conflict. For it is not just coincidental that at this point in his scheme, Marx's predictions about class revolutions in capitalistic societies begin to go wrong. Thus, the Marxian legacy points rather dramatically to a needed area of theoretical and empirical research: Under what conditions is conflict likely to be violent? And more specifically, under what conditions is conflict involving *highly organized and mobilized* subordinates likely to be violent and under what conditions are less combative forms of conflict likely to occur?

The final proposition in the Marxian inventory also appears to follow more from a philosophical commitment to the dialectic than carefully reasoned conclusions:

6. The more violent the conflict, the greater will be the structural change of the system and the redistribution of scarce resources.

This proposition reveals Marx's faith in the success of the revolution as well as his assertion that new sets of super-subordinate relations of power would be established by these successful revolutionaries. As such, the proposition is ideology rephrased in the language of theory, especially since no conditional statements are offered on just when violent conflict leads to change and redistribution and just when it does not. Had Marx not *assumed* conflicts to become polarized and violent, then he would have paid more attention to the *degrees* of violence and nonviolence in the conflict process, and this in turn, would have alerted him to the variable outcomes of conflict for social systems. In fact, as suggestive as Marx's propositions are, the entire scheme suffers from a failure to specify clearly the interaction of variables. For example, the schema begs questions like: What *kinds* or *types* of inequality create *what types* of conflict of interest? What *types* of awareness and questioning actually lead to *what degrees* of overt violence and what *types* of ideological unification and political leadership, producing what *types* of polarization leading to what *types* of violent conflict causing what *types* of structural change? It is to answering these questions in Marx's theory that contemporary social theorists have begun to address their efforts.

In contrast to Marx's inventory of basic propositions, Simmel's had no propositions on the ultimate causes of conflict. Rather, Simmel's propositions focus on the intensity or degree of violence or combativeness of conflict once initiated and on the consequences of conflicts for the parties to the conflict and for the systemic whole. While it is regrettable that Simmel chose not to examine the causes of conflict, his emphasis on the varying outcomes of conflict does provide some necessary corrections for Marx's scheme. For it is clear that Marx's inventory begins to break down at just this point in his analysis, since for Marx, conflict among organized groups pursuing divergent interests will be violent and lead to dramatic social reorganization. Simmel's propositions offer some clues as to where Marx went wrong in these presumptions; and in so doing, they helped recast the foundations of conflict sociology.

Simmel's propositions are not always easy to abstract from his rambling prose, especially since he tends to argue by example and analogy. As a result of this type of exposition, he constantly shifts the units and levels of analysis—from intrafamily conflict to wars between nation-states. To appreciate Simmel's significance for a theory of conflict, then, it is best to abstract above his discursive prose and thereby present only what appear to be the most generic propositions.[15] Simmel's primary concern in analyzing the forms of dissociation in social systems was with the degree of combativeness or violence of conflict. These basic propositions can be summarized as:

1. The greater the degree of emotional involvement of parties to a conflict, the more likely is the conflict to be violent.
   A. The greater the respective solidarity among members of conflict parties, the greater is the degree of their emotional involvement.
   B. The greater the previous harmony between members of conflict parties, the greater is the degree of their emotional involvement.
2. The more that conflict is perceived by members of conflict groups to transcend individual aims and interests, the more likely is the conflict to be violent.
3. The more that conflict is a means to an end, the less likely is the conflict to be violent.

Propositions 1, 1A, 1B overlap somewhat with those developed by Marx. In a vein similar to Marx, Simmel emphasized that violent conflict is the result of emotional arousal. Such arousal is particularly likely when conflict groups possess a great deal of internal solidarity and when these conflict groups emerge out of previously harmonious relations. Marx postulated a similar process in his contention that polarization of groups previously involved in social relations (albeit exploitive ones) leads to violent conflict. In proposition 2 Simmel indicated that, coupled with emotional arousal, the extent to which members see the conflict as transcending their individual aims increases the likelihood of violent conflict. Marx analyzed, of course, in considerably more detail just how such a state of consciousness is created, since his concern with erasing false consciousness through communication and creation of a common belief

---

[15] These propositions are abstracted from Simmel's essay on conflict in Kurt H. Wolff's translation of *Conflict and the Web of Group Affiliations* (1956). The propositional inventory presented here and elsewhere differs considerably from Coser's, primarily because many of what Coser chose to call "propositions" are, in my view, definitions or assumptions. I have also taken more liberty than Coser to rephrase and state more generically Simmel's propositions. Further, in some instances I have omitted propositions which are not critical to the basic argument. For a complete listing of Simmel's propositions, see Lewis A. Coser, *The Functions of Social Conflict* (New York: The Free Press, 1956), and Jonathan H. Turner, "Marx and Simmel Revisited," *Social Forces* 53 (June), 1975.

system represents a more precise way of stating Simmel's proposition.

Proposition 3 is Simmel's most important, because it appears to contradict Marx's hypothesis that objective consciousness of interests will lead to organization for violent conflict. In this proposition, Simmel argued that the more clearly articulated their interests, the more focused are the goals of conflict groups. With clearly articulated goals, it becomes possible to view violent conflict as only one of many means for their achievement, since other less combative conflicts, such as bargaining and compromise, can often serve to meet the now limited objectives of the group. Thus for Simmel, consciousness of common interests (Simmel's proposition 2) can, under unspecified conditions, lead to highly instrumental and nonviolent conflict. Marx's analysis precludes this possibility; and while Simmel's propositions leave many questions unanswered, they do provide a corrective to the Marxian analysis: Conflict among highly organized groups of emotionally aroused actors pursuing collective goals can, under conditions which need to be specified, lead to the use of violent conflict as only one means to an end which, under other conditions that need to be specified, can actually lower the probability of violent conflict. In the context of labor-management relations, for example, Simmel's proposition appears to have been more accurate than Marx's, since violence has more often accompanied labor-management disputes, especially in the initial formation of unions, when interests and goals are not well articulated. As interests become clarified, violent conflict has been increasingly replaced by less violent forms of social interaction.[16]

Thus, both Simmel and Marx provided an interesting set of propositions on how conflict groups become organized and mobilized to pursue violent conflict, but as Simmel seemed to be pointing out, this very process of mobilization and organization can, in the end, cause less violent forms of conflict. Violence appears to be an interim result of initial organization and mobilization, but as groups become highly organized, they become more instrumental, thereby decreasing the probability of violent conflict.

The curvilinear nature of the conflict process is further clarified by Simmel's subsequent attention to the consequences or functions of conflict for the conflict parties and for the systemic whole within which the conflict occurs. For Simmel first analyzed how violent conflicts

---

[16] Admittedly, Marx's late awareness of the union movement in the United States forced him to begin pondering this possibility, but he did not incorporate this insight into his theoretical scheme.

increase solidarity and internal organization of the conflict parties, but when he shifted to an analysis of the functions of conflict for the social whole, he drew attention primarily to the fact that conflict promotes system integration and adaptation. How can violent conflicts promoting increasing organization and solidarity of the conflict groups suddenly have these positive functions for the systemic whole in which the conflict occurs? For Marx, such a process was seen to lead to polarization of conflict groups and then to *the* violent conflicts which would radically alter the systemic whole. But for Simmel, the organization of conflict groups enables them to realize many of their goals without overt violence (but perhaps with a covert threat of violence), and such partial realization of clearly defined goals cuts down internal system tension, and hence promotes integration.

To document this argument, Simmel's key propositions on how violent conflicts can increase the organization of conflict parties are first summarized:

1. The more violent intergroup hostilities and the more frequent conflict among groups, the less likely are group boundaries to disappear.
2. The more violent the conflict, and the less integrated the group, the more likely is despotic centralization of conflict groups.
3. The more violent the conflict, the greater will be the internal solidarity of conflict groups.
    A. The more violent the conflict, and the smaller the conflict groups, the greater will be their internal solidarity.
        (1) The more violent the conflict and the smaller the conflict groups, the less will be the tolerance of deviance and dissent in each group.
    B. The more violent the conflict, and the more a group represents a minority position in a system, the greater will be the internal solidarity of the group.
    C. The more violent the conflict, and the more a group is engaged in purely self-defense, the greater will be the internal solidarity.

In these propositions, violent conflict, under varying conditions, will lead to a clearer definition of the boundaries of the conflict groups, centralization of the groups, and increases in internal solidarity of the groups. When viewed in the narrow context, most of these propositions overlap with Marx's, but they diverge considerably when their place in Simmel's over-all propositional inventory is examined. Unlike Marx's inventory, Simmel's does not assume that conflict begets increasingly violent conflicts between increasingly polarized segments in a system which, in the end, will cause radical change in the system. This difference between Marx's and Simmel's analyses is dramatically exposed when Simmel's propositions on the consequences of conflict for the systemic whole are reviewed. The most notable feature of several key propositions, listed below, is that Simmel was concerned with less violent conflicts and with their integrative functions for the social whole:

1.   The less violent the conflict between groups of different degrees of power in a system, the more likely is the conflict to have integrative consequences for the social whole.
     A.   The less violent and more frequent the conflict, the more likely is the conflict to have integrative consequences for the social whole.
          (1)   The less violent and more frequent the conflict, the more members of subordinate groups can release hostilities and have a sense of control over their destiny, and thereby maintain the integration of the social whole.
          (2)   The less violent and more frequent the conflict, the more likely are norms regularizing the conflict to be created by the conflict parties.
     B.   The less violent the conflict, and the more the social whole is based on functional interdependence, the more likely is the conflict to have integrative consequences for the social whole.
          (1)   The less violent the conflict in systems with high degrees of functional interdependence, the more likely it is to encourage the creation of norms regularizing the conflict.

These propositions provide an important qualification to Marx's analysis, since Marx visualized mild conflicts between super- and subordinate as intensifying as the conflict groups become increasingly polarized; and in the end, the resulting violent conflict would lead to radical social change in the system. In contrast, Simmel argued that conflicts of low intensity and high frequency in systems of high degrees of interdependence do not necessarily intensify, or lead to radical social change. On the contrary, they release tensions and become normatively regulated, thereby promoting stability in social systems. Further, Simmel's previous propositions on violent conflicts present the possibility that with the increasing organization of the conflicting groups, the degree of violence of their conflict will decrease as their goals become better articulated. The end result of such organization and articulation of interests will be a greater disposition to initiate milder forms of conflict, involving competition, bargaining and compromise. What is critical for developing a sociology of conflict is that Simmel's analysis provides more options than Marx's propositions on conflict outcomes. First, conflicts do not necessarily intensify to the point of violence, and when they do not, they can have, under conditions which need to be further explored, integrative outcomes for the social whole. Marx's analysis precludes exploration of these processes. Second, Simmel's propositions allow for inquiry into the conditions under which initially violent conflicts can become less intense and thereby have integrative consequences for the social whole. This insight dictates a search for the conditions under which the level of conflict violence and its consequences for system parts and the social whole can shift and change over the course of the conflict process. This expansion of options represents a much broader and firmer foundation for building a theory of conflict.

Finally, Simmel presents two basic propositions on the positive functions of violent conflict for expanding the basis of integration of systemic wholes:

2. The more violent and the more prolonged the conflict relations between groups, the more likely is the formation of coalitions among previously unrelated groups in a system.
3. The more prolonged the threat of violent conflict between groups, the more enduring are the coalitions of each of the conflict parties.

These propositions could represent a somewhat different way to state Marx's polarization hypothesis, since conflict was seen by Simmel as drawing together diverse elements in a system as their respective interests become more clearly recognized. But Simmel was not ideologically committed to dialectical assumptions, and thus, unlike Marx, he appeared to be arguing only that violent conflicts pose threats to many system units which, depending upon calculations of their diverse interests, will unite to form larger social wholes. Such unification will persist as long as the threat of violent conflict remains. Should violent conflict no longer be seen as necessary, with increasing articulation of interests and the initiation of bargaining relations, then Simmel's propositions 1A and 1B on the consequences of conflict for the social whole would become operative. Thus, once again, Simmel's analysis on conflict offers more options in developing a theory of how varying types of conflict can have diverse outcomes for different system referents at different points in the conflict process.

THE EMERGENCE OF CONFLICT THEORY:
AN OVERVIEW

While both Marx and Simmel viewed conflict as a pervasive and inevitable feature of social systems, their respective intellectual purposes as well as their assumptions about the nature of society were vastly different. Marx emphasized the divisiveness of conflict; Simmel, the integrative consequences of conflict. These differences are reflected in the types of propositions they chose to develop, with Marx addressing the conditions under which violent conflict would be accelerated and Simmel asking questions about the conditions under which the intensity of conflict might vary. Furthermore, Marx was vitally concerned with the social structural causes of conflict, whereas Simmel tended to concentrate attention on the form and consequences of conflict once it was initiated, while making only vague references to "fighting instincts."

These differences in analytical emphasis are sufficiently great to suggest that, when taken together, they offer a more complete set of theoretical statements about the causes, intensity, and consequences of conflict in social systems than when taken separately. For Marx, the sources of conflict must be sought within the distribution of resources and the conflicts of interest inherent in unequal distribution. For both Marx and Simmel, the intensity of conflict appears to reflect the relative degree of internal solidarity of groups involved in conflict, with both thinkers specifying additional structural conditions in the more inclusive social system that might also influence the intensity of conflict between opposed parties.

Equally intriguing in comparisons of Marx and Simmel are the contradictory propositions that can be uncovered. For example, Simmel argued that the more clear-cut the goals pursued by conflicting parties, the more likely was conflict to be viewed as merely a means to an end, with the result that both parties to a conflict would be motivated to seek compromises and alternative means in an effort to avoid the high costs of intense or violent conflict. On the other hand, Marx argued just the opposite in holding that once a social class recognizes its true interests (hence, has a clear conception of its goals), then violent conflict is highly probable. The divergence of these propositions probably stems from the different assumptions of their authors, for Marx assumes that intense conflict is an inevitable and inexorable feature of social systems and their change, whereas Simmel merely assumes that conflict is simply one process, varying in intensity and consequences, within a social whole.

In this particular instance, Simmel may have been more "correct" in that his proposition would seemingly fit the facts of what really happened in labor-management relations in capitalist economic systems, since compromise became typical once labor was organized to pursue specific goals. On the other hand, violent conflict appears to have occurred when labor did not have a clear conception of goals but only a sense of diffuse frustration. Naturally, this argument is open to debate and is not central to the current discussion. What is of more importance for present purposes is the recognition that by reducing the Marxian and Simmelian propositions to their most generic form, it is possible to compare the overlaps, gaps, and contradictions among them and thereby gain some insight into possible strategies for effecting reformulation.

To some extent, modern conflict theory has attempted to combine the promising features in the schemes of both Marx and Simmel. Even when this has been done, however, contemporary theorists have tended to embrace more enthusiastically the assumptions and propositions of either one or the other of these thinkers. Such selectivity has created two dominant contemporary conflict perspectives in sociological theory, each owing its inspiration to either Marx or Simmel: (1) dialectical conflict theory, and (2) conflict functionalism. These perspectives are the ones most often seen as promising a "new" alternative to functional theory in sociology, and hence a more adequate solution to the Hobbesian problem of order: How and why is society possible?

7

DIALECTICAL CONFLICT THEORY: RALF DAHRENDORF

Ralf Dahrendorf has persistently argued that the Parsonian scheme, and functionalism in general, offers an overly consensual, integrated, and static vision of society. While society is seen as having "two faces"— one of consensus, the other of conflict—Dahrendorf has maintained that it is time to begin analysis of the "ugly face" of society and abandon the utopian image of society created by functionalism. To leave utopia, Dahrendorf offers the following advice:

> Concentrate in the future not only on concrete problems but on such problems as involve explanations in terms of constraint, conflict, and change. This second face of society may aesthetically be rather less pleasing than the social system—but, if all sociology had to offer were an easy escape to Utopian tranquility, it would hardly be worth our efforts.[1]

To escape out of utopia therefore requires that a one-sided conflict model be substituted for the one-sided functional model. While this conflict perspective is not considered by Dahrendorf to be the only face of society, it is a necessary supplement that will make amends for the past inadequacies of functional theory.[2] The model that emerges

---

[1] Ralf Dahrendorf, "Out of Utopia: Toward a Reorientation of Sociological Analysis," *American Journal of Sociology* 64 (September 1958): 127.

[2] As Dahrendorf emphasizes: "I do not intend to fall victim to the mistake of many structural-functional theorists and advance for the conflict model a claim to comprehensive and exclusive applicability . . . it may well be that in a philosophical sense, society has two faces of equal reality: one of stability, harmony, and consensus and one of change, conflict, and constraint" (ibid.). Such disclaimers are, in reality, justifications for arguing for the primacy of conflict in society. By claiming that functionalists are one-sided, it becomes fair game to be equally one-sided in order to "balance" past one-sidedness.

from this theoretical calling is a dialectical-conflict perspective, which, Dahrendorf claims, has more correspondence to what occurs in the actual world than functionalism and is therefore the only path out of utopia. In his analysis, Dahrendorf is careful to note that processes other than conflict are evident in social systems and that even the conflict phenomena he examines are not the only kinds of conflict in societies. Having said this, however, Dahrendorf then launches into an analysis that appears to contradict these qualifications. There is a persistent hint that the conflict model presented represents a more comprehensive "theory" of society, providing a more adequate solution to the Hobbesian problem of order.

DAHRENDORF'S IMAGE OF THE SOCIAL ORDER

For Dahrendorf, institutionalization involves the creation of "imperatively coordinated associations" (hereafter referred to as ICAs), which, in terms of criteria not specified, represent a distinguishable organization of roles.[3] This organization is characterized by power relationships, with some clusters of roles having power to extract conformity from others. While Dahrendorf is somewhat vague on the point, it appears that *any* social unit—from a small group or formal organization to a community or an entire society—can be considered for analytical purposes an ICA if an organization of roles displaying power differentials exists. Furthermore, while power denotes the coercion of some by others, these power relations in ICAs tend to become legitimated and can therefore be viewed as *authority* relations in which some positions have the "accepted" or "normative right" to dominate others.[4] The "social order" is thus conceived by Dahrendorf to be maintained by processes creating authority relations in the various types of ICAs existing throughout all layers of social systems.

At the same time, however, power and authority are the scare resources over which subgroups within a designated ICA compete and fight. They

---

[3] There are a number of contemporary dialectical conflict models that could be discussed in this chapter. For example, John Rex (*Key Issues in Sociological Theory* [London: Routledge & Kegan Paul, 1961]) has presented a model similar to Dahrendorf's. But since Dahrendorf is the most conspicuous conflict theorist in contemporary sociology, it is considered best to examine his model intensely rather than spread analysis across several dialectical-conflict models.

[4] Ralf Dahrendorf, "Toward a Theory of Social Conflict," *Journal of Conflict Resolution* 2 (June 1958): 170–83; Ralf Dahrendorf, *Class and Class Conflict in Industrial Society* (Stanford, Calif.: Stanford University Press, 1959), pp. 168–69; Ralf Dahrendorf, *Gesellschaft un Freiheit* (Munich: R. Piper, 1961); Ralf Dahrendorf, *Essays in the Theory of Society* (Stanford, Calif.: Stanford University Press, 1967).

are thus the major sources of conflict and change in these institutionalized patterns. This conflict is ultimately a reflection of where clusters of roles in an ICA stand in relation to authority, since the "objective interests" inhering to any role is a direct function of whether that role possesses authority and power over other roles. However, even though roles in ICAs possess varying degrees of authority, any particular ICA can be typified in terms of just two basic types of roles, ruling and ruled, with the ruling clusters of roles having an "interest" in preserving the status quo and the ruled clusters having an "interest" in redistributing power, or authority. Under certain specified conditions, awareness of these contradictory interests increases, with the result that ICAs polarize into two conflict groups, each now aware of its objective interests, which then engage in a contest over authority. The "resolution" of this contest or conflict involves the redistribution of authority in the ICA, thus making conflict the source of social change in social systems. In turn, the redistribution of authority represents the institutionalization of a new cluster of ruling and ruled roles, which under certain conditions polarizes into two interest groups that initiate another contest for authority. Social reality is thus typified in terms of this unending cycle of conflict over authority within the various types of ICAs comprising a social system. Sometimes the conflicts within diverse ICAs in a society overlap, leading to major conflicts cutting across large segments of the society, while, at other times and under different conditions, these conflicts are confined to a particular ICA.

As is clearly acknowledged by Dahrendorf, this image of social organization represents a revision of Marx's portrayal of social reality:

1. Social systems are seen by both Dahrendorf and Marx as in a continual state of conflict.
2. Such conflict is presumed by both authors to be generated by the opposed interests that inevitably inhere in the social structure of society.
3. Opposed interests are viewed by both Marx and Dahrendorf as reflections of differences in the distribution of power among dominant and subjugated groups.
4. Interests are seen by both as tending to polarize into two conflict groups.
5. For both, conflict is dialectical, with resolution of one conflict creating a new set of opposed interests, which, under certain conditions, will generate further conflict.
6. Social change is thus seen by both as a ubiquitous feature of social

systems and the result of inevitable conflict dialectics within various types of institutionalized patterns.

This image of institutionalization as a cyclical or dialectic process has led Dahrendorf, much like Marx before him, into the analysis of only certain key causal relations: (1) Conflict is assumed to be an inexorable process arising out of opposing forces within social structural arrangements; (2) such conflict is accelerated or retarded by a series of intervening structural conditions or variables; (3) conflict "resolution" at one point in time creates a structural situation, which, under specifiable conditions, inevitably leads to further conflict among opposed forces.

For Marx, the source of conflict ultimately lay beneath cultural values and institutional arrangements, which represented edifices constructed by those with power. In reality, the dynamics of a society are found in society's "substructure," where the differential distribution of property and power inevitably initiates a sequence of events leading, under specifiable conditions, to revolutionary class conflict. While borrowing much of Marx's rhetoric about power and coercion in social systems, Dahrendorf actually ends up positing a much different source of conflict: the institutionalized authority relations of ICAs. Such a position is much different from that of Marx, who viewed such authority relations as simply a "superstructure" erected by the dominant classes, which, in the long run, would be destroyed by the conflict dynamics occurring below institutional arrangements. While Dahrendorf acknowledges that authority relations are imposed by the dominant groups in ICAs, and frequently makes reference to such things as "factual substrates," the source of conflict becomes, upon close examination, the legitimated authority role relations of ICAs. This drift away from Marx's emphasis on the institutional "substructure" forces Dahrendorf's analysis to seek the source of conflict in those very same relations that integrate, albeit temporarily, an ICA. By itself, this shift in emphasis is perhaps desirable, since Dahrendorf clearly recognizes that not all power is a reflection of property ownership—a fact Marx's polemics tended to underemphasize. But as will become evident, to view power as only authority can lead to analytical problems that are easily as severe as those encountered in the polemical extremes of Marx's model.

Although they emphasize different sources of conflict, the models of both Dahrendorf and Marx reveal a similar causal chain of events leading to conflict and reorganization of social structure: Relations of domination and subjugation lead to the "objective" opposition of interests; awareness or consciousness by the subjugated of this inherent opposition of interests occurs under certain specifiable conditions; under other conditions this new-found awareness leads to the political organization and then polarization of subjugated groups, who then join in conflict with the dominant group; the outcome of the conflict will usher in a new pattern of social organization; this new pattern of social organization will have within it relations of domination and subjugation which set off another sequence of events leading to conflict and then change in patterns of social organization.

The intervening conditions affecting these processes are outlined by both Marx and Dahrendorf only with respect to the formation of awareness of opposed interests by the subjugated, the politicization and polarization of the subjugated into a conflict group, and the outcome of the conflict. The intervening conditions under which institutionalized patterns generate dominant and subjugated groups and the conditions under which these can be typified as having opposed interests remain unspecified—apparently because they are in the nature of institutionalization, or ICAs, and hence do not have to be explained.

In Figure 7–1, an attempt is made to outline the causal imagery of Marx and Dahrendorf. At the top of the figure are Marx's analytical categories, stated in their most abstract form. The other two rows specify the empirical categories of Marx and Dahrendorf, respectively. Separate analytical categories for the Dahrendorf model are not enumerated because they are the same as those in the Marxian model. As is clear, the empirical categories of the Dahrendorf scheme differ greatly from those of Marx. But the form of analysis is much the same, since each considers as nonproblematic and not in need of causal analysis the empirical conditions of social organization, the transformation of this organization into relations of domination and subjugation, and the creation of opposed interests. The causal analysis for both Marx and Dahrendorf begins with an elaboration of the conditions leading to growing class consciousness (Marx) or awareness among quasi groups (Dahrendorf) of their objective interests; then analysis shifts to the creation of a politicized class "for itself" (Marx) or a true "conflict group" (Dahrendorf); and finally, emphasis focuses on the emergence of conflict between polarized and politicized classes (Marx) or conflict groups (Dahrendorf).

CRITICISMS OF THE DIALECTICAL CONFLICT MODEL

Problems in the Causal Analysis

The most conspicuous criticism of Dahrendorf's causal imagery comes from Peter Weingart, who has argued that in deviating from Marx's

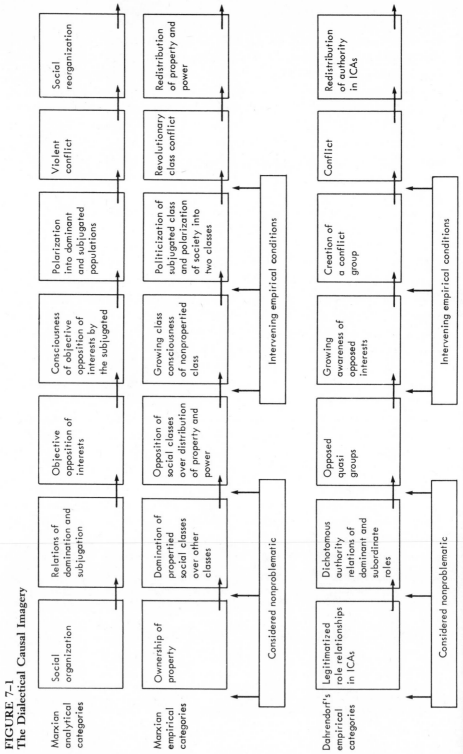

FIGURE 7–1
The Dialectical Causal Imagery

conception of the "substructure" of opposed interests existing below the cultural and institutional edifices of the ruling classes, Dahrendorf forfeits a genuine causal analysis of conflict, and therefore of how patterns of social organization are changed.[5] This criticism asks questions reminiscent of Dahrendorf's portrayal of Parsonian functionalism: How is it that conflict emerges from legitimated authority relations among roles in an ICA? How is it that the same structure that generates integration also generates conflict? Although for the Marxian scheme there are empirical problems, the causal analysis does not pose an analytical problem, since the source of conflict—the opposition of economic interests—is clearly distinguished from the institutional and cultural arrangements maintaining a temporary order—the societal superstructure. Dahrendorf, however, has failed to make explicit this distinction and thus falls into the very analytical trap he has imputed to functional theory: Change inducing conflict must mysteriously arise from the legimated relations of the social system.

In an attempt to escape this analytical trap, the causal analysis often becomes confusing. One tack Dahrendorf employs is to assert that many roles also have a nonintegrative aspect, because they represent fundamentally opposed interests of their incumbents. These opposed interests are reflected in role conflict, which seemingly reduces the issues of role strain and conflict to dilemmas created by objectively opposed interests— surely a dubious assertion that is correct only some of the time. In equating interests and role expectations, Dahrendorf would seemingly have to hypothesize that all institutionalized patterns, or ICAs, display two mutually contradictory sets of role expectations—one to obey, the other to revolt—and that actors must "decide" which set they will follow. Presumably, actors "wish" to realize their "objective interests" and hence revolt against the role expectations imposed upon them by the dominant group. This approach forces the Dahrendorf model to reduce the origins of conflict to the wishes, wills, and sentiments of a person or group— a reductionist imperative that Dahrendorf would reject, but one which his causal imagery would seemingly dictate.[6]

Many of these problems might be overcome if Dahrendorf had provided a series of existence and relational statements that would indicate the conditions under which legitimatized role relationships in ICAs create

---

[5] Peter Weingart, "Beyond Parsons? A Critique of Ralf Dahrendorf's Conflict Theory," *Social Forces* 48 (December 1969): 151–65. See also Jonathan H. Turner, "From Utopia to Where: A Strategy for Reformulating the Dahrendorf Conflict Model," *Social Forces*, 52 (December 1973), pps. 236–44.

[6] Weingart, "Beyond Parsons?"

dichotomous authority relations of domination and subjugation. To simply assume that this is the case is to avoid the critical causal link in his analytical scheme. These kinds of necessary propositions—or, as Dahrendorf describes them, "intervening empirical conditions"—are a necessary part of the model. Without them it is unclear how the types of authority, coercion, and domination which lead to conflict ever emerge in the first place. Assuming that they just emerge, or are an endemic part of social structure, is to define away the theoretically important question about what types of authority in what types of ICAs lead to what types of domination and subjugation, which, in turn, lead to what types of opposed interests and what types of conflict.[7] These are all phenomena that must be conceptualized as variables and incorporated into the causal chains of the dialectical-conflict model. Referring back to Figure 7–1, this task would involve stating the "intervening empirical conditions" at each juncture of all of Dahrendorf's empirical categories. What is now considered "nonproblematic" would become as problematic as subsequent empirical conditions.

Initiating this task is difficult, but to do so would enable Dahrendorf to avoid some of the more standard criticisms of his causal imagery:[8] (1) Conflict not only causes change of social structure, but changes of structure also cause conflict (under conditions that need to be specified); (2) not all conflict leads to change (under conditions that need to be specified in greater detail than Simmel's initial analysis); and (3) conflict can inhibit change (again, under conditions that need to be specified). Unless these conditions are part of the causal imagery, conflict theory merely states the rather obvious fact that change occurs, without answering the theoretical question of *why, when,* and *where* does such change occur?

Despite the vagueness of Dahrendorf's causal analysis, he has attempted to state systematically the "intervening empirical conditions" that cause "quasi groups" to become "conflict groups," as well as the conditions affecting the intensity (involvement of group members) and violence (degree of regulation) of the confict and the degree and the rate of structural change caused by conflict. More formally, Dahrendorf outlines three types of intervening empirical conditions: (1) "conditions of organization" which affect the transformation of latent quasi groups into manifest conflict groups; (2) "conditions of conflict" which deter-

---

[7] Alvin Boskoff, *The Mosaic of Sociological Theory* (New York: Thomas Y. Crowell Co., 1972), p. 83.

[8] For a convenient summary of these, see Percy Cohen, *Modern Sociological Theory* (New York: Basic Books, 1968), pp. 183–91.

mine the form and intensity of conflict; and (3) "conditions of structural change" which influence the kind, speed, and the depth of the changes in social structure.[9]

Thus, the explicitly acknowledged variables in the theoretical scheme are the (1) degree of conflict-group formation; (2) the degree of intensity of the conflict; (3) the degree of violence of the conflict; (4) the degree of change of social structure; and (5) the rate of such change. It is significant, for criticisms to be delineated later, that concepts such as ICAs, legitimacy, authority, coercion, domination, and subjugation are not *explicitly* characterized as variables requiring statements on the conditions affecting their variability. Rather, these concepts are simply defined and interrelated to each other in terms of definitional overlap or stated as assumptions about the nature of social reality.

For those phenomena that are conceptualized as variables, Dahrendorf's propositions appear to be an elaboration of those developed by Marx, as can be seen in Table 7–1.[10]

These propositions follow Marx's substantive and formal legacy and represent, in terms of explicitness, considerable improvement over functional formulations, in which there is a noticeable absence of systematically interrelated propositions. Furthermore, Dahrendorf is to be commended for actually attempting to place the propositions in a reasonably systematic format—a difficult task too infrequently performed by theorists in sociology. However, even though this propositional inventory represents a promising attempt, a number of criticisms have been leveled against the scheme and should be summarized here with an eye toward the improvements they suggest.

One of the most obvious criticisms of the Dahrendorf perspective is the failure to visualize crucial concepts as *variables.* Most conspicuous of these are the concepts of authority, domination-subjugation, and interest. Since it is from legitimated authority relations that conflict ultimately springs, it is somewhat surprising that this concept is not viewed as a variable, varying at a minimum in terms of such properties as intensity, scope, and legitimacy. Rather Dahrendorf has chosen to define away the problem:

> No attempt will be made in this study to develop a typology of authority. But it is assumed throughout that the existence of domination and subjec-

---

[9] Dahrendorf, "Toward a Theory of Social Conflict."

[10] The propositions listed below differ from a list provided by Dahrendorf, *Class and Class Conflict,* pp. 239–40 in two respects: (1) they are phrased consistently as statements of co-variance and (2) they are phrased somewhat more abstractly without reference to "class," which in this particular work was Dahrendorf's primary concern.

TABLE 7-1
The Propositions of the Dahrendorf Scheme

I. The more members of quasi groups in ICAs can become aware of their objective interests and form a conflict group, the more likely is conflict to occur
   A. The more the "technical" conditions of organization can be met, the more likely is the formation of a conflict group
      1. The more a leadership cadre among quasi groups can be developed, the more likely are the "technical" conditions of organization to be met
      2. The more a codified idea system, or charter, can be developed, the more likely are the "technical" conditions of organization to be met
   B. The more the "political" conditions of organization can be met, the more likely is the formation of a conflict group
      1. The more the dominant groups permit organization of opposed interests, the more likely are the "political" conditions of organization to be met
   C. The more the "social" conditions of organization can be met, the more likely is the formation of a conflict group
      1. The more opportunity for members of quasi groups to communicate, the more likely are the "social" conditions of organization to be met
      2. The more recruiting is permitted by structural arrangements (such as propinquity), the more likely are the "social" conditions of organization to be met
II. The more the "technical," "political," and "social" conditions of organization are met, the more intense is the conflict
III. The more the distribution of authority and other rewards are associated with each other (superimposed), the more intense is the conflict
IV. The less the mobility between super- and subordinate groups, the more intense is the conflict
V. The less the "technical," "political," and "social" conditions of organization are met, the more violent is the conflict
VI. The more the deprivations of the subjugated in the distribution of rewards shifts from an absolute to relative basis, the more violent is the conflict
VII. The less the ability of conflict groups to develop regulatory agreements, the more violent is the conflict
VIII. The more intense the conflict, the more structural change and reorganization it will generate
IX. The more violent the conflict, the greater is the rate of structural change and reorganization

---

tion is a common feature of all possible types of authority and, indeed, of all possible types of association and organization.[11]

A typology of authority would give some indication of the variable states of authority and related concepts—a fact Dahrendorf appears content to ignore by simply arguing that authority implies domination and subjugation, which in turn gives him the structural dichotomy necessary for his dialectical theory of conflicting interests. He refuses to speculate on *what types* of authority displaying *what variable states* lead to *what types of variations* in domination and subjugation, which in turn cause *what variable types* of opposed interests leading to *what variable types* of conflict groups. Thus, Dahrendorf links only by assumption and defini-

---

[11] Ibid., p. 169.

tion crucial variables that causally influence each other as well as the more explicit variables of his scheme: the degree of conflict, the degree of intensity of conflict, the degree of violence in conflict, the degree of change, and the rate of change. In fact, it is likely that these unstated variable properties of authority, domination, and interests have as much influence on the explicit variables in the scheme as the "intervening empirical conditions" Dahrendorf chooses to emphasize. Furthermore, as noted earlier, when viewed as variables, the concepts of authority, domination-subjugation, and interests require their own "intervening empirical conditions." These conditions may in turn influence other, subsequent intervening conditions in much the same way as the "conditions of organization" also influence the subsequent intensity and violence of conflict in the scheme.

Inattention to these questions greatly reduces the predictive value of the Dahrendorf model, but it does more: It reduces much of the model to a tautology. Conflict groups would appear to follow from the definition of ICAs as dichotomous authority structures composed of opposed interests. This tautology is made more bearable by Dahrendorf's insertion of the notion of "quasi groups" (members of ICAs not yet aware of the true interests), which, under the "conditions of organization," lead to true conflict-group formation. But this distinction simply delays the question of how opposed quasi groups emerged, to which Dahrendorf should answer: by definition and assumption. Instead, he chooses to answer: "As to the . . . statement, the one with the dichotomy of authority positions in imperatively coordinated associations, it is not, I suggest, either an assumption or an empirical hypothesis, but an analytical statement." Just what an "analytical statement" is in this context is left vague, but it appears to be a way to avoid concluding that a major portion of his propositions about conflict-group formation are little more than rephrasings of his definitions and assumptions about the nature of ICAs and society.

These criticisms suggest an obvious solution: to conceptualize ICAs, legitimacy, authority, domination-subjugation, and interests as variable phenomena and to attempt a statement of the "intervening empirical conditions" influencing their variability. Expanding the propositional inventory in this way would reduce the vagueness of the causal imagery and make less tautologous the specific propositions. Such an alteration would also cut down on the rather protracted set of dialectical assumptions—which are of dubious isomorphism with all of reality—and address a theoretical (rather than philosophical) question: Under what conditions do ICAs create legitimated authority relations that generate clear relations of domination and subjugation leading to strongly opposed interests? Coupled with Dahrendorf's tentative answer to the subsequent question—Under what conditions do conflict groups emerge and cause what kinds of conflict and change?—these additional propositions, and their inverse, would provide a significant theoretical advance in answering the ultimate theoretical question of "how and why society is possible."

Methodological Problems

Dahrendorf is careful to provide formal definitions of major concepts and to suggest operational clues about their application in concrete empirical settings, as is evident in his analysis of class conflict in industrial societies.[12] Furthermore, the incorporation of at least *some* concepts into an explicit propositional inventory—albeit an incomplete one—makes the scheme *appear* more testable and amenable to refutation.

However, a number of methodological problems remain, one of which concerns the extremely general definitions given to concepts. While these definitions are stated formally, they are often so general that they can be used in an *ad hoc* and ex post facto fashion to apply to such a wide variety of phenomena that their current utility for the development and testing of theory can be questioned. For example, power, legitimacy, authority, interests, domination, and even conflict are defined so broadly that instances of these concepts can be found in almost any empirical situation that Dahrendorf desires—a strategy that insures confirmation of his assumptions about the nature of social life, but which inhibits empirical investigation of these assumptions. This problem was emphasized in an earlier discussion in which it was noted that Dahrendorf appeared reluctant to view crucial concepts, such as authority and domination, as variables. If these concepts were so conceptualized, it would be easier for investigators to put empirical "handles" on them, since definitional statements about their variable states would specify more precisely the phenomena denoted by the concept. Dahrendorf rarely does this service, preferring to avoid typologies; and even when concepts are defined as variables, Dahrendorf avoids the issue with such statements as the following: "The intensity of class conflict varies on a scale (from 0 to 1)." Coupled with the formal definition of conflict intensity as the "energy expenditure and degree of involvement of conflicting parties," empirical investigators are given few operational guidelines about how such a concept might be measured. Were these definitions supple-

---

[12] Ibid., pp. 241–318.

mented with, at a minimum, a few examples of prominent points along the "0 to 1" scale, then the concepts and propositions of the scheme would be more amenable to empirical investigation. As the definitions stand now, Dahrendorf does the very thing for which he has so resoundingly criticized Parsons: He uses concepts in an ad hoc and ex post facto fashion to interpret past events in such a way that they confirm the overall scheme. More attention by Dahrendorf to providing operational definitions would give the concepts as incorporated into propositions a priori predictive power of future events—a more fruitful theoretical enterprise.

Another related methodological problem with the scheme stems from the tautologous character of the entire theoretical perspective. To the extent that the propositions of the scheme are true more by definition than derivation, then the entire theoretical scheme is not refutable—even in principle—and hence is of little use in the development of scientific theory. As long as dichotomous authority relations of domination-subjugation leading to objectively opposed interests are part of the definition of social reality, it is difficult to see how the formation of conflict groups and emergence of open conflict follows other than by definition—despite the scientific appearance of specific propositions about "intervening empirical conditions" that "cause" such conflict to occur. As noted earlier, this danger of tautology can be corrected by conceptualizing as variables such central concepts as legitimacy, authority, domination-subjugation, and interests and by providing a tentative list of "intervening empirical conditions" affecting their variability.

In sum, then, the Dahrendorf scheme presents a number of problems for empirical investigators. Such a statement can be made for almost all theoretical perspectives in sociology and by itself is not a unique indictment. For the Dahrendorf scheme, however, it appears that methodological problems could be minimized with just a little additional work. To the extent that the suggested corrections are made, it is likely that the dialectical-conflict perspective will offer a fruitful strategy for developing sociological theory.

FROM UTOPIA TO WHERE?
A CONCLUDING COMMENT

As was emphasized at the beginning of this chapter, Dahrendorf has been one of the harshest critics of functional forms of theorizing, likening them to an ideological utopia. In order to set sociological theorizing on the road "out of utopia," Dahrendorf has felt compelled to delineate a dialectical-conflict scheme, which presumably mirrors more accurately than Parsonian functionalism the "real character" of the social world. In so doing, Dahrendorf would view his theoretical perspective and strategy as providing a more adequate set of theoretical guidelines for resolving the Hobbesian problem of order: How and why is society possible? And under what conditions are various patterns of organization likely to be created, maintained, and changed?

What is curious about Dahrendorf's "solution" to the "problem of order" is that, upon close examination, it appears quite similar to that he has imputed to Parsonian functionalism.[13] For example, a number of commentators have noted that both Parsons and Dahrendorf view the social world in terms of institutionalized patterns—for Parsons, the "social systems"; for Dahrendorf, "imperatively coordinated associations."[14] Both view societies as composed of subsystems involving the organization of roles in terms of legitimate normative prescriptions. For Dahrendorf, these legitimated normative patterns reflect power differentials in a system; and, despite his rhetoric about the "coercive" nature of these relations, this vision of power is remarkably similar to Parsons' conception of power as the legitimate right of some status roles to regulate the expectations attendant upon other statuses.[15] Furthermore, in Dahrendorf's model, deviation from the norms established by them will lead dominant groups to attempt to employ negative sanctions—a position that is very close to Parsons' view that power exists to correct for deviations within a system.[16]

The apparent difference in Dahrendorf's and Parsons's emphasis with respect to the "functions" of power in "social systems" (or ICAs) is that Dahrendorf argues explicitly that power differentials cause both integration (through legitimated authority relations) and disintegration (through the persistence of opposed interests). However, to state that conflict emerges out of legitimated authority is nothing more than to state, a priori, that opposed interests exist and cause conflict. The emergence of conflict follows from vague assumptions about such processes as the "inner dialectic of power and authority" and the "historical function of authority,"[17] rather than from carefully documented causal se-

---

[13] For the best of these critiques, see Weingart, "Beyond Parsons."

[14] Ibid.; Pierre L. van den Berghe, "Dialectic and Functionalism: Toward a Theoretical Synthesis," *American Sociological Review* 28 (October 1963): 695–705.

[15] For example, see Talcott Parsons and Edward Shils, eds., *Toward a General Theory of Action* (New York: Harper & Row, 1962), pp. 197–205.

[16] Ibid., p. 230.

[17] Weingart, "Beyond Parsons," p. 161.

quences. Thus, the genesis of conflict in Dahrendorf's own model remains as unexplained as it does in his portrayal of the inadequacies of the functional utopia, primarily because its emergence is set against a background of unexplained conceptions of "system" norms and legitimated authority.[18]

Dahrendorf's problem in explaining why and how conflict groups can emerge from a legitimated authority structure is partly a reflection of his hidden assumptions of "functional requisites." In a subtle and yet consistent fashion, he assumes that authority is a functional requisite for system integration and that the conflict that somehow emerges from authority relations is a functional requisite for social change. The "purpose and the consequence," or "the historical function of authority," is to generate conflict, and thereby, presumably, maintain the vitality of social systems. From this notion of the requisite for change, it is all too easy to assert that conflict exists to meet the system's "needs" for change—an illegitimate teleology that transforms Marx's teleological assumption that cycles of dialectical change are necessary to create the "communist" utopia.

More fundamentally, however, Dahrendorf's inability to explain how conflict and change emerge stems from his inability to address the problem of order seriously: How and why is the organization of ICAs possible? To assert that they are organized in terms of power and authority defines away the problem of how, why, and through what processes the institutionalized patterns generating both integration and conflict come to exist. Parsons's analysis does attempt—however inadequately—to account for how institutionalized patterns, or "social systems," become organized: Through actors adjusting their various orientations, normative prescriptions emerge which affect the subsequent organization of action; such organization is maintained by various mechanisms of social control—interpersonal sanctions, ritual activity, safety-valve structures, role segregation, and, on some occasions, power—and mechanisms of socialization—the internalization of relevant values and the acquisition of critical interpersonal skills. Quite naturally, because of his commitment to developing "systems of concepts" instead of formats of propositions, Parsons gives only a vague clue about the variables involved in the process of institutionalization by which the types of opposed interests that lead to the organization of conflict groups and social change are created. However, Parsons at least attempts to conceptualize—albeit inadequately—the variables involved in creating and maintaining the very

---

[18] Boskoff, "Mosaic of Sociological Theory," pp. 82–83.

social order that Dahrendorf glosses over in his formulation of the ICA concept. Yet, it is from the institutionalized relations in ICAs that conflict-ridden cycles of change are supposed to emerge. Asserting one's way out of utopia, as Dahrendorf prefers to do, will not obviate the fundamental theoretical question facing sociological theory: How is society, in all its varied and changing forms, possible?

In sum, then, the critics would contend that Dahrendorf has used the rhetoric of "coercion," "dialectics," "domination and subjugation," and "conflict" to mask a vision of social reality which is close to the utopian image he has imputed to Parsons's work: In Dahrendorf's ICA is Parsons's "social system"; in his concepts of roles and authority is Parsons's concern with social control; in his portrayal of conflict, the origin of conflict is just as unclear as he assumes it to be in Parsons's work; and even in the analysis of social change, conflict is considered, in a way reminiscent of Parsons, to meet the functional need for change. One extreme conclusion to be drawn from these facts is that little progress has been made on the road out of utopia.

8

CONFLICT FUNCTIONALISM: LEWIS A. COSER

As the criticisms of functionalism began to look much the same—berating Parsons and others for viewing society as overly institutionalized and equilibrating—the conflict schemes offered as alternatives revealed considerable diversity. The divergence in conflict theory is particularly evident when the conflict functionalism of Lewis Coser is compared with Ralf Dahrendorf's dialectical-conflict perspective. Although Coser has consistently criticized Parsonian functionalism for its failure to address the issue of conflict, he has also been sharply critical of Dahrendorf for underemphasizing the positive functions of conflict for maintaining social systems. This two-pronged indictment has allowed Coser to formulate a theoretical scheme that can supplement both functional and dialectical-conflict forms of theorizing.

In his first major work on conflict, Coser launched what was to become the typical polemic against functionalism: Conflict is not given sufficient attention, with related phenomena such as deviance and dissent too easily viewed as "pathological" for the equilibrium of the social system.[1] In his concern for developing a system of concepts denoting how the process of institutionalization resolves the "problem of order," Parsons has come to underemphasize conflict in his formal analytical works, seemingly viewing conflict as a "disease" that needs to be "treated" by the "mechanisms" of the "body social."[2] From this interpretation

---

[1] Lewis A. Coser, *The Functions of Social Conflict* (London: Free Press of Glencoe, 1956).

[2] Ibid., pp. 22–23.

of Parsonian functionalism, Coser then posits the need for balancing the assumed one-sidedness of Parsonian functionalism with another kind of analytical one-sidedness focusing on conflict phenomena. Apparently such analytical compensation was to be carried out for well over a decade, since after the tenth anniversary of his first polemic Coser was moved to reassert his earlier claim that it was "high time to tilt the scale in the direction of greater attention to social conflict."[3]

While Coser has consistently maintained, much like Dahrendorf, that functional theorizing "has too often neglected the dimensions of power and interest," he has not followed either Marx's or Dahrendorf's emphasis on the disruptive consequences of violent conflict.[4] On the contrary, he has tended to correct for what he views as Dahrendorf's analytical excesses by emphasizing primarily the integrative and "adaptability" functions of conflict for social systems. Thus, in effect, Coser has been able to justify his efforts through criticism of functionalism for ignoring conflict, and of conflict theory for underemphasizing the functions of conflict. In so doing, Coser has provided a somewhat unique "solution" to the problem of order, for in a vein similar to Georg Simmel, even open conflict is seen, under certain conditions, as maintaining the vitality and flexibility of institutionalized patterns of social organization.[5]

IMAGES OF SOCIAL ORGANIZATION

To the extent that Émile Durkheim can be considered one of the fathers of functionalism, it is significant that Coser has devoted a critical essay to Durkheim's image of social reality.[6] Most particularly, Durkheim

---

[3] Lewis A. Coser, "Some Social Functions of Violence," *Annals of the American Academy of Political and Social Science* 364 (March 1966): 10.

[4] Lewis A. Coser, *Continuities in the Study of Social Conflict* (New York: Free Press, 1967), p. 141.

[5] A listing of some of Coser's prominent works, to be utilized in subsequent analysis reveals the functional flavor of his conflict perspective: Coser, *Functions of Social Conflict*: Coser, "Some Social Functions of Violence"; Lewis A. Coser, "Some Functions of Deviant Behavior and Normative Flexibility," *American Journal of Sociology* 68 (September 1962): 172–81; and "The Functions of Dissent," in *The Dynamics of Dissent* (New York: Grune & Stratton, 1968), pp. 158–70. Other prominent works with less revealing titles, but critical substance, include: "Social Conflict and the Theory of Social Change," *British Journal of Sociology* 8 (September 1957): 197–207; "Violence and the Social Structure" in *Science and Psychoanalysis*, ed. J. Masserman, vol. 7 (New York: Grune & Stratton, 1963), pp. 30–42. These and other essays are collected in Coser's *Continuities in the Study of Social Conflict*. One should also consult his *Masters of Sociological Thought* (New York: Harcourt, Brace, Jovanovich, 1977).

[6] Lewis Coser, "Durkheim's Conservatism and Its Implications for His Sociological Theory," in *Émile Durkheim, 1858–1917: A Collection of Essays*, ed. K. H. Wolff (Columbus: Ohio State University Press, 1960) (also reprinted in Coser's *Continuities*, pp. 153–80).

is viewed as taking a conservative orientation to the study of society, an orientation that "prevented him from taking due cognizance of a variety of societal processes, among which social conflict is the most conspicuous." Furthermore, this abiding conservatism forced Durkheim to view crises such as violence and dissent as deviant and pathological to the social equilibrium, rather than as opportunities for constructive social changes. While Coser appears intent on rejecting the organicism of Durkheim's sociology, his own work is filled with organismic analogies. For example, in describing the "functions of violence" Coser likens violence to pain in the human body, since both can serve as a danger signal that allows the "body social" to readjust itself.[7] To take another example, in his analysis of the "functions of dissent" Coser rejects the notion that dissent is explainable in terms of individual "sickness" and embraces the assumption that "dissent may more readily be explained as a reaction to what is perceived as a sickness in the body social."[8] This form of analogizing does not necessarily reduce the power of Coser's analysis, but it does reveal that he has not rejected organicism. Apparently, Coser has felt compelled to criticize Durkheim's organicism because it did not allow the analysis of conflict as a process that could promote the further adaptation and integration of the "body social."[9]

In rejecting the analytical constraints of Durkheim's analogizing, Coser was led to embrace Georg Simmel's organicism (see Chapter 6). For now, conflict can be viewed as a process that, under certain conditions, "functions" to maintain the "body social" or some of its vital parts. From this vantage point, Coser has developed an image of society that stresses:

1. The social world can be viewed as a system of variously interrelated parts.
2. All social systems reveal imbalances, tensions, and conflicts of interests among variously interrelated parts.
3. Processes within and between the system's constituent parts operate under different conditions to maintain, change, and increase or decrease a system's integration and "adaptability."
4. Many processes, such as violence, dissent, deviance, and conflict,

---

[7] Coser, "Some Functions of Violence," pp. 12–13.

[8] Coser, "The Functions of Dissent," pp. 159–60.

[9] It is of interest to note that such an emphasis on the "positive functions" of conflict could be construed as the pinnacle of conservative ideology—surpassing that attributed to Parsons. Even conflict promotes integration rather than disruption, malintegration, and change. Such a society, as Dahrendorf would argue, no longer has an ugly face and is as utopian as that of Parsons'. For Coser's reply to this kind of charge, see *Continuities*, pp. 1, 5.

which are typically viewed as disruptive to the system can also be viewed, under specifiable conditions, as strengthening the system's basis of integration as well as its "adaptability" to the environment.

It is from these assumptions that Coser has developed a rather extensive set of propositions about the functions (and to a limited extent the dysfunctions) of conflict for social systems. While Coser does offer some propositions about the conditions under which conflict leads to disruption and malintegration of social systems, the main thrust of his analysis revolves around sorting out the causal chains involved in how conflict maintains or reestablishes system integration and adaptability to changing conditions. This imagery reveals a consistent series of causal nexuses: (1) Imbalances in the integration of constituent parts of a social whole leads to (2) the outbreak of varying types of conflict among constituent parts, which, in turn, causes (3) temporary reintegration of the systemic whole, which, under certain conditions, causes (4) increased flexibility in the system's structure, which, in turn, (5) increases the system's capability to resolve future imbalances through conflict, leading to a system that (6) reveals a high level of adaptability to changing conditions.

This causal imagery presents a number of obvious problems, the most important of which is that, much like the functional imperativism of Parsons, system processes are too frequently viewed as contributing to system integration and adaptation. Such an emphasis on the positive functions of conflict may reveal hidden assumptions of system "needs" that can be met only through the functions of conflict. While Coser is careful to point out that he is simply correcting for analytical inattention to the positive consequences of conflict, the strategy is nonetheless one-sided.[10] Despite these shortcomings, however, Coser's image of social organization has been translated into a series of suggestive propositions about the functions of conflict in social systems. As such, the scheme takes on considerably more clarity than when stated as a cluster of assumptions and causal images. Equally significant, the scheme becomes more testable and amenable to reformulation on the basis of empirical findings.

---

[10] It is somewhat tragic for theory building in sociology that the early promising lead of Robin M. Williams, Jr., in his *The Reduction of Intergroup Tensions: A Survey of Research on Problems of Ethnic, Social, and Religious Group Relations* (New York: Social Science Research Council, 1947) was not consistently followed. Most of the propositions developed by Dahrendorf and Coser were summarized in this volume ten years prior to their major works. More important, they are phrased more neutrally, without an attempt to reveal society's "ugly face" or correct for inattention to the "functions of conflict."

PROPOSITIONS ON CONFLICT PROCESSES

Using both the substance and style of Georg Simmel's provocative analysis, Coser has expanded the scope of Simmel's initial insights, incorporating propositions not only from Marx but also from diverse sources in the contemporary literature on conflict. While his scheme reveals a large number of problems, steming from his primary concern with the functions of conflict, Coser's conflict perspective still remains one of the most comprehensive in the current literature. This comprehensiveness is revealed in the broad range of variable phenomena covered by the propositions: (1) the causes of conflict; (2) the intensity of conflict; (3) the violence of conflict; (4) the duration of conflict; and (5) the functions of conflict. Under each of these headings a variety of specific variables are incorporated into relational statements among abstract concepts.

One drawback to Coser's propositional inventory is that, unlike Dahrendorf's efforts, it has not been presented in a systematic or ordered format. Rather, the propositions appear in a number of discursive essays on substantive topics and in his analysis of Simmel's essay on conflict. While each discrete proposition is usually stated quite clearly, it is often necessary to interpret—with some danger of misinterpretation—the exact interrelationships among the various propositions. This fact makes the attempt at a systematic presentation of Coser's propositions an *ad hoc* exercise that not only rips propositions from their substantive context, but also runs the danger of misinterpreting the intended significance of certain propositions.[11]

The Causes of Conflict

Dialectical theorists such as Dahrendorf tend to view the causes of conflict as residing in "contradictions," or "conflicts of interests." As subordinates become aware of their interests, they pursue conflict; and hence, the major theoretical task is to specify the conditions raising levels of awareness. In contrast, Coser's first proposition on the causes of conflict focuses on the issue of legitimacy:

---

[11] Again, it should be emphasized that it is dangerous and difficult to pull from diverse sources discrete propositions and attempt to relate them systematically without doing some injustice to the theorist's intent. However, unless this kind of exercise is performed the propositions will contribute little to the development of sociological theory.

1. The more deprived members of a system question the legitimacy
    of the existing distribution of scarce resources, the more likely they
    are to initiate conflict.[12]
    A. The fewer channels for redressing grievances over the distrib-
        ution of scarce resources by the deprived, the more likely they
        are to question legitimacy.[13]
        (1) The fewer internal organizations there are segmenting
             emotional energies of the deprived, the more likely are
             the deprived to be without grievance alternatives to ques-
             tion legitimacy.
        (2) The greater the ego deprivations of those without grievance
             channels, the more likely they are to question legitimacy.
    B. The more membership in privileged groups is sought by the
        deprived, and the less mobility allowed, the more likely they
        are to withdraw legitimacy.[14]

To the extent that "conflicting interests" initiate conflict, Coser appears
to argue, such conflicts of interest are likely to be exposed only after
the deprived withdraw legitimacy from the system. As with most functional sociologists, Coser emphasizes that the social order is maintained
by some degree of consensus over existing arrangements and that "disorder" through conflict occurs when conditions decreasing this consensus
or legitimacy over existing arrangements are present. Two such conditions
are specified in propositions 1A and 1B above. Proposition 1A argues
that the degree to which channels for expressing grievances do not exist,
the greater the likelihood of a withdrawal of legitimacy, especially if
there are few organizations to deflect and occupy people's energy (1A–
1) and if there are felt ego deprivations (1A–2). Proposition 1B specifies
that if the deprived desire memebership in higher ranks, or if they have
been led to believe that some mobility is possible, a withdrawal of legitimacy will be likely when little mobility is allowed.

Coser's propositions indicate, however, that the withdrawal of legitimacy, in itself, is not likely to result in conflict. People must first become
emotionally aroused. The theoretical task then becomes one of specifying
the conditions that translate the withdrawal of legitimacy into emotional

12 Coser, *The Functions of Social Conflict,* p. 8, "Social Conflict and the Theory
of Social Change," pp. 197–207; "Internal Violence as a Mechanism for Conflict Resolution."
13 Coser, "Social Conflict and the Theory of Social Change," p. 203.
14 Coser, *The Functions of Social Conflict,* pp. 37–38.

arousal, as opposed to some other emotional state, such as apathy and resignation:

2.   The more that deprivations are transformed from absolute to relative, the more likely are the deprived to initiate conflict.[15]

   A.   The less the degree to which socialization experiences of the deprived generate internal ego constraints, the more likely they are to experience relative deprivation.

   B.   The less the external constraints applied to the deprived, the more likely they are to experience relative deprivation.

These propositions are somewhat vague, but they emphasize, much as Parsons did with his notions of mechanisms of socialization and social control, that the aroused states necessary to pursue conflict are influenced by the effectiveness of socialization and social control processes. As Marx observed and as a number of empirical studies have documented,[16] absolute deprivation does not always foster revolt. It is when peoples' *expectations* for a better future suddenly begin to exceed perceived avenues for realizing these expectations that people become aroused to pursue conflict. The level of arousal will, in turn, be influenced by peoples' commitments to the existing system, by the degree to which they have developed strong internal constraints, and on the nature and amount of social control revealed by a system. Such propositions, for example, lead to predictions that in systems with absolute dictators, who ruthlessly repress the masses, revolt by the masses is less likely than in systems where some "freedoms" have been granted and where the deprived have been led to believe that things will be getting better. Under these conditions, the withdrawal of legitimacy can be accompanied by released passions and emotions.

Thus, in contrast to Dahrendorf and many dialectical theorists, Coser does not view conflict as being released with the deprived's awareness of their true interests. Following Simmel, his propositions deal with the problems of *overcoming* the "inertia" and organic interdependence of the system. Thus, his propositions focus first on the conditions leading to a breakdown of legitimacy, and then on the mobilization of people's emotional energies to pursue conflict.

---

[15] Coser, "Social Conflict and the Theory of Social Change" and "Violence and Social Structure," pp. 30–42.

[16] James Davies, "Toward a Theory of Revolution," *American Journal of Sociology*, 27 (1962):5–19; Ted Robert Gurr, *Why Men Rebel* (Princeton, N.J.: Princeton University Press, 1970); and "Sources of Rebellion in Western Societies: Some Quantitative Evidence," *The Annals* 38 (1973):495–501.

The Intensity of Conflict

Coser is somewhat vague in his definition of intensity, but the concept appears to denote the degree of emotional commitment to pursue conflict. Thus, proposition 2 above indicates that a threshold of emotional arousal is necessary if people are to initiate conflict, but there are other conditions influencing, as Simmel might have phrased the matter, the subsequent "form" of the conflict. For Coser, the most important of these conditions are those influencing intensity:

3. The more the conditions causing the outbreak of conflict are realized, the more intense the conflict.[17]
4. The greater the emotional involvement of members in a conflict, the more intense the conflict.[18]
    A. The more primary the relations among parties to a conflict, the more emotional involvement.[19]
        (1) The more primary the groups where conflict occurs, the more emotional involvement.[20]
        (2) The more primary the relations among parties, the less likely the open expression of hostilities, but the more intense their expression in a conflict situation.[21]
    B. The more secondary relations among parties to a conflict, the more segmental their participation and the less emotional involvement.[22]
        (1) The more secondary relations, the more frequent the conflict, but the less the emotional involvement.[23]
        (2) The larger the secondary group, the more frequent the conflict, but the less the emotional involvement.[24]

In these first two propositions on conflict intensity, Coser initially restates that the more the conditions causing conflict are perpetuated, the more parties will be committed to the conflict. The next proposition then states that the greater the emotional involvement of members, the greater will be their commitment to pursue conflict. This proposition comes close to being a tautology, because "emotional involvement" and

---

17 Coser, *Continuities in the Study of Social Conflict*, p. 3.
18 Coser, *The Functions of Social Conflict*, p. 59.
19 Ibid., pp. 98–100.
20 Ibid.
21 Ibid., pp. 62–63, 68.
22 Ibid., p. 85.
23 Ibid.
24 Ibid., pp. 98–99.

"psychological commitment"—the two variables in the proposition—could be viewed as denoting the same processes. What Coser has in mind is that commitment to pursue conflict is not simply the result of sudden emotional arousal, nor rational and dispassionate calculations of interest. Where parties to the conflict are involved in and dependent upon groups engaged in conflict, then their commitments to pursue conflict, as opposed to withdrawal, opting out, or apathy, will be greater. States of emotional arousal must become focused on the conflict alternative. And as 4A and 4B underscore, "involvement" is a reflection of the nature of social relations in the system where conflict occurs. The more primary the relations, the more involvement and the more intense—that is, the more commitment to pursue—the conflict. Moreover, propositions 4A and 4B emphasize an important point: The more involving the social relations, the less frequent conflict, but the more intense it is likely to be when the conditions causing conflict (propositions 1 and 2 above) are met. In less involving social, or secondary, relations, conflict is likely to break out more frequently, but it will be less intense and thus less disruptive to people's lives and to the more inclusive system. For example, a feud between families is likely to be far more intense than the competition between two corporations.

In Coser's next proposition, he seeks to indicate that emotionally aroused actors must develop unifying beliefs about the collective purpose of conflict. As long as conflict simply represents the expression of each individual's idiosyncratic emotions, it will not be highly intense. But if individual self-interest can be subordinated to a collective interest, then emotional commitment to pursue more organized conflict, as opposed to individual outbursts of emotion, are likely. As the propositons below underscore, Coser hypothesizes that ideological unification—that is, commitment to beliefs about the worthiness of a cause—will increase intensity:

5. The more conflicts are objectified above and beyond individual self-interest, the more intense the conflict.[25]
    A. The more ideologically unified a group, the more conflicts transcend self-interest.[26]
        (1) The more ideologically unified a group, the more common its goals, and the more they transcend individual self-interest.[27]

---

[25] Ibid., pp. 85, 68–70.
[26] Ibid., pp. 83–85.
[27] Ibid.

(2)   The more ideologically unified a group, the more conflicts
      will be entered with a clear conscience, and the more
      they transcend individual self-interest.[28]

In these propositions, then, Coser has sought to specify conditions
increasing psychological commitment to pursue conflict. In many ways,
these propositions qualify those developed by Marx and Dahrendorf on
what makes individuals committed to pursue conflict as opposed to other
alternative behaviors. The next issue discussed by Coser concerns the
degree of violence that conflict among committed persons and groups
will reveal.

The Violence of Conflict

Coser is somewhat vague in his definition of conflict violence, but
he appears to be denoting the degree to which conflict parties seek to
injure or eliminate each other. As most functional theorists are likely
to emphasize, Coser's initial proposition is directed at specifying the
conditions under which conflict will be *less* violent. In contrast, dialectical
theorists, such as Marx, often pursue just the opposite fact: to specify
the conditions under which conflict will be *more* violent. Yet, the inverse
of Coser's first proposition can indicate a condition under which conflict
will be violent—a fact which should diffuse severe criticism of the
proposition.

6.   The more groups engage in conflicts over their "realistic" (objective)
     interests, the less violent the conflict.[29]
     A.   The more groups conflict over realistic interests, the more likely
          they are to seek compromises over means to realize their
          interests.
          (1)   The greater the power differentials between groups in con-
                flict, the less likely that alternative means are to be sought.
          (2)   The more rigid the system where conflict occurs, the less
                the availability of alternative means.

The key concept in these propositions is "realistic" interests. For
Coser, realistic conflict involves the pursuit of specific aims against real
sources of hostility, with some estimation of the costs to be incurred
in such pursuit. As was noted in the earlier discussion of Simmel and

---

[28] Ibid.
[29] Coser, *The Functions of Social Conflict*, pp. 45, 49, 50.

Marx in Chapter 6, Simmel recognized that when clear goals are sought, compromise and conciliation are likely alternatives to violence. Coser restates this proposition, but adds two importnat qualifications. In systems where power differentials are great, the subordinates have little to bargain with or compromise, and thus, violence may be pursued for lack of an alternative. And in systems which are rigidly structured and, for whatever reason, unable to provide alternatives to the deprived, then violence is likely to increase. These basic insights are then expanded by Coser into a supplemental proposition:

7.   The more groups conflict over nonrealistic issues, the more violent the conflict.[30]
   A.   The more that conflict occurs over nonrealistic issues, the greater the emotional involvement of the parties in the conflict, and the more intense the conflict.
   B.   The more rigid the system where conflict occurs, the more likely is the conflict to be nonrealistic.
   C.   The more that realistic conflict endures, the more nonrealistic issues are likely to emerge.

These propositions underscore Coser's recognition that when parties do not have clear goals, the more likely is violence, especially in situations where emotions are aroused (7A), in systems that are rigid, and in conflict relations that endure and create animosities which transcend object interests or goals. Coser then turns his attention to issues raised in propositions 6A–2 and 7B, the degree of rigidity in the system where the conflict occurs. This emphasis will take on additional significance when Coser's analysis of the "functions" of conflict are analyzed, since "system rigidity" is a critical variable.

8.   The more rigid the social structure, the less the availability of institutional means for absorbing conflicts and tensions, and the more violent the conflict.[31]
   A.   The more primary the relations among parties where conflict occurs, the more rigid the structure.
   B.   The more secondary (functionally interdependent) the relations among parties where conflict occurs, the less rigid the social structure, and hence, the less violent the conflict.
   C.   The greater the control mechanisms, the more rigid the structure.

---

[30] Ibid., p. 50.
[31] Coser, *The Functions of Social Conflict.*

In these propositions, Coser recognizes that in systems such as smaller groups or communities based upon primary (emotional, affective, and personal) relations, social structure tends to be rigid. Implicitly, as 8 underscores, such systems evidence considerable social control. And while conflict is less likely in such systems (see 4A–1, 2 above), it will tend to be violent when it does emerge, since there are no means for absorbing and regulating conflict relations. In contrast, systems based upon functional interdependence in which members do not invest their total emotional energies are likely to be more flexible and able to regularize the conflict in ways that do not disrupt relations of interdependence.

Coser's final proposition on conflict violence underscores an important variable, the issue over which conflict occurs.

9.   The more that conflict occurs over core values, the more violent the conflict.
     A.   The more rigid the structure where conflict occurs, the more likely is conflict to occur over core values.
     B.   The more emotional involvement in a conflict situation, the more likely this involvement to reflect commitments to core values.

In these propositions, Coser is emphasizing that where groups hold different values, or differing interpretations of what is "good" and "proper," compromise and reconciliation are likely to be difficult, since such values hold deep emotional significance for members of conflict parties. Such conflicts are most likely in rigid systems held together by strong commitments to values. Thus, in looking at propositions 6 through 9, a clear picture of crucial variables influencing the violence of conflict emerges: The less realistic the interests over which conflict occurs, the more rigid the system in which a conflict erupts, and the more conflict occurs over core values, then the more violent is the conflict. These variables are, as Coser implies, interrelated: Conflict over values is more likely in rigid systems, and nonrealistic conflict is more likely in rigid systems and where values are strongly held. While the propositions do not sort out the interrelations among these and other variables, Coser has expanded upon the Simmelian legacy and offered at least a series of suggestive leads for developing propositions on conflict violence.

The Duration of Conflict

Despite the recognition that conflict is a *process*, unfolding over time, surprisingly few theorists have incorporated the variable of "time" in

their work. This oversight is not just true of conflict theory, but also
of all theory in sociology. However, Coser's incorporation of the time
variable is extremely limited. He views time as "the duration of conflict,"
but then views duration as a dependent variable. Just how the duration
of conflicts operates as an independent variable, influencing such variables
as conflict intensity, violence, or "functions" is never specified. Thus,
Coser's analysis is confined to the more limited question: What variables
influence the length of conflict relations?

10. The less limited the goals of the opposing parties to a conflict,
    the more prolonged the conflict.[32]
    A. The more emotional involvement of members, rigidity of struc-
       ture in which the conflict occurs, and nonrealistic the character
       of the conflict, the less likely are goals to be limited.
11. The less the consensus over the goals of conflict, the more prolonged
    the conflict.[33]

    In these two propositions, Coser underscores the fact that conflicts
in which a broad range of goals are pursued or in which goals are vague
will be prolonged. When goals are limited and articulated, it is possible
to know when they have been attained, and with perception of attainment, the conflict can be terminated. Conversely, with such a wide
variety or long list of goals, a sense of attainment is less likely to occur—
thus prolonging the conflict.

12. The less the parties in a conflict can interpret their adversary's
    symbolic points of victory and defeat, the more prolonged the
    conflict.
13. The more leaders of conflicting parties can perceive that complete
    attainment of goals is possible only at a cost higher than those
    required for victory, the less prolonged the conflict.
    A. The more equal the power between conflicting groups, the
       more likely are leaders to perceive the high costs of complete
       attainment of goals.[34]
    B. The more clear-cut the indexes of defeat or victory in a conflict,
       the more likely are leaders to perceive the high costs of com-
       plete attainment of goals.[35]

---

[32] Coser, "The Termination of Conflict" in *Continuities in the Study of Social Conflict*, pp. 37–52.
[33] Coser, *The Functions of Social Conflict*, pp. 48–55, 59.
[34] Coser, *The Functions of Conflict*, p. 20.
[35] Coser, "The Termination of Conflict."

14. The greater the capacity of leaders of each conflict party to persuade followers to terminate conflict, the less prolonged the conflict.

    A.   The more centralized the conflict parties, the greater leaders' capacity to persuade followers.[36]

    B.   The fewer the internal cleavages within conflict parties, the greater leaders' capacity to persuade followers.

In these propositions, Coser emphasizes that knowledge of what would symbolically constitute victory and defeat (attainment) will influence the length of conflict. Without the ability to recognize defeat or victory, then conflict is likely to be prolonged to a point where one party destroys the other.

Propositions 13 and 14 deal with the role of leadership in conflict processes. The more leaders can perceive that complete attainment is not possible and the greater their ability to convince followers to terminate conflict, the less prolonged the conflict. Thus, the over-all image of conflict duration communicated in these propositions can be stated as follows: Where the goals of conflict parties are extensive, where there is dissensus over goals, where conflict parties cannot interpret symbolic points of victory and defeat, where leaders cannot assess the costs of victory, and where leaders cannot effectively persuade followers, then the conflict will be of longer duration than when the converse conditions hold true. In turn, as is evident, these variables are interrelated. For example, clear and limited goals help members to determine symbolic points of victory or defeat and leaders to assess the costs of victory. While these interrelations are not fully or systematically developed, Coser has, once again, provided an important lead in the study of the time dimension in the conflict process.

The Functions of Social Conflict

As was emphasized in the chapters on functionalism in the last section, the concept of "function" presents a number of problems. If some process or structure has "functions" for some other feature of a system, there is often an implicit assumption about what is "good" and "bad" for a system. If this implicit evaluation is not operative, how does one assess when an item is functional or dysfunctional? Even seemingly neutral concepts, such as "survival" or "adaptability," merely mask the implicit evaluation that is taking place. Sociologists are usually not in a position to determine what is "survival" or *more* survival and "adaptation" or

---

[36] Coser, *The Functions of Social Conflict*, pp. 128–33.

increased adaptation. To say that an item has more survival value or increases adaptation is frequently a way that sociologists have hidden their evaluation of what is good.

In Coser's propositions on the functions of conflict, this problem is evident: Conflict is "good" when it promotes integration based on solidarity, clear authority, functional interdependence, and normative control. In Coser's terms it is more adaptive. Other conflict theorists might argue that "conflict" in such a system is "bad" because integration and adaptability in this specific context could be "exploitive." With these qualifications on the hidden biases of functional propositions, Coser's suggestive propositions can now be analyzed.

Coser divides his analysis of the functions of conflict along lines similar to those presented by Simmel: The functions of conflict for (1) the respective parties to the conflict and (2) the systemic whole in which the conflict occurs. The propositions on the functions for the parties to the conflict will be presented first:

15. The more intense the conflict, the more clear-cut the boundaries of each respective conflict party.[37]
16. The more intense the conflict and the more differentiated the division of labor of each conflict party, the more likely each to centralize its decision-making structure.[38]
    A. The more intense the conflict, the less differentiated the structure; and the less stable the structure and internal solidarity, the more centralization is despotic.
17. The more intense the conflict and the more it is perceived to affect all segments of each group, the more conflict promotes structural and ideological solidarity among members of respective conflict groups.
18. The more primary the relations among the members of respective conflict groups, and the more intense the conflict, the more conflict leads to suppression of dissent and deviance within each conflict group and to forced conformity to norms and values.
    A. The more conflict between groups leads to forced conformity, the more the accumulation of hostilities and the more likely internal group conflict in the long run.

In these propositions, Coser views the intensity of conflict—that is, people's involvement in and commitment to pursue the conflict—as

---

[37] Ibid., pp. 37–38.

[38] For this and following propositions, ibid., pp. 95; 92; 93; 69–72; and 48, respectively.

increasing demarcation of boundaries, centralization of authority, ideological solidarity, and suppression of dissent and deviance within each of the conflict parties. Conflict intensity is presumably "functional" because it increases integration, although Coser implies that despotic centralization and suppression of deviance and dissent create "in the long run" malintegrative pressures. Thus, there appears to be an inherent dialectic in conflict group unification—one which creates pressures toward disunification. Unfortunately, Coser does not specify the conditions under which these malintegrative pressures are likely to be realized. In focusing on functions—that is, forces promoting integration—Coser has skewed his analysis away from a promising area of inquiry.

This bias becomes even more evident when Coser shifts attention to the functions of conflict for the systemic whole within which the conflict occurs.

19. The less rigid the social structure where conflict between groups occurs and the more frequent and less intense the conflict, the more likely is conflict to change the system in ways promoting adaptability and integration.[39]

A. The less rigid the system, the more likely is conflict to promote innovation and creativity in the system.

B. The less rigid the system, the less likely is conflict to involve displacement of hostilities to alternative objects and the more likely is conflict to confront realistic sources of tension.[40]

(1) The more a system is based upon functional interdependence, the more frequent and less intense the conflict and the more likely it is to release tensions without polarizing the system.

(2) The more stable the primary relations in a system and the more frequent and less intense is the conflict, the more likely it is to release tensions without polarizing the system, but not to the extent of a system based upon secondary relations.

C. The less rigid the system, the more likely is conflict to be

---

[39] Ibid., pp. 45–48; Lewis A. Coser, "Internal Violence as Mechanisms for Conflict resolution"; Lewis A. Coser, "Social Conflict and the Theory of Social Change," *British Journal of Sociology* 8 (September 1957):197–207. This proposition is implied in the others that follow and is thus considered crucial in determining whether conflict is functional or dysfunctional for system integration and adaptability.

[40] Lewis A. Coser, "Internal Violence as a Mechanism for Conflict Resolution"; Coser, *Functions of Social Conflict*, pp. 45–48; for following two propositions, see *Functions of Social Conflict*, pp. 85; and 83 and 85, respectively.

perceived by those in power as signals of maladjustment that need to be addressed.[41]

20. The more frequently conflict occurs, the less likely it is to reflect dissensus over core values, and the more functional for maintaining equilibrium it is likely to be.[42]

   A. The more a conflict group can appeal to the core values of a system, the less likely the conflict is to create dissensus over these values and the more likely it is to promote integration of the system.[43]

   B. The more a conflict group does not advocate extreme interpretations of core values, the less likely is a counterconflict group to form and the less disruptive the conflict for the system.

21. The more frequent and less intense are conflicts, the more likely they are to promote normative regulation of conflict.

   A. The less rigid a system, the more frequent and less intense the conflict.[44]

      (1) The less rigid the system, the more likely conflict to revitalize existent norms.[45]

      (2) The less rigid the system, the more likely conflict to generate new norms.

   B. The more frequent and less intense conflicts, the more likely groups are to centralize in an effort to promote conformity of each group's membership to norms governing the conflict.[46]

      (1) The more equal the power of conflict groups, the more likely is conflict to generate centralization promoting normative conformity.

22. The less rigid the system, the more likely it is that conflict can establish balances and hierarchies of power in a system.

   A. The less knowledge of the adversary's strength and the fewer the indexes of such strength, the more likely is conflict between two groups vying for power to promote a balance of power relations in a system.

---

[41] Lewis A. Coser, "Some Social Functions of Violence," *Annals of the American Academy of Political and Social Science* 364 (March 1966): 10; Coser, "Internal Violence as a Mechanism for Conflict Resolution."

[42] Coser, *Functions of Social Conflict*, p. 73.

[43] See Lewis A. Coser, "The Functions of Dissent," in Coser, *The Dynamics of Dissent* (New York: Greene & Stratton, 1968), for this and the following proposition.

[44] Coser, "Social Conflict and the Theory of Social Change," and *Functions of Social Conflict*, p. 125.

[45] Ibid. for this and the following proposition.

[46] Ibid., p. 129; for the following propositions, see ibid., pp. 129; 133–38; 136; 140; 148; 142; 143; 149; 142; 146; and 146, respectively.

23.   The less rigid the system, the more likely is conflict to cause forma-
      tion of associative coalitions that increase the cohesiveness and
      integration of the system.
   A.   The more other parties in a system are threatened by coalitions
        of other parties, the more likely they are to form associative
        coalitions.
   B.   The more a system is based upon functional interdependence,
        the more likely coalitions are to be instrumental and less
        enduring.
        (1)   The more a system reveals crosscutting cleavages, the
              more likely groups in a coalition are to have their own
              conflicts of interests, and the more likely is the coalition
              to be instrumental.
        (2)   The more a coalition is formed for purely defensive pur-
              poses, the more likely it is to be instrumental.
   C.   The more tightly structured and primary the relations in a
        system, the more likely coalitions are to develop common
        norms and values and form a more permanent group.
        (1)   The more coalitions are formed of individuals (or, more
              generally, the smaller the units forming a coalition), the
              more likely they are to develop into a permanent group.
        (2)   The more interaction required among the parties of a
              coalition, the more likely it is to form a permanent group.

In these propositions, the rather vague states of "cohesiveness," "integration," "balances," "normative regulation," "equilibrium," and "adaptability" are promoted by frequent conflicts of low intensity in flexible
social systems. Unfortunately, the outcomes of less frequent and more
intense, violent, long or short conflicts in less flexible system are not
examined. Coser's functional assumptions have thus biased his propositions in the direction portraying a system in harmony, or in Dahrendorf's
works, a "utopia." One could, if so inclined, criticize Coser's analysis
on the same grounds as Parsons' portrayal of "the social system."

Thus, in effect, Coser has fallen into the same analytical trap that
he has imputed to Parsons. The net impact of his propositions is to
portray a world in which conflict promotes only institutionalization and
integration. While this portrayal is not quite the same as "Parsons' utopia," it is perhaps no less unrealistic.

STRATEGIES FOR REFORMULATING COSER'S SCHEME

As has been emphasized, Coser's approach represents an analytical
one-sidedness, which, if followed exclusively, would produce a skewed

vision of the social world. While Coser begins with statements about
the inevitability of force, coercion, constraint, and conflict, his analysis
quickly turns to the integrative and adaptive consequences of such processes. This analytical emphasis could rather easily transform the integrative and adaptive "functions" of conflict into functional "needs" and
"requisites" that necessitate, or even cause, conflict to occur. Such teleology was inherent in Marx's work, where revolutionary conflict was viewed
as necessary to meet the "need" for a communist society. But Coser's
teleological inspiration appears to have come more from Simmel's organic
model than Marx's dialectical scheme. Once he became committed to
documenting how conflict contributes to the systemic whole, or "body
social," as he is prone to say, it is sometimes inadvertently implied that
the body social causes conflict in order to meet its integrative needs.
While conflict is acknowledged to cause change in social systems, it is
still viewed primarily as a crucial process in promoting integration or
equilibrium—albeit a "moving equilibrium" as Parsons likes to call it.

Dahrendorf has noted with respect to Parsonian functionalism:

> The difference between utopia and a cemetery is that occasionally some
> things do happen in utopia. But . . . all processes going on in utopian
> societies follow recurrent patterns and occur within . . . the design of
> the whole. Not only do they not upset the status quo: they affirm and
> sustain it, and it is in order to do so that most utopias allow them to
> happen at all.[47]

Does Coser's model reveal a similar weakness? On the one hand, it is
possible to note that Coser has continually emphasized the limitations
and "corrective" one-sidedness of his scheme, while, on the other hand,
critics can charge that Parsons's scheme, no less than Coser's, also started
out with good intentions, but in the end was weakened by implicit
organicism.

Looking at the bulk of Coser's work, this assessment is perhaps the
most appropriate, since Coser's assumptions, images of causal processes,
and abstract propositional statements, all point to a system in which
conflict functions in positive ways to either maintain the system or change
it in such a way as to increase adaptability.

To correct for this problem, little substantive redirection of Coser's
propositions on the causes, intensity, violence, and duration of conflict
appears necessary. These propositions address important questions neutrally and do not attempt to "balance" or "correct for" past theoretical
one-sidedness with another kind of one-sidedness. In fact, they display

---

[47] Ralf Dahrendorf, "Out of Utopia: Toward a Reorientation of Sociological Analysis,"
American Journal of Sociology 64 (September 1958):115–27.

an awareness of key aspects of conflict in social systems; and, with obviously needed supplementation and reformulation, they offer an important theoretical lead. The substantive one-sidedness in the scheme comes with his borrowing and then supplementing Simmel's functional propositions; and it is here that drastic changes in the scheme must come. One corrective strategy, which does not smack of another form of one-sidedness, is to ask the more neutral theoretical question: Under what conditions can what kinds of outcomes of conflict for what types of systems and subsystems be expected? While this is not a startling theoretical revelation, it keeps assessments of conflict processes in systems away from what ultimately must be evaluative questions of "functions" and "dysfunctions." If the question of outcomes of conflicts were more rigorously pursued, the resulting propositions would present a more balanced and substantively accurate view of social reality.

Given the long and unfortunate organic connotations of words such as "function" it might be wise to drop their use in sociology, since they all too frequently create logical and substantive problems of interpretation. While Coser appears well aware of these dangers, he has invited misinterpretation by continually juxtaposing notions of "the body social" and the "functions" of various conflict processes and related phenomena such as dissent and violence. Had he not done this, he would have better achieved his goal of correcting for the inadequacies of functional and conflict theorizing in sociology.

In sum, then, it would make little sense to have more "new perspectives" that "correct" for the deficiencies of either dialectical- or functional-conflict theory. Sociological theory has far too long engaged in this kind of activity and it is now a wiser strategy to begin reconciling the propositions in order to: (1) specify more clearly the units of analysis (classes, groups, organizations, societies) to which they apply; (2) close the gaps among the propositions; (3) reconcile the divergent conclusions; and (4) supplement them with the generalization from the research literature. Such a strategy offers a greater payoff for ascertaining the conditions under which different patterns of social organization emerge, persist, change, and break down. For only in this way will sociological theory be capable of providing a scientific solution to the Hobbesian problem of order.

9

THE FUTURE
OF CONFLICT THEORY

Conflict theory currently enjoys much popularity among sociologists. The rediscovery of Marx has stimulated efforts at theoretical synthesis and research endeavor.[1,2] It would be a mistake, however, to pretend that this "New Sociology," as Irving Louis Horowitz has termed it, is really new. Contrary to the claims of theorists such as Dahrendorf and Coser, concern with conflict is not new, nor has it been ignored. Indeed, it could be argued that no single social process in sociological theory has received as much conceptual attention as conflict. There are, no doubt, good reasons for this emphasis: Conflict appears to be a ubiquitous process and seems to help account for how and why patterns of social organization are created, maintained, and changed. Yet, the recognition

---

[1] For example, see William Gamson, *The Strategy of Social Protest* (Homewood, Ill.: Dorsey Press, 1975); Louis Kriesberg, *The Sociology of Social Conflict* (Englewood Cliffs, N.J.: Prentice-Hall, 1973); Anthony Oberschall, *Social Conflict and Social Movements* (Englewood Cliffs, N.J.: Prentice-Hall, 1973); Robin M. Williams, Jr., *Mutual Accommodation: Ethnic Conflict and Cooperation* (Minneapolis: University of Minnesota Press, 1977); and Randall Collins, *Conflict Sociology,* (New York: Academic Press, 1975).

[2] A list of such recent endeavors is long, but a sample of prominent studies would include: Ted Gurr, "Sources of Rebellion in Western Societies: Some Quantitative Evidence," *The Annals* 391 (September 1970): 128–44; A. L. Jacobson, "Intrasocietal Conflict: A Preliminary Test of a Structural Level Theory," *Comparative Political Studies* 6 (1973): 62–83; David Synder, "Institutional Setting and Industrial Conflict," *American Sociological Review* 40 (June 1975): 259–78; and David Britt and Omer R. Galle, "Industrial Conflict and Unionization," *American Sociological Review* 37 (February 1972): 46–57.

of this fact is not recent as only a cursory review of the theoretical literature in sociology would underscore.[3]

And yet, despite all of the promising work being done on the theory of conflict, certain controversies and issues persist. This persistence of unresolved issues is, perhaps, endemic to theory building. Yet it is also possible that the failure to address and resolve these issues will inhibit the efforts of theorists and researchers. Thus, these issues must be examined if the future of conflict theory is to be assessed. And it is in the context of these issues that Dahrendorf's, Coser's, and other theorists' ideas must be examined.

In this chapter, then, certain unresolved issues will first be examined. Then, Coser's and Dahrendorf's theories will be analyzed in terms of how much they are likely to contribute to the future of conflict theory.

UNRESOLVED ISSUES IN CONFLICT THEORY

What Is Conflict?

Probably the most controversial issue in conflict theory is the definition of conflict. What is, and what is not, conflict? A quick review of the conflict theory literature will produce a surprisingly diverse array of terms denoting different aspects of conflict: hostilities, war, competition, antagonism, tension, contradiction, quarrels, disagreements, inconsistencies, controversy, violence, opposition, revolution, dispute, and many other terms.[4] This issue boils down to the question of what kind of behavior

---

[3] The list of conflict theories and theorists is long. See for example, E. McNeil, ed., *The Nature of Human Conflict* (Englewood Cliffs, N.J.: Prentice-Hall, 1965); Jessie Bernard, *American Community Behavior* (New York: Dryden Press, 1949), "Where is the Modern Sociology of Conflict?" *American Journal of Sociology* 56 (1950): 111–16, "Parties and Issues in Conflict," *Journal of Conflict Resolution* 1 (June 1957): 111–21; Kenneth Boulding, *Conflict and Defense: A General Theory* (New York: Harper & Row, 1962); Thomas Carver, "The Basis of Social Conflict," *American Journal of Sociology* 13 (1908): 628–37; James Coleman, *Community Conflict* (Glencoe, Ill.: Free Press, 1957); James C. Davies, "Toward A Theory of Revolution," *American Journal of Sociology,* 27 (1962): 5–19; Charles P. Loomis, "In Praise of Conflict and Its Resolution," *American Sociological Review* 32 (December 1967): 875–890; Raymond Mack and Richard C. Snyder, "The Analysis of Social Conflict," *Journal of Conflict Resolution* 1 (June 1957) 2:388–97; John S. Patterson, *Conflict in Nature and Life* (New York: Appleton, 1883); Anatol Rapoport, *Fights, Games and Debates* (Ann Arbor: University of Michigan Press, 1960); Thomas C. Schelling, *The Strategy of Conflict* (Cambridge: Harvard University Press, 1960); Pitirim Sorokin, "Solidary, Antagonistic, and Mixed Systems of Interaction" in *Society, Culture, and Personality* (New York: Harper, 1947); Nicholas S. Timasheff, *War and Revolution* (New York: Sheed and Ward, 1965); and Robin M. Williams, Jr., *The Reduction of Intergroup Tensions* (New York: Social Science Research Council, 1947). Moreover, most of the basic texts by the first two generations of professional sociologists revealed prominent treatments of conflict. See for example: E. A. Ross, *Principles of Sociology* (Boston: Houghton Mifflin, 1942); Robert McIver, *Society* (New York: Farrar and Rinehart, 1937).

[4] For a more extended discussion of this issue, see Clinton F. Fink, "Some Conceptual Difficulties in the Theory of Social Conflict," *Journal of Conflict Resolution* 12 (December 1968): 429–431.

among either individuals or collective units is to be defined as conflict? For example, does conflict involve only overt action of one party against another? Or can it include covert tensions among these parties? Or, does conflict embrace "competition" where parties strive for mutually exclusive goals without directly confronting each other? Or, is conflict only antagonisms involving overt violence and efforts to injure another party?

There is no consensus on these issues. Dahrendorf and Coser both employed broad definitions. For example, Dahrendorf uses the concept of conflict for "contests, competitions, disputes, and tensions as well as for manifest clashes between social forces."[5] Dahrendorf's definition is consistent with his dialectical assumptions: ICAs reveal "conflicts of interest" among quasi groups which, under technical, social, and political conditions, become true conflict groups willing to engage in overt action against each other. As long as one is disposed to prove that the social world is rife with contradictions, a broad definition of conflict is likely to be used. When conflict can be *any* overt or covert state which hints of antagonism, then it is easy to "document" the ubiquity of conflict. And demonstrating the pervasiveness of conflict has indeed been one of Dahrendorf's primary intellectual goals.

Similarly, Coser's broad definition serves his intellectual purposes: to demonstrate the ubiquity of conflict *and* to document its functions for system integration. If Coser viewed conflict as only violent confrontations, then its integrative functions might be less visible, since conflict parties might indeed destroy each other. But if conflict can be any antagonistic, or potentially antagonistic, disposition or action of subgroups in a system, one is more likely to find instances where these antagonisms have promoted integration and adaptability among the parties to the "conflict" or within the systemic whole where this "conflict" is evident.

Presently, most conflict theorists appear to favor such broad definitions. After exhaustively reviewing a large number of definitions, for example, Clinton Fink argues for a broad definition: Conflict is "any social situation or process in which two or more entities are linked by at least one form of antgonistic psychological relation or at least one form of antagonistic interaction."[6] In turn, the concept of "antagonism" embraces such states as "incompatable goals," "mutually exclusive interests," "emotional hostility," "dissensus," "violent struggle," "regulated mutual interference," and the like.

---

[5] Ralf Dahrendorf, *Class and Class Conflict in Industrial Society* (Stanford: Stanford University Press, 1957), p. 135.

[6] Fink, "Some Conceptual Difficulties," p. 456.

Few would, for example, want to consider a narrow definition such as: "Conflict is direct and overt interaction between parties in which the actions of each party are directed at inhibiting their adversary's attainment of its goals." Such a definition makes conflict an *overt and direct interaction* between parties, but it allows for considerable variability in how one party inhibits the actions of the other. Such actions can be normatively regulated, unregulated and violent, or any other state. Other forms of interaction could be labeled with different terms, and thus avoid what is probably a lumping together of "apples and oranges" under the generic rubric of conflict. At present, the term is so global and encompassing that it embraces diverse forms of relationships which, in all probability, are highly distinctive and reveal somewhat different laws of operation.

One of the few conflict theorists who has sought to develop a more limited definition which, at the same time, embraces diverse forms of conflict is Robin Williams, Jr. Although he is not always this explicit, he defines conflict in one important essay as:

> . . . interaction in which one party intends to deprive, control, injure, or eliminate another, against the will of that other. Pure conflict is a *fight;* its goal is to immobilize, neutralize, destroy, or otherwise harm an opponent. In the impure world of actuality, some overt struggles are conducted accordingly to rules and for limited goals; oppositional behavior may then have the primary goal of winning rather than of injuring the opponent; we then usually call the encounter a *game.* Some games merge into *debates* in which the primary aim is to convince or persuade opponents or others of the rightness or correctness or attractiveness of one's views or claims.[7]

Such a definition views conflict as direct interaction which takes a variety of specific forms but which still involves efforts to "deprive, control, injure, or eliminate" the other. It is attention to this kind of explicit definition of conflict that is needed in conflict theory. As long as the background conditions, such as "contradictions," "oppositions of interests," or "hostilities," are viewed as conflict, then it will be difficult to separate out the causes of conflict—that is, these and other background conditions—from the conflict itself. When the preconditions of conflict are lumped together with the actual emission of conflict acts, then theo-

---

[7] Robin M. Williams, Jr., "Social Order and Social Conflict," *Proceedings of the American Philosophical Society* 114 (June 1970): 217–25. Yet, in a more thorough analysis of the "law of social conflict," Williams does not present this kind of explicit definition. See "Conflict and Social Order: A Research Strategy for Complex Propositions," *Journal of Social Issues* 28 (1972) 1:11–26.

ries are likely to be vague. The future of conflict theory thus depends upon making explicit what is, and what is not, conflict and in distinguishing different types or forms of conflict from each other.

Conflict among or between What?

Conflict theory evidences "unit of analysis" problems. Typically just what units are in conflict is left vague—whether they be individuals, groups, organizations, classes, nations, communities, and the like. For example, in Dahrendorf's scheme, conflict occurs between such units as "quasi groups" and "conflict groups" in equally vague "ICAs." In Coser's portrayal, "parties" and "groups" are the units in conflict, although Coser's essays often deal with explicit empirical referents.

Leaving the units vague has the virtue of making theory abstract and hence applicable to all social units, from individuals to nation states. Thus, theoretical statements can potentially be more powerful, explaining conflict among all social forms. On the other hand, however, it is likely that the nature of the units influences the nature of the conflict among them. While conflict between individuals and nations may have certain common properties, and thus be subsumable under some general laws, there are also likely to be clear differences in conflict between such disparate units.[8]

Conflict theory reveals a bipolarity: On the one hand, there are a number of abstract schemes, such as Dahrendorf's and Coser's, which seek to uncover basic laws of conflict among a wide variety of social units, while on the other hand, there are a large number of specific theories of international, interpersonal, racial, class, sexual, religious, ethical, organizational, community, and occupational conflict, to name just a few empirical areas where research and theory on conflict are prominent.

Recognizing this polarity, a number of theorists have sought to isolate those basic units which might reveal their own laws of conflict. For example, Dahrendorf's work posits conflict between and within five different levels of organization: roles, groups, sectors, societies, and suprasocietal units.[9] Other classifications, such as one by Johan Galtung,[10] distinguish conflicts between and within two levels: the individual and collective. In this scheme, intrapersonal and interpersonal conflicts are

---

[8] Fink, "Some Conceptual Difficulties," pp. 417–25, for a summary of various efforts to specify different types of conflict units.

[9] These distinctions are made in Dahrendorf's untranslated work. Cited in Robert C. Angel "The Sociology of Human Conflict," in E. McNeil, ed., *The Nature of Human Conflict*.

[10] Johan Galtung, "Institutionalized Conflict Resolution: A Theoretical Paradigm," *Journal of Peace Research* 2, (1965) 4:348–96.

presumed to be of a different nature than intranational and international conflicts. In turn, intrapersonal (within a person) differ from interpersonal (between person) conflicts, while intranational (within society) and international (between society) reveal fundamental differences.

At present, then, conflict theory has yet to agree on how conflict varies among different types of units. It is significant, however, that conflict theory has at least addressed the issue of units, for sociological theory has rarely concerned itself with how social relations vary with different types of units. For example, Parsonian functionalism developed an elaborate conceptual scheme around processes occurring in one type of unit—the "social system"—which could be anything from a small group to a system of societies. Little attention was devoted to indicating how social processes varied with different types of social units. This problem will also be evident in the subsequent analysis of other theoretical perspectives. For the present, it can be emphasized that since conflict theory is about social relations—that is, conflict relations—it is inevitably drawn to the issue of conflict between and among what types of units.

As conflict theorists begin to define conflict more explicitly and to develop theories that distinguish among phenomena denoted by such labels as fights, games, war, revolution, competitions, disputes, and the like, the issue of units of analysis will become even more relevant. It is likely that the type of conflict will vary with the type of unit. Or, at least, certain types of units will be found to be more likely to engage in one type of conflict than in another. For example, a "fight" may be an "interpersonal conflict," whereas a "revolution" is a type of conflict among other types of social units, such as social classes. Until these kinds of problems in distinguishing types of units and types of conflicts are resolved, conflict theory will tend to remain somewhat vague and abstract. Coser's and Dahrendorf's schemes illustrate this fact, for while they are highly insightful, they are vague.[11]

Escape from Functionalism?

A number of recent commentaries have sought to document the implicit functionalism in dialectical conflict theory.[12] Such functional im-

---

[11] Lest there be a misunderstanding, I should emphasize that this point is not intended as a critique of highly abstract conflict schemes. Indeed, these tend to be far superior to the lower-level empirical analyses which abound in the literature. But the schemes of Coser, Dahrendorf, Williams, Gamson, Gurr, and others are now sufficiently developed that unit of analysis questions can be profitably addressed.

[12] Arthur L. Stinchcombe, *Constructing Social Theories* (New York: Harcourt, 1968), p. 94; Piotr Sztompka, *System and Function: Toward a Theory of Society* (New York: Academic Press, 1974).

agery is, of course, explicit in the conflict functionalism of Lewis Coser. In asserting an implicit functionalism in conflict theory, the charge is made that end states or the consequences of conflict often take analytical precedence over the causes of conflict. Such a charge is perhaps bothersome to dialectical theorists who have sought to take sociology out of its "functional utopia," and yet, it has the ring of truth.

There can be little doubt that the consequences of conflict processes are given prominent attention by many theorists. The issue of whether or not this emphasis on consequences distorts causal analysis is, however, less clear. In Figure 9–1, the over-all causal imagery in Dahrendorf's

FIGURE 9–1
Over-All Causal Imagery of Conflict Theory

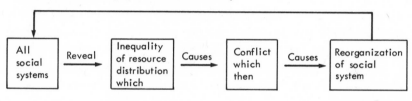

and Coser's analysis, as well as the analyses of most conflict theorists, is presented. In Figure 9–1, it is evident that conflict theory emphasizes inequality as the ultimate source of conflict. Under varying conditions, which differ in each theory, inequality causes conflict, which then, under differing conditions, changes the organization of the social system. The feedback arrow at the top of the figure underscores the dialectical assumption that reorganization of the system sets off the conflict producing process again. This sequence is unending, because social systems are always assumed to reveal inherent conflict-producing tendencies. As is obvious, of course, dialectical and functional conflict theories focus on different types of conflict and on varying forms of system reorganization. Dialectical theories concentrate on more severe and violent conflicts causing redistribution of resources into a new pattern of inequality which, in turn, will cause a new wave of conflict and resource distribution. In contrast, functional theories focus on less severe and violent conflicts and on their consequences for promoting integration within and between conflict parties and for increasing over-all system "adaptability" and "flexibility."

Both dialectical and functional conflict theories, then, are not merely interested in what causes conflict. They are also interested in what conflict "does for" the systemic whole in which it occurs. Conflict is both a dependent variable—that is, a process which is caused by other forces—and an independent variable—that is, a process which causes alterations in still other processes. This distinction between conflict as a dependent and independent variable is not always clear, however. It often appears that theorists' desire to present social organization as either constantly in change or in adaptive upgrading obscures the causes of conflict. Conflict is seen to emerge and cause changes, but theories sometimes fail to specify what kind of conflict revealing what properties causes what alterations in what subsystems or systemic wholes.

This problem is compounded by the failure to define conflict and to specify what conflict units are involved in what kinds of conflict. The result is a vagueness about what conflict theorists are trying to explain: the causes of different forms of conflict or the social functions of ill-defined conflict processes? Was Marx, for example, attempting to explain conflict or promote a certain end-state in social systems? Is Dahrendorf seeking to explain conflict or to assert an image of social organization as constantly in change? It can be recalled that the nature of conflict is never specified by Dahrendorf, for as he notes, such matters as "conflict intensity" and "conflict violence" vary on "a scale of 0 to 1 according to the operation of certain factors."[13] Similarly, is Coser attempting to explain conflict or system integration? His distinctions between "violence" and "intensity," it can be recalled, are not much more explicit than Dahrendorf's.

The simple answer to these questions about the "causes" or "consequences" of conflict is that both are being explained. Yet, as with all other forms of functionalism, the desire to explain the functions of a social phenomena—whether it be conflict, religion, or a mechanism of social control—sometimes leads theorists to "short circuit" the explanation of what caused the phenomena in the first place. Coser and Dahrendorf do provide suggestive causal statements, but their analysis of functions also appears to be obscured by their desire, respectively, to demonstrate the system change and system integration consequences of conflict.

Thus, one of the issues which conflict theorists must address more squarely is this: Is conflict an independent, intervening, or dependent variable? And as a variable, what are its *varying* states? What causes these varying states? And what variations in other social processes and structures do these varying states of conflict cause? Behind these questions, however, is the more fundamental issue of sorting out causes and consequences—the issue which has plagued functionalism (see Chapters

---

[13] Dahrendorf, *Class and Class Conflict*, p. 239.

2, 3, 4, 5). To delineate the causes of varying types of conflicts is a much easier task than specifying what "they do" for system parts and systemic wholes. For example, it might be possible to document the causes of violent revolution between social classes, but to assess what this revolution "did for" the social whole can prove illusive. What the violence brought in the first week is different from the first year, and the first year's results will differ, in all probability, from the first decade. Or, what were the consequencs of the revolution for what units—individuals, classes, political parties, the integration of the nation, international affairs, and so on for any conceivable system referent? Thus, the scope, time, and structures influenced by a particular state of conflict present problems of analysis—problems which inhere in a functional orientation.

In sum, then, these three problems—the definition of conflict, the units of conflict, and the confusion over causes and functions—present a challenge to conflict theory. Theorists must first decide what is, and what is not conflict. If the definition remains too broad, then almost any social process can be labeled conflict, since all that must be revealed is a hint of antagonism, psychological hostility, frustration, dissensus, or any of the hundreds of terms currently subsumed under the concept of conflict.

Theorists will also have to decide on the scope and level of abstraction of their theories. Are they seeking to develop general laws which can subsume all the more specific conflict processes in the world? Or are they seeking to develop a theory of conflict about a specific type of social unit—if so, what type of unit? And, finally, theorists must make clear what they are seeking to do: Explain the causes or functions of conflict? As Durkheim emphasized, "causal" and "functional" analysis are separate tasks. It is unlikely, as the deficiencies in Durkheim's, Malinowski's, Parsons', and Merton's theories underscore, that *one* theory can do *both* a causal and functional analysis.

It is in the context of these unresolved problems, then, that the future of conflict theory must be assessed. As was noted earlier, this task will be approached by assessing and reformulating Coser's and Dahrendorf's theories.

ASSESSING AND REFORMULATING DAHRENDORF'S AND COSER'S THEORIES

In assessing and reformulating Coser's and Dahrendorf's theories of conflict, it is necessary to perform several analytical operations.[14] First,

---

[14] This section draws heavily from my "A Strategy for Reformulating the Dialectical and Functional Theories of Conflict," *Social Forces* 53 (March 1975):433–44.

efforts at limiting the scope of their theories should be made. In the following discussion, this goal will be reached by (a) ignoring all discussion of the functions or consequences of conflict, (b) visualizing conflict as a variable which can reach different states of violence, (c) recognizing that conflict is a form of overt interaction which can be defined as observable efforts of parties to thwart each other's access to scarce resources, and which involves mutual awareness and contact of conflict parties with each other. Second, the high level of abstraction in their theories should be retained, for the variables and propositions of the theories probably have wide-ranging implications for many different types of social units. Third, it must be recognized that conflict for both Coser and Dahrendorf's is a *process* which goes through stages, and thus it is necessary to reconcile their somewhat different views on the stages in the conflict process. Fourth, the major concepts and propositions of each theory must be retained, and yet reconciled to form a more comprehensive scheme which is logically consistent and empirically relevant.

Thus, this effort will view conflict as a process of events leading to overt conflict of varying degrees of violence among two interacting parties. It is felt that it is in this area that Coser's and Dahrendorf's theories have the most to offer conflict theory. The future of conflict theory hinges upon efforts such as this to reconcile divergent, and yet overlapping, concepts and propositions as they bear on the analysis of conditions which lead to different forms of social conflict.

The Over-All Causal Model

Figure 9–2 schematically outlines the combined causal sequence of Dahrendorf's and Coser's theories. By briefly examining this diagram, a general overview of a composite theory emerges. This overview, of course, will need to be "filled in" with the actual propositions of Coser's and Dahrendorf's theories. As the numbers above each box in the diagram emphasize, the theories are sequential; there are steps in the processes leading to overt conflict. The arrows connecting each box mark the direction of this sequence. The arrows pointing upward between boxes represent propositions that each theorist develops for indicating the conditions under which the state of affairs described in each box will be realized. As can be seen, however, neither Dahrendorf nor Coser present propositions for why social systems reveal interdependence (box 1) or why an unequal distribution of scarce resources (box 2) should exist. They are simply boundary conditions of the theory. That is, in social systems which reveal the unequal distribution of scarce resources among interdependent units, stages 3, 4, 5, 6, 7, 8, and 9 will be activated if certain conditions at each stage are met. The theory is thus devoted to specifying the conditions under which sequences of events will occur, ultimately resulting in overt conflict.

The feedback arrows at the top of the diagram connecting various boxes emphasize that the causal model is more complex than just indicated. Events at various stages feed back and influence the weights of variables at earlier stages, making the conflict process a sequence with many built-in cycles. For example, efforts at "organization of conflict groups" (box 8) will feed back and influence "awareness of objective interests" (box 4). If the feedback loop is "positive"—that is, organization is successful and thus increases awareness—then the weights of variables in steps 5, 6, and 7 are altered. In turn, the increased emotional arousal (box 5), the occurrence, if any, of collective outbursts (box 6), and increased emotional involvement (box 7) will shape, along with other conditions (denoted by the arrow between boxes 7 and 8), the degree of organization of conflict groups (box 8). Similar feedback cycles for other stages within the over-all causal sequence are also postulated by Coser and Dahrendorf, as is indicated by the feedback arrows.

While this over-all causal model appears complex, it actually represents a simplification of Coser's and Dahrendorf's theories. Yet, it is these causal linkages that mark Coser's and Dahrendorf's contribution to a theory of conflict. And it is in testing the plausibility of the propositions linking these stages, and those postulated by other theorists, that the future of conflict theory resides.

To fill in the model, it is necessary to summarize the conditions which influence the states described in each box of the conflict sequence. These conditions are specified in the inventories of propositions that were presented for Dahrendorf's and Coser's theories in Chapters 6 and 7. The present analysis will seek to summarize the most relevant of these propositions and indicate how they are implicated in the conflict sequence delineated in Figure 9–2.

Key Theoretical Propositions

To analyze the key propositions in Coser's and Dahrendorf's schemes, it is necessary to specify the conditions under which the state of affairs described in each box in Figure 9–2 are realized. Thus, in this section, stages presented in Figure 9–2 will be discussed separately, with an emphasis on specifying the key propositions influencing the weights of variables at each point in the conflict process.

Stage 3.   Withdrawal of Legitimacy.   As was noted in Chapter 7, Coser and Dahrendorf differ in their conceptualization of how inequalities initiate the conflict process. Dahrendorf emphasizes awareness, Coser the withdrawal of legitimacy. Figure 9–2 indicates that the combined

FIGURE 9–2
Coser's and Dahrendorf's Composite Causal Model of Conflict

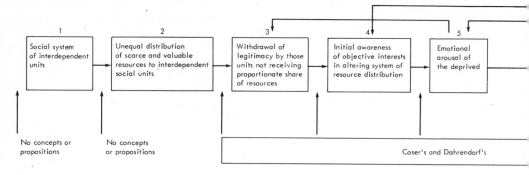

model hypothesizes that an initial withdrawal of legitimacy with respect to inequality is the first step in the conflict process. Such withdrawal is likely when: (*a*) channels of upward mobility are insufficient to accommodate people's aspirations, thus creating a sense of blockage among deprived segments of the population: (*b*) channels for redressing grievances against the system of inequality are insufficient relative to the demand for expressing grievances; and (*c*) rewards and deprivations are superimposed on each other—that is, having (or not having) access to one resource is highly correlated with access (or lack of access) to other scarce resources.[15] Hence, those with money also enjoy power, prestige, health, and other rewards, whereas the reverse is true for the deprived. These propositions, as will be recalled from Chapter 7, are borrowed from Coser's analysis. The presumption in placing these propositions first in the causal sequence is that people must begin to question the system before they will begin to perceive their objective interests in altering the system of resource distribution.

Stage 4   Initial Awareness of Objective Interests.   In Dahrendorf's theory, a group's awareness is influenced, as will be recalled from Chapter 7, by the technical (leaders, ideology, and so forth), political (creation

---

[15] Both Coser and Dahrendorf present their hypotheses but at different places in their causal schemes. It is felt that this is the most appropriate place for these key propositions. Moreover, placing this proposition here helps resolve the dispute over the "structural conditions" versus the "psychological tensions" hypotheses of conflict. Withdrawal of legitimacy occurs under specifiable structural conditions—thus underscoring the interaction of structural and social psychological variables. For a more detailed discussion of this issue, see: Robin M. Williams, Jr., "Relative Deprivation Versus Power Struggle?: Tension and Structural Explanations of Collective Conflict," *Cornell Journal of Social Relations* 11 (1976)1:31–38 and his article, "Relative Deprivation," in Lewis A. Coser, ed., *The Idea of Social Structure: Papers in Honor of Robert K. Merton* (New York: Harcourt, Bruce, Jovanovich, 1975):355–78.

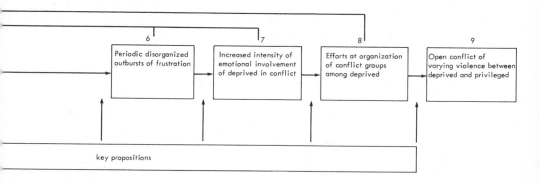

of opposition organizations), and social (opportunities to communicate, to recruit members) conditions. The more these technical, political, and social conditions can be met, the more likely are the deprived to be aware of their objective interests in altering the present system of resource distribution. However, Coser's theory emphasizes the inadequacy of this formulation. As people withdraw legitimacy from a system, they do not suddenly become "aware" of their interests. Only an *initial* awareness is likely. Thus, Dahrendorf's technical, political, and social conditions are premature. It is unlikely that they exert their full impact until later in the causal sequence, when actors have become disillusioned, initially aware, and emotionally aroused. It is then that they will begin to seek leaders, organization, unifying beliefs, and means for communication.

Stage 5. Emotional Arousal of Deprived. The major failing of Dahrendorf's scheme is that it is too "mechanical." Actors do not seem to have emotion, and, in fact, Dahrendorf stays clear of the psychology of the deprived. Coser's emphasis upon emotional arousal of the deprived is thus an important supplement to Dahrendorf's analysis. For Coser appears to recognize that withdrawal of legitimacy and initial awareness of an interest in altering the system leads to emotional arousal, to passions which, under other conditions, drive actors to pursue conflict. Coser postulates two conditions influencing arousal: (*a*) the degree to which socialization practices among the deprived, and socialization agents in the broader system, create internal psychological controls in actors; and (*b*) the extent to which social control mechanisms can suppress, channel, or deflect emotional arousal. Thus, the greater the internal psychological constraints and the more effective the external social control, the less likely is overt emotional arousal among the deprived. The reverse is true under conditions of weak social and psychological control.

Stage 6. Periodic Collective Outbursts. The conflict process is often marked by individual and collective outbursts of emotion and frustration. These often result in conflict as the agencies of social control in a system seek to suppress these outbursts. Ghetto riots in U.S. society in the 1960s were an example of collective outbursts which reflected the withdrawal of legitimacy, the initial awareness of objective interests, and the sudden escalation of emotions.

Such outbursts are, of course, a form of conflict in themselves, but they are also a stage in a process leading to other forms of conflict, such as a society-wide revolution or serious "collective bargaining" relations among conflict parties. Collective outbursts occur, as Simmel initially emphasized, when the technical, political, and social conditions postulated by Dahrendorf have not been realized.[16] The impact of critical feedback loops outlined in Figure 9–2 must be recognized in this process. Aroused emotions (box 5) feed back upon questions about legitimacy. Aroused emotions will decrease commitments to the system and foster a sense of increased awareness of interests. In turn, increased withdrawal of legitimacy and awareness escalates emotions to a point where collective outbursts are more likely. Another critical feedback loop comes from stages 6, 7, and 8 in the conflict process. When outbursts occur, they release frustrations; but if social control is harsh and highly repressive, they also increase the level of emotional arousal (hence, the feedback loop between boxes 6 and 5).[17] Moreover, as actors become more motivated to channel emotions into conflict activities (box 7), this too increases emotional arousal (box 5). And, finally, if highly motivated actors can become organized—in accordance with technical, political, and social conditions (box 8)—then this fact will influence awareness of objective interests (box 4), which in turn will arouse emotions, but as Simmel understood more than Marx, this arousal is now focused and less likely to lead to collective outbursts. Rather, deprived actors will become motivated to increase their organization and bargain with superordinates over resource redistribution.

Stage 7. Increased Intensity. Intensity is the degree to which actors are motivated to pursue their interests and engage in conflict. Intensity involves emotional arousal, but it denotes the channeling of emotional

---

16 Naturally, there are many other conditions influencing such outbursts. For examples of a specific analysis of particular empirical cases, see Jeffrey M. Paige, *Agrarian Revolution* (Riverside, N.J.: Free Press, 1975); and "Political Orientation and Riot Participation," *American Sociological Review* 36 (October, 1971): 810–20.

17 For a more thorough analysis of this proposition, see Williams, "Relative Deprivation Versus Power Struggle?" p. 35.

energies and the willingness to sustain these energies in the pursuit of objective interests. One condition increasing intensity is the failure of collective outbursts. In the wake of an outburst—a ghetto riot or a wildcat strike, for example—some people become more committed to pursue conflict once they recognize that others would be prepared to join them. Moreover, the use of social control agents—police and troops, for instance—to suppress outbursts often helps solidify emotional commitments and bring into sharper perspective the targets of conflict-oriented activity.

Stage 8. Efforts at Organization. Once the deprived have withdrawn legitimacy, become somewhat aware of their interests, been emotionally aroused, participated in, or observed, outbursts of their fellows, and become committed to realizing their interests, then people are likely to become receptive to organization. Their ability to organize, as Dahrendorf emphasizes, is a function of: (*a*) the availability of leaders and unifying beliefs (technical conditions); (*b*) the tolerance of political organization and the resources to organize (political conditions); and (*c*) the capacity to communicate grievances and to recruit members into organizations.

With increased organization, articulation of objective interests becomes more explicit (thus, feeding back to box 4), and hence, the emotional arousal of actors (box 5) will be less likely to result in spontaneous outbursts (box 6), but to a growing commitment (or intensity) to use organizations to pursue objective interests (box 7).

Stages 3 to 8 have thus set the stage for open conflict. While conflict in the form of collective or individual outbursts may have preceded stage 9, these outbursts can also be viewed as steps in a more inclusive conflict process. Moreover, there are a number of feedback cycles in the over-all process which will influence not only the probability of outbursts, but also subsequent forms of conflict. Before presenting Coser's and Dahrendorf's propositions influencing the nature of conflict at stage 9, it is wise to summarize and assess those presented thus far. In Figure 9–3, the basic causal scheme is presented again, but this time, the key propositions are inserted at the appropriate point in this causal sequence.[18] As can be seen, certain stages lack propositions. For example, propositions specifying the conditions under which awareness of objective interests follows the withdrawal of legitimacy need to be specified (stage 4). Perhaps some incipient level of technical, political, and social conditions must exist, as Dahrendorf's theory emphasizes. Another proposi-

---

[18] Turner, "A Strategy," p. 437.

FIGURE 9–3
Propositions on the Conflict Process

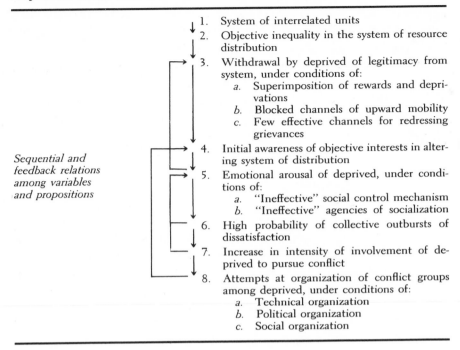

1. System of interrelated units
2. Objective inequality in the system of resource distribution
3. Withdrawal by deprived of legitimacy from system, under conditions of:
    a. Superimposition of rewards and deprivations
    b. Blocked channels of upward mobility
    c. Few effective channels for redressing grievances
4. Initial awareness of objective interests in altering system of distribution
5. Emotional arousal of deprived, under conditions of:
    a. "Ineffective" social control mechanism
    b. "Ineffective" agencies of socialization
6. High probability of collective outbursts of dissatisfaction
7. Increase in intensity of involvement of deprived to pursue conflict
8. Attempts at organization of conflict groups among deprived, under conditions of:
    a. Technical organization
    b. Political organization
    c. Social organization

Sequential and feedback relations among variables and propositions

tional gap can be seen for step 6. The conditions under which emotional arousal leads to collective outbursts have not been specified. The literature on "collective behavior" emphasizes such variables as:[19] (a) a "precipitating incident" which symbolizes the situation of the deprived and suddenly escalates their emotions to a point where internal psychological inhibitions and external agents of social control are temporarily ineffective in preventing an outburst; (b) a high degree of propinquity among the deprived who witness the precipitating event, thus increasing mutual communication of hostilities and frustrations; and (c) the availability of objects—persons, organizations, or symbols—which can serve as "targets" of frustrations. Thus, for example, ghetto riots of the 1960s usually occurred in situations where: (a) the police were arresting a resident; (b) the heat of the summer evening had brought people in propinquity to the incident and each other; and (c) the stores, businesses, and the

---

[19] For a more thorough review of this literature, see: Neil J. Smelser, *A Theory of Collective Behavior* (New York: Free Press, 1963); Ralph H. Turner and Lewis M. Killian, *Collective Behavior* (Englewood Cliffs, N.J.: Prentice-Hall, 1957).

slum housing owned by white, absentee entrepreneurs provided a clear target for venting frustrations.[20]

Another propositional gap can be observed at stage 7. Coser lists some conditions increasing commitment to pursue conflict, such as the degree of ideological unification (one of Dahrendorf's "technical conditions") and the degree of "primariness" of relations among the deprived. These propositions were not inserted in the causal model because they are vague and do not clearly specify conditions increasing people's commitment to channel their energies in pursuit of conflict. This issue is one where further thinking and research are needed.

In presenting Coser's and Dahrendorf's propositions in Figure 9–3, however, it is at least possible to visualize the strengths and weaknesses of the theory. The theory specifies why people withdraw legitimacy, why they might become aroused, and why they become organized to pursue conflict. Less clear are propositions about why people become aware of their interests, why they sometimes individually or collectively protest, and why they increase the intensity of their involvement to pursue conflict. Some propositions can be inserted, as was done above, but the theory still requires additional propositions to account for the weights of variables at these stages.

Stage 9. The Degree of Violence in the Conflict. Coser's and Dahrendorf's propositional inventories offer three propositions on the conditions influencing the degree of violence of a conflict: (*a*) The extent to which the technical, political, and social conditions are met is negatively related to violence; that is, the less the conditions are met, the more likely is conflict to be violent. (*b*) The failure to define true interests, independently of core values, is negatively related to the violence of conflict. Thus, if conflict parties cannot distinguish between their core values and specific goals for realizing their interests, then the conflict is likely to be "moral" rather than "instrumental," with the result that compromises over "moral" issues become difficult to make. In contrast, compromises over specific goals are easier to make, because they do not involve a moral issue which evokes great emotion. (*c*) A system which does not have a means for regularizing conflict interaction through legal norms and agencies of mediation is likely to reveal high rates of violent conflict. If a system cannot regulate conflicts between parties with laws, courts, mediating agencies, and other structures, it is difficult for conflict parties to bargain, compromise, and trust each other, since

---

[20] Otto Kerner et al, *Report of the National Advisory Commission on Civil Disorders* (Washington, D.C.: Government Printing Office, 1972).

there is no mechanism for mediating conflicts of interest and for enforcing agreed-upon compromises.

These three propositions bear important interrelationships. A conflict group that realizes the technical, political, and social conditions of organization is likely to be able to articulate its interests, independently of values and beliefs. A system revealing well-organized conflict groups is also likely to have developed regulatory mechanisms; and if it has not, the potential for conflict may force the emergence of such regulatory mechanisms. Or, the existence of regulating mechanisms may actually facilitate the organization of conflict groups (constituting another "political condition" of conflict group organization). Of course, it is indeed possible for well-organized groups to mix values and goals, or to view them as inseparable. And it is possible for well organized conflict groups to confront one another in the absence of any regulation. Under these conditions, then, conflict violence is likely to increase. These propositions and their interrelations are summarized in Figure 9–4.[21]

FIGURE 9–4
Propositions on the Degree of Conflict Violence

	8. Attempts at organization of conflict groups among deprived	
	9A. More violent conflict, under conditions of:	9B. Less violent conflict, under conditions of:
Sequential and feedback relations among variables and propositions	a. Failure to realize technical, political, and social conditions of organization	a. Capacity to realize technical, political, and social conditions of organization
	b. Failure to define clearly true interests, independently of core values	b. Articulation of true interests, independently of core values
	c. Incapacity of inclusive system to regularize conflict relations	c. Capacity of system to regularize conflict relations

COSER'S AND DAHRENDORF'S THEORIES: AN OVERVIEW

In this long and complex presentation of Coser's and Dahrendorf's combined theory of conflict, the goal has been to illustrate where the

---

[21] Turner, "A Strategy," p. 440.

future of conflict theory resides. By seeking to define conflict explicitly and to state more clearly relationships among variables and propositions, it is possible to build suggestive and testable theory. The above exercise suggests one strategy for developing a formal theory of conflict processes. This exercise has retained the essence of Coser's and Dahrendorf's theories: abstract statements about the conditions under which varying types of conflict are likely to emerge. But it has sought to avoid some of the limitations in their theories: the excessive concern with the functions of conflict for system change or integration and global claims about the ubiquity of conflict in social systems.

In many ways, the problem with much conflict theory is its excessive claims: to visualize all social relationships in all social systems as rife with conflict. The only way to sustain this claim is to define conflict so broadly that virtually any social relationship will reveal "conflict." Coser's and Dahrendorf's theories are much more powerful when their insights are used to develop a composite theory about the degree of violence in conflict. And by ignoring the issue of the functions of this conflict for the social whole, the temptation to let theorists' assumptions about what *should* occur in social systems influence their analyses has been avoided. Too often, conflict theorists *want* to view the world as rife with conflict and change, creating intellectual pressures for distorting their analyses. It is, of course, a tribute to Coser and Dahrendorf that, despite the existence of these pressures, they have developed theories which offer considerable insight into a most prominent process. By viewing conflict as only one of many processes in human affairs, then it is more likely that theory will be directed to understanding the conditions under which various types of conflicts are likely to occur. This is a more laudable goal than attempting to reveal "the ugly face of society" or lead sociology "out of utopia."

The future of conflict theory resides not in polemics and excessive claims about the ubiquity of conflict, but in the careful analysis of the conditions under which different forms of conflict are likely to occur among different types of social units. Such theory will be a theory of *conflict*, not of social organization. Yet, because conflict does appear to be a pervasive phenomenon, greater understanding of human organization will ensue. Moreover, in understanding the conditions under which conflict occurs, considerable insight into the conditions of social integration will also be gained. For what drives society apart is often the reverse side of what drives society together. Thus, conflict theory, as theory and not polemics, has much to offer in understanding how and why patterns of social organization are created, maintained, and changed.

PART III

Exchange Theorizing

10

THE INTELLECTUAL ROOTS OF EXCHANGE THEORY

The intellectural heritage culminating in modern exchange theory is diverse, drawing from sources in economics, anthropology, and psychology. What typifies this heritage as much as its diversity are the frequently vague connections between contemporary exchange theorists and their predecessors. Indeed, current exchange theories appear to be a curious and unspecified mixture of utilitarian economics, functional anthropology, and behavioral psychology. When this mixture is coupled with each contemporary author's attempts to provide an exchange-theoretic alternative to Parsonian functionalism, the development over the last two decades of sociological exchange theories presents a complex picture of selective borrowing of long standing concepts and principles from other disciplines and reaction to imputed inadequacies of functional forms of theorizing. In this chapter, then, a tentative overview of the traditions toward which sociologists turned in seeking the exchange alternative to functionalism is provided.

UTILITARIANISM: THE LEGACY OF "CLASSICAL" ECONOMICS

The names of Adam Smith, David Ricardo, John Stuart Mill, and Jeremy Bentham loom large in the history of economic theorizing between 1750–1850. While each made a unique contribution to both economic and social thought, certain core assumptions about the nature of humans and their relation with each other, especially in the economic marketplace, enabled their thought to be labeled "utilitarianism." Although the extreme formulations of utilitarianism have long since been rejected, several key ideas still continue to inform theorizing in the social sciences. For example, as was noted in the discussion of Talcott Parsons' voluntaristic theory of action, there is a clearly acknowledged intellectual debt to utilitarian thought. And so it is with modern exchange theorists, although their intellectual debt is not so thoroughly documented or clearly understood as was the case with Parsons.

Underlying all contemporary exchange theories are reformulations of certain basic utilitarian assumptions and concepts. For classical economists, humans were viewed as rationally seeking to maximize their material benefits, or "utility," from transactions or exchanges with others in a free and competitive marketplace. As rational units in a free marketplace, people would have access to all necessary information, could consider all available alternatives, and, on the basis of this consideration, rationally select the course of activity which would maximize material benefits. Entering into these rational considerations were calculations of the "costs" involved in pursuing various alternatives. Such costs must be weighted against material benefits in an effort to determine which alternative would yield the maximum payoff or profit (benefits less costs).[1]

With the emergence of sociology as a self-conscious discipline, there was considerable borrowing, revision, and reaction to this conception of humans and their transactions with each other. In fact, the debate between the intellectual descendants of utilitarianism and those reacting to this perspective has raged since sociology's inception. For example, the formulations of Durkheim were in large part an attempt to devise an alternative to the utilitarian thought in the various works of Herbert Spencer. More recently, as was noted in the discussion of functionalism, Parsons has attempted to reformulate utilitarian principles and weld them to other theoretical traditions in an effort to correct for Spencer's oversights. Similarly, modern exchange theorists have attempted to reformulate utilitarian principles into various theories of social exchange.

This reformulation has involved the recognition that: (a) rarely do people attempt to maximize profits; (b) humans are not always rational; (c) their transactions with each other, whether in an economic marketplace or elsewhere, are not free from external regulation and constraint; and (d) individuals do not have perfect information on all available alternatives. Recognition of these facts has led to a series of alternative

---

[1] For interesting discussions of utilitarian thought as it bears on the present discussion, see Elie Halévy, *The Growth of Philosophical Radicalism* (London: Farber & Farber, 1928); John Plamenatz, *Man and Society* (New York: McGraw-Hill, Book Co., 1963).

utilitarian assumptions: (1) While humans do not seek to maximize prof-its, they always attempt to make some profit in their social transactions with others. (2) While they are not perfectly rational, they engage in calculations of costs and benefits in social transactions. (3) While actors do not have perfect information on all available alternatives, they are usually aware of at least some alternatives, which form the basis for assessments of costs and benefits. (4) While there are always constraints on human activity, people compete with each other in seeking to make a profit in their transactions. In addition to these alterations of utilitarian assumptions, exchange theory removes human interaction from the limi-tations of material transactions in an economic marketplace: (5) While economic transactions in a clearly defined marketplace occur in all socie-ties, they are only a special case of more general exchange relations occurring among individuals in virtually all social contexts. (6) While material goals typify exchanges in an economic marketplace, individuals also exchange other, nonmaterial commodities, such as sentiments and services of various kinds.

Aside from the substantive legacy of utilitarianism, some forms of modern exchange theory have also adopted the *strategy* of the utilitarians for constructing social theory. In assuming humans to be rational, utilitari-ans argued that exchanges among people could also be studied by a rational science, one in which the "laws of human nature" would stand at the top of a deductive system of explanation. Thus, utilitarians bor-rowed the early physical science conception of theory as a logico-deductive system of axioms or laws and various layers of lower-order propositions that could be "rationally" deduced from the laws of "economic man." As will be emphasized at the close of this chapter, utilitarianism inspired the development of psychological behaviorism, which not only adjusted the concepts and assumptions of classical economic theory to its purposes, but also adopted the commitment to axiomatic forms of theorizing. This commitment, as inherited directly and indirectly through behavior-ism, has persisted to the present day and dominates much of the ex-change-theoretic literature.

However, in reviewing the tenets of utilitarianism, only part of the historical legacy of exchange theory is exposed. In addition to influencing behaviorists, who in turn were to have a separate impact on modern exchange theory, utilitarianism excited considerable debate and contro-versy in early anthropology. In fact, much of the influence of utilitarian-ism on current exchange theory appears to have been indirect, passing simultaneously through behaviorism and social anthropology around the turn of this century. Thus, while the exchange theories of sociology may now exert the most impact on social theory, sociological exchange theories have been built upon the pioneering efforts of social anthropologists.

EXCHANGE THEORY IN ANTHROPOLOGY[2]

Sir James Frazer

In 1919 Sir James George Frazer, in the second volume of his *Folklore in the Old Testament*, conducted what was probably the first explicitly exchange-theoretic analysis of social institutions.[3] In examining a wide variety of kinship and marriage practices among primitive societies, Frazer was struck by the clear preference of Australian aboriginals for cross-cousin over parallel-cousin marriages: "Why is the marriage of cross-cousins so often favored? Why is the marriage of ortho-cousins [that is, parallel cousins] so uniformly prohibited?"[4]

While the substantive details of Frazer's descriptions of the aboriginals' practices are fascinating in themselves (if only for their inaccuracy), it is the *form* of his explanation that marks his theoretical contribution. In a manner clearly indebted to utilitarian economics, Frazer launched an economic interpretation of the predominance of cross-cousin marriage patterns. In this explanation, Frazer invoked the "law" of "economic motives," since, in having "no equivalent in property to give for a wife, an Australian aboriginal is generally obliged to get her in exchange for a female relative, usually a sister or daughter."[5] Thus, the material or economic motives of individuals in society (lack of property and desire for a wife) explain various social patterns (cross-cousin marriages). What is more, Frazer went on to postulate that once a particular pattern, emanating from economic motives, becomes established in a culture, it circumscribes and constrains other social patterns that can potentially emerge.

For Frazer, then, the institutionalized patterns that come to typify a particular culture are a reflection of economic motives in humans

---

[2] For a similar treatment of these materials, see Peter Ekeh, *Social Exchange Theory and the Two Sociological Traditions* (Cambridge: Harvard University Press, 1975).

[3] Sir James George Frazer, *Folklore in the Old Testament*, vol. 2 (New York: Macmillan Co., 1919); see also his *Totemism and Exogamy: A Treatise on Certain Early Forms of Superstition and Society* (London: Dawsons of Pall Mall, 1968) (original publication 1910); and his Preface to *Argonauts of the Western Pacific*, by Bronislaw Malinowski (London: Routledge & Kegan Paul, 1922), pp. vii–xiv.

[4] Quote taken from Ekeh's *Social Exchange Theory*, pp. 41–42, discussion of Frazer (original quote in Frazer, *Folklore*, p. 199).

[5] Ibid., p. 195.

who, in exchanging commodities, attempt to satisfy their basic economic needs. While Frazer's specific explanation was to be found sadly wanting by subsequent generations of anthropologists, especially Malinowski and Lévi-Strauss, much modern exchange theory in sociology invokes a similar conception of social organization:

1. Exchange processes are the result of motives among people to realize their needs.
2. When yielding payoffs for those involved, exchange processes lead to the institutionalization or patterning of interaction.
3. Such institutionalized networks of interaction not only serve the needs of individuals, but they also constrain the kinds of social structures that can subsequently emerge in a social system.

In addition to anticipating the general profile of modern explanations on how elementary-exchange processes create more complex institutional patterns in a society, Frazer's analysis also foreshadowed another concern of contemporary exchange theory: the differentiation of social systems in terms of privilege and power. Exchange systems, Frazer noted, allow those who possessed commodities of high economic value to "exploit" those who had few such commodities, thereby enabling the former to possess high privilege and presumably power over the latter. Hence, the exchange of women among the aboriginals was observed by Frazer to lead to the differentiation of power and privilege in at least two separate ways:[6] First, "Since among the Australian aboriginals women had a high economic and commercial value, a man who had many sisters or daughters was rich and a man who had none was poor and might be unable to procure a wife at all."[7] Second, "the old men availed themselves of the system of exchange in order to procure a number of wives for themselves from among the young women, while the young men having no women to give in exchange, were often obliged to remain single or to put up with the cast-off wives of their elders."[8] Thus, at least implicitly, Frazer anticipated a fourth principle of social organization which was to be elaborated upon by contemporary exchange theory:

4. Exchange processes operate to differentiate groups in terms of their relative access to valued commodities, resulting in differences in power, prestige, and privilege.

---

[6] This insight comes from Ekeh's provocative *Social Exchange Theory*, p. 44.
[7] Frazer, *Folklore*, p. 198.
[8] Ibid., pp. 200–201.

As provocative and seemingly seminal as Frazer's analysis appears, it has had little direct impact on modern exchange theory. Rather, it is to those in anthropology who reacted to, and attempted to improve upon, Frazer's brand of utilitarianism that contemporary theory in sociology remains indebted.

Bronislaw Malinowski and Exchange Psychologism

Despite Malinowski's close ties with Frazer, he was to develop an exchange perspective that radically altered the utilitarian slant of Frazer's analysis of cross-cousin marriage. Indeed, Frazer himself in his preface to Malinowski's *Argonauts of the Western Pacific* recognized the importance of Malinowski's contribution to the analysis of exchange relations.[9] In his now-famous ethnography of the Trobriand Islanders—a group of South Seas Island cultures—Malinowski observed an exchange system termed the "Kula Ring," a closed circle of exchange relations among individuals in communities inhabiting a wide ring of islands.[10] What was distinctive in this closed circle, Malinowski observed, was the predominance of exchange of two articles—armlets and necklaces—which constantly traveled in opposite directions. In one direction around the Kula Ring, armlets traveled and were exchanged by individuals for necklaces moving in the opposite direction around the ring. In any particular exchange between individuals, then, an armshell would always be exchanged for a necklace.

In interpreting this unique exchange network, Malinowski was led to distinguish material, or economic, from nonmaterial, or symbolic, exchanges. In contrast with the utilitarians and Frazer, who were unable to conceptualize nonmaterial exchange relations, Malinowski recognized that the Kula was not an economic, or material, exchange network. Rather it was a symbolic exchange, cementing a web of social relationships: "One transaction does not finish the Kula relationship, the rule being 'once in the Kula, always in the Kula,' and a partnership between two men is a permanent and lifelong affair."[11] While purely economic transactions could occur within the rules of the Kula, the ceremonial exchange of armlets and necklaces was observed by Malinowski to be the principle "function" of the Kula.

The natives themselves, Malinowski emphasized, recognized the distinction between purely economic commodities and the symbolic signifi-

---

[9] Frazer, Preface to *Argonauts*.

[10] Bronislaw Malinowski, *Argonauts of the Western Pacific* (London: Routledge & Kegan Paul, 1922), p. 81.

[11] Ibid., pp. 82–83.

cance of armlets and necklaces. However, to distinguish economic from symbolic commodities should not be interpreted to mean that the Trobriand Islanders did not assign graded values to the symbolic commodities; indeed, they did make such gradations and used them to express and confirm the nature of the relationships among exchange partners as equals, superordinates, or subordinates. But, as Malinowski noted, "in all forms of [Kula] exchange in the Trobriands, there is not even a trace of gain, nor is there any reason for looking at it from the purely utilitarian and economic standpoint, since there is no enhancement of mutual utility through the exchange."[12] Rather, the motives behind the Kula were social psychological, for the exchanges in the Kula Ring were viewed by Malinowski to have implications for the "needs" of both individuals and society. From Malinowski's typical functionalist framework (see Chapter 2), he interpreted the Kula to meet "the fundamental impulse to display, to share, to bestow [and] the deep tendency to create social ties."[13] For Malinowski, then, an enduring social pattern such as the Kula Ring is considered to have positively functional consequences for satisfying *individual* psychological needs and *societal* needs for social integration and solidarity.

As Robert Merton and others were to emphasize (see Chapter 4), this form of functional analysis presents many logical difficulties. Despite the difficulties, however, Malinowski's analysis made several enduring contributions to modern exchange theory:

1. In Malinowski's words, "the meaning of the Kula will consist in being instrumental to dispel [the] conception of a rational being who wants nothing but to satisfy his simplest needs and does it according to the economic principle of least effort."[14]
2. Psychological rather than economic needs are the force that initiate and sustain exchange relations and are therefore critical in the explanation of social behavior.
3. Exchange relations can also have implications beyond two parties, for, as the Kula demonstrates, complex patterns of indirect exchange can operate to maintain extended and protracted social networks.
4. Symbolic exchange relations are the basic social process underlying both differentiation of ranks in a society and the integration of society into a cohesive and solidary whole.

---

[12] Ibid., p. 175.
[13] Ibid., p. 175.
[14] Ibid., p. 516.

Malinowski thus freed exchange theory from the limiting confines of utilitarianism by introducing the importance of symbolic exchanges for both individual psychological processes and patterns of social integration and solidarity. In so doing, he provided the conceptual base for two basic types of exchange perspectives, one emphasizing the importance of psychological processes, and the other stressing the significance of emergent cultural and structural forces on exchange relations. As subsequent chapters will document, modern sociological exchange theories appear to have diverged around these two nodes of emphasis in Malinowski's work.

Marcel Mauss and the Emergence of Exchange Structuralism

Reacting to what he perceived as Malinowski's tendency to overemphasize psychological over social needs, Marcel Mauss was led to reinterpret Malinowski's analysis of the Kula.[15] In this effort, he was to formulate the broad outlines of a "collectivistic," or structural exchange, perspective.[16] For Mauss, the critical question in examining an exchange network as complex as that of the Kula was:

> In primitive or archaic types of societies what is the principle whereby the gift received has to be repaid? What force is there in the thing which compels the recipient to make a return?[17]

The "force" compelling reciprocity was, for Mauss, society or the group. As he noted: "It is groups, and not individuals, which carry on exchange, make contracts, and are bound by obligations."[18] The individuals actually engaged in an exchange are "persons" who represent the moral codes of the group. Exchange transactions among individuals are conducted in accordance with the rules of the group, while, at the same time, reinforcing these rules and codes. Thus, for Mauss, the individual

---

[15] Marcel Mauss, *The Gift*, trans. Ian Cunnison (New York: Free Press, 1954) (originally published as *Essai sur le don en sociologie et anthropologie* [Paris: Presses universitaires de France, 1925]). It should be noted that Mauss rather consistently misinterpreted Malinowski's ethnography, but it is through such misinterpretation that he came to visualize a "structural" alternative to "psychological" exchange theories.

[16] In Peter Ekeh's excellent discussion of Mauss and Lévi-Strauss (*Social Exchange Theory*, pp. 55–122), the term "collectivist" is used in preference to "structural" and is posited as the alternative to "individualistic" or "psychological" exchange perspectives. I prefer the terms "structural" and "psychological"; thus, while I am indebted to Ekeh's discussion, these terms will be used to make essentially the same distinction. My preference for these terms will become more evident in subsequent chapters, since, in contrast with Ekeh's analysis, I consider Peter M. Blau and George C. Homans to have developed, respectively, structural and psychological theories. Ekeh considers the theories of both Blau and Homans to be "individualistic," or psychological.

[17] Mauss, *The Gift*, p. 1 (italics in original).

[18] Ibid., p. 3.

self-interest of utilitarians and the needs of Malinowski's psychologisms are replaced by a conception of individuals as mere representatives of social groups. In the end, exchange relations create, reinforce, and serve a group morality that is an entity *sui generis*, to borrow a famous phrase from Mauss's colleague, Émile Durkheim. Furthermore, in a vein similar to that of Frazer, once such a morality emerges and is reinforced by exchange activities, it comes to regulate other activities in the social life of a group, above and beyond particular exchange transactions.

While Mauss's work has received but scant attention from sociologists, he was the first to forge a reconciliation between the exchange principles of utilitarianism and the structural, or collectivistic, thought of Durkheim. In recognizing that exchange transactions give rise to and, at the same time, reinforce the normative structure of society, Mauss anticipated the structural position of some contemporary exchange theories, such as that advocated by Blau (see Chapter 12). Mauss's influence on modern theory, however, was indirect, for it is only through Lévi-Strauss's structuralism that the French collectivist tradition of Durkheim has had a major impact on both the psychological and structural exchange perspectives of contemporary sociological theorizing.

Claude Lévi-Strauss and Structuralism

In 1949, Claude Lévi-Strauss launched an analysis of cross-cousin marriage in his classic work, *The Elementary Structures of Kinship*.[19] In restating Durkheim's objections to utilitarians such as Spencer, Lévi-Strauss took exception to Frazer's utilitarian interpretation of cross-cousin marriage patterns. And in a manner similar to Mauss's opposition to Malinowski's emphasis on psychological needs, Lévi-Strauss developed the most sophisticated of the structural exchange perspectives to predate modern sociological theory's concern with exchange processes.[20]

In reacting to Frazer's interpretation of cross-cousin marriage, Lévi-Strauss first rejects the substance of Frazer's utilitarian conceptualization. Frazer, he notes, "depicts the poor Australian aborigine wondering how he is going to obtain a wife since he has no material goods with which to purchase her, and discovering exchange as the solution to this appar-

---

[19] Claude Lévi-Strauss, *The Elementary Structures of Kinship* (Boston: Beacon Press, 1969). This is a translation of Lévi-Strauss's 1967 revision of the original *Les structures élémentaires de la parenté* (Paris: Presses universitaires de France, 1949). The full impact of this work was probably never felt in sociology, since until 1969 it was not available in English. Yet, as will be noted in chapter 10 on Homans, it did have a profound impact on Homans' thinking, primarily because Homans felt compelled to reject Lévi-Strauss's analysis.

[20] See Ekeh's discussions for a more detailed analysis of Lévi-Strauss.

ently insoluble problem: 'men exchange their sisters in marriage because that was the cheapest way of getting a wife.' "[21] In contrast, Lévi-Strauss emphasizes that "it is the exchange which counts and not the things exchanged." Exchange for Lévi-Strauss must be viewed in terms of its functions for integrating the larger social structure. Lévi-Strauss then attacks Frazer's and the utilitarian's assumption that the first principles of social behavior are economic. Such an assumption flies in the face of the fact that social structure is an emergent phenomenon that operates in terms of its own irreducible laws and principles.

Lévi-Strauss also rejects psychological interpretations of exchange processes, especially the position advocated by behaviorists (see later section). In contrast with psychological behaviorists, who see little real difference between the laws of behavior among animals and humans, Lévi-Strauss emphasizes that humans possess a cultural heritage of norms and values which separates their behavior and organization into society apart from the behavior and organization of animal species. Human behavior is thus qualitatively different from animal behavior, especially with respect to social exchange. Animals are not guided by values and rules that specify when, where, and how they are to carry out social transactions. Unlike animals, humans carry with them into any exchange situation learned and institutionalized definitions of how they are to behave— thus assuring the principles of human exchange will be distinctive.

Furthermore, exchange is more than the result of psychological needs, even those that have been acquired through socialization. Exchange cannot be understood solely in terms of individual motives, because exchange relations are a reflection of patterns of social organization which exist as an entity, *sui generis*, to the psychological dispositions of individuals. Exchange behavior is thus regulated from without by norms and values, with the result that exchange processes can only be analyzed in terms of their "consequences," or "functions," for these norms and values.

In arguing this point of view, Lévi-Strauss posits several fundamental exchange principles: First, all exchange relations involve costs for individuals, but, in contrast with economic or psychological explanations of exchange, such costs are attributed to society—to its customs, rules, laws, and values. These features of society require behaviors that incur costs. Yet, individuals do not assess the costs to themselves, but to the "social order" requiring that costly behavior be emitted. Second, for all those scarce and valued resources in society—whether material objects,

---

[21] Lévi-Strauss, *Elementary Structures of Kinship*, p. 138.

such as wives, or symbolic resources like esteem and prestige—their distribution is regulated by norms and values. As long as resources are in abundant supply or not highly valued in a society, their distribution goes unregulated, but once they become scarce and highly valued, their distribution is soon institutionalized. Third, all exchange relations are regulated by a norm of reciprocity, requiring those receiving valued resources to bestow on their benefactors other valued resources. What is critical in Lévi-Strauss's conception of reciprocity is that there are various patterns of reciprocity specified by norms and values. In some situations, following norms of reciprocity requires "mutual" and direct rewarding of one's benefactor, whereas in other situations the reciprocity can be "univocal" involving diverse patterns of indirect exchange in which actors do not reciprocate directly but only through various third (fourth, fifth, and so forth) parties. Within these two general types of exchange reciprocity—mutual and univocal—numerous subtypes of exchange networks can be normatively regulated.

Lévi-Strauss's enumeration of these three principles offered for him a more useful set of concepts to describe cross-cousin marriage patterns. Now these patterns can be viewed in terms of their functions for the larger social structure. Particular marriage patterns and other features of kinship organization no longer need be interpreted merely as direct exchanges among individuals, but can be conceptualized as univocal exchanges between individuals and society. In freeing exchange from concepts forcing the analysis of only direct and mutual exchanges, Lévi-Strauss goes on to offer a tentative theory of societal integration and solidarity. His explanation represents an attempt to extend Durkheim's provocative analysis and involves an effort to indicate how various subtypes of direct and univocal exchange both reflect and reinforce different patterns of societal integration and organization.

This theory of integration is, in itself, of theoretical importance, but more significant for present purposes is Lévi-Strauss's impact on current sociological exchange perspectives. As will become evident in subsequent chapters, two of his concepts appear to have had a strong influence on modern sociological theory:

1. Various forms of social structure rather than individual motives are the critical variables in the analysis of exchange relations.
2. Exchange relations in social systems are frequently not restricted to direct interaction among individuals, but protracted into complex networks of indirect exchange. On the one hand, these exchange

processes are caused by patterns of social integration and organization; on the other hand, they promote diverse forms of such organization.

In looking back on the anthropological heritage, Lévi-Strauss's work can be seen to represent the culmination of reaction to economic utilitarianism as it was originally incorporated into anthropology by Frazer. Malinowski recognized the limitations of Frazer's analysis of only material or economic motives in direct exchange transactions. As the Kula Ring demonstrated, exchange could be generalized into protracted networks involving noneconomic motives which had implications for societal integration. Mauss drew explicit attention to the significance of social structure in regulating exchange processes and to the consequences of such processes for maintaining social structure. Finally, in this intellectual chain of events in anthropology, Lévi-Strauss began to indicate how different types of direct and indirect exchange were linked to different patterns of social organization. While this intellectual heritage has influenced both the substance and strategy of exchange theory in sociology, it has done so only after considerable modification of assumptions and concepts by a particular strain of psychology: behaviorism.

PSYCHOLOGICAL BEHAVIORISM AND EXCHANGE THEORY

Psychological behaviorism as a theoretical perspective has historically drawn its principles from the observation of subhuman, animal behavior. From the first observations of Pavlov on the responses of dogs to a light that had previously been associated with food to the experimental manipulations of pigeons and mice in the famous Skinner box, it has been assumed by many behaviorists that the elementary principles describing animal behavior will form the core of a deductive system of propositions explaining human behavior. Of critical importance in understanding the position of some behaviorists is the presumption that it is unnecessary to delve into the "black box" of human thought and cognition, since it is quite possible and desirable to study only *overt* behavior as a response to *observable* stimuli in the environment. Although this extreme position is not accepted by all behaviorists, it has been the guiding assumption behind the work of the scholars, such as B. F. Skinner,[22] who have had the most influence on sociological exchange theory.

----

[22] See, for example, B. F. Skinner, *The Behavior of Organisms* (New York: Appleton-Century-Crofts, 1938); and B. F. Skinner, *Science and Human Behavior* (New York: Macmillan, 1953).

In many ways, behaviorism is an extreme variant of utilitarianism, since it operates on the principle that animals and humans are both reward-seeking organisms that pursue alternatives that will yield the most reward and least punishment. Rewards are simply a way of rephrasing the economist's concept of "utility," while "punishment" is a somewhat revised notion of "cost." For the behaviorist, reward is any behavior that reinforces or meets the needs of the organism, whereas punishment is behavior of the organism, or of other organisms in the environment, which inhibits an organism from meeting its needs—most typically, the need to avoid pain.

Modern exchange theories have borrowed from behaviorists the notion of reward and used it to reinterpret the utilitarian exchange heritage. In place of utility, the concept of reward has been inserted, primarily because it allows exchange theorists to view behavior as motivated by psychological needs. However, the utilitarian concept of cost appears to have been retained in preference to the behaviorist's vague formulation of "punishment," since the notion of "cost" allows exchange theorists to visualize more completely the alternative rewards that organisms forego in seeking to achieve a particular reward. Seemingly, "punishment" is too closely associated with the concept of "pain," which does not necessarily allow for the conceptualization of humans as choice-making organisms who not only seek to avoid pain, but who also can choose among several rewarding alternatives in most situations.

Despite these modifications of the basic concepts of behaviorism, several of its key theoretical generalizations have been incorporated, with relatively little change, into some forms of sociological exchange theory:

1. In any given situation, organisms will emit those behaviors that will yield the most reward and least punishment.
2. Organisms will repeat those behaviors which have proved rewarding in the past.
3. Organisms will repeat behaviors in situations that are similar to those in the past in which behaviors were rewarded.
4. Present stimuli that on past occasions have been associated with rewards will evoke behaviors similar to those emitted in the past.
5. Repetition of behaviors will occur only as long as they continue to yield rewards.
6. An organism will display emotion if a behavior that has previously been rewarded in the same, or similar, situation suddenly goes unrewarded.
7. The more an organism receives rewards from a particular behavior,

the less rewarding that behavior becomes (due to satiation) and the more likely the organism to emit alternative behaviors in search of other rewards.

Since these principles were discovered in laboratory situations where experimenters typically manipulated the environment of the organism, it is difficult to visualize the experimental situation as *interaction*. The tight control of the situation by the experimenter precludes the possibility that the animal will affect significantly the responses of the experimenter. This fact has forced modern exchange theories using behaviorist principles to incorporate the utilitarian's concern with "transaction," or "exchanges." In this way humans can be seen as mutually affecting each other's opportunities for rewards. In contrast with animals in a Skinner box or some similar laboratory situation, humans exchange rewards, with the result that each person represents a potentially rewarding stimulus situation for the other.

As sociological exchange theorists have attempted to apply behaviorist principles to the study of human behavior, they have inevitably confronted the problem of "the black box": Humans differ from laboratory animals in their greater ability to engage in a wide variety of complex cognitive processes. Indeed, as the utilitarians were the first to emphasize, what is distinctly human is the capacity to abstract, to calculate, to project outcomes, to weight alternatives, and to perform a wide number of other covert cognitive manipulations. Furthermore, in borrowing behaviorist's concepts, contemporary exchange theorists have also had to introduce the concepts of an introspective psychology and structural sociology. Humans not only think in complex ways; their thinking is emotional and circumscribed by many social and cultural forces (first incorporated into the exchange theories of Mauss and Lévi-Strauss). Once it is recognized that behaviorist principles must incorporate concepts denoting both internal psychological processes and constraints of social structure and culture, it is also necessary to visualize exchange as frequently transcending the mutually rewarding activities of individuals in direct interaction. The organization of behavior by social structure and culture, coupled with humans' complex cognitive abilities, allows protracted and indirect exchange networks to exist.

In looking back upon the impact of behaviorism on some forms of contemporary exchange theory, then, a curious marriage of concepts and principles appears to have occurred. While the vocabulary and general principles of behaviorism are clearly evident, the concepts have been redefined and the principles altered to incorporate the insights of the early utilitarians as well as the anthropological reaction to utilitarianism. The end result has been for proponents of an exchange perspective employing behaviorist concepts and principles to abandon much of what made behaviorism a unique perspective as they have dealt with the complexities introduced by human cognitive capacities and their organization into socio-cultural groupings.

MODERN EXCHANGE THEORY: A PREVIEW

Exchange theory is now one of the most prominent theoretical perspectives in sociology. A number of exchange perspectives have emerged in recent decades. Typically, they begin with inspiration from either the behaviorist tradition in psychology or the utilitarian heritage in economic theory. But as will become evident, these two traditions merge in modern exchange theory. They address similar problems and have a similar view of how and why society is possible.

In the chapters to follow, two prominent theorists from the behaviorist and economic traditions will be examined. The "exchange behaviorism" of George C. Homans is explored first. Then, the "exchange structuralism" of Peter M. Blau is presented. And finally, in a chapter on the future of exchange theory, the issues, problems, and efforts at their resolution will be examined.

11

EXCHANGE
BEHAVIORISM:
GEORGE C. HOMANS

One of the most eloquent contemporary spokesmen for the exchange perspective is George C. Homans. In a long career devoted to theoretical explanation, Homans has increasingly advocated a particular strategy for building sociological theory which has become predicated upon exchange principles. Much of Homans's advocacy is directed toward providing an alternative to Talcott Parsons' theoretical strategy and conceptual edifice. Yet curiously, in light of the widespread acceptance of criticisms against Parsonian functionalism, Homans' exchange scheme has been subjected to a barrage of criticism usually reserved only for functional theorizing. Interestingly, this criticism comes not just from "functional" theorists, but from all theoretical camps. The purpose of this chapter, therefore, is to trace the development of Homans' exchange perspective and then to explicate and analyze the reasons behind the widespread criticisms of the perspective.

HOMANS ON THEORY BUILDING IN SOCIOLOGY

The Early Inductive Strategy

By 1950, with the publication of *The Human Group*, Homans' work revealed a clear commitment to an inductive strategy for building sociological theory.[1] In studies ranging from the analysis of a work group in a factory and a street gang, to the kinship system of a primitive

---

[1] From *The Human Group* by George C. Homans, copyright, 1950, by Harcourt Brace Jovanovich, Inc., and reprinted with their permission.

216

society and the structure of an entire New England community, he stressed the importance of observing people's actual behaviors and activities in various types of groups. By observing what people actually do, it would be possible to develop concepts that are "attached" to the ongoing processes of social systems. Such concepts were termed by Homans "first-order abstractions," since they merely represent "names" that observers use to signify a "single class of observations" in a group. Homans chose the words "first-order abstractions" carefully. He wanted to emphasize their difference from the "second-order abstractions" commonly employed by sociologists. As distinct from the abstractions he prefers, second-order abstractions refer to several classes of observations and are thereby somewhat detached from ongoing events in actual groups. For example, "status" and "role" are favorite concepts used by sociologists to denote processes in groups, but upon careful reflection, it is evident that one does not observe directly a "status" or "role"; rather, they are highly abstract names which subsume numerous types and classes of events occurring in groups.

The typical practice of jumping to second-order abstractions in building theory was viewed by Homans as premature:

> [Sociologists should initially] attempt to climb down from the big words of social science, at least as far as common sense observation. Then, if we wish, we can start climbing up again, but this time with a ladder we can depend on.[2]

In constructing a firm "bottom rung" to the abstraction ladder, Homans introduced three first-order abstractions that provided labels or names to the actual events occurring in groups: activities, interaction, and sentiments. Activities pertain to what people do in a given situation; interaction denotes the process in which one unit of activity stimulates a unit of activity in another person; and sentiments refer to the internal psychological states of people engaged in activities and interaction.

The three first-order abstractions, or "elements," as Homans was fond of calling them, were seen as existing within an "external system." For Homans, this "external system" represented the environmental parameters of a particular group under study. As he was to later label this analytical approach, the external system represented the "givens" of a particular situation, which, for the purposes at hand, are not examined extensively. Of more interest, however, was the "internal system," which operated within the constraints imposed by the external system and which was composed of the interrelated activities, interactions, and senti-

---

[2] Ibid., p. 13.

ments of group members. The fact that activities, interactions, and sentiments were interrelated was of great analytical significance: Changes
in one element led to changes in the other elements.

Of critical importance in the analysis of internal systems is the process
of "elaboration" in which new patterns of organization among activities,
interaction, and sentiments are constantly emerging by virtue of their
interrelatedness with each other and with the external system. A group
thus "elaborates itself, complicates itself, beyond the demands of the
original situation"; in so doing, it brings about new types of activities,
forms of interaction, and types of sentiments.

In *The Human Group*, Homans' strategy was to present a descriptive
summary of five case studies on diverse groups. From each summary,
Homans attempted to incorporate the "elements" of the internal system
into propositions that described the empirical regularities he "observed"
in the case study.[3] As he proceeded in his summaries of the case studies,
Homans attempted to substantiate the generalizations from one study
in the next, while at the same time using each successive study as a
source for additional generalizations. With this strategy, it was hoped
that a body of interrelated generalizations describing the various ways
different types of groups elaborate their internal systems of activities,
interactions, and sentiments would emerge. In this way, the first rungs
of the abstraction ladder used in sociological theorizing would be "de-
pendable," providing a firm base for subsequent theorizing at a more
abstract level.

For example, in Homans' summary of the now-famous Bank Wiring
Room in the Hawthorne Western Electric Plant, Homans observed these
regularities:[4] (1) If the frequency of interaction between two or more
persons increases, the degree of their liking for one another will increase,
and vice versa.[5] (2) Persons whose sentiments of liking for one another
increase will express these sentiments in increased activity, and vice
versa.[6] (3) The more frequently persons interact with one another, the
more alike their activities and their sentiments tend to become, and

---

[3] In Homans' work, he rarely makes direct observations himself. Rather, he has tended
to rely upon the observations of others, making from their reports inferences about
events. As would be expected, Homans has often been criticized for accepting too
readily the imprecise, and perhaps inaccurate, observations of others as an inductive
base for theorizing.

[4] This extended example is adapted from Mulkay's discussion of Homans' propositions
in M. J. Mulkay, *Functionalism and Exchange and Theoretical Strategy* (New York:
Schocken Books, 1971), pp. 135–41. As was done by Mulkay, some of Homans' propositions are reworded in an effort at simplification.

[5] Homans, *Human Group*, p. 112.

[6] Ibid., p. 118.

vice versa.[7] (4) The higher the rank of a person within a group, the more nearly his activities conform to the norms of the group, and vice versa.[8] (5) The higher the person's social rank, the wider will be the range of his interactions.[9]

These propositions describe some of the group-elaboration processes that Homans "observed" in the Bank Wiring Room. Propositions 1 and 2 summarize Homans' observation that the more the workers in the Bank Wiring Room interacted, the more they appeared to like one another, which, in turn, seemed to cause further interactions above and beyond the work requirements of the external system. Such elaboration of interactions, sentiments, and activities was also seen as resulting in the differentiation of subgroups which revealed their own levels of output, topics of conversation, and patterns of work assistance. This tendency is denoted by proposition 3. Another pattern of differentiation in the Bank Wiring Room is described by proposition 4, whereby the ranking of individuals and subgroups was viewed to occur when group members compared their activities with those of other members and the output norms of the group. Proposition 5 describes the tendency in the Bank Wiring Room of high-ranking members to interact more frequently with all members of the group, offering more on-the-job assistance.

Having tentatively established these, and other, empirical regularities in the Bank Wiring Room, Homans then analyzed the equally famous Norton Street Gang, described in William Whyte's *Street Corner Society*. In this second case study, Homans followed his strategy of confirming his earlier propositions, while inducing further generalizations: (6) The higher a person's social rank, the larger will be the number of persons that originate interaction for him or her, either directly or through intermediaries.[10] (7) The higher a person's social rank, the larger will be the number of persons toward whom interaction is initiated, either directly or through intermediaries.[11] (8) The more nearly equal in social rank a number of people are, the more frequently they will interact with one another.[12]

Propositions 6 and 7 are simply corollaries of proposition 5. It follows, almost by definition, that those with a wide range of interactions will receive and initiate more interaction. However, propositions 6 and 7

---

[7] Ibid., p. 120.
[8] Ibid., p. 141.
[9] Ibid., p. 145.
[10] Ibid., p. 182.
[11] Ibid.
[12] Ibid., p. 184.

were induced separately from Homans's "observation" that Doc, the leader of the Norton Street Gang, was in the center of a complex network of communication. Such a pattern of communication was not observable in the Bank Wiring Room because stable leadership ranks had not emerged. Proposition 8 describes another process Homans observed in groups with clear leadership: The internal system tended to differentiate into super- and subordinate subgroups, whose members appeared to interact more with each other than those of higher or lower rank.

After using the group-elaboration processes in the Norton Street Gang to confirm and supplement the propositions induced from the Bank Wiring Room, Homans then examined the Tikopia family, as described in Raymond Firth's famous ethnography. As with the Norton Street Gang, the Tikopia family system was used to confirm earlier propositions and as a field from which to induce further propositions: (9) The more frequently persons interact with one another, when no one of them originates interaction with much greater frequency than the others, the greater is their liking for one another and their feeling of ease in one another's presence.[13] (10) When two persons interact with one another, the more frequently one of the two originates interaction for the other, the stronger will be the latter's sentiment of respect (or hostility), and the more nearly will the frequency of interaction be kept to a minimum.[14]

These propositions reveal another facet of Homans's inductive strategy. They establish some conditions under which proposition 1 will hold. In proposition 1, Homans noted that increased interaction between two persons increases their liking, but in the Tikopia family system Homans "discovered" that this generalization holds true only under conditions where authority of one person over another is low. In the Tikopia family system, brothers revealed sentiments of liking as a result of their frequent interactions, primarily because they did not have authority over one another. However, frequent interaction with their father, who did have authority, was tense, because the father initiated the interaction and because it usually involved the exercise of his authority.

Perhaps less critical than the substance of propositions 9 and 10 is the strategy they reveal. Homans had used an inductive technique to develop a large number of propositions that described empirical regularities. By continually "testing" them in different types of groups, he was able to "confirm" them, or, as is the case with propositions 9 and 10, qualify these earlier propositions. By following this strategy, Homans

---

[13] Ibid., p. 243.
[14] Ibid., p. 247.

argued that it was possible to develop a large body of empirical statements that reveal the form: y varies with x, under C_1, C_2, C_3, . . . , C_n. Stated in this form and with a clear connection to actual events in human groupings, such propositions would encourage the development of more abstract concepts and theoretical statements. In addition, Homans hoped, these statements would be induced from a firm empirical footing—a footing that would allow the abstract statements of sociology to be tested against the facts of ongoing group life.

In recent decades, however, Homans appears to have abandoned this strategy. In its place, he has advocated a deductive approach. Ostensibly, Homans has become concerned with explanations of empirical regularities, such as those described in *The Human Group* and in the research literature that has accumulated since 1950. As will be examined in some detail shortly, Homans views explanation as involving the construction of deductive systems of propositions. This fact will help account for Homans' concern with *deducing to*, as opposed to *inducing from*, empirical findings. However, the critics of Homans' recent theoretical strategy, and the exchange perspective it has inspired, contend that Homans' switch in strategy stems from basic problems contained in his inductive efforts. Discussion of these problems might ordinarily be omitted, since primary concern in this chapter is with Homans' exchange perspective, regardless of why he abandoned the strategy advocated in *The Human Group*. But, as the critics argue, Homans repeats many of the same conceptual mistakes of his inductive strategy in his deductive approach to theory building.

An inductive strategy to theory building requires two important tasks to be continually performed: (*a*) Generalizations induced from one body of data should be tested against other data so that propositions abstracted from one study can be confirmed, altered, expanded, and refined in another (much as Homans did in his five case studies in *The Human Group*). (*b*) The first-order abstractions of inductive theory should continually be refined so that the propositions of such theorizing may offer precise indicators of actual events in the empirical world and thereby provide higher-order concepts and statements with a firm empirical base. After *The Human Group*, Homans makes few attempts to perform either of these tasks, with the result that the generalizations of *The Human Group* provide a poor set of generalizations for either an inductive or a deductive strategy.

The difficulties in *The Human Group* stem primarily from the imprecision of the critical variables of his propositions: activity, interaction, and sentiments. Homans's attempt to climb down from the "big words" and abstractions of social science is not complete. In fact, his first-order abstractions are more complex and abstract than he admits. For example, the term "sentiment" is used to encompass "affection," "sympathy," "rage," "thirst," "hunger," "nostalgia," "scorn," or any "internal state of the human body."[15] The diversity of phenomena subsumed under the concept of "sentiment" would seemingly make it highly abstract and in need of refinement if various types of sentiment are to refer, in Homans' words, to "a single class of observable data." From the logic of an inductive strategy, then, Homans should have begun the difficult task of developing true first-order abstractions, with clear empirical referents, to be incorporated into a more precise body of empirical propositions. Instead, Homans chose to bypass this task and began to "explain" in the vocabulary of deductive theory a body of empirical generalizations that were in need of considerable refinement.[16]

The Recent Deductive Strategy

The logic of Homans' inductive strategy would have dictated that, after reasonable attempts at improving the precision of his first-order concepts and propositions, he make an effort to induce more abstract and general propositions from a survey of his own (and others') empirical generalizations. Whether due to the inadequacy of his empirical generalizations or a new found excitement with abstract exchange principles, Homans adopts a much simpler strategy for developing sociological theorizing, that is, borrowing from economics and psychology some basic principles that could become the axioms of a deductive system of theoretical statements. In an effort to maintain the illusion of continuity between the strategy of *The Human Group* and that now advocated, Homans has chosen to call the development of abstract exchange principles "induction":

> The process of borrowing or inventing the more general propositions I call *induction*, whether or not it is the induction of the philosophers; the process of deriving the empirical propositions from the more general ones I call explanation, and this is the *explanation* of the philosophers.[17]

Assuredly, Homans' notion of induction is not that of the philosophers, nor that of *The Human Group*. But his portrayal of explanation is that

---

[15] Ibid., pp. 36–40.

[16] Mulkay, *Functionalism and Exchange*, pp. 161–63 and Pitirim Sorokin, *Sociological Theories of Today* (New York: Harper & Row, 1966), pp. 34–36, are particularly unkind to Homans in this regard.

[17] From *Social Behavior; Its Elementary Forms* by George C. Homans, © 1961, by Harcourt Brace Jovanovich, Inc., and reprinted with their permission.

of some philosophers—especially those advocating a natural science interpretation of scientific explanation. Since it is this somewhat distorted
notion of induction and more accurate conception of explanation that
has guided the development of Homans' exchange perspective, it is wise
to discern just what Homans now considers explanation in the social
sciences to be.[18]

Since the publication of *The Human Group*, Homans has mounted
an increasingly pointed criticism of sociological theorizing, with the hope
that "we bring what we say about theory into line with what we actually
do, and so put an end to our intellectual hypocrisy." First on the road
out of "intellectual hypocrisy" is a rejection of the Parsonian strategy
of developing systems of concepts and categorical schemes:

> Some students get so much intellectual security out of such a scheme,
> because it allows them to give names to, and to pigeonhole, almost any
> social phenomenon, that they are hesitant to embark on the dangerous
> waters of actually saying something about the relations between the phe-
> nomena—because they must actually take the risk of being found wrong.[19]

For Homans, a more proper strategy—one that allows theories to
be proven wrong—is the construction of deductive systems of propositions. At the top of the deductive system are the general axioms, from
which lower-order propositions are logically deduced. The lowest-order
propositions in the scheme are those composed of first-order abstractions
that describe actual events in the empirical world. Because these empirical
generalizations are logically related to a hierarchy of increasingly abstract
propositions, culminating in logical articulation with the axioms, the
empirical generalizations are assumed to be explained by the axioms.
Thus, for Homans, to have deduced logically an empirical regularity
from a set of more general propositions and axioms is to have *explained*
the regularity.[20]

---

[18] Ibid.

[19] George C. Homans, *The Nature of Social Science* (New York: Harcourt, Brace,
& World, 1967), p. 13. Parsons has replied that such systems of concepts can be theory:
"I emphatically dispute this [deductive theory] is all that can legitimately be called
theory. In biology, for example, I should certainly regard the basic classificatory schemes
of taxonomy, for example in particular the comparative anatomy of vertebrates, to be
theoretical. Moreover very important things are, with a few additional facts, explained
on such levels such as the inability of organisms with lungs and no gills to live for
long periods under water" (Talcott Parsons, "Levels of Organization and the Mediation
of Social Interaction," *Sociological Inquiry* 34 [Spring 1964]: 219–20).

[20] Homans has championed this conception of theory in a large number of works;
see, for example, Homans, *Social Behavior;* Homans, *Nature of Social Science;* George
C Homans, "Fundamental Social Processes," in *Sociology,* ed. N. J. Smelser (New
York: John Wiley & Sons, 1967), pp. 27–78; George C. Homans, "Contemporary Theory

THE EXCHANGE MODEL

Sources of Homans' Psychological Exchange Perspective

Homans' exchange scheme first surfaced as a polemical reaction to Lévi-Strauss' structural analysis of cross-cousin marriage patterns. In collaboration with David Schneider, Homans in 1955 previewed what were to become the persistent themes in his recent writings: (1) a skeptical view of any form of functional theorizing, (2) an emphasis on psychological principles as the axioms of social theory, and (3) a preoccupation with exchange-theoretic concepts.[21]

In their assessment of Lévi-Strauss' exchange functionalism, Homans and Schneider took exception to virtually all that made Lévi-Strauss' theory an important contribution to social theory. First, the conceptualization of different forms of indirect, generalized exchange was rejected. In so conceptualizing exchange, it was argued, Lévi-Strauss "thinned the meaning out of it." Second, the Lévi-Straussian position that different forms of exchange symbolically reaffirmed and integrated different patterns of social organization was questioned, for an "institution is what it is because it results from the drives, or meets the immediate needs, of individuals or subgroups within a society."[22] The end result of this rejection of Lévi-Strauss's thought was for Homans and Schneider to argue that exchange theory must initially emphasize face-to-face interaction, focus primarily on limited and direct exchanges among individuals, and recognize the psychological (as opposed to social structural) impetus to exchange relations.

With this extreme polemic against the anthropological tradition that had flourished as a reaction to utilitarianism, Homans resurrected the utilitarian's concern with individual self-interest in the conceptual trappings of psychological behaviorism. For indeed, as Homans and Schneider emphasized: "We may call this an individual self-interest theory, if we remember that interests may be other than economic."[23] As was to become evident by the early 1960s, this self-interest theory was to be

in Sociology," in *Handbook of Modern Sociology,* ed. R. E. L. Faris (Chicago: Rand-McNally, 1964), pp. 251–77; and George C. Homans, "Bringing Men Back In," *American Sociological Review* 29 (December 1964): 809–18. For an early statement of his position, see George C. Homans "Social Behavior as Exchange," *American Journal of Sociology* 63 (August): 597–606.

21 George C. Homans and David M. Schneider, *Marriage, Authority, and Final Causes: A Study of Unilateral Cross-Cousin Marriage* (New York: Free Press, 1955). There are, however, hints of this interest in exchange theory in Homans' first major work, *English Villagers of the 13th Century* (New York: Russell & Russell, 1941).

22 Homans and Schneider, *Marriage,* p. 15.

23 Ibid.

cast in the behaviorist language of B. F. Skinner. Given Homans' commitment to axiomatic theorizing and his concern with face-to-face interaction
among individuals, it was perhaps inevitable that he would look toward
Skinner and borrow concepts and principles from his colleague's controlled laboratory experiments with animals.[24] Stripped of its subtlety,
as Homans prefers, Skinnerian behaviorism states, as its basic principle,
that if an animal has a need it will perform activities that in the past
have satisfied that need. A first corollary to this principle is that organisms
will attempt to avoid unpleasant experiences, but will endure limited
amounts of such experiences as a cost in emitting the behaviors that
satisfy an overriding need. A second corollary is that organisms will
continue emitting certain behaviors only as long as they continue to
produce desired and expected effects. A third corollary of Skinnerian
psychology emphasizes that as needs are satisfied by a particular behavior,
animals are less likely to emit the behavior. A fourth corollary states
that if in the recent past a behavior has brought rewards and if these
rewards suddenly stop, the organism will appear angry and gradually
cease emitting the behavior that formerly satisfied its needs. A final
corollary holds that if an event has consistently occurred at the same
time as a behavior that was rewarded or punished, the event becomes
a stimulus and is likely to produce the behavior or its avoidance.

These principles were derived from behavioral psychologists' highly
controlled observations of animals, whose needs could be inferred from
deprivations imposed by the investigators. Although human needs are
much more difficult to ascertain than those of laboratory pigeons and
mice and despite the fact that humans interact in groupings that defy
experimental controls, Homans perceived that the principles of operant
psychology could be applied to the explanation of human behavior in
both simple and complex groupings. One of the most important adjustments of Skinnerian principles to fit the facts of human social organization
involves the recognition that needs are satisfied by other people and
that people reward and punish each other. In contrast with Skinner's
animals, which only indirectly interact with Skinner through the apparatus of the laboratory and which have little ability to reward Skinner

---

[24] Homans, *Social Behavior*, pp. 1–83. For an excellent summary of the Skinnerian
principles incorporated into Homans' scheme, see Richard L. Simpson, "Theories of
Social Exchange" (Morristown, N.Y.: General Learning Press, 1972), pp. 3–4. As an
interesting aside, Peter P. Ekeh, *Social Exchange Theory and the Two Sociological
Traditions* (Cambridge: Harvard University Press, 1975) has argued that had Homans
not felt so compelled to reject Lévi-Strauss, he would not have embraced Skinnerian
principles. Ekeh goes so far as to offer a hypothetical list of axioms that Homans would
have postulated, had he not cast his scheme into the terminology of behaviorism.

(except perhaps to confirm his principles), humans constantly give and take, or exchange, rewards and punishments.[25]

The conceptualization of human behavior as exchanges of rewards (and punishments) among interacting individuals led Homans to incorporate, in altered form, the first principle of elementary economics: Humans rationally calculate the long-range consequences of their actions in a marketplace and attempt to maximize their material profits in their market transactions. However, as Homans emphasized, this simple economic principle needed reformulation:

> Indeed we are out to rehabilitate the economic man. The trouble with him was not that he was economic, that he used resources to some advantage, but that he was antisocial and materialistic, interested only in money and material goods and ready to sacrifice even his old mother to get them.[26]

Thus, to be an appropriate explanation of human behavior, this basic economic assumption needed to be altered in four ways: (a) People do not always attempt to maximize profits; they seek only to make some profit in exchange relations. (b) Humans do not usually make either long-run or rational calculations in exchanges, for, in everyday life, "the theory of Games is good advice for human behavior but a poor description of it." (c) The things exchanged involve more than money, but other commodities, including approval, esteem, compliance, love, affection, and other less materialistic goods. (d) The "marketplace" is not a separate domain in human exchanges, for all interaction involves individuals exchanging rewards (and punishments) and seeking to derive profits.

The Basic Concepts

Homans has altered somewhat his concepts since the original publication of his theory. He has sought to eliminate terms, such as "activity," "interaction," and "sentiment," that presented so many problems in *The Human Group*. He has also sought to refine the theory and respond to the charges of his critics. These changes culminated in a revised

---

[25] For a more detailed analysis of this point and the problems it presents, see Richard M. Emerson, "Social Exchange Theory," in *Annual Review At Sociology*, 2 (Palo Alto: Annual Reviews, Inc., 1976).

[26] Homans, *Social Behavior*, p. 79. Kenneth Boulding ("An Economist's View of 'Social Behavior: Its Elementary Forms,'" *American Journal of Sociology* 67 [January 1962]: 458) has noted that in Homans' work "economic man is crossed with the psychological pigeon to produce what the unkind might call the Economic Pigeon theory of human interaction." For a more detailed and serious analysis of Homans' meshing of elementary economics and psychology, see Ekeh, *Social Exchange Theory*, pp. 162–71.

edition of his major exchange work, *Social Behavior: Its Elementary Forms.*[27]

In this new edition, Homans abandons efforts to show continuity with the inductive effort in *The Human Group.* His concepts thus become fewer and more explicitly in the behaviorist tradition: *stimulus*—cues in the environment to which an organism responds with action; *action*—behaviors emitted by organisms directed at getting rewards and avoiding punishments; *reward*—the capacity to bestow gratification, or to meet the needs of an organism, that a stimulus possesses; *punishment*—the capacity to harm, injure, or to block the satisfaction of needs that a stimulus possesses; *value*—the degree of reward that a stimulus possesses; *cost*—rewards forgone, or punishment incurred, in engaging in one line of action; *perception*—the capacity to perceive, weigh, and assess rewards and costs; *expectation*—the level of rewards, punishments, or costs that an organism has come to associate with a particular stimulus.[28]

These are the key concepts used in Homans' statement of his "elementary exchange principles."[29] He adds other concepts when applying these principles to human behavior. These new concepts, however, merely extend those listed here.

Elementary Principles of Social Behavior

Homans labels each proposition in terms of the variables that each highlights.[30] These labels are listed alongside the appropriate propositions:

1. *Success Proposition:* For all actions taken by persons, the more often a particular action of a person is rewarded, the more likely the person is to perform that action.
2. *Stimulus Proposition:* If in the past the occurrence of a particular stimulus, or set of stimuli, has been the occasion on which a person's action has been rewarded, then the more similar the present stimuli

---

[27] George Casper Homans, *Social Behavior: Its Elementary Forms* (New York: Harcourt Brace Jovanovich, 1974). In contrast to the earlier edition of *The Structure of Sociological Theory,* which concentrated on the earlier edition of Homans' book, I have relied almost exclusively on the revised edition of *Social Behavior.* For a discussion of Homans' original formulation of his exchange theory, the reader is referred to pp. 235–47 of *The Structure of Sociological Theory* (Homewood, Ill.: The Dorsey Press, 1974).

[28] *Social Behavior,* pp. 15–47.

[29] The concept of "cost" does not appear in Homans' actual axioms, but it is so prominent in his scheme that it is listed here along with the other important concepts of his theoretical scheme.

[30] See *Social Behavior,* pp. 11–68.

are to the past ones, the more likely the person is to perform the action, or some similar action, now.

3.   *Value Proposition:* The more valuable to a person is the result of his action, the more likely he is to perform the action.

4.   *Deprivation-Satiation Proposition:* The more often in the recent past a person has received a particular reward, the less valuable any further unit of that reward becomes for him.

5.   *Aggression-Approval Propositions:* (*a*) When a person's action does not receive the reward he expected, or receives punishment he did not expect, he will be angry; he becomes more likely to perform aggressive behavior, and the results of such behavior become more valuable to him. (*b*) When a person's action receives the reward he expected, especially greater reward than expected, or does not receive punishment he expected, he will be pleased; he becomes more likely to perform approving behavior, and the results of such behavior become more valuable to him.

In propositions 1 through 3, the principles of Skinnerian psychology are restated in greatly simplified form. The more valuable an activity (3), the more frequently or often such activity is rewarded (1), and the more a situation approximates one in which activity has been rewarded in the past (2), then the more likely a particular activity will be emitted. Proposition 4 indicates the condition under which the first three fall into temporary abeyance. In accordance with the reinforcement principle of satiation or the economic law of marginal utility, humans eventually define as less valuable rewarded activities and begin to emit other activities in search of different rewards (again, however, in accordance with the principles enumerated in propositions 1–3). Proposition 5 introduces a more complicated set of conditions which qualifies propositions 1 through 4. From Skinner's observation that pigeons reveal "anger" and "frustration" when they do not receive an expected reward, Homans reasons that humans will probably reveal basically the same behavior.

In addition to these principles, Homans introduces a "rationality proposition" which summarizes the stimulus, success, and value propositions:

6.   *Rationality Proposition:* In choosing between alternative actions, a person will choose that one for which, as perceived by him at the time, the value of the result, multiplied by the probability of getting that result, is greater.

To translate: People make calculations about various alternative lines of action. They "perceive" or calculate the value of the rewards that might be yielded by various actions. But they also temper this calculation in terms of the perceptions of how probable the receipt of rewards will be. Low probability of receiving highly valued rewards would lower their reward potential. Conversely, high probability of receiving a lower valued reward increases their over-all reward potential. This relationship can be stated by the following formula:

$$\text{Action} = \text{Value} \times \text{Probability}$$

People are, Homans asserts, rational in the sense that they are likely to emit that behavior, or action, among alternatives in which value on the right side of the equation is largest. For example, if $Action_1$ is highly valued (say, 10) but the probability of getting it by emitting $Action_1$ is low (.20) and if $Action_2$ is less valued (say, 5), but the probability of receiving it is greater (.50) than $Action_1$, the actor will emit $Action_2$ (because $10 \times .20 = 2$ yields less reward than $5 \times .50 = 2.5$).

This proposition was implicit in Homans' earlier exchange theory, but now, he has made it explicit. This proposition, as noted above, summarizes the implications of the stimulus, value, and success propositions, because it indicates why actors would choose one stimulus situation which has been rewarding over another. And in fact, Homans had tended to use it in his explanations long before he made it explicit.[31] Such a proposition re-evokes utilitarian notions of rational calculation in the vocabulary of psychological behaviorism.

These basic principles or "laws" of human behavior are intended to explain, in the sense of deductive explanation, patterns of human organization. As is obvious, they are psychological in nature. What is more, these psychological axioms constitute the only general sociological propositions, since "there are no general sociological propositions that hold good of all societies or social groups as such."[32]

However, the fact that psychological propositions are the most general does not make any less relevant or important sociological propositions stating the relationships among group properties or between group properties and those of individuals. On the contrary, these are the very propositions that are to be deduced from the psychological axioms. Thus, sociological propositions will be conspicuous in the deductive system emanating from the psychological principles. Homans stresses that sociology will finally bring what it says about theory into what it actually

---

[31] See the earlier edition of *The Structure of Sociological Theory* and my "Building Social Theory: Some Questions about Homans' Strategy," *Pacific Sociological Review* 20 (April 1977): 203–20.

[32] Homans, "Bringing Men Back In."

does when it arranges both abstract sociological statements and specific empirical generalizations in a deductive system with the psychological axioms at its top. For, as he continually emphasizes, to deduce propositions from one another is to explain them.

Homans' Construction of Deductive Systems

The fact that the basic axioms to be used in sociological explanation seem to be "obvious truisms" should not be a cause for dismay. Too often, Homans insists, social scientists assume that the basic laws of social organization will be more esoteric—and certainly less familiar— since for them the game of science involves the startling discovery of new, unfamiliar, and, presumably, profound principles. In reference to these social scientists, Homans writes:

> All this familiarity has bred contempt, a contempt that has got in the way of the development of social science. Its fundamental propositions seem so obvious as to be boring, and an intellectual, by definition a wit and a man of the world, will go to great lengths to avoid the obvious.[33]

However, if the first principles of sociology are obvious, despite the best efforts of "scientists" to the contrary, Homans suggests that sociology cease its vain search for the esoteric and begin constructing deductive systems that recognize the fact that the most general propositions are not only psychological but familiar. In fact, if sociologists crave complexity, this task should certainly be satisfying, since the deductive systems connecting these "simple" principles to observed empirical regularities will be incredibly complex.

Unfortunately, Homans himself has never offered a well-developed explanation. He has tended to simply invoke, in a rather *ad hoc* fashion, his axioms and reconciled them in a very loose and imprecise manner with empirical regularities. Or, he has constructed brief deductive schemes to illustrate his strategy. These limitations, in themselves, constitute an important criticism of Homans' work: He has not implemented his own theoretical strategy. Yet, Homans' failure to actually do what he says should be done does not negate the utility of the strategy. It is necessary, therefore, to examine one of Homans' deductive schemes to assess its *potential* as well as its problems.

Since Homans' clearest deductive statements appeared before the revision of his major exchange work, it is necessary to draw an example that pre-dates this revision. Yet, as was noted earlier, Homans' "rationality proposition" has been used for a considerable period of time, and thus

---

[33] Homans, *Nature of Social Science*, p. 73.

the substance and form of his argument is unchanged. Only certain terms in the propositions have been altered. It is possible, then, to examine Homans' deductive strategy with an example appearing before the most recent edition of *Social Behavior*.

Below, one of Homans' explanations is reproduced. Homans recognizes that this is not a complete explanation, but he argues that it is as good as any other that exists. Moreover, while certain steps in the deductive scheme are omitted, its form is, in Homans' mind, the proper way to develop scientific explanations. In this scheme, Homans was trying to explain "Golden's Law" that industrialization and the level of literacy in the population are highly correlated. In deductive formats, the empirical generalization to be explained will appear at the bottom of the deductive scheme. Propositions move from the most abstract statement, or the axiom(s), to the specific empirical regularity to be explained. "Golden's Law" is thus explained in the following manner.[34]

1. Men are more likely to perform an activity, the more valuable they perceive the reward of that activity to be.
2. Men are more likely to perform an activity, the more successful they perceive the activity to be in getting that reward.
3. Compared with agricultural societies, a higher proportion of men in industrial societies are prepared to reward activities that involve literacy. (Industrialists want to hire bookkeepers, clerks, persons who can make and read blueprints, manuals, and so forth)
4. Therefore a higher proportion of men in industrial societies will perceive the acquisition of literacy as rewarding.
5. And [by (1)] a higher proportion will attempt to acquire literacy.
6. The provision of schooling costs money, directly or indirectly.
7. Compared with agricultural societies, a higher proportion of men in industrial societies is, by some standard, wealthy.
8. Therefore a higher proportion is able to provide schooling (through government or private charity), and a higher proportion is able to pay for their own schooling without charity.
9. And a higher proportion will perceive the effort to acquire literacy as apt to be successful.
10. And [by (2) as by (1)] a higher proportion will attempt to acquire literacy.

---

[34] George C. Homans, "Reply to Blain," *Sociological Inquiry* 41 (Winter, 1971):19–24. This article was written in response to a challenge by Robert Blain for Homans to explain a sociological law: "On Homans' Psychological Reductionism," *Sociological Inquiry* 41 (Winter, 1971):3–25.

11.   Since their perceptions are in general accurate, a higher proportion
      of men in industrial societies will in fact acquire literacy. That is,
      the literacy rate is apt to be higher in an industrial than in an
      agricultural society.

Propositions 1 and 2 are an earlier statement of the "rationality proposition" which, as will be recalled, summarizes the success, stimulus, and
value propositions. It is from these first two propositions, or axioms,
that others are derived in an effort to "explain" "Golden's Law" (proposition 11 in the scheme above). Examining some of the features of this
explanation can provide insight into Homans' deductive strategy.

In this example, the transition between propositions 2 and 3 ignores
so many necessary variables as to simply *describe* in the words of
behavioral psychology what Homans *perceives* to have occurred. Why
are people in industrial societies prepared to reward literacy? This statement does not explain; it describes and thus opens a large gap in the
logic of the deductive system. For Homans, this statement is a "given."
It states a boundary condition, for the theory is not trying to explain
why people are prepared to reward literacy. Another theory is required
to explain this event. Thus, Homans argues that "no theory can explain
everything" and that it is necessary to ignore some things and assume
them to be "givens" for the purposes of explanation at hand. The issue
remains, however: Has not Homans defined away the most interesting
sociological issue, what makes people ready to reward literacy in a society's
historical development? For Homans, people are just ready to do so.

Another problem in this scheme comes with the placement of the
word "therefore." It can be noted that this transitive is typically used
immediately following a statement of "givens" which, as noted, define
away important classes of sociological variables. For example, the "therefore" preceding key propositions begs questions such as: *Why* do people
perceive literacy as rewarding? *What* level of industrialization would
make this so? *What* level of educational development? *What* feedback
consequences does desire for literacy have for educational development?
By ignoring the "why" and "what" of these questions, Homans can
then in propositions 5 and 10 reinsert the higher order axioms (1 and
2) of the explanation, thereby giving the scheme an appearance of deductive continuity. In fact, however, answers to the critical sociological questions have been avoided, such as why "men" perceive as valuable and
rewarding certain crucial activities.

While "no theory can explain everything," it must explain something.
The unsympathetic critics conclude, however, that Homans' prose gives

the form, but not the substance, of axiomatic explanation. While this deductive system is offered as an example and not as a complete explanation, critics charge that it is misleading because it ignores key sociological questions. In so doing, it sustains the illusion, critics charge, that psychological laws have, or at least could have, explained something. In fact, the unsympathetic reader can maintain that these laws explain little without the sociological propositions which would explain what Homans takes as a "given."

There can be little doubt that the inclusion of the sociological propositions—Why are people prepared to reward literacy? Why are people wealthy? Why do people see literacy as rewarding?—in this explanation of "Golden's Law" would yield a better explanation. Just whether or not the psychological axioms would be necessary would be a matter of preference. In terms of Homans' conception of explanation—subsumption in a deductive system under ever more abstract laws of less abstract propositions—the psychological laws would be necessary. Adopting a different strategy of explanation, such as causal modeling (see Chapter 1), others would be satisfied with the sociological propositions and the causal explanations of empirical events they allow. However, this example should warn that to search for the ultimate laws of explanation in deductive forms of theorizing—whether they be psychological, biological, chemical, or whatever—can tempt the theorist to ignore the very sociological laws which can account for critical social phenomena.

Homans' incorporation of an exchange perspective into a deductive strategy has raised many questions. Some of these problems are endemic to exchange theory in general, and therefore, will be discussed in more detail in Chapter 13 on "The Future of Exchange Theory." A number of criticisms and issues have been raised about Homans' strategy and perspective in particular, and hence, these should be explored in more detail.

CRITICISMS OF HOMANS' STRATEGY
AND EXCHANGE PERSPECTIVE

The Issues of Rationality

Homans' proposition on rationality could potentially open his exchange scheme to criticisms leveled against utilitarianism: Do actors *rationally calculate* the costs and rewards to be made by engaging in a line of conduct? Homans partially meets this criticism by recognizing that people make calculations by weighing costs, rewards, and the probabilities of receiving rewards, or avoiding punishments. But they do so in terms of value—that is, in terms of *what bestows gratifications on them*. What is rewarding is thus a personal matter and unique to all individuals. Depending upon their past experiences, people establish their own values. "Rationality," then, is made in terms of universal values, but it is a personal matter involving "calculations" of personal value.[35]

There is, however, another implicit assumption that leaves Homans, and most exchange schemes, open to criticism. Do all human actions involve calculations? Do people always weigh and assess costs and rewards in all situations?[36] Often, critics argue, people just receive rewards without prior calculations. For example, when a person receives a gift or becomes the beneficiary of another's desires to bestow rewards, prior calculations are not involved. Rewards or reinforcement are, of course, still involved, but the principle of rationality excludes much interaction. Thus, Homans may have unduly limited his theory.

The Issue of Tautology

More fundamental to the exchange perspective is the problem of tautology. If one examines the definition of key concepts—value, reward, and action—they appear to be defined in terms of each other. Rewards are gratifications which have value. Value is the degree of reward, or reinforcement. Action is reward-seeking activity. The question arises, then, as to whether it is possible to build a theory from axioms which are tautological. For example, Homans' proposition that "The more valuable to a person is the result of his action, the more likely he is to perform the action" could be considered a tautology. "Value" is defined as the degree of reward and "action" is defined as reward-seeking behavior. All of Homans' axioms suffer from this problem and Homans has taken great care in dealing with the issue.[37]

---

[35] Parsons, who similarly has dealt with the rationality issue ("Levels of Organization," in H. Turk and R. L. Simpson, eds., *Institutions and Social Exchange* [Indianapolis: Bobbs-Merrill, 1971], p. 219), notes: "History thus seems to become for Homans the ultimate residual category, recourse to which can solve any embarrassment which arises from inadequacy of the more specific parts of the conceptual scheme. The very extent to which he has narrowed his conceptualization of the variables, in particular adopting the atomistic conception of values, . . . increases the burden thrown upon history and with it the confession of ignorance embodied in the statement, 'things are as they are because of ways in which they have come to be that way.' "

[36] Robert Bierstedt, "Review of Blain's Exchange and Power," *American Sociological Review*, 30 (1965):789–90.

[37] For enlightening discussions of this problem, see Morton Deutsch, "Homans in the Skinner Box," in H. Turk and R. L. Simpson, eds., *Institutions & Social Exchange*, pp. 81–92; Bengt Abrahamsson, "Homans on Exchange: Hedonism Revived," *American Journal of Sociology* 76 (September 1970):273–85; Pitirim Sorokin, *Sociological Theories of Today* (New York: Harper & Row, 1966), especially chap. 15, "Pseudo-Behavioral and Empirical Sociologies;" and M. J. Mulkay, *Functionalism and Exchange*, pp. 166–69.

Homans acknowledges the circularity, but views the problem as resolved by the use of deductive theory. If the axioms are viewed as part of a deductive system, the problem of tautology is soon obviated. While "value" and "action" cannot be measured independently when stated so abstractly, the deductive system allows for their independent measurement at the empirical level. Thus, "a tautology can take part in the deductive system whose conclusion is not a tautology."[38] Thus, Homans argues that the tautological nature of highly abstract axioms in a deductive system can be obviated when precise and clear derivations from the axioms are performed. In this process, independent definitions and indicators of key concepts can be provided. If these deductive steps are left out, however, and vague axioms are simply reconciled in an ad hoc fashion to empirical events, the problem of tautology will persist. And it is here that critics note: in virtually every "explanation" of social behavior in his recent work,[39] rigorous deductive systems are absent. But in fairness, Homans has been only attempting to *suggest* the utility of his concepts for future construction of deductive systems.

Yet, if we examine Homans' explanation of "Golden's Law," important deductive steps are left out.[40] Homans actually presents an argument that reveals the following form:

1. Why does literacy increase with industrialization?
    a. People do things because they are rewarding ("Rationality Proposition").
    b. People at some point in history were ready to reward literacy.
    c. Other people thus calculated that they should become literate ("Rationality Proposition").
    d. Therefore, literacy increases.

There is a circularity to this argument. People become literate because they perceive literacy as rewarding; they perceive literacy as rewarding

---

[38] *Social Behavior*, p. 35.

[39] Ibid., pp. 51–339.

[40] Ronald Maris ("The Logical Adequacy of Homans' Social Theory," *American Sociological Review* 35 [December 1970]:1069–81) came to a somewhat different conclusion about the logical adequacy of Homans's theoretical manipulations. With the aid of symbolic logic, and the addition of some assumptions, "Homans' theory of elementary social behavior has not been proven inadequate." But the criticisms of Maris' logical manipulation are sufficient to suggest that his analysis is not the definitive answer to the logical adequacy of Homans's deductions. For examples of these criticisms, see Don Gray, "Some Comments concerning Maris on 'Logical Adequacy' "; Stephen Turner, "The Logical Adequacy of 'The Logical Adequacy of Homans' Social Theory' "; and Robert Price, "On Maris and the Logic of Time"; all in *American Sociological Review* 36 (August 1971):706–13. Maris' "Second Thoughts: Uses of Logic in Theory Construction" can also be found in this issue. For a more adequate construction of a logically sophisticated exchange perspective, see B. F. Meeker, "Decisions and Exchange," *American Sociological Review* 36 (June 1971):485–95.

because others are ready to reward literacy; these others are ready to reward literacy because they see having literacy as rewarding. What really has been explained in this argument? Has Homans provided independent operationalizations of "reward" and "action" in his deductions? And do we now understand more with the concepts of value and reward than we would have without these concepts?

The Issue of Prediction versus Ad Hoc Reasoning

The problem of tautology points to another problem in exchange theory: Can predictions be made about what will occur with the use of these exchange axioms? Or, have descriptions of a process—industrialization and literacy, for example—simply been recast into a new vocabulary *after* the fact of literacy and industrialization. Explanation is ex post facto; it is hindsight rather than prediction. Of course, the relationship between literacy and industrialization is an historical issue, and therefore, it must be interpreted through hindsight. Thus, we need to examine a case where actual prediction would be involved to highlight this problem.

Richard Emerson has provided an illustrative example of the problem.[41] Politicians need money to get elected; politicians therefore value campaign contributions; Person X is a politician; and Group Y contributes heavily to Person X's campaign. Prediction: Person X, once elected, will advocate policies favorable to Group Y. This seems reasonable, and it might come to pass. But what if Person X did not favor policies for Group Y? Would the theory be rejected? This is unlikely; rather, the theorist would proclaim that accurate measurement of Person X's values had not occurred, or other information about more valuable alternatives—say, maintaining one's "personal integrity in one's constituent's eyes"—offered more rewards. This kind of problem will almost always occur with exchange theory because it is difficult to measure the key concept, "value," before the actual emission of the behavior that "value" is supposed to explain. Thus, theorists are often left with constructing new ad hoc "explanations" *after* one set of predictions goes wrong. As a result, there is no way to refute the theory; "faulty measurement" is always the villain, not the theory.

It is typically difficult to measure value until after the action to be explained has been emitted. And if this is all that can be done, then the problem of tautology surfaces again. Why did Person X vote in favor of policies favorable to Group Y? Answer: Because this line of

---

[41] Richard Emerson, "Social Exchange Theory," p. 344.

activity was rewarding (after all, Group Y had been a heavy campaign contributor). Such an explanation is ad hoc; if this one were considered insufficient, it would be possible to construct another; and still another; and yet, one more until the audience evaluating the theory was satisfied. As long as it is difficult to measure "value," prediction will also prove difficult. At best, interesting ad hoc, after the fact "explanations" can be offered.

The Issue of Reductionism

Periodically old philosophical issues are resurrected and debated fervently. Homans' exchange perspective has rekindled one such debate: the issue of reductionism. Homans' statements on the issue are sometimes tempered and at other times polemic, but the thrust of his argument has been made amply clear. He writes:

> The institutions, organizations, and societies that sociologists study can always be analyzed, without residue, into the behavior of individual men. They must therefore be explained by propositions about the behavior of individual men.[42]

This position has been particularly disturbing to some sociologists, since it appears to pose a problem: If it is accepted that sociological propositions are reducible to those about individuals, then those about individuals are reducible to physiological propositions, which, in turn, are reducible to biochemical propositions, and so on in a reductionist sequence ending in the basic laws of physical matter. Homans has not been very helpful in alleviating sociologists' concern with whether he is advocating this kind of reductionism. In fact, he is advocating the position that while the psychological axioms "cannot be derived from physiological propositions, . . . this condition is unlikely to last forever."[43]

However, Homans fortunately avoids a related, and equally old, philosophical debate: the realist-nominalist issue. Homans is clearly not a nominalist, for he is not asserting that, to put the matter simply, society and its various collective forms (groups, institutions, organizations, and so forth) are mere names sociologists arbitrarily assign to the only "really real" phenomenon, the individual:

> I, for one, am not going to back into the position of denying the reality of social institutions. . . . The question is not whether the individual is

---

[42] Homans, "Commentary," *Sociological Inquiry* 34 (Spring 1964):229–31.
[43] Homans, "Commentary," p. 373.

the ultimate reality or whether social behavior involves something more than the behavior of individuals. The question is, always, *how social phenomena are to be explained* [Emphasis added].[44]

It is the thrust of the last phrase above which has seemingly been underemphasized in the criticisms of Homans' reductionism. Critics have too often implied that his reductionism forces him to embrace a particular variety of nominalism. Yet, for Homans, the issue has always been one of how to explain with deductive—or axiomatic—systems the groups and institutions studied by sociologists.

Homans and the Fallacy of "Misplaced Concreteness." The most persistent criticism of Homans's reductionist strategy has revolved around the assertion that he has fallen into the fallacy of "misplaced concreteness."[45] As originally conceived by the philosopher Alfred North Whitehead,[46] scientists had at one time fallen into the trap of thinking that they could analyze the universe into its constituent parts and thereby eventually discover the basic elements or building blocks of all matter. Once *the* basic building block had been found, it would only then be necessary to comprehend the laws of its operation for an understanding of everything else in the universe. In the eyes of Whitehead and others, these scientists had erroneously assumed that the basic parts of the universe were the only reality of phenomena. In so doing, they had "misplaced" the concreteness of phenomena. In reality, the *relationships* among parts forming a whole is just as "real" as the constituent parts. The organization of parts is not the "sum of the parts," but rather, the constitution of a new kind of reality.

Has Homans fallen into this fallacy? Numerous critics think that he has when he implies that the behavior of persons or "men" are the basic units, whose laws need only be understood to explain more complex sociocultural arrangements. These critics appear to be overreacting to Homans' reductionism, perhaps confusing his reductionist strategy with the mistaken assumption that Homans is a nominalist in disguise. Actually, Homans has never denied the importance of sociological laws describing complex sociocultural processes; on the contrary, they are critical propositions in any deductive systems that attempts to *explain* these processes. All that Homans has asserted is: These sociological laws are

[44] Homans, *Nature of Social Science*, pp. 61–62.

[45] For examples of this line of criticism, see Parsons, "Levels of Organization"; and Blain, "On Homans' Psychological Reductionism," *Sociological Inquiry* 41 (Winter, 1971): 10–19.

[46] Alfred North Whitehead, *Science and The Modern World* (New York: Macmillan Co., 1925).

not the most general; they are subsumable under more general psychological laws (his axioms), which eventually, with more knowledge and sophisticated intellectual techniques, will be subsumable under a still more general set of laws. At no point in this reductionist philosophy is Homans
asserting that the propositions subsumed by a more general set of laws
are irrelevant or unimportant. Thus, Homans has not "misplaced the
concreteness" of reality. He has not denied the existence of emergent
properties such as groups, organizations, and institutions, nor the theoretical significance of the laws describing these emergent phenomena.
Homans is not a nominalist in disguise, but a sociological realist, who is advocating a particular *strategy for understanding sociocultural phenomena.*

The Utility of Homans' Reductionist Strategy. Once it becomes
evident that Homans's reductionism is a theoretical strategy that does
not deny the metaphysical or ontological existence of emergent phenomena, the next question in need of an answer becomes: Is this strategy
useful in explaining phenomena? Some critics have emphasized that a
reductionist strategy will affect the kinds of theoretical and research
questions sociologist will ask.[47] If one is concerned primarily with psychological laws as explanatory principles, it is likely that research questions
and theoretical generalizations will begin to revolve around psychological
and social psychological phenomena, because these phenomena are the
most readily derived from psychological axioms. Thus, despite a recognition that complex sociological phenomena are real, the adoption of a
reductionist strategy for building theory will inadvertently result in the
avoidance of the macro patterns of social organization studied by many
sociologists. To the extent that such one-sided research and theory building is the result of a reductionist strategy, then this strategy is undesirable
and can be questioned on these grounds alone. However, critics charge
that there are more fundamental grounds on which to reject Homans'
strategy: Adherence to his strategy at the present time will lead to logically
imprecise and empirically empty theoretical formulations.

This indictment is, of course, severe and needs to be documented.
Homans may be correct in holding that logically a deductive axiomatic
strategy necessitates reductionism, for the goal of such a strategy is to
subsume under ever more general axioms what we previously considered
the most general axioms. Such a process of subsumption may indeed
lead first to the subsumption of sociological axioms under psychological
axioms, and then to the subsequent subsumption of these latter axioms

---

[47] For example, see Blain, "On Homans' Psychological Reductionism"; Buckley,
Sociology and Modern Systems Theory (Englewood Cliffs, N.J.: Prentice-Hall, Inc.,
1967), pp. 109–11.

under physiological, biochemical, and physical laws. Just as many of the laws of chemistry can be subsumed under the laws of physics, so sociological laws may be subsumed by the laws of psychology. However, some have argued that deduction of sociological laws from psychological axioms should occur in a two-step process:[48] (1) First, a series of well-established sociological laws, from which it is possible to deduce a wide variety of sociological propositions that have received consistent empirical support, must be developed. Then, *and only then*, (2) a clear body of psychological axioms, which are amenable to similar reductions and which have received consistent empirical support, can be used to explain the sociological laws. Step 1 must occur prior to step 2, as it typically has in the physical sciences. Homans has recognized the fact that the social sciences have not achieved step 1 when he notes that the "issue for the social sciences is not whether we should be reductionists, but rather, if we were reductionists, whether we could find any propositions to reduce."[49]

Homans has failed, however, to realize the full implications of his statement. Without well-established sociological laws to subsume, the critics can correctly ask: What is the utility of attempting to subsume what does not exist? Would it not be far wiser to expend our efforts in developing sociological laws and let the issue of reductionism take care of itself when these laws are established? To attempt prematurely to develop psychological axioms and then deduce sociological propositions from them in the absence of well-established sociological laws is likely to generate tautologous axioms and logically imprecise deductions, as has been demonstrated earlier for "Golden's Law." What Homans typically does in his "deductions" is to (*a*) state in an ad hoc manner some general psychological propositions that are not logically derived from his axioms, and (*b*) take as givens all the interesting sociological questions, answers to which would lead to the development of the sociological laws needed to fill out properly his deductive system. The end result of Homans' pseudo-deductions is that an empirical generalization—say Golden's Law—may be "explained" without any of the logically necessary components of a deductive system—clear sociological laws and psychological axioms.

Such deductive systems will ultimately boil down to statements like the following: Things are as they are because they are rewarding. What this does is to repeat the empirical generalization to be "explained" in

---

[48] Turner, "Building Social Theory."

[49] Homans, *Nature of Social Science*, p. 86.

the words of behavior psychology, without *logically* reducing the generalization to *clear* psychological axioms.[50]

HOMANS' IMAGE OF SOCIETY

Homans' eloquent advocacy of his theoretical strategy has failed to convert many sociologists, primarily because his exchange scheme is filled with many conceptual and logical problems. Coupled with the methodological difficulties of operationalizing concepts such as value and reward independently of actions, it is not surprising that Homans' exchange perspective has received considerable criticism. Yet, Homans is probably correct in his assertion that at the elementary level of interaction the processes that his concepts denote do indeed occur, as only a small degree of introspection will reveal.

It is the latter fact that perhaps marks the appeal of Homans's theoretical efforts. For all its logical difficulties, and attendant methodological problems, Homans offers an image of society and social processes that is, if only intuitively, pleasing. The *substantive* vision of the social world first communicated in *The Human Group* and expanded upon in the later exchange works is provocative and likely to be the most enduring feature of Homans' theoretical perspective.

In *The Human Group*, Homans' numerous empirical generalizations described the processes of group elaboration and disintegration. Groups were observed to differentiate into subgroups, to form leadership ranks, to codify norms, to establish temporary equilibriums, and then, in his last case study of a dying New England town, to reveal the converse of these processes. In the later exchange works, the concepts of "activities," "interactions," and "sentiments," which have been incorporated into the propositions describing such group elaboration, are redefined in order to give Homans the opportunity to explain why these processes

---

[50] The concepts of behavioral psychology do not have to muddle empirical generalizations, so long as one does not prematurely try to deduce sociological propositions to crude psychological propositions. In fact, operant principles can be used quite fruitfully to *build* (note: not reduce) more complex exchange principles that pertain to sociological processes (note: not psychological). For an impressive attempt at employing operant principles as a starting point, and then changing them to fit the facts of emergent properties, see Richard M. Emerson's various works, especially "Power-Dependence Relations," *American Sociological Review* 27 (February 1962):31–41; "Power-Dependent Relations: Two Experiments," *Sociometry* 27 (September 1964):282–98; "Operant Psychology and Exchange Theory," in *Behavior Sociology: The Experimental Analysis of Social Process*, ed. R. L. Burgess and D. Bushell, Jr. (New York: Columbia University Press, 1969), pp. 379–405; and "Exchange Theory, Part I: A Psychological Basis for Social Exchange" and "Exchange Theory, Part II: Exchange Relations and Network Structures," in *Sociological Theories in Progress*, ed. J. Berger, M. Zelditch, Jr., and B. Anderson (New York: Houghton Mifflin Co., 1972), pp. 38–87.

should occur. Human activity has become viewed as action directed toward the attainment of rewards and avoidance of punishments. Interaction has become social behavior where the mutual actions of individuals have cost and reward implications for the parties to the interaction. People are now seen as emitting those activities that would increase the likelihood of profits—rewards less costs—measured against a set of expectations. Such rewarding and costly exchanges of activities were not viewed as necessarily involving the exchange of material rewards and punishments, but more frequently "psychic profits."

Just as he did in *The Human Group*, in his recent works Homans enumerates concepts that enable him to denote processes of group elaboration. In *Social Behavior*, the particular ad hoc explanations are of less interest than Homans' descriptions (as opposed to "explanations") of how vital group processes—interaction, influence, conformity, competition, bestowal of esteem, justice, ranking, and innovation—ebb and flow as actors seek psychic profits in their exchanges of rewards and punishments. In these descriptions, considerable intuitive insight into the basic processes of human interaction is evident. It was these insights that made *The Human Group* appealing, and it is this same feature of *Social Behavior* that makes it an important work.

Despite the suggestiveness of his descriptions of basic processes, however, the most theoretically interesting section of *Social Behavior* is the closing chapter on "The Institutional and the Subinstitutional." Introduced apologetically as a last-gasp "orgy," Homans nevertheless returns to an issue first raised in *The Human Group:* the relationship of processes in groups to the structures of larger societies, or "civilizations," as he phrased the issue at the time. As he emphasized in the last paragraph of *The Human Group*, the development of civilizations ultimately is carried out by persons in groups:

> At the level of the small group, society has always been able to cohere. We infer, therefore, that if civilization is to stand, it must maintain, in the relation between the groups that make up society and the central direction of society, some of the features of the small group itself.[51]

In *Social Behavior*, Homans has a more sophisticated answer to why it appears that society coheres around the small group: Society is like a group in that it is elaborated and structured from fundamentally the same exchange processes that structure and cause the elaboration of the small group. All social structures are thus built up from basically

---

[51] Homans, *Human Group*, p. 468.

the same exchange processes; in the explication of why this should be so, Homans provides an interesting image of how patterns of social organization are created, maintained, changed, and broken down. This image is not developed into what can be considered adequate theory—as has already been shown. But it does provide a vision of the social world which can perhaps initiate a more useful exchange-theoretic perspective on the processes underlying various patterns of social organization.

To explicate the relationship between elementary exchange processes and more complex patterns of social organization, Homans—much like Parsons a decade earlier—provides a sketch of the process of institutionalization:[52] At points in history, some people have the "capital" to reinforce or provide rewards for others, whether it comes from their possessing a surplus of food, money, a moral code, or valued leadership qualities. With such capital, "institutional elaboration" can occur, since some can "invest" their capital by trying to induce others (through rewards or threats of punishments) to engage in novel activities. These new activities can involve an "intermeshing of the behavior of a large number of persons in a more complicated or roundabout way than has hitherto been the custom." Whether this "investment" involves conquering territory and organizing a kingdom or creating a new form of business organization, those making the investment must have the resources—whether an army to threaten punishment, a charismatic personality to morally persuade followers, or the ability to provide for peoples' subsistence needs—to keep those so organized in a situation where they derive some profit. At some point in this process, such organization can become more efficient and hence rewarding to all when the rewards are clearly specified in terms of generalized reinforcers, such as money, and when the activities expended to get their rewards are more clearly specified, such as in the case when explicit norms and rules emerge. In turn, this increased efficiency allows for greater organization of activities. This new efficiency increases the likelihood that generalized reinforcers and explicit norms will be used to regulate exchange relations and hence increase the profits of those involved. Eventually, the exchange networks involving generalized reinforcers and an increasingly complex body of rules require differentiation or subunits—such as a legal and banking

---

[52] Homans, *Social Behavior*, chap. 16. The reader should find interesting a comparison of this model of institutionalization and that provided by Parsons, since Homans implicitly sees this model as an alternative to that presented by functionalists such as Parsons. But a careful reading of Talcott Parsons, *The Social System* (New York: Free Press, 1951), pp. 1–91, and his more recent work on evolution would reveal a remarkable similarity between his conceptualization of this basic process and that of Homans.

system—that can maintain the stability of the generalized reinforcers and the integrity of the norms.

Out of this kind of exchange process, then, social organization—whether at a societal, group, organizational, or institutional level—is constructed. The emergence of most patterns of organization is frequently buried in the recesses of history, but such emergence is typified by these accelerating process: (1) People with "capital" (reward capacity) "invest" in creating more complex social relations that increase their rewards and allow those whose activities are organized to realize a "profit." (2) With increased rewards, these people can invest in more complex patterns of organization. (3) Increasingly complex patterns of organization require, first of all, the use of generalized reinforcers, and then, the codification of norms to regulate activity. (4) With this organizational base, it then becomes possible to elaborate further the pattern of organization, creating the necessity for differentiation of subunits that assure the stability of the generalized reinforcers and the integrity of norms. (5) With this differentiation, it is possible to expand even further the networks of interaction, since there are standardized means for rewarding activities and codifying new norms as well as enforcing old rules.

However, these complex patterns of social organization employing formal rules and "secondary" or "generalized" reinforcers can never cease to meet the more "primary" needs of individuals.[53] Institutions first emerged to meet these needs; and no matter how complex institutional arrangements become and how many norms and formal rules are elaborated, these extended interaction networks must ultimately reinforce humans' more primary needs. When these arrangements cease meeting the primary needs from which they ultimately sprang, an institution is vulnerable and apt to collapse if alternative actions, which can provide primary rewards, present themselves as a possibility. In this situation, low- or high-status persons, or someone who has little to lose by nonconformity to existing prescriptions, will break from established ways to expose to others a more rewarding alternative. While institutions may continue to extract conformity for a period, they will cease to do so when they lose the capacity to provide primary rewards. Thus, complex institutional arrangements must ultimately be satisfying to individuals, not simply because of the weight of culture or norms, but because they are constructed to serve people:

---

[53] Homans, *Social Behavior;* unfortunately, just what a "primary reward" in this context means is not specified.

> Institutions do not keep going just because they are enshrined in norms, and it seems extraordinary that anyone should ever talk as if they did. They keep going because they have pay-offs, ultimately pay-offs for individuals. Nor is society a perpetual-motion machine, supplying its own fuel. It cannot keep itself going by planting in the young a desire for these goods and only those goods that it happens to be in shape to provide. It must provide goods that men find rewarding not simply because they are sharers in a particular culture but because they are men.[54]

The fact that institutions of society must also meet "primary" needs sets the stage for a continual conflict between institutional elaboration and the primary needs of humans. As one form of institutional elaboration meets one set of needs, it may deprive people of other important rewards—opening the way for deviation and innovation by those presenting the alternative rewards that have been suppressed by dominant institutional arrangements. In turn, the new institutional elaborations that may ensue from innovators who have the capital to reward others will suppress other needs, which, through processes similar to its inception, will set off another process of institutional elaboration.

In sum, this sketch of how social organization is linked to elementary processes of exchange represents an interesting perspective for analyzing how patterns of social organization are built up, maintained, altered, and broken down. While there are obvious conceptual problems—say, for example, the difficulty of distinguishing "primary rewards" from "other types"—the *image of society* presented by Homans is provocative. It can perhaps lead Homans to a fruitful strategy for developing a theory of exchange relations.

---

[54] Ibid., p. 390.

12

EXCHANGE STRUCTURALISM: PETER M. BLAU

Major theoretical developments in sociology seemingly occur in a spirit of reaction and overreaction to functional forms of theorizing. As preceding chapters have attempted to document, dialectical and functional conflict theories, and the exchange psychologism of George C. Homans have been viewed by their proponents as more desirable alternatives to functional theory, especially that of Talcott Parsons. Yet, as has been argued at various points, Parsonian functionalism and the proposed alternatives have more in common than the framers of conflict theories, and some forms of exchange theory have admitted. In only one of the theoretical perspectives to be discussed in this volume is this latent commonality utilized to build an alternative to functionalism which incorporates the "useful" concepts not only from Parsonian functionalism but also from other theoretical perspectives.

This perspective has been advanced by Peter M. Blau. Although his theoretical scheme is an exchange model, it seeks to incorporate many of the assumptions and concepts of functional, conflict, and interactionist theory. In this way, Blau's exchange perspective attempts to bridge the gap between the micro processes of interaction, conflict, and exchange among individuals and the emergent structural units—such as groups, communities, organizations and institutions—at the macro level of analysis.

BLAU'S THEORETICAL STRATEGY

In contrast with Homans' concern with developing deductive explanations, Blau offers what he terms a theoretical "prolegomenon"—or, in other words, a conceptual sketch—which can serve as a preliminary to more mature forms of theorizing.[1] In many ways, Blau's strategy resembles Parsons', for he appears less concerned with developing a rigorous system of propositions than with enumerating concepts that can capture in loosely phrased and related propositions the fundamental processes occurring at diverse levels of social organization. While there is less categorization than in Parsons' conceptual efforts, Blau is concerned with developing an initial "bundle" of concepts and propositions that can provide insight into the operation of a wide range of sociological processes, from the behavior of individuals in small-group contexts to the operation of whole societies.

To execute this strategy, Blau's major theoretical work undertakes two fundamental tasks: (1) to conceptualize some of the simple and direct exchange processes occurring in relatively small interaction networks, and (2) then expand the conceptual edifice to include some of the complexities inherent in less direct exchange processes in larger social systems. In a vein similar to Homans' analysis, Blau first examines "elementary" forms of social exchange with an eye to how they help in the analysis of "subinstitutional" behavior. Where Homans terminates his analysis by simply presenting a conceptual "orgy" in the last chapter of *Social Behavior*, Blau begins to supplement the exchange concepts describing elementary processes in an effort to understand more completely the complex processes of institutionalization.[2]

Thus, in a manner reminiscent of Parsons' analysis of the process of institutionalization in *The Social System* (see Chapter 3), Blau begins with a conceptualization of basic interactive processes; then, utilizing and supplementing the concepts developed in this analysis, he shifts to the conceptualization of how more elaborate institutional complexes are created, maintained, changed, and broken down.[3]

---

[1] Peter M. Blau's major exchange work is *Exchange and Power in Social Life* (New York: John Wiley & Sons, 1964). This formal and expanded statement on his exchange perspective was anticipated in earlier works. For example, see Peter M. Blau, "A Theory of Social Integration," *American Journal of Sociology* 65 (May 1960):545–56; and Peter M. Blau, *The Dynamics of Bureaucracy*, 1st and 2d eds. (Chicago: University of Chicago Press, 1955 and 1963). It is of interest to note that George C. Homans in *Social Behavior: Its Elementary Forms* (New York: Harcourt, Brace & World, 1961) makes frequent reference to the data summarized in this latter work. For a more recent statement of Blau's position see Peter M. Blau, "Interaction: Social Exchange," in *International Encyclopaedia of the Social Sciences*, vol. 7 (New York: Macmillian Co., 1968), pp. 452–58.

[2] Homans, "The Institutional and the Subinstitutional, *Social Behavior*, rev. ed., chap. 16.

[3] Talcott Parsons, *The Social System* (New York: Free Press, 1951), especially pp. 1–200.

BASIC EXCHANGE PRINCIPLES

Blau does not define as explicitly as Homans the variables in his exchange scheme. Rather, considerably more attention is devoted to defining exchange as a particular type of association, involving "actions that are contingent on rewarding reactions from others and that cease when these expected reactions are not forthcoming."[4] For Blau, exchange occurs only among those relationships in which rewards are *expected and received from designated others.* Much like Parsons's conception of voluntarism, or Homans' rationality proposition, Blau conceptualizes as exchange "activities" only those behaviors that are oriented to specified goals, or *rewards,* and that involve actors selecting from various potential alternatives, or *costs,* a particular line of action which will yield an expected reward. In pursuing rewards and selecting alternative lines of behaviors, actors are conceptualized as seeking a *profit* (rewards less costs) from their relations with others. Thus, Blau employs the basic concepts of all exchange theories—reward, cost, and profit—but he limits their application to relations with *others* from whom rewards are *expected* and *received.* This definition of exchange is considerably more limited than Homans' definition, which encompasses *all* activity as exchange, regardless of whether rewards are expected or received.

In common with Homans, however, Blau recognizes that in focusing on associations involving "an exchange of activity, tangible or intangible, and more or less rewarding and costly, between two persons," an elementary economic model is being employed.[5] Indeed, social life is conceived to be a "marketplace" in which actors negotiate with each other in an effort to make a profit. However, Blau shares the skepticism that led Homans to reject the "theory of games" as "good advice" but a "poor description" of human behavior and that induced Parsons' earlier in *The Structure of Social Action* to discard the extremes of utilitarianism.[6] Blau recognizes that, unlike the simple "economic man" of classical economics (and of more recent rationalistic models of human behavior), humans (1) rarely pursue one specific goal to the exclusion of all others, (2) are frequently inconsistent in their preferences, (3) virtually never have complete information of alternatives, and (4) are never free from social commitments limiting the available alternatives. Furthermore, in contrast with a purely economic model of human transactions, social

---

[4] Blau, *Exchange and Power,* p. 6.

[5] Ibid., p. 88.

[6] Talcott Parsons, *The Structure of Social Action* (New York: McGraw-Hill Book Co., 1937).

associations involve the exchange of rewards whose value varies from one transaction to another without a fixed market value, and whose value cannot be expressed precisely in terms of a single, accepted medium of exchange (such as money). In fact, the vagueness of the values exchanged in social life is a "substantive fact, not simply a methodological problem."[7] As Blau emphasizes, the values people hold are inherently diffuse and ill defined.[8]

Unlike Homans, Blau does not state a formal set of exchange principles, primarily because he is not concerned with developing the higher order axioms of a deductive theoretic system. In a less explicit manner, Blau does employ a series of exchange principles. Since these principles are not always enumerated, it is often unclear whether they represent assumptions or statements of covariance among the variables of his exchange system. Despite the vagueness with which they are stated, Blau's theoretical perspective is not comprehensible without an understanding of the "principles" or "laws" he views as guiding the dynamics of the exchange process. For convenience, these principles will be phrased as statements of co-variance among exchange variables, despite the fact that Blau may have preferred to state them as assumptions.

Principle 1. The more profit people expect from one another in emitting a particular activity, the more likely they are to emit that activity.

This principle combines Homans' axioms 1, 2, and 3, where rewarding stimulus situations, the frequency of rewards, and the value of rewards were seen as increasing the likelihood that actions would be emitted. Actually, in Homans' own deductive systems—for example, the one he constructed to "explain" Golden's Law—Homans usually collapses his first three axioms into his rationality principle: "In choosing between alternative actions, a person will choose that one for which as perceived by him at the time, the value of the result, multiplied by the probability of getting the result, is greater.[9] In practice, then, Homans and Blau utilize the same basic principle. Blau's use of the concept "reward expectation" would encompass the same phenomena denoted by Homans' use of the concepts "perception of reward" and "probability" of getting a reward.

---

[7] Blau, *Exchange and Power*, p. 95.

[8] As was noted for Homans' scheme, this "fact" creates both methodological and logical problems. If value cannot be precisely measured, how is it possible to discern just how value influences behavior? If value cannot be measured independently of the behavior it is supposed to regulate, then propositions will be tautologous and of little use in building sociological theory.

[9] Homans, *Social Behavior*, p. 43.

Principle 2.   The more people have exchanged rewards with one another, the more likely are reciprocal obligations to emerge and guide subsequent exchanges among these persons.

Drawing from Malinowski's and Lévi-Strauss's initial discussion as reinterpreted by Alvin Gouldner,[10] Blau postulates that "the need to reciprocate for benefits received in order to continue receiving them serves as a 'starting mechanism' of social interaction."[11] Equally important, once exchanges have occurred, a "fundamental and ubiquitous norm of reciprocity" emerges to regulate subsequent exchanges. Thus, inherent in the exchange process, per se, is a principle of reciprocity. Over time, and as the conditions of principle 1 are met, this principle of reciprocity becomes codified into a social *norm* of reciprocity, whose violation brings about social disapproval and other negative sanctions. Since violations of the norm of reciprocity become significant in Blau's subsequent analysis of opposition and conflict, it is wise to formulate explicitly a corollary of principle 2, stated here as a separate principle.

Principle 3.   The more the reciprocal obligations of an exchange relationship are violated, the more are deprived parties disposed to sanction negatively those violating the norm of reciprocity.

Following economists' analyses of transactions in the marketplace, Blau introduces in his fourth principle the economic "law" of "marginal utility." The more a person has received a reward, the more satiated he or she is with that reward, and the less valuable further increments of the reward (principle 4 is the equivalent to Homans' axiom 4). Actors will therefore seek alternative rewards until their level of satiation declines.

Principle 4.   The more expected rewards have been forthcoming from the emission of a particular activity, the less valuable the activity, and the less likely its emission.[12]

Much like Homans, Blau recognizes that people establish expectations about what level of reward particular exchange relations should yield. Unlike Homans, however, Blau recognizes that these expectations are normatively regulated.[13] These norms are termed "norms of fair ex-

---

[10] Alvin W. Gouldner, "The Norm of Reciprocity," *American Sociological Review* 25 (April 1960): 161–78.

[11] Blau, *Power and Exchange*, p. 92.

[12] Ibid., p. 90.

[13] See Peter M. Blau, "Justice in Social Exchange," in *Institutions and Social Exchange: The Sociologies of Talcott Parsons and George C. Homans*, ed. H. Turk and R. L. Simpson (New York: Bobbs-Merrill Co., 1971), pp. 56–68; see also: Blau, *Power and Exchange*, pp. 156–57.

change" since they determine what the proportion of rewards to costs *should* be in a given exchange relation.[14] Hence, Blau enumerates a fifth principle:

Principle 5.   The more exchange relations have been established, the more likely they are to be governed by norms of "fair exchange."

A corollary to this principle modifies Homans' assertion that aggression is forthcoming when these norms are violated. For convenience, this corollary can be stated as a separate principle.

Principle 6.   The less norms of fairness are realized in an exchange, the more are deprived parties disposed to sanction negatively those violating the norms.

Since Blau's exchange model is vitally concerned with the conditions under which conflict and change occur in social systems, principle 6 becomes a crucial generalization. In his subsequent analysis, the deprivations arising from violating the norms of fair exchange are viewed as translated, under specified conditions, into retaliation against violators. This concern with enumerating exchange principles that can account for conflict in social relations is underscored by Blau's final exchange principle:[15]

Principle 7.   The more stabilized and balanced some exchange relations among social units, the more likely other exchange relations are to become imbalanced and unstable.

All established exchange relations involve "costs" or alternative rewards forgone. Since most actors *must* engage in more than one exchange relation, the balance and stabilization of one exchange relation (in accordance with principles 1, 2, and 4) is likely to create imbalance and strain in other necessary exchange relations. For Blau, social life is thus filled with "dilemmas" in which people must successively trade off stability and balance in one exchange relation for strain in others as they attempt to cope with the variety of relations they must maintain. In his last chapter on institutionalization, Homans hinted at this principle when he emphasized that, in satisfying some needs, institutional arrangements deny others and thereby set into motion a perpetual dialectic between dominant institutions and change-oriented acts of innovation and deviance.[16] It is from this concluding insight of Homans into the dialecti-

---

[14] Blau, "Justice in Social Exchange," p. 68.

[15] Blau, *Exchange and Power*, p. 14.

[16] Homans, *Social Behavior*, pp. 390–98.

cal nature of relationships between established social patterns and forces of opposition that Blau is to begin his analysis of exchange in social life.

BASIC EXCHANGE PROCESSES IN SOCIAL LIFE

Elementary Systems of Exchange

Blau initiates his discussion of elementary exchange processes with the assumption that people enter into social exchange because they perceive the possibility of deriving rewards (principle 1). Blau labels this perception *social attraction* and postulates that unless relationships involve such attraction, they are not relationships of exchange. In entering an exchange relationship, each actor assumes the perspective of another, and thereby derives some perception of the other's needs. Actors then manipulate their presentation of self so as to convince each other that they have the valued qualities others appear to desire. In adjusting role behaviors in an effort to impress others with the resources they have to offer, people operate under the principle of reciprocity, for, by indicating that one possesses valued qualities, each person is attempting to establish a claim on others for the receipt of rewards from them. All exchange operates under the presumption that people who bestow rewards will receive rewards in turn as payment for value received.

Actors attempt to impress each other through *competition* in which they reveal the rewards they have to offer in an effort to force others, in accordance with the norm of reciprocity, to reciprocate with an even more valuable reward. Social life is thus rife with people's competitive efforts to impress each other and thereby extract valuable rewards. But as interaction proceeds, it inevitably becomes evident to the parties to an exchange that some people have more valued resources to offer than others, putting them in a unique position to extract rewards from all others who value the resources they have to offer.

It is at this point in exchange relations that groups of individuals become *differentiated* in terms of the resources they possess and the kinds of reciprocal demands they can make on others. Blau then asks an analytical question that Homans typically ignored: What generic types or classes of rewards can those with resources extract in return for bestowing their valued resources upon others? Blau conceptualizes four general classes of such rewards: money, social approval, esteem or respect, and compliance. While Homans discussed extensively each of these rewards, he failed to conceptualize them as an exhaustive categorization of types of rewards that could be incorporated into abstract theoretical statements. It is to this end that Blau devotes considerable attention. Although he does not make full use of his categorization of classes of rewards, he offers some suggestive clues about how these abstract theoretical statements can be formulated.

Blau first ranks these generalized reinforcers in terms of their value to those in a position to extract rewards from others in exchange for services rendered. In most social relations, money is an inappropriate reward and hence is the least valuable reward. Social approval is an appropriate reward, but for most humans it is not very valuable, thus forcing those who derive valued services to offer with great frequency the more valuable reward of esteem or respect to those providing valued services. In many situations, the services offered can command no more than respect and esteem from those receiving the benefit of services. At times, however, the services offered are sufficiently valuable to require those receiving them to offer, in accordance with the principles of reciprocity and fair exchange, the most valuable class of rewards—compliance with one's requests.

When people can extract compliance in an exchange relationship, they have "power," since they have the capacity to withhold rewarding services and thereby punish or inflict heavy costs on those who might withhold compliance. To conceptualize the degree of power possessed by individuals, Blau formulates four general propositions that determine the capacity of powerful individuals to extract compliance:[17]

1. The more services people can supply in return for the receipt of particularly valued services, the less those providing these particularly valued services can extract compliance.
2. The more alternative sources of rewards people have, the less those providing valuable services can extract compliance.
3. The more those receiving valuable services from particular individuals can employ physical force and coercion, the less those providing the services can extract compliance.
4. The more those receiving the valuable services can do without them, the less those providing the services can extract compliance.

These four propositions list the conditions leading to differentiation of members in social groups in terms of power. To the extent that group members can supply some services in return, seek alternative rewards, potentially use physical force, or do without certain valuable

---

[17] Blau, *Exchange and Power*, pp. 118–19.

services, individuals who can provide valuable services will be able to extract only esteem and approval from group members; thus, groups will be differentiated in terms of prestige rankings but not power. Naturally, as Blau emphasizes, most social groups reveal complex patterns of differentiation of power, prestige, and patterns of approval; but, of particular interest to him, are the dynamics involved in generating power, authority, and opposition.

In focusing almost exclusively on the questions of power, authority, and opposition, Blau fails to complete his analysis of how different types of social structures are influenced by the exchange of different classes of rewards. The logic of Blau's argument would require additional propositions that would indicate how various types of rewards lead to the differentiation of groups, not only in terms of power and authority, but also with respect to esteem and prestige rankings and networks of social approval. Interesting theoretical questions left unanswered include: What are the "conditions" for the emergence of different types of prestige rankings? What are the "conditions" for the creation of various types of approval networks? Presumably, answers to these questions are left to others to provide. Blau chooses to focus primarily on the problem of how power is converted into authority and how, in accordance with his seven basic exchange principles, various patterns of integration and opposition become evident in human groupings.

For Blau, power differentials in groups create two contradictory forces: (1) strains toward *integration* and (2) strains toward *opposition* and conflict.

Strains toward Integration.   Differences in power inevitably create the potential for conflict. However, such potential is frequently suspended by a series of forces promoting the conversion of power into authority, in which subordinates accept as legitimate the demands of leaders for compliance. Principles 2 and 5 denote two processes fostering such group integration: Exchange relations always operate under the presumption of reciprocity, forcing those deriving valued services to provide other rewards in payment (principle 2). In providing these rewards, subordinates are guided by norms of fair exchange, in which the costs they incur in offering compliance are to be "proportional" to the value of the services they receive from leaders (principle 5). Thus, to the extent that actors engage in exchanges with leaders, and to the degree that the services provided by leaders are considered highly valuable, subordination must be accepted as legitimate in accordance with the norms of reciprocity and fairness which emerge in all exchanges. Under these conditions, groups "elaborate" additional norms specifying just how exchanges with leaders are to be conducted in order to regularize the requirements for reciprocity and to maintain fair rates of exchange. Leaders who conform to these emergent norms can usually assure themselves that their leadership will be considered legitimate. In fact, Blau emphasizes that if leaders abide by the norms regulating exchange of their services for compliance, norms carrying negative sanctions typically emerge among subordinates stressing the need for compliance to leaders' requests. Through this process, subordinates exercise considerable social control over each others' actions and thereby promote the integration of super- and subordinate segments of groupings.

Authority, therefore, "rests on the common norms in a collectivity of subordinates that constrain its individual members to conform to the orders of a superior."[18] In many patterns of social organization these norms simply emerge out of the competitive exchanges among collective groups of actors. Frequently, however, in order for such "normative agreements" to be struck, participants in an exchange must be socialized into a common set of values which define not only what constitutes "fair exchange" in a given situation, but also the way such exchange should be institutionalized into norms for both leaders and superiors. Although it is quite possible for actors to arrive at normative consensus in the course of the exchange process itself, an initial set of common values facilitates the legitimation of power. Actors can now enter into exchanges with a common "definition of the situation," which can provide a general framework for the normative regulation of emerging power differentials. Without common values, the competition for power is likely to be severe. In the absence of guidelines about what should constitute "reciprocity" and "fair exchange," considerable strain and tension will persist as definitions of reciprocity and fair exchange are worked out. For Blau, then, legitimation "entails not merely tolerant approval but active confirmation and promotion of social patterns by common values, either preexisting ones or those that emerge in a collectivity in the course of social interaction."[19]

With the legitimation of power through the normative regulation of interaction, as "confirmed" by common values, the structure of collective organization is altered. One of the most evident changes is the decline in interpersonal competition, for now actors' presentations of

---

[18] Ibid., p. 208.
[19] Ibid., p. 221.

self shift from a concern with impressing others with their valuable qualities to an emphasis on confirming their statuses as loyal group members. Subordinates come to accept their statuses and manipulate their role behaviors in an effort to assure that they receive social approval from their peers as a reward for conformity to group norms. Leaders can typically assume a lower profile, since it is no longer necessary to demonstrate in each and every encounter with subordinates their superior qualities—especially since norms now define *when* and *how* they should extract conformity and esteem for providing their valued services. Thus, with the legitimation of power as authority, the interactive processes, involving the way group members define the situation and present themselves to others, undergoes a dramatic change, reducing the degree of competition and thereby fostering group integration.

With these events, the amount of direct interaction between leaders and subordinates usually declines, since power and ranking no longer must be constantly negotiated. This decline in direct interaction marks the formation of distinct subgroupings as members seek to interact with those of their own social rank, avoiding the costs of interacting with either their inferiors or superiors.[20] In interacting primarily among themselves, subordinates avoid the high costs of interacting with leaders; while social approval from their peers is not a particularly valuable reward, it can be extracted with comparatively few costs—thus allowing for a sufficient profit. Conversely, leaders can avoid the high costs (in terms of time and energy) of constantly competing and negotiating with inferiors over when and how compliance and esteem are to be bestowed upon them. Instead, by having relatively limited and well-defined contact with subordinates, they can derive the high rewards that come from compliance and esteem without incurring excessive costs in interacting with subordinates—thereby allowing for a profit.

Strains toward Opposition. Thus far, Blau's exchange perspective is decidedly functional. Social exchange processes—attraction, competition, differentiation, and integration—have been viewed in terms of how they contribute to creating a legitimated set of normatively regulated relations. In a manner similar to Parsons's discussion of institutionalization, Blau has also emphasized the importance of common values as a significant force in creating patterns of social organization. However, Blau is keenly aware that social organization is always rife with conflict and opposition, creating an inevitable dialectic between integration and

---

[20] As will be recalled from Chapter 11, these processes were insightfully described by George C. Homans in *The Human Group* (New York: Harcourt, Brace & World, 1950).

opposition in social structures. Recognition of this fact has led Blau to assert:[21]

> The functional approach reinforces the overemphasis on integrative social forces . . . whereas the dialectical perspective counteracts it by requiring explicit concern with disruptive tendencies in social structures. The pursuit of systematic analysis and the adoption of a dialectical perspective create a dilemma for the sociologist, who must rivet his attention on consistent social patterns for the sake of the former and on inconsistencies in accordance with the latter. This dilemma, like others, is likely to give rise to alternating developments, making him veer in one direction at one time and in the opposite at another.

What is important about Blau's perspective is that, in adopting dialectical assumptions, he does not reject polemically the useful tenets of functionalism. Blau recognizes that patterns of social organization are created and maintained *as well as* changed and broken down, leading him to seek the principles that can explain this spectrum of events. Thus, unlike Dahrendorf's conflict model, in which the organization of authority relations in "imperatively coordinated associations" (ICAs) and the opposition of "quasi groups" were merely taken *as givens,* Blau has sought to address the question of how, and through what processes, authority structures such as ICAs are created. In so doing, Blau is in a much better analytical position than Dahrendorf and other dialectical theorists to document how the creation of social structure can also, under specifiable conditions, set in motion forces for conflict and change. As was emphasized in the earlier discussion of conflict theory, to *assert* that conflict is endemic to authority relations in social structure, and then to analyze how such conflict changes such structure, is to define away the interesting theoretical question: Under *what* conditions, in *what* types of structures, revealing *what* types of authority which have arisen through *what* processes, is *what* type of conflict likely to emerge? Blau's discussion of "strains for integration" represents an attempt to answer this question and provide a more balanced theoretical framework for discussing opposition and conflict in social systems.

Much as Parsons' emphasis in *The Social System*[22] on the "mechanisms" of socialization and social control implied that a failure in these mechanisms would generate deviance, conflict, and change, so Blau's

---

[21] Peter M. Blau, "Dialectical Sociology: Comments," *Sociological Inquiry* 42 (Spring 1972): 185. This article was written in reply to an attempt to document Blau's shift from a functional to dialectical perspective; see Michael A. Weinstein and Deena Weinstein, "Blau's Dialectical Sociology," ibid., pp. 173–82.

[22] Parsons, *Social System,* pp. 201–325.

emphasis on the failure to enter exchange with, or develop through the exchange process, a common set of values and regulative norms reveals how those processes that create patterns of social organization can also operate to create opposition, conflict, and change in social systems. Unlike Parsons, however, Blau has formulated abstract theoretical statements that help conceptualize more precisely the events that operate to cause a failure in those processes maintaining institutionalized patterns. The first of these abstract theoretical statements can be found in principles 3, 6, and 7. As principle 3 documents, the failure to receive "expected" rewards in return for various activities leads actors to attempt to apply negative sanctions which, when ineffective, can drive people to violent "retaliation" against those who have denied them an expected reward. Such retaliation is intensified by principle 5 on "fair exchange," since when they violate such norms, those in power inflict excessive costs on subordinates, creating a situation, which, at a minimum, leads to attempts to sanction negatively and, at most, to retaliation. Finally, principle 6 on the inevitable imbalances emerging from multiple exchange relations emphasizes that to balance relations in one exchange context by meeting reciprocal obligations and conforming to norms of fairness is to put into imbalance other relations. Thus, the imbalances potentially encourage a cyclical process in which actors seek to balance previously unbalanced relations and thereby throw into imbalance currently balanced exchanges. In turn, exchange relations that are thrown into imbalance violate the norms of reciprocity and fair exchange, thus causing attempts at negative sanctioning, and, under some conditions, retaliation. For Blau, then, built into *all* exchange relationships are sources of imbalance. When severely violating norms of reciprocity and fair exchange, these imbalances can lead to open conflict among individuals in group contexts.

At this level of generality, however, these suggestive principles simply state what *can* occur, without specifying the conditions under which the forces they denote will actually be set into motion. Unfortunately, despite this promising analytical lead, Blau provides few specific propositions that delineate when the propensities for opposition are activated. It is perhaps at this point that propositions similar to those developed by Dahrendorf could prove useful, since they specify some of the conditions under which those exchange processes leading to patterns of social organization also cause conflict. It is no coincidence, then, that when Blau does undertake a limited discussion of the conditions leading to increasingly intense forms of opposition, his analysis resembles

Dahrendorf's discussion of the technical, political, and social conditions of conflict group organization:

1. The more exchange relations between super- and subordinates become imbalanced, the greater the probability of opposition to those with power.
   (a) The more norms of reciprocity are violated by the superordinates, the greater the imbalance.
   (b) The more norms of fair exchange are violated by superordinates, the greater the imbalance.
2. The more individuals experience *collectively* relations of imbalance with superordinates, the greater their sense of deprivation, and the greater the probability of opposition to those with power.
   (a) The less the spatial dispersion of subordinates, the more likely they are to experience collectively relations of imbalance with superordinates.
   (b) The more subordinates can communicate with each other, the more likely they are to experience collectively relations of imbalance with superordinates.
3. The more subordinates can experience collectively deprivations in exchange relations with superordinates, the more likely they are to codify ideologically their deprivations and the greater their opposition to those with power.
4. The more deprivations of subordinates are ideologically codified, the greater the sense of solidarity among subordinates, and the greater the probability of opposition.
5. The greater the sense of solidarity among subordinates, the more they can define their opposition as a noble and worthy cause, and the greater the probability of their opposition to those with power.
6. The greater the sense of ideological solidarity, the more likely are subordinates to view opposition as an end in itself, and the greater the probability of opposition to those with power.[23]

At best, what emerges from these propositions and the somewhat discursive context in which they are imbedded is a general sense of how Blau conceptualizes opposition to emerge.[24] Blau seemingly hypothesizes that the more imbalanced exchange relations are experienced collectively, the greater the sense of deprivation and the greater

---

[23] Blau, *Exchange and Power*, pp. 224–52.
[24] Ibid.

is the potential for opposition. While he does not explicitly state the case, he appears to hold that increasing ideological codification of deprivations, the formation of group solidarity, and the emergence of conflict as a way of life will increase the intensity of the opposition—that is, members' emotional involvement in and commitment to opposition to those with power.

The vagueness of Blau's model on the various *types* and *classes* of opposition that can emerge from imbalanced exchange relations offers little more than a suggestive lead for conceptualizing inherent processes of opposition in exchange relations. Unlike Dahrendorf's dialectical model, Blau's scheme does offer some important theoretical insights into how the creation of relations of authority can also cause opposition. Beyond the analytical clues provided by principles 3, 6, and 7 of his general exchange perspective, however, the variables specifying the subsequent course of the opposition—for example, its intensity, violence, duration, and outcomes—remain unspecified.

Blau's conceptualization of the processes of institutionalization *and* conflict in terms of the same abstract exchange principles does represent a significant improvement over Parsons' portrayal of institutionalization, which lacked an explicit formulation of principles governing conflict and change. It also goes beyond Dahrendorf's model, which failed to specify either how institutionalized patterns or latent conflicts first emerged in authority systems. Further, Blau's presentation represents an improvement over Homans' analysis of institutionalization and of the inherent conflict between the institutional and subinstitutional, since in Blau's scheme there is a more adequate conceptualization of the process of institutionalization of the power relations from which opposition, innovation, and deviance ultimately spring. Thus, despite the weakness of his discussion of the dialectical forces of opposition, Blau's efforts do suggest ways the model can be improved: (*a*) by more precise formulation of the conditions under which exchange imbalances are likely for various types of social units; and then (*b*) by specification of the conditions leading to various levels of intensity, violence, and duration in relations of opposition among various types of social units.

In looking back on Blau's discussion of micro exchange processes, it is clear that he visualizes a series of basic exchange processes in human groupings: attraction, competition, differentiation, integration, and opposition. Of particular interest are the processes of differentiation in terms of power and how this pattern of differentiation creates strains for both integration and opposition—thus giving social reality a dialectical character. Also noteworthy in the perspective is the attempt to utilize concepts developed in the analysis of elementary exchange processes in order to examine more complex exchange processes among the macro social units of social systems. Of great significance is the fact that Blau recognizes the necessity for reformulating and supplementing elementary exchange concepts when analyzing more complex social processes. As will become evident, he also realizes that the basic social processes of attraction, competition, differentiation, integration, and opposition still typify exchanges even among macro social units—thus giving social life a degree of continuity.

Complex Exchange Systems

While the general processes of attraction, competition, differentiation, integration, and opposition are evident in the exchanges among macro structures, there are several fundamental differences between these exchanges and those among micro structures:

1. In complex exchanges among macro structures, the significance of "shared values" increases, for it is through such values that indirect exchanges among macro structures are mediated.
2. Exchange networks among macro structures are typically institutionalized. While spontaneous exchange is a ubiquitous feature of social life, there are usually well-established historical arrangements that circumscribe the operation of the basic exchange processes of attraction, competition, differentiation, integration, and even opposition among collective units.
3. Since macro structures are themselves the product of more elementary exchange processes, the analysis of macro structures requires the analysis of more than one level of social organization.[25]

Mediating Values. For Blau, the "interpersonal attraction" of elementary exchange among individuals is replaced by "shared values" at the macro level. These values can be conceptualized as "media of social transactions" in that they provide a common set of standards for conducting the complex chains of indirect exchanges among social structures and their individual members. Such values are viewed by Blau as providing effective mediation of complex exchanges by virtue of the fact that the individual members of social structures have usually been socialized into a set of common values, leading them to accept them as "appropriate." Furthermore, when coupled with codification into laws and enforcement procedures by those groups and organizations with power, shared

---

[25] Ibid., pp. 253–311.

values provide a means for mediating the complex and indirect exchanges among the macro structures of large-scale systems. In mediating indirect exchanges among groups and organizations, shared values provide standards for the calculation of: (a) expected rewards (principle 1), (b) reciprocity (principle 2), and (c) fair exchange (principle 5).

Thus, since individual people are not the units of complex exchanges, Blau emphasizes that, in order for complex patterns of social organization to emerge and persist, it is necessary for a "functional equivalent" of direct interpersonal attraction to exist. This "functional equivalent" assures that exchange can proceed in accordance with principles 1, 2, and 5. And even when complex exchanges do involve people, their interactions are frequently so protracted and indirect that one individual's rewards are contingent on others who are far removed, requiring that common values guide and regulate the exchanges.

There is considerable similarity between Blau's concern with "mediating values" and Parsons' recent interest in "generalized media of exchange."[26] While the respective conceptualizations of the general classes and types of media differ, each is concerned with how social relationships utilize in varying contexts distinctive "symbols," not only to establish the respective "values" of actions among exchange units, but also to specify just how the exchange should be conducted. The similarity of their strategies is particularly evident by the fact that Blau employs Parsons' pattern variable, universalism-particularism, in attempting to conceptualize the most generic types of "mediating values" for the processes of attraction, competition, and differentiation. For Blau, "particularistic values" are the media of "integration" and "solidarity" in complex exchange systems. By providing the parties to complex exchange relations with a set of unique standards for judging and evaluating themselves as distinct from other groupings, particularistic values "unite members of a collectivity in common solidarity and extend the scope of integrative bonds far beyond the limits of personal feelings of attraction."[27] Particularistic values thus represent a set of symbols for identifying a group from other collectivities, thereby providing a "medium through which

[26] See discussion in Chapter 3, as well as Talcott Parsons, "On the Concept of Political Power," *Proceedings of the American Philosophical Society* 107 (June 1963): 232–62; Talcott Parsons, "On the Concept of Influence," *Public Opinion Quarterly* 27 (Spring 1963): 37–67; and Talcott Parsons, "Some Problems of General Theory," in *Theoretical Sociology: Perspectives and Developments*, ed. J. C. McKinney and E. A. Tiryakian (New York: Appleton-Century-Crofts, 1970), pp. 28–68. See also T. S. Turner, "Parsons' Concept of Generalized Media of Social Interaction and Its Relevance for Social Anthropology," *Sociological Inquiry* 38 (Spring 1968): 121–34.

[27] Blau, *Exchange and Power*, p. 267.

its members are bound together into a cohesive community."[28] So, once accepted and shared by group members, particularistic values serve as "functional substitutes for sentiments of personal attraction that integrate the members of a face-to-face group into a cohesive unit."[29] "Universalistic values" are media of "exchange and differentiation" in complex exchange systems.[30] One of the fundamental problems facing indirect exchange relationships revolves around how to standardize the "value" of various types of activity. Universalistic values perform this "function" of standardizing and making comparable the value of activities across extended networks of exchange relations. Much as money in economic transactions represents a measure of value for widely diverse and extended exchanges, so universalistic values provide common standards for measuring an exchange party's "contributions" and the kinds and amounts of variously valued rewards it should receive. In doing so, universalistic values allow for the unequal, but "fair," distribution of rewards and privileges across extended exchange networks. Without such values, social competition and differentiation of super- and subordinates beyond immediate face-to-face relations could not occur, since there would be no way to assess either the value of the services provided by superordinates in large social groupings or the rewards they should receive in return for providing these services. Universalistic values therefore allow ranking and stratification to occur in macro systems, where most exchange relations are indirect.

Thus, the Parsonian concept, universalism-particularism, provides Blau with a way to classify the values necessary for the basic processes of attraction, competition, and differentiation to occur in complex exchange systems. Particularistic values "attract" members of collectivities toward each other, facilitating the expectation of rewards. Universalistic values establish standards for assessing the "winners" and "losers" in competition, while specifying the rate of exchange between services and rewards among subordinates and superordinates in larger collectivities.

In discussing the other two basic social processes—integration and opposition—Blau does not find a convenient parallel in Parsons' pattern variables. He thus must posit two additional types of mediating values: "legitimating values" and "opposition values." Values legitimating authority are "media of organization, which extend the scope of organized social control."[31] In direct interpersonal exchanges, the exercise of power

[28] Ibid.
[29] Ibid.
[30] Ibid., pp. 268–70.
[31] Ibid., p. 270.

(demands for compliance in exchange for valuable services) is mediated by norms enforced directly by the participants to the exchange. Values legitimating authority remove regulation of power from the individuals in the exchange by bestowing on various "positions" and "offices," rather than on individuals, the right to demand compliance in some situations. By removing power from the realm of "personal influence," and vesting it in the rights of offices and positions, the range and scope of power is expanded. It now becomes possible to have authority that organizes, for example, an entire nation, as is the case when a government or body of administrative offices is legitimated and given the right to extract compliance in exchange for providing certain services.

"Opposition values" are the media of social change and reorganization in a complex exchange system.[32] Such values allow for the organization of opposition beyond the limits of individual influence and proselytizing, because they provide a set of common symbols that can potentially codify the grievances of large and diverse segments of collectivities into a "countervailing force against entrenched powers and existing institutions in the society."[33] These symbols unite those who have suffered deprivations in existing exchange relations and make them willing, under various conditions, to sacrifice their present material welfare in pursuit of change and reorganization of the current exchange system.

In sum, then, complex exchange systems are dependent upon "shared values," which "mediate" exchange relations between individuals and macro structures as well as between various types of macro structures. Without shared values, exchange is tied to the direct interpersonal interactions of individual people. Since virtually all known social systems involve indirect exchange relations among various types of social units—from individuals and groups to organizations and communities—it is necessary to conceptualize just how this can occur. For Blau, mediating values are a critical condition for complex exchange systems to emerge, persist, and break down. Without them, social organization beyond face-to-face interaction would not be possible.

Institutionalization. While values facilitate processes of indirect exchange among diverse types of social units, institutionalization denotes those processes that regularize and stabilize complex exchange processes.[34] As people and various forms of collective organization become dependent upon particular networks of indirect exchange for ex-

---

[32] Ibid., p. 271.

[33] Ibid.

[34] Ibid., pp. 273–80.

pected rewards, pressures for formalizing exchange networks through explicit norms increase. This formalization and regularization of complex exchange systems can be effective under three minimal conditions: (*a*) The formalized exchange networks must have profitable payoffs for most parties to the exchange. (*b*) Most individuals organized into collective units must have internalized through prior socialization the mediating values used to build exchange networks. And (*c*) those units with power in the exchange system must receive a level of rewards that moves them to seek actively the formalization of rules governing exchange relations.

Institutions are historical products, whose norms and underlying mediating values are handed down from one generation to another, thereby limiting and circumscribing the kinds of indirect exchange networks that can emerge. Institutions exert a kind of "external constraint" on individuals and various types of collective units, bending exchange processes to fit their prescriptions and proscriptions. Institutions thus represent a set of relatively stable and general norms regularizing different patterns of indirect and complex exchange relations among diverse social units.

This conception of institutionalization is similar to the somewhat divergent formulations of both Parsons and Homans. While institutions represent for both thinkers the regularization through norms of interaction patterns, Parsons visualizes institutions as normative structures, infused with values, which allow for the patterning of interaction among diversely oriented and goal-seeking actors, while Homans considers institutions as the formalization through norms and generalized reinforcers of exchange relations that ultimately have payoffs for each individual person involved. Despite their respective points of emphasis, however, both are concerned with the basic process through which norms emerge to facilitate the attainment of "goals" and "rewards" by social units. The formalization of such institutional norms is viewed by both to allow for expanded networks of "interaction" or "exchange" among various social units: for Homans, the "Person"; and for Parsons, the "Actor." Blau's conceptualization draws from both these perspectives by emphasizing, in a vein similar to Homans, that institutionalized patterns of interaction must have payoffs for the reward-seeking individuals involved and, in a way reminiscent of Parsons, that shared values must exist prior to effective institutionalization of indirect exchange relations. In this way, Blau apparently has sought to weld exchange-theoretical principles to the functionalist's concern with how values and norms account for the emergence and persistence of complex social systems.

In doing so, Blau apparently recognizes Homans' failure to develop concepts that describe the various types and classes of institutionalized exchange systems. In an effort to correct for this oversight, Blau develops a typology of institutions embracing both the substance and style of the Parsonian formulation. Just as Parsons employed the pattern variables to describe the values guiding institutionalized patterns, Blau attempts to classify institutions in terms of the values they appear to embody in their normative structure. He posits three generic types of institutions: (a) *integrative institutions* "perpetuate particularistic values, maintain social solidarity, and preserve the distinctive character and identity of the social structure";[35] (b) *distributive institutions* embody universalistic values and operate to "preserve the social arrangements that have been developed for the production and distribution of needed social facilities, contributions, and rewards of various kinds";[36] and (c) *organizational institutions* utilize values legitimating authority and serve "to perpetuate the authority and organization necessary to mobilize resources and coordinate collective effort in the pursuit of social objectives."[37]

However, Blau also recognizes that in this form of typologizing the potential is great for connoting an image of society as static and equilibrium maintaining. Thus, drawing from Homans' recognition that institutions are accepted only as long as they have payoffs for humans' "primary needs" and from Dahrendorf's concern with the inherent sources of conflict and change in all relations of authority, Blau stresses that all institutionalized exchange systems reveal a *counterinstitutional component*, "consisting of those basic values and ideals that have not been realized and have not found expression in explicit institutional forms, and which are the ultimate source of social change."[38] To the extent that these values remain unrealized in institutionalized exchange relations, individuals who have internalized them will derive little payoff from existing institutional arrangements and will therefore feel deprived, seeking alternatives to dominant institutions. These unrealized values, even when codified into an opposition ideology advocating open revolution, usually contain at least some of the ideals and ultimate objectives legitimated by the prevailing culture, indicating that institutional arrangements "contain the seeds of their potential destruction" by failing to

---

[35] Ibid., p. 278.

[36] Ibid.

[37] Ibid., p. 279. It is of interest to note that Blau implicitly defines institutions in terms of their functions for the social whole. While these functions are not made explicit, they are similar to Parsons's requisites. For example, "integrative institutions" appear to meet "needs" for "latency"; "distributive institutions," for "adaptation"; and "organizational institutions," for "integration" and "goal attainment."

[38] Ibid., p. 279.

meet all of the expectations of reward raised by institutionalized values.

While Blau does not enumerate extensively the conditions leading to the mobilization of individuals into conflict groups, his scheme explicitly denotes the source of conflict and change: counterinstitutional values whose failure of realization by dominant institutional arrangements create deprivations that, under unspecified conditions, can lead to conflict and change in social systems. In this way, Blau attempts to avoid the predictable charges leveled against almost any form of functional analysis for failing to account for the sources of conflict, deviance, and change in social systems. Unlike the Dahrendorf model of dialectical conflict, however, Blau's scheme does not just assert the pervasiveness of conflict and change in social systems, but attempts to document how opposition forces, culminating in conflict and change, are created by the very processes that lead to the institutionalization of power in complex exchange systems.

Such tendencies for complex exchange systems to generate opposition are explicable in terms of the basic principles of exchange.[39] When certain mediating values are not institutionalized in a social system, exchange relations will not be viewed as "reciprocated" by those who have internalized these values. Thus, in accordance with Blau's principle 3 on "reciprocity," the more likely are these segments of a collectivity to feel deprived and seek ways of retaliating against the dominant institutional arrangements which, from the perspective dictated by their values, have failed to reciprocate. For those who have internalized values that are not institutionalized, it is also likely that perceptions of fair exchange have been violated, leading them, in accordance with principle 6, to attempt to sanction negatively those arrangements that violate alternative norms of fair exchange. Finally, the operation of principles 3 and 6 in complex exchange systems is assured by the fact that, in accordance with principle 7, in institutionalized exchange networks the balancing of exchange relations with some segments of a collectivity inevitably create imbalances in relations with other segments, thereby violating norms of reciprocity and fairness and setting into motion forces of opposition.

Unlike direct interpersonal exchanges, however, opposition in complex exchange systems is between large collective units of organization, which in their internal dynamics reveal their own propensities for integration and opposition. This fact requires that the analysis of integration and opposition in complex exchange networks be attuned to various levels

---

[39] Ibid., see chap. 12, "Dialectical Forces," pp. 312–38.

of social organization. Such analysis needs to show, in particular, how exchange processes among macro structures, whether for integration or opposition, are partly influenced by the exchange processes occurring among their constituent substructures.

Levels of Social Organization. To a great extent, the "dynamics of macro structures rests on the manifold interdependence between the social forces within and among their substructures."[40] The patterns of interdependence among the substructures of distinguishable macro structures are various, including: (*a*) joint membership by some members of macro structures in constituent substructures; (*b*) mobility of members between various substructures of macro structures; and (*c*) direct exchange relations among the substructures of different macro structures.

To discern these dynamics of substructures and how they influence exchanges among macro structures, Blau first raises the question of what generic types of substructures exist, resulting in the isolation of four classes of substructures: categories, communities, organized collectivities, and social systems. *Categories* refer to an attribute, such as race, sex, and age, that "actually governs the relations among people and their orientations to each other."[41] *Communities* are "collectivities organized in given territories, which typically have their own government and geographical boundaries that preclude their being overlapping, though every community includes smaller and is part of larger territorial organizations."[42] *Organized collectivities* are "associations of people with a distinctive social organization, which may range from a small informal friendship clique to a large bureaucratized formal organization."[43] *Social systems* "consist not of the social relations in specific collectivities but of analytical principles of organization, such as the economy of a society or its political institutions."[44]

Values mediate the processes within these various types of substructures. "Particularistic values" allow for each substructure to create segregating boundaries; "universalistic values" allow for differentiation of units with substructures; "legitimating values" stabilize relations of authority; and "opposition values" give substructures their own internal sources of dialectical change. Discerning the complex relationships between the mediating values of substructures and those of macro structures poses one of the most difficult problems of analysis. On the one hand, some

---

40 Ibid., p. 284.
41 Ibid., p. 285.
42 Ibid.
43 Ibid.
44 Ibid.

values must cut across the substructures of a macro structure if the latter is to remain minimally integrated; on the other hand, values of various substructures not only can segregate substructures from each other, but also generate conflict among them. Further, the relations among substructures involve the same basic exchange processes of attraction, competition, and differentiation in terms of the services they can provide for each other. It thus becomes evident that the analysis of exchange networks among macro structures forces examination of the exchange processes of their substructures. Additionally, the relations among these substructures are complicated by the fact that they often have overlapping memberships or mobility of members between them, making the analysis of attraction, competition, differentiation, integration, and opposition increasingly difficult.

Blau simplifies the complex analytical task of examining the dynamics of substructures by positing that organized collectivities, especially formal organizations, are the most important substructures in the analysis of macro structures. As explicitly goal (reward) seeking structures that frequently cut across social categories and communities and that form the substructures of analytical social systems, they are mainly responsible for the dynamics of macro structures. Thus, the theoretical analysis of complex exchange systems among macro structures requires that primary attention be drawn to the relations of attraction, competition, differentiation, integration, and opposition among various types of complex organizations. In emphasizing the pivotal significance of complex organizations, Blau posits a particular image of society that should guide the ultimate construction of sociological theory.

BLAU'S IMAGE OF SOCIETY

Organizations in a society must typically derive rewards from each other, thus creating a situation in which they are both "attracted" to, and in competition with, each other. Out of this competition, hierarchical differentiation between successful and less successful organizations operating in the same sphere emerges. Such differentiation usually creates strains toward specialization in different fields among less successful organizations as they seek to provide particular goods and services for dominant organizations and each other. If such differentiation and specialization among organizations is to provide effective means for integration, separate political organizations must also emerge to regulate their exchanges. Such political organizations possess power and are viewed as legitimate only as long as they are considered by individuals and organizations to follow the dictates of shared cultural values. Typically political organizations are charged with several objectives: (a) regulating complex networks of indirect exchange by the enactment of laws; (b) controlling through law competition among dominant organizations, thereby assuring the latter of scarce resources; (c) protecting existing exchange networks among organizations, especially those with power, from encroachment on these rewards by organizations opposing the current distribution of resources.

For Blau, then, it is out of the competition among organizations in a society that differentiation and specialization occurs among macro structures. While mediating values allow differentiation and specialization among organizations to occur, it is also necessary for separate political organizations to exist and regularize, through laws and the use of force, existent patterns of exchange among other organizations. Such political organizations will be viewed as legitimate as long as they normatively regulate exchanges that reflect the tenets of mediating values and protect the payoffs for most organizations, especially the most powerful. However, the existence of political authority inevitably encourages opposition movements, for now opposition groups have a clear target—the political organizations—against which to address their grievances. As long as political authority remains diffuse, opposition organizations can only compete unsuccessfully against various dominant organizations. With the legitimation of clear-cut political organizations charged with preserving current patterns of organization, opposition movements can concentrate their energies against one organization, the political system.

In addition to providing deprived groups with a target for their aggressions, political organizations inevitably must aggravate the deprivations of various segments of a population, because political control involves exerting constraints and distributing resources unequally. Those segments of the population that must bear the brunt of such constraint and unequal distribution usually experience an escalated sense of deprivation in terms of the principles of reciprocity and fair exchange which, under various conditions, cause their *organization* into a movement against the existing political authorities. To the extent that this organized opposition forces redistribution of rewards, other segments of the population are likely to feel constrained and deprived, leading them to organize into an opposition movement. These facts indicate that the organization of political authority assures that, in accordance with principle 7, attempts to balance one set of exchange relations among organizations throws into imbalance other exchange relations, causing the formation of opposition organizations. Thus, built into the structure of political authority in a society are inherent forces of opposition that give society a dialectical and dynamic character.

Echoing the assumptions of Dahrendorf and Coser, Blau conceptualizes opposition as representing "a regenerative force that interjects new vitality into a social structure and becomes the basis of social reorganization."[45] However, the extent to which opposition can result in dramatic social change is limited by several counterforces inhering in patterns of organization in complex exchange systems among organizations:[46] (a) The interdependence of the majority of organizations upon each other for rewards gives each a vested interest in the status quo, thus providing strong resistance to opposition organizations. (b) Dominant organizations that have considerable power to bestow rewards on other organizations independently of political organizations have a particularly strong vested interest in existing arrangements, thereby assuring their resistence to change-oriented organizations. (c) By virtue of controlling the distribution of valued resources, both dominant and political organizations are in a strategic position to make necessary concessions to opposition groups, thereby diffusing their effective organization. (d) Opposition movements must overcome the internalization of values by the majority; and without control of the means of socialization, their ideological call for organization is likely to fall on unsympathetic ears. (e) Societies composed of exchange networks among complex organizations typically reveal high levels of social mobility up the organizational hierarchy, thus increasing the difficulties involved in organizing a stable constituency.[47]

In reviewing Blau's analysis of exchanges among organizations in a society, it is evident that he has attempted to cast many of the assumptions and propositions of Parsons, Dahrendorf, and Coser into an exchange perspective that extends Homans' insights beyond the analysis of individuals. In discussing the development of exchange systems among organizations, and the emergence of political authority, Blau focuses on the institutionalization of relations among what Parsons termed "social systems." The fact that such institutionalization rests upon the internalization of shared values and that institutional patterns can be typologized in terms of the dominance of various clusters of values further underscores Blau's analytical debt to Parsons. In contrast with Parsons' less explicit

---

[45] Ibid., p. 301. Such a position is inevitable in light of Blau's explicitly stated belief that "our society is in need of fundamental reforms" (Blau, "Dialectical Sociology," p. 184).

[46] Blau, "Dialectical Sociology," p. 187; Blau, *Exchange and Power*, pp. 301–9.

[47] However, Blau recognizes that high rates of mobility in a society can also increase the sense of relative deprivation of those who are denied opportunities for advancement—thereby making them likely constituents of an opposition organization.

analysis, Blau's analysis is concerned with "mechanisms" of social change. Embracing Marx's and Dahrendorf's assumptions of the dialectical forces of opposition inherent in all micro and macro relations of power and authority, Blau visualizes the source of conflict as lying in the unbalanced exchange relations, violating norms of reciprocity and fairness, which are inevitable concomitants of some organizations having a disproportionate hold upon valued resources.

Blau does not enumerate as explicitly as did either Marx or Dahrendorf the conditions leading to the organization of opposition ("conflict groups" for Dahrendorf and "class" for Marx). But his debt to Marx's insightful analysis (see Chapter 6) is evident in his analysis on how levels of deprivation are influenced by (a) the degree of ecological concentration and the capacity to communicate among the deprived, (b) the capacity to codify an opposition ideology, (c) the degree of social solidarity among the deprived, and (d) the degree to which opposition organization is politicized and directed against the political organizations. Furthermore, Blau's incorporation of Dahrendorf's key propositions is shown in his recognition that the capacity of the deprived segments of a population to organize opposition is affected by such variables as the rate of social mobility, the capacity of dominant groups to make strategic concessions, and the number of cross-cutting conflicts resulting from multigroup affiliations. Finally, although Blau does not develop his argument extensively, he clearly has followed Simmel's and Coser's lead in emphasizing that conflict and opposition are a regenerative force in societies, which "constitute countervailing forces against . . . institutional rigidities, rooted in vested powers as well as traditional values, and . . . [which] are essential for speeding social change."[48]

In sum, then, Blau has offered a most varied "image of society." By incorporating—albeit in an unsystematic manner—the fruitful leads of sociology's other dominant conceptual perspectives, Blau has indeed offered a suggestive theoretical "prolegomenon" that can serve as a guide to more explicit theoretical formulations. Despite its suggestiveness, the scheme presents analytical problems that must eventually be resolved. While Blau's solutions are certainly more elegant than Homans' formative efforts, several serious problems with the scheme remain.

CRITICISMS OF BLAU'S EXCHANGE PERSPECTIVE

Blau's theoretical scheme has been subjected to relatively few criticisms, especially when compared with the controversy generated by Ho-

---

[48] Blau, *Exchange and Power,* p. 302.

mans' exchange perspective. Part of the reason for this dearth of critical review stems from the fact that, in synthesizing into an exchange perspective previously diverse theoretical traditions, Blau offers "something for everyone."[49] For the functionalist, Blau offers the concept of mediating values, types of institutions, and the counterpart of mechanisms of socialization and control that operate to maintain macro social wholes. For the conflict theorist, Blau presents a dialectical-conflict perspective emphasizing the inevitable forces of opposition in relations of power and authority. For those concerned with interactions among individuals, Blau's analysis of elementary exchange processes places considerable emphasis on the actions of people in interaction. And, for the critic of Homans' reductionism, Blau provides an insightful portrayal of exchanges among emergent social structures which leaves the "integrity" of sociological theorizing intact.

In offering a theoretical resting place for the major perspectives in sociology, Blau has perhaps provided a clue about how sociological theorizing should proceed: Rather than becoming bogged down in controversies and debates among proponents of various schools, it is much wiser to incorporate the useful concepts and assumptions of diverse perspectives into one theoretical "prolegomenon" describing how and why patterns of social organization emerge, persist, change, and break down. However, in offering this alternative to continued debate, Blau has left a number of theoretical issues unresolved. These issues are obscured by the insightfulness of his synthesis, and yet their resolution constitutes a critical "next step" in his theoretical strategy.

A System of Concepts or Propositions?   Blau's analysis is a mixture of conceptual taxonomies and implicit theoretical generalizations. As was emphasized in the earlier enumeration of the seven exchange principles, these abstract principles are not made explicit. Why should this be so, especially in light of the fact that they so obviously guide his analysis? Perhaps Blau has shied away from statements of sociological laws or axioms, for fear of arousing the avalanche of criticism that accompanied Homans' efforts at stating sociology's first principles. But his failure to make explicit these principles probably has a more deep seated cause: To enumerate sociological laws requires that other concepts be

---

[49] For examples of the few criticisms of Blau's work, see M. J. Mulkay, "A Conceptual Elaboration of Exchange Theory: Blau," in his *Functionalism, Exchange, Theoretical Strategy* (New York: Schocken Books, 1971), especially pp. 206–12; Percy S. Cohen, *Modern Sociological Theory* (New York: Basic Books, 1968), pp. 123–27; and Anthony Heath, "Economic Theory and Sociology: A Critique of P. M. Blau's 'Exchange and Power in Social Life,' " *Sociology* 2 (September 1968): 273–92.

incorporated into the propositions which are to be logically articulated to the laws.

Blau was clearly not prepared to perform this exacting task, preferring instead to delineate, much like Parsons, "bundles of concepts." Such "bundles of concepts" allow Blau considerable analytical leeway, for concepts like mediating values; integrative, distributive, and organizational institutions; counterinstitutional forces; social categories; communities; organized collectivities; and analytical social systems, all appear to overlap conceptually without denoting very precisely the phenomena to which they refer. As such, they can be bent and redefined in an ad hoc fashion to fit whatever the "facts may dictate." Thus, just as Parsons's system of concepts is not tightly interconnected into a logical system, thereby allowing enormous latitude in its use, so Blau's prolegomenon offers the same luxury of applying loosely articulated concepts to empirical phenomena without much possibility of their refutation.

Blau has a ready defense for such criticisms: His goal is not to develop a mature theory, but a scheme that can serve as a "preliminary" to the construction of such theory. The suggestiveness of Blau's perspective gives this defense some credibility; but, unfortunately, few have undertaken the task of making the scheme more theoretically mature. Just why this has been so, especially now that the scheme is 15 years old, is difficult to determine, but part of the reason may lie in Blau's failure to grapple successfully with several additional issues.

The Issue of Tautology.   At the very outset of his presentation, Blau suggests that in limiting his definition of exchange to relations in which rewards are expected and forthcoming, his perspective can avoid charges of tautology. Furthermore, if a theoretical perspective allows for the formulation of testable hypotheses, it is not tautologous, for ultimately "the question of whether the theoretical principles are tautologous depends upon the possibility of *inferring* empirically testable hypotheses from them, and some operational hypotheses will be *inferred* to *illustrate* that this possibility exists" (italics added).[50] However, Blau's consistent lack of logical rigor in making empirical "inferences" from more abstract exchange principles does not obviate the potential for tautology, for without clear-cut use of *logical rules of inference,*[51] empirical hypotheses cannot be considered to have been derived from a theory.

---

[50] *Exchange and Power,* p. 6.

[51] For an interesting discussion of logical rules of influence, see Karl Popper, "Why Are the Calculi of Logic and Arithmetic Applicable to Reality," in his *Conjectures and Refutations: The Growth of Scientific Knowledge* (Routledge & Kegan Paul, 1963), pp. 201–14.

Thus, the theory has not necessarily been vindicated against charges of tautology, since the empirical hypotheses illustrating instances of non-tautology do not bear the necessary logical connections to the theory.

Blau's disclaimers aside, the issue of tautology in exchange theory hinges on the question of whether the value of rewards are conceptualized and measurable independently of the "activities" value is supposed to regulate. As was emphasized in the last chapter, Homans failed to provide such independently defined concepts and empirical indicators of these concepts. However, Blau's scheme reveals a more elegant solution to the problem, for he attempts to define generic types of rewards—money, approval, esteem, and compliance[52]—in terms of their value for participants to an exchange. By analytically distinguishing classes of rewards, it is more likely that reward will be defined independently of the activities to be influenced by rewards. In Blau's scheme, such is especially likely to be the case, since he attempts to define generic types of institutional activities—integrative, distributive, and organizational—in various generic types of social units—categories, communities, organized collectivities, and social systems. While he does not develop the abstract theoretical statements describing what type of rewards in what type of social units will influence what type of institutional activities, the potential for performing this difficult, but critical, theoretical task remains. In fact, instead of "illustrating" with examples his implicit exchange principles as they apply to various types of institutionalized relations in various social contexts, Blau could have more profitably devoted his effort to linking explicitly his exchange principles to abstract theoretical statements on the relationship among different types of rewards for various types of activities in diverse types of social settings. When this difficult analytical task is performed, the problem of tautology will be greatly reduced. It is perhaps the difficulty of this task that has kept sociological theorists from embracing more enthusiastically Blau's suggestive lead.

Bridging the Micro-Macro Gap. One of the most important analytical problems facing sociological theorizing revolves around the questions: To what extent are structures and processes at micro *and* macro levels of social organization subject to analysis by the same concepts and to description by the same sociological laws? At what levels of sociological organization do emergent properties require use of additional concepts

---

[52] Homans makes these distinctions in his discussion of empirical phenomena. For example, chap. 16 on "Status, Conformity, and Innovation," in *Social Behavior*, employs a similar set of distinctions. Unlike Blau's scheme, such distinctions are made *after* analysis of data and are not considered to constitute generic types of rewards that can be incorporated into abstract corollaries to his axioms.

and description in terms of their own unique social laws? In what ways are groups, organizations, communities, or social systems similar and different? These questions are extremely troublesome for sociological theorizing and constitute one of its most enduring problems. Blau has attempted to resolve this problem in several ways: (a) by assuming that the basic exchange processes of attraction, competition, differentiation, integration, and opposition occur at all levels of social organization; (b) by explicating general exchange principles, incorporating abstract exchange concepts, that can account for the unfolding of these processes at all levels of organization; (c) by enumerating additional concepts, such as mediating values and institutionalization, to account for emergent phenomena at increasingly macro levels of social organization; and (d) by classifying the generic types of organization—categories, communities, organized collectivities, and social systems—which denote different levels of organization, requiring somewhat different concepts for explication of their operation.

Such an effort constitutes a useful beginning to bridging the micro-macro analytical gap that exists in sociological theorizing. However, a number of problems remain; and it is to their resolution that efforts to improve upon Blau's scheme should be directed. First, Blau defines "organized collectivities" so broadly that they include phenomena ranging from small groups to complex organizations. It is likely that the concepts and theoretical generalizations appropriate to the small primary group, the secondary group, a crowd, a social movement, a small organization, and a large corporate bureaucracy will be somewhat different. Surely there are emergent properties of social organization in a spectrum ranging from a small group to a complex organization. In fact, aside from the study of community, most subfields in sociology fall within Blau's category of "organized collectivity." Thus, Blau has not resolved the problem of emergent properties; rather it has been defined away with an excessively broad category that subsumes most of the emergent properties of interest to sociologists.

Second, the delineation of additional concepts to account for differences in level of organizations only highlights the micro-macro gap without providing a sense of what concepts are needed to understand increasingly macro levels of social organization. What Blau does is to assert that there are certainly elementary exchange processes which occur at macro levels of organization and which require the addition of the concept "mediating values" if these emergent levels of organization are to be understood. But such an analysis begs the key question: When and at what levels of organization do such concepts become critical? Among dyads? triads? primary groups? secondary groups? small organizations? large organizations? To phrase the issue differently, at what point do what kinds of values, operating in accordance with what laws, become analytically significant? Blau simply says that at some point mediating values become critical, and he thereby avoids answering the theoretically interesting question.

· .Third, as has already been emphasized, Blau's presentation of exchange concepts and their incorporation into exchange principles is vague. Much of the analysis in this chapter has attempted to make more explicit the implicit exchange principles employed in his analysis. Without explicit statements of the exchange laws that cut across levels of organization, Blau fails to address an issue that he claims to be of great significance in the opening pages of his major work.

> The problem *is to derive* the social processes that govern the complex structures of communities and societies from the simpler processes that pervade the daily intercourse among individuals and their interpersonal relations [emphasis added].[53]

To make such "derivations," it is necessary to formulate explicitly the laws from which derivations from simpler to more complex structures are to be made. Too often, Blau hides behind the fact that, to use his words, his "intent is not to present a systematic theory of social structure; it is more modest than that."[54] Yet, even in its "modesty," Blau has synthesized diverse theoretical traditions into a suggestive exchange perspective.

---

[53] Blau, *Exchange and Power*, p. 2.
[54] Ibid.

13

THE FUTURE OF EXCHANGE THEORY

THE APPEAL OF EXCHANGE THEORY

The Eclectic Appeal of Exchange Theory

Exchange theory has gained wide appeal in sociological theorizing.[1] Much of this appeal stems from its capacity to incorporate diverse intellectual traditions. Exchange theory, for example, draws from utilitarianism and economics, psychological behaviorism, dialectical conflict theory, and even functionalism. Much as Talcott Parsons' early synthesis in *The Structure of Social Action* of diverse scholars and traditions fell upon sympathetic ears, so contemporary exchange theory has found a large and receptive audience.[2] By viewing actors as decision-makers who seek rewards, and yet who also organize themselves into complex exchange structures rife with imbalance and potential conflict, exchange theory

---

[1] It would be difficult to list all of the exchange perspectives that have been developed over the last decades. In addition to the perspectives of Blau and Homans, the most important, I feel, include J. Thibault and H. H. Kelley, *The Social Psychology of Groups* (New York: Wiley, 1959); J. S. Coleman, "Foundations for a Theory of Collective Decisions," *American Journal of Sociology* 71 (1966):615–27; A. Kuhn, *Unified Social Science: A System-Based Introduction* (Homewood, Ill.: Dorsey Press, 1975); and R. M. Emerson, "Exchange Theory, Parts I and II," in J. Berger, M. Zelditch and B. Anderson, eds., *Sociological Theories in Progress, Volume 2* (Boston: Houghton-Mifflin, 1972). There are several important secondary analyses of exchange theory. See, for example, J. K. Chadwick-Jones, *Social Exchange Theory: Its Structure and Influence in Social Psychology* (London: Academic Press, 1976); M. J. Mulkay, *Functionalism Exchange and Theoretical Strategy* (London: Routledge and Kegan Paul, 1971); R. L. Simpson, *Theories of Social Exchange* (General Learning Press, 1972).

[2] Talcott Parsons, *The Structure of Social Action* (New York: McGraw-Hill, 1937).

has "something for everyone." For the behaviorist, it offers a view of the world as operating in terms of the principle of reinforcement. For the economically-inclined analyst, it presents a vision of human action and organization as exchanges of utility, or value. For conflict theorists, the emphasis on power and dialectics affirms their vision of the social world. And for functionalists, there is a strong emphasis on the process of institutionalization and the patterning of social relations.

The Strategic Appeal of Exchange Theory

Another source of the appeal of exchange theory resides in the theoretical strategy offered by such thinkers as Homans and Blau. Each presents basic principles from which additional principles can be derived as analysis moves from simple to complex structures. By viewing patterns of social organization as guided by a relatively few "laws" or "principles," hope for a rigorous, deductive "science of society" is rekindled—a science that emulates the more respected "hard sciences."

The Substantive Appeal of Exchange Theory

Still another source of exchange theory's appeal comes from the substantive vision of social organization that it connotes. In both Blau's and Homans' analysis, patterns of social organization are constructed from basic exchange processes. And while the increased complexity of emerging social patterns requires that new concepts be introduced into the exchange perspective, the basic exchange principles remain unaltered.

Homans' Substantive Imagery. Homans visualizes the elaboration of structure to occur in the following manner: Individuals with valued resources invest their resources in new social relations which bring them a return on their investment, while providing rewards for those who have been drawn into these new social relations. New patterns of organization create the potential for increased rewards, since with organization more can be accomplished and greater resources can be secured. For example, people can farm more productively and efficiently; they can conquer others; and they can do many other activities to increase their rewards. At some point, organization begins to employ "secondary reinforcers," such as money, resulting in a situation where activities can be more precisely coordinated. It is now possible to establish exact exchange ratios for different activities. With money, people can more readily exchange with each other because they do not have to negotiate over less precise rewards such as power and esteem, but over rewards measured in terms of money.

FIGURE 13–1
Homans' Image of Social Organization

1	2	3
Individuals with capital or resources	New patterns of social organization which provide capital for investors and payoffs for followers.	Creating elaborated social patterns employing secondary reinforcers and explicit norms.

Invest in

Organization allows for expanded investment

In turn, this elaborated organizational base allows for expanded social organization

Norms also facilitate the growth of organizational complexity. They allow for specification of expectations for actors, thereby regularizing exchange relations and eliminating much time-consuming bargaining.

With generalized reinforcers and explicit rules, enforcement of norms becomes necessary in complex exchange systems. Thus, specialized units of social control emerge to regulate social affairs. And with secondary reinforcers, clear norms, and enforcement capacities, even more complex patterns of social organization can be elaborated.

It is through these processes, then, that social organization is constructed. Yet there is an inherent dialectic in these processes. Homans assumes that humans have "primary needs" which are often at variance with the rewards that elaborated social structures are able to provide. If other individuals or organizations can provide new rewards that meet these unfulfilled needs, then new paths of social organization are likely to be followed—paths that may come into conflict with existing social patterns.[3]

This image of social organization is diagrammed in Figure 13–1. As the figure underscores, Homans visualizes social structure as elaborated through a series of stages, with organization at one stage providing the

---

[3] See George C. Homans, *Social Behavior: Its Elementary Forms*, rev. ed., (New York: Harcourt Brace Jovanovich, 1974), chap. 16.

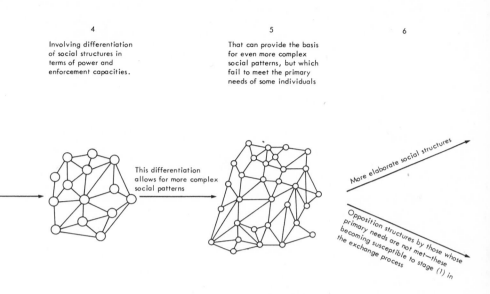

base for even more elaborate patterns of social organization. At some point, when "primary needs" of people are no longer met, new processes of elaboration are initiated as opposition groups form to challenge and change dominant social patterns. Such an image contains elements of utilitarian economics, behaviorism, and dialectical conflict theory—underscoring the eclectic appeal of exchange imagery.

Blau's Substantive Imagery.   Blau appears to accept the general image of society provided by Homans. He recognizes, of course, that this image is vague and in need of considerable specification. For this reason, Blau addresses a number of issues: (1) What types of reinforcers are there? An answer to this question can help analysts specify Homans' vague notions of "secondary" and "generalized" reinforcers. (2) How is power and control implicated in the elaboration of social patterns? An answer to this question can make less vague Homans' imprecise vision of "social control" by specialized subunits. (3) In what ways are cultural components, such as values and norms, involved in regulating the elaboration of complex exchange relations? An answer to this question can help theorists specify in ways never done by Homans the manner in which different cultural components operate to facilitate, or hinder, exchange relations. (4) What types of structures are elaborated from exchange relations? An answer to this query can remove the vagueness from Homans' notions of "sub-institution," "institutional," "institutional piles"

FIGURE 13–2
Blau's Image of Social Organization

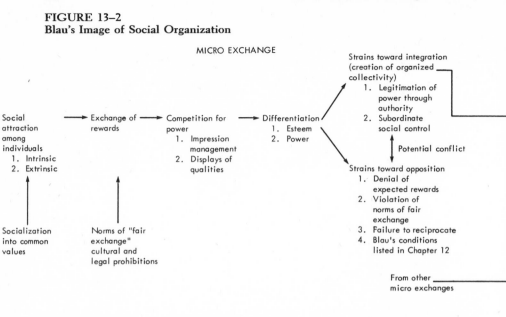

and "civilization." (5) And, finally, what is the nature of the dialectic in human affairs? Is it only a conflict between humans' primary needs and the capacities of elaborated social structures to provide only certain rewards? Or are there built-in sources for perceived deprivations in all complex exchange relations? Answers to these inquiries can help delineate the inherent sources of imbalance and change in elaborated social structures.

It is because of his concern with these unanswered questions that Blau appears to have begun his substantive analysis of human organization. Blau's model on the elaboration of social structure is more detailed than Homans' and places considerable emphasis on norms and values, power, differentiation, integration, and conflict among varying types of social units. The basic social process is conceptualized as a more explicit series of stages: attraction, exchange, competition for power, differentiation, integration, and opposition.[4] Values and norms regulate these processes by influencing what is rewarding, what actors will find "attractive" in each other, what forms the competition for power will assume, and what cultural components will be used to either legitimate power differentials or to codify opposition groupings.

Once patterns of social organization are created out of elementary exchange processes, the organizations themselves become the "actors"

---

[4] See Peter M. Blau, *Exchange and Power in Social Life* (New York: Wiley, 1967).

MACRO EXCHANGE

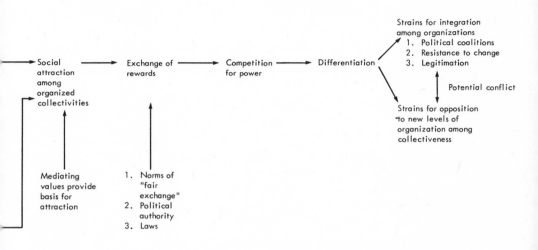

in the exchange. In describing these exchanges, Blau devotes most of his effort to specifying the values and norms that will affect the flow of the attraction, exchange, competition, differentiation, and opposition process.

Human social structure is thus viewed as exchange relations among different types of social units, the most important of which are "organized collectives" which become differentiated in terms of power and which reveal vacillating patterns of legitimation and opposition. Blau's imagery is delineated in Figure 13–2.

This kind of imagery is appealing to a variety of theoretical perspectives. It addresses the issues that most concerned Parsons and other functionalists: How does structure become built up and institutionalized? And what is the place of ideas or cultural symbols in legitimating patterns of social organization? It maintains the basic dynamic of utilitarian economics and psychological reinforcement theories: Individual humans, and collective actors like complex organizations, pursue lines of conduct in an effort to receive rewards. And it emphasizes the consequences of differences in power. When distributed unequally, power is a resource which creates pressures for perpetual conflict and change.

As appealing as this strategy is, it currently encounters a number of severe difficulties. These have been alluded to in the discussion of the emergence of exchange theory as well as in the more detailed review of Homans' and Blau's work. The future of exchange theory resides in the resolution of these difficulties, and hence it is wise to review them and explore potential solutions.

THE THEORETICAL PROBLEMS OF EXCHANGE THEORY

Logical Problems: The Issue of Tautology

The propositions of exchange theories run the risk of becoming tautologies. This issue boils down to the question: How are the "values" of actors to be defined and measured independently of the "behaviors" they they supposedly influence? For example, how is it known what a person values? Answer: By observing their behaviors. In such a case, values are inferred from behavior, with the result that values are not defined or measured independently of the behaviors that they influence. Propositions with "value" or "reward" and "behavior" or "actions" as their key variables can thus become tautologies.

The problem of tautology involves more than the measurement issue, however. It is often the case that value or reward, on the one hand, and behavior, on the other, are not defined independently from each other. Reward or value is often defined as gratification-producing, or punishment-avoiding, behavior. Behavior is then defined as reward-seeking, or punishment-avoiding, responses to stimuli. Rarely is the tautology this obvious, but there is a tendency for the concepts of exchange propositions to be defined in terms of each other.

There have been a number of attempts to resolve this issue. Homans' effort at a solution was reviewed earlier, and thus his argument will be briefly recapitulated, and then other arguments will be examined.

Homans' "Solution." All of Homans' axioms, as was noted earlier, are definitional tautologies. "Value" is defined as the degree of reward and "action" is defined as reward-seeking behavior. Homans acknowledges this circularity, but defends it with the following argument: While "value" and "action" are defined in terms of each other, independent indicators of value and action can be found as deductions from the tautologous axioms to the empirical world are performed. But as was noted earlier, precise deductions and clear operational definitions for "value" and "action" must be developed if this "solution" is to prove viable. Homans himself never reveals the necessary rigor in his deductions, but he has at least presented theorists with one possible solution to the problem of tautology.

Blau's "Solution." Blau skirts around the issue of tautology. He presents two kinds of arguments. One simply states that the tautological nature of value and action is a problematic fact of social life, not just a methodological or logical problem. Blau is thus arguing that in "real life" values and actions are connected to each other and this is a substantive fact of human action. This fact may make theories of human action and organization difficult to develop, but it is, nonetheless, a substantive constraint imposed by the nature of humans. Unfortunately, as will be evident shortly in an examination of Richard Emerson's "solution," Blau does not develop fully the implications of his argument. If action and value are substantively inseparable, then theoretical propositions should not attempt to separate them. If value and action constitute a substantive unit, then they should be treated as such.

Blau's other attempt at resolving the issue of tautology revolves around limiting just what constitutes social exchange. Blau believes that by limiting the definition of social exchange "to those actions that are contingent on rewarding reactions from others and that cease when these expected reactions are not forthcoming," the problem of tautology is obviated.[5] Without the capacity to measure specific quantities of rewards from others, it is not possible to measure actions of one person independently of the rewards received from another. For example, an action on the part of a person that does not reveal measurable rewards from others is not, in Blau's eyes, a social exchange. A person who gives a gift without expectation of any reward in return is not involved in social exchange. Blau excludes such actions because the problem of tautology becomes severe, since the only way to explain the gift-giver's actions is to say: "The gift is given because the person finds gift-giving rewarding." Such a statement is a tautology, because the values of the gift-giver can only be inferred from the actions of gift-giving.

Thus, Blau provides for a more limited definition of social exchange than does Homans. Exchange exists only when actions are directed toward receiving measurable rewards from others. Such a strategy, however, does not completely eliminate the problem of tautology. Actions are still defined as reward-seeking behaviors; and value is defined as that which bestows gratification on actions. Blau must then resort to Homans' solution to the problem: At the abstract level, propositions with "value" and "action" as the key variables are tautologies which will be obviated when deductions to specific empirical cases are made. Once at the empirical level, "actions" and "reward" can be measured independently of each other, and hence, the problem of tautology is "eliminated."

The Methodological Chauvinism "Solution." Much of the controversy surrounding the issue of tautology centers on the question of meas-

---

[5] Blau, *Exchange and Power,* p. 6.

urement. How are values to be measured independently of actions? Blau and Homans have seemingly given up trying to define action and value in totally nontautologous ways, and instead have emphasized the importance of independent measurement of these two variables. It can be argued that this solution presupposes that the concepts in exchange theory cannot be defined, in the abstract, independently from each other. It also assumes that it is necessary, in the present, to have measures of key concepts in a theory. Both of these presumptions can, from one point of view, be questioned.

In regard to the definitional issue, it would seem that nontautologous definitions can be developed. For example, Meeker has noted that "value" is a part of a person's cognitive structure and can be defined independently of that person's overt action.[6] It can be defined, for purposes of illustration, as a series of cognitive orientations which establish what people will perceive as gratifying and ungratifying. Action can then be defined as overt behavior of a person. In this illustration, "action" and "value" are not defined in terms of each other, and thus, the definitions are not tautologous.

The issue then turns on the question of measurement. Can value and action, as defined above, be measured independently? It would seem possible, at least in principle, to develop separate measures of cognitions and overt behavior. But even if measurement of cognitions independently of the behavior influenced by these cognitions proves difficult, is this a theoretical or methodological problem? Is this a problem with the theory or is it a problem of inadequate methodologies? The history of science reveals many instances where measurement of key concepts—for example, many of those in Albert Einstein's "theory of relativity"—had to wait for improved methodologies.

Social sciences tend to be dominated by a concern with measurement techniques. Such concern is, of course, a reaction against the highly speculative, and suspect, "arm chair" theorizing of the past. And yet, an overconcern with measurement could conceivably hinder the development of abstract theory, since if a concept cannot be measured by today's limited methodologies, its utility is considered minimal. Such methodological chauvinism could account for many of the problems perceived to exist for exchange theory.

Emerson's Exchange Unit "Solution." Richard Emerson has sought to bypass the issue of tautology by viewing exchange relations between

---

[6] B. F. Meeker, "Decisions and Exchange," *American Sociological Review* 36 (June 1971): 485–95.

two or more actors as a unit.[7] Rather than viewing each actor as a unit, the social relationship that they form becomes the unit of sociological analysis. Questions about each actor's values become less central in such a scheme, because attention is focused on the relationship between actors who exchange resources.

This line of argument, of course, abandons explanation in terms of an individual actor's values. The emphasis is on the ratio of rewards exchanged among actors and on how this ratio shifts or stabilizes over the course of the exchange relationship. Propositions thus focus on explaining the variables outside the actors in the broader context of the social relationship that might influence the ratio of rewards in a given social relationship. Thus, behavior is no longer the dependent variable in propositions, but rather it is the exchange relationship that becomes the variable to be explained. The theorist now seeks to discover laws which help account for particular types of exchange units. These laws do not make reference to the values of the actors involved but to variables in the social environment which will influence the ratio of rewards exchanged in a given social relationship.

Traditional exchange theory will seek to explain why a person enters into an exchange relationship in terms of that person's values. But if the relationship is the unit of analysis, then the question of why the individual enters the relationship is no longer of prime concern. The fact is that the individual has entered a relationship and is willing to exchange rewards with another. When this exchange relationship among actors becomes the unit of analysis, Emerson argues, theory seeks to discover what events could effect variations in the entire unit, not in the individual behaviors of actors. For example, in a hypothetical exchange, person A gives esteem and respect to person B in return for advice. With the $A;B$ relationship as the unit of analysis, the question is not what made either A or B enter the relationship. Answers to such a question take theory into A's and B's cognitive structure and thereby increase the probability of tautologous propositions. Rather, since the $A;B$ unit already exists as an entity, theoretical questions should focus on what events would influence the ratio of esteem and advice exchanged in the $A;B$ unit.

This vision of social exchange develops the implications of Blau's assertion that the reciprocal giving and receiving of rewards among actors

---

[7] Richard Emerson, "Social Exchange Theory" in Alex Inkeles and Neil J. Smelser, eds., *Annual Review of Sociology*, vol. 2 (Palo Alto: Annual Reviews, 1976), pp. 335–62.

is the defining characteristic of exchange. Moreover, it also follows Blau's recognition that value and action are, in actual social life, often fused and meshed together. Rather than attempt to separate them and run the risk of tautologous statements, Emerson argues that it makes more conceptual sense to view social relationships among actors exchanging rewards as *the* unit of exchange theory. Attention then shifts to the properties of the unit, per se, not those of the actors comprising the unit. And in this way, the problem of defining and measuring values and behaviors independently from each other is bypassed.

In sum, then, it is possible to view a variety of arguments developed to obviate the problem of tautology. As long as the major independent variable of exchange theory—value—is difficult to separate from the principal dependent variable—behavior—the problem of tautology will continue to surface in exchange theory. To a very great extent, the future of exchange theory hinges upon how this conceptual problem is resolved. Other problems, such as the issue of ad hoc explanation are less severe. Moreover, resolution of the problem of tautology can obviate most of these other problems. The "solutions" discussed in this section, however, have not silenced the critics, and thus, it is likely that the issue of tautology will continue to haunt exchange theory.

Substantive Problems: The Metaphorical Image of Society

Exchange theory in sociology is a curious mixture of abstract theoretical principles and vague images of human organization. Much of this vagueness stems from a chronic issue in sociological theorizing: micro versus macro theory. How are micro processes among individual actors related to macro processes among collective or corporate actors, and vice versa? Parsons' *The Social System* represented one of the first efforts to analyze the process of institutionalization from small groups of individuals to more complex collectivities.[8] All were viewed as "social systems" and all could be analyzed in terms of the mechanisms integrating culture, personality, and social systems (see Chapter 3). Parsons' subsequent elaboration of his scheme similarly represented an effort to employ the same concepts, or "system of concepts," for analyzing simple and complex social patterns.

The initial appeal of the Parsonsian scheme soon vanished in the face of criticisms from conflict sociology, which has rarely addressed the issue of micro versus macro phenomena. And it is in this context that exchange theory has found its appeal; it offers a common set of

---

[8] Talcott Parsons, *The Social System* (New York: Free Press, 1951).

principles or "laws" for analyzing both individual and collective actions. Its proponents, despite their varying orientations, appear united in the presumption that basically the same processes, describable in terms of a relatively small set of laws, operate at all levels of social organization. Unfortunately, as is evident for both Homans' and Blau's schemes, these princicples are virtually abandoned as analysis moves further and further away from direct exchanges among particular individuals. Homans, as was noted in Chapter 11, simply defines away as "givens" most of the complexities introduced by macro social organization when constructing explanations, or he abandons all systematic efforts to use his principles when presenting his conceptual "orgy" on how complex social forms are elaborated (see Figure 13–1). Blau is somewhat more precise, but since he never intended to enumerate principles but only to provide a conceptual "prolegomenon," he merely develops series of categories for visualizing complex exchanges among collective or corporate actors (see Figure 13–2).

In the end, these exchange perspectives are as suggestive and imprecise as Parsons' model was imputed to be. There is a lack of precision in the definition of social structure and on how social structure becomes elaborated. Concepts such as "institutional piles," "civilizations," and "organized collectivities" do not define social structure, nor do they indicate its varying properties as it increases in complexity. The image of social organization communicated is thus metaphorical. It connotes, but does not delineate how clearly defined structural properties of complex social patterns operate under exchange principles. As Figures 13–1 and 13–2 should underscore, the substantive image of social organization presented in these models is not focused.

The future of exchange theory, therefore, depends not only on resolving the logical problem of tautology, but also on developing a more focused image of the patterns of social organization that are to be explained by nontautologous principles. At present, of course, no theoretical perspective in sociology can come close to resolving these problems. But the future of exchange theory, and all theoretical perspectives in sociology, hinges upon dealing more effectively with these issues.

Homans' and Blau's schemes do not address the issue of tautology or the problem of defining and analyzing social structure nonmetaphorically. They have offered, however, important beginnings. Further development of the exchange perspective now appears to have shifted to a somewhat different theoretical strategy which borrows the early insights of Homans' and Blau's, as well as the ideas of other pioneers of the perspective, and has used these to develop a perspective which can more effectively deal with the issue of tautology and the problem of developing a more focused image of social organization. Thus, before closing this discussion on the future of exchange theory, the broad contours of this alternative theoretical strategy should be outlined.

EXCHANGE NETWORK ANALYSIS: RICHARD EMERSON

Richard Emerson's exchange theoretic strategy represents an important development in sociological theorizing.[9] More than other exchange perspectives, it is less vulnerable to the logical and substantive problems that have plagued this orientation. The future of exchange theory may rest on the further execution of Emerson's strategy for developing a more viable form of exchange theorizing.

Much like Homans, Emerson begins with a discussion of psychological behaviorism. His purpose is to extract basic concepts and principles of operant psychology which could prove useful in analyzing more complex social patterns. Unlike Homans, however, Emerson does not stop theoretical efforts once basic reinforcement principles are isolated. As was noted in the discussion of his scheme, Homans tended to define away the complexities of social structure by viewing them as "givens" and then to reconcile in an ad hoc and ex post facto manner psychological axioms and empirical generalizations. And as we noted earlier in this chapter, when Homans does address the sociological question of how patterns of social organization are created, maintained, and changed, he becomes metaphorical and abandons even the illusion of logical rigor in favor of what he termed an "intellectual orgy."

In contrast, Emerson's strategy involves a careful analysis of the logic of operant psychology, a selective borrowing of concepts and principles and, most important, an extension of these principles that allows for a less metaphorical analysis of the complexity of social organization. His

---

[9] Emerson's perspective is best stated in his "Exchange Theory, Part I: A Psychological Basis for Social Exchange" and "Exchange Theory, Part II: Exchange Relations and Network Structures" in Berger, Zelditch, and Anderson, *Sociological Theories*, pp. 38–87. Earlier empirical work which provided the initial impetus to, or the empirical support of, this theoretical perspective include: "Power-Dependence Relations," *American Sociological Review* 17 (February 1962): 31–41; "Power-Dependence Relations: Two Experiments," *Sociometry* 27 (September 1964): 282–98; John F. Stolte and Richard M. Emerson, "Structural Inequality: Position and Power in Network Structures," in Robert Hamblin, ed., *Behavioral Theory in Sociology* (forthcoming, Transaction Books). Other more conceptual works include "Operant Psychology and Exchange Theory" in Burgess and Bushell, eds., *Behavioral Sociology* (New York: Columbia University Press, 1969) and "Social Exchange Theory" in Inkeles and Smelser, *Annual Review*.

efforts represent, of course, only a tentative beginning. And perhaps more important than the present state of his theory is the strategy it personifies. This section will thus concentrate on delineating the strategy's potential rather than on its substantive accomplishments.

The Over-All Strategy

Emerson begins by enumerating the basic propositions of operant psychology. Then, through the development of corollaries, he extends these propositions and makes them more relevant to human social organization. Finally, he derives from these propositions and their corollaries a series of theorems to account for the operation of different social patterns. At various points in the development of his system of propositions, corollaries, and theorems, he defines new concepts that will be incorporated into the corollaries and theorems.

Emerson does not perform the logical operations in deriving corollaries from basic operant propositions and in developing theorems from these propositions and corollaries. Yet in contrast to Homans' strategy, Emerson's work is extremely rigorous. Concepts are precisely defined and represented by symbolic notation. Propositions, corollaries, and theorems are stated in terms of co-variance among these clearly defined concepts. Thus, considerable attention is devoted to concept-formation and then to the use of these concepts in a system of propositions, corollaries, and theorems. Rarely do sociological theories reveal this degree of rigor.[10]

Emerson follows the substantive strategy of other exchange theorists by moving from micro processes in simple structures to processes in more complex structures. As the structures under investigation become more complex, additional corollaries and theorems are developed. But the most important difference between Emerson's substantive approach and that of other perspectives is his concern with the *forms* of exchange relations. The theorems delineate the processes inhering in a given form of exchange relationship. The nature of the units in this relationship can be either micro or macro—individual persons or corporate units such as groups, organizations, or nations. Much as the German sociologist Georg Simmel (see Chapter 6) focused on the "forms of sociation," so Emerson has sought to develop a set of theoretical principles which explain social form. In this way, the distinction between micro and macro analysis is rendered less obstructive, because it is the *form of*

---

[10] There are, of course, notable exceptions to this statement. See, for examples: Kuhn, *Unified Social Science*, and the articles in Berger, Zelditch and Anderson, *Sociological Theories*.

the relationship rather than the properties of the units that is being explained.

Emerson's strategy involves many problems of exposition, however. His concern with rigorous concept-formation involves the creation of a new language. Acquiring a familiarity with this language requires considerable time and effort. Moreover, the system of definitions, concepts, propositions, corollaries, and theorems soon becomes exceedingly complex, even though Emerson only explores a few basic types, or forms, of social relationships. This analysis of Emerson's work must therefore retranslate terms into discursive language and omit discussion of certain corollaries and theorems. In this way, the logic of Emerson's approach and its substantive implications can be more readily communicated. Some rigor—one of the appeals of the approach—is lost in such a discussion. Yet the essentials of the strategy are more readily communicated. Also, in an effort to communicate succinctly the essence of Emerson's approach, the exact sequence of his argument will not be followed.

The discussion will be divided into several sections: (1) the basic concepts, (2) the basic processes, (3) the basic propositions, and (4) the basic social forms. Throughout the discussion in these sections, attention will focus on the potential of Emerson's strategy for obviating the logical problem of tautology and the substantive problems of micro versus macro analysis.

The Basic Exchange Concepts

Below is an incomplete list of key concepts in Emerson's exchange perspective. While the definitions for each concept appear, on the surface, to be similar to those developed by Homans, important differences exist. These differences will become increasingly evident. The definitions are:

Actor: An individual or collective unit which is capable of receiving reinforcement from its environment.

Reinforcement: Features of the environment which are capable of bestowing gratification upon an actor.

Behaviors: Actions or movements of actors on their environment.

Exchange: Behaviors by actors which yield reinforcement from the environment.

Value: The strength of reinforcers to evoke and reinforce behavioral initiations by an actor, relative to other reinforcers and holding deprivation constant and greater than zero.

Reward: The degree of value attached to a given type of reinforcement.

Alternatives: The number of sources in the environment of an actor that can bestow a given type of reinforcer.

Cost: The magnitude and number of rewards of one type foregone to receive rewards of another type.

Exchange Relation: Opportunities across time for an actor to initiate behaviors which lead to relatively enduring exchange transactions with other actors in the environment.

Dependence: A situation where an actor's reinforcement is contingent upon behaviors on the part of another actor, with the degree of dependence being a dual function of the strength of reinforcement associated with behavior and the number of alternatives for rewards.

Balance: The degree to which the dependency of one actor, A, for rewards from actor B is equal to the dependency of actor B for rewards from actor A.

Power: The degree to which one actor can force another actor to incur costs in an exchange relation.

Resources: Any reward that an actor can use in an exchange relation with other actors.

This list of concepts does not exhaust those employed by Emerson. With these concepts, however, it is possible to gain considerable insight into his approach. There are several points that need to be made about this list of concepts. First, emphasis is placed upon the exchange *relation* between actors. As was noted earlier, Emerson seeks to bypass the problem of tautology by viewing an established relation—not the actors in the relation—as the smallest unit of analysis. Second, the concepts of actor, reinforcement, exchange, value, reward, cost, and resource are all defined in terms of each other, but since they are not analyzed independently of the exchange relation, the problem of tautology is bypassed. They are the "givens" of any existing exchange relation. Third, in accordance with the emphasis on the attributes of the exchange relation, as opposed to the characteristics of the actors, the concepts of (a) dependence, (b) power, and (c) balance in exchange relations become central. The key questions in Emerson's scheme thus revolve around how dependence, power, and balance in exchange relations help explain the operation of more complex social patterns. Fourth, actors are viewed as either individuals or collective units. The same processes in exchange relations are presumed to apply to both individuals and collectivities of individuals, thus obviating many problems in the micro versus macro schism in sociological theorizing. This emphasis is possible when attention is shifted away from the attributes of actors to the *form* of their exchange relationship.

Thus, while this partial list of Emerson's concepts appears to be similar to that developed by Homans, and other behavioristically oriented exchange theorists, there is a subtle shift in definitions and emphasis. The shift is away from concern with the "values" and other cognitive properties of actors to a concern with existence of an exchange relation which takes as a "given" the flow of valued resources among those involved in the exchange. Theoretical attention then focuses on the attributes of the exchange relation and on the processes that maintain or change the form of an ongoing exchange relationship.

The Basic Exchange Processes

In Emerson's scheme, it is a given that an exchange relation exists between at least two actors. This relationship has been formed from (*a*) perceived opportunities by at least one actor, (*b*) the initiation of behaviors, and (*c*) the consummation of a transaction between actors mutually reinforcing each other. If initiations go unreinforced, then an exchange relation does not exist. And unless the exchange transaction between actors endures for at least some period of time, it is theoretically uninteresting.

Emerson's approach thus begins with an established exchange relation, and then asks: To what basic processes is this relationship subject? His answer: (1) *the use of power* and (2) *balancing.* If exchange relations reveal high dependency of one actor, *A,* on another, *B,* for reinforcement, or rewards, then *A* has what Emerson terms a "power advantage" over *B.* This conceptualization of power is similar to Blau's formulation, although Emerson develops a different set of propositions for explaining its dynamics. To have a power advantage is to use it, with the result that actor *A* forces increasing costs on actor *B* within the exchange relationship.

In Emerson's view, a power advantage represents an imbalanced exchange relation. A basic proposition in Emerson's scheme is that over time imbalanced exchange relations tend toward balance. He visualizes such balancing as occurring through a number of "balancing operations."

1. A decrease in the value for actor *B* of reinforcers, or rewards, from actor *A.*
2. An increase in the number of alternative sources for the reinforcers, or rewards, provided to *B* by *A.*

3. An increase in the value of reinforcers provided by B for A.
4. A reduction in the alternative sources for the rewards provided by B for A.

These "balancing operations" are somewhat similar to the propositions enumerated by Blau on the conditions for differentiation of power (see Chapter 12). But in contrast to Blau's emphasis on the inherent and incessant dialectic for change resulting from power imbalances, Emerson stresses that relations tend toward balance. Through at least one of these four balancing operations the dependency of B and A on each other for rewards will reach an equilibrium.

The basic process, then, is for exchange transactions to reveal differences in power which, over time, tend toward balance. Naturally, in complex exchange relations involving many actors, $A, B, C, D \ldots n$, the basic processes of dependence, power, and balance will ebb and flow as new actors and new reinforcers or resources enter the exchange relations.

The Basic Exchange Propositions

As was emphasized in the earlier discussion of his over-all theoretical strategy, Emerson has sought to develop a system of corollaries and theorems, derived from basic operant propositions, to explain human social relationships. In this section, the processes just described will be viewed in terms of Emerson's system of propositions, corollaries, and theorems. In this way, a sense for the formal nature of Emerson's strategy can be communicated.

In Table 13–1, Emerson's basic operant propositions are listed. These,

TABLE 13–1
The Operant Propositions and Initial Corollaries

Proposition 1:	The greater the behavioral repertoire of actor A in a situation and the greater the variations in rewards for behaviors, the more likely A to emit those behaviors yielding the greatest rewards.
Corollary 1.1:	The more rewards decrease for A in an established exchange relation, the more variation in A's behavior.
Corollary 1.2:	The more rewards in an established exchange relation approach a zero level of reinforcement, the fewer initiations by A.
Corollary 1.3:	The greater the power advantage of A over B in an exchange relation, the more A will use its power advantage across continuing transactions.
Corollary 1.4:	The more power is balanced in an exchange relation between A and B, and the more A increases its use of power, the more B will increase its use of power.

TABLE 13–1 *(continued)*

Proposition 2:   The more frequent and valuable the rewards received by actor A for a given behavior in a situation, the less likely actor A to emit similar behaviors immediately.

Corollary 2.1:   The more rewards of a given type received by A, the less frequent A's initiations for rewards of this type.

Proposition 3:   The more actor A must emit a given behavior for a given type of reward, and the greater strength and number of rewards of this type in a situation, the more likely is actor A to emit behaviors of a given type in that situation.

Corollary 3.1:   The greater the number of alternatives available to A for a given reward, the less dependent A upon that situation.

Corollary 3.2:   The more a situation provides multiple sources of reward for A, the more dependent is A on that situation.

Corollary 3.3:   The greater the value of rewards received by A in a given situation, the greater is the dependency of A on that situation.

Corollary 3.4:   The greater the uncertainty of A over receiving a given reward in a given situation, and the fewer alternative situations for receiving this reward, the greater is the dependency of A on that situation.

Corollary 3.5:   The less the value of a reward for A in an $A;B$ exchange relation, and the greater the alternative sources of that reward for A, the less cohesive the exchange relation between A and B; or conversely, the more the value of a reward for A, and the fewer alternative sources of that reward for A, the more cohesive the relationship between A and B.

Corollary 3.6:   The more an $A;B$ exchange relationship at one point in time is transformed to $A \rightarrow B \rightarrow C$ relationship, the greater the dependency of B upon A, and the fewer the alternatives for B in the $A;B$ relationship, then B's dependency upon A will be greater than B's dependency upon C.

Proposition 4:   The more uncertain an actor A of receiving a given type of reward in recent transactions, the more valuable that reward for actor A.

Corollary 4.1:   In a set of potential exchange relations, the more maintenance of one transaction precludes other transactions in this set, the greater the initial costs of this one transaction, but the less the costs across continuing transactions.

___

Emerson feels, are the basic principles from operant psychology that will prove useful in examining exchange relationships. From each of these propositions, a number of corollaries are developed. These four propositions and their corollaries serve as a basis from which other corollaries and theorems are derived to explain processes in exchange relationships.

As can be seen, the corollaries for propositions 1 and 3 move from

TABLE 13–2
The Initial Theorems

Theorem 1:	The greater the value of rewards to A in a situation, the more initiations by A reveal a curvilinear pattern, with initiations increasing over early transactions and then decreasing over time (From corollaries 1.2 and 2.1).
Theorem 2:	The greater the dependency of A on a set of exchange relations, the more likely A to initiate behaviors in this set of relations (From propositions 1 and 3).
Theorem 3:	The more the uncertainty of A increases in an exchange relation, the more the dependency of A on that situation increases, and vice versa. (From corollary 3.3 and proposition 4).
Theorem 4:	The more the dependency of B on A for rewards in an $A;B$ exchange relationship, the greater the power of A over B and the more imbalanced the relationship between A and B (From propositions 1 and 3, and definitions of cost, dependence, and power).
Theorem 5:	The greater the imbalance of an $A;B$ exchange relation at one point in time, the more likely it is to be balanced at a subsequent point in time (From corollaries 1.1, 1.3, 3.1, 3.3, and proposition 4).

statements on actors in situations to actors, A and B, engaging in exchange relations. What Emerson has done is to recognize that operant principles are *not* exchange principles. Rats and pigeons in a Skinner Box do not exchange rewards with the experimenter. Rather, they respond to a situation contrived and controlled by an experimenter. Operant principles must therefore be transformed into exchange principles in which the situation for an actor is another actor. Thus, the corollaries eventually begin to address properties of the $A;B$ exchange relationship.

In Table 13–2, the first six theorems developed by Emerson are listed. This same pattern is evident: Movement from theorems about actor; situation processes to actor; actor exchanges.

The logical steps in the derivations of corollaries and theorems are not enumerated, giving the propositions, corollaries, and theorems in Tables 13–1 and 13–2 an ad hoc character. Yet Emerson has faithfully sought to show the source of additional corollaries and theorems that will be used to explain more complex exchange relationships among multiple actors, A, B, C . . . n. The propositions and initial corollaries and theorems have been presented at this point to illustrate the substance of Emerson's strategy and to give an indication of where additional corollaries and theorems fit in a larger inventory of propositions. It is from this base of propositions that Emerson seeks to develop additional corollaries and theorems which can begin to explain—in a sense that Homans would appreciate—more complex social forms. In seeking to extend this system of theoretical statements, Emerson has drawn upon the concept of "networks."

The Basic Social Forms: Exchange Networks

By viewing exchange relations, rather than the individual actor, as the basic unit of analysis, Emerson has provided at least one potential solution to the logical problem of tautology (see earlier discussion). The substantive problem of moving from exchanges among individuals to exchanges among collective units, such as groups, parties, classes, organizations, and nations, is resolved by viewing *actors* as either individuals or collective units and then concentrating on the formal properties of their relationship. With this emphasis, the nature of the actor, whether an individual or corporate unit, is viewed as subject to the laws governing the relationship, rather than any laws that might be unique to each type of actor.

In addressing the forms of exchange relations, Emerson was led to represent graphically networks of relations among actors. While he follows the conventions of diagraph theory and develops a number of definitions, only two critical definitions are offered below.

Actors: points A, B, C . . . n in a network of relations. Different letters represent actors with different resources to exchange. The same letters— that is, A_1, A_2, A_3, and so forth—represent different actors exchanging similar resources.
Exchange relations: A————B, A————B————C, A_1————A_2, and other patterns which can connect different actors to each other forming a network of relations.

With these two definitions, the basic thrust of Emerson's network approach can be reviewed. The next conceptual task is to visualize the forms of networks that can be represented with these two definitions. For each basic form, new corollaries and theorems are added as Emerson seeks to document the way in which the basic processes of dependence, power, and balance operate. His discussion is only preliminary, but it does illustrate the perspective's potential.

Several basic social forms are given special treatment: (*a*) unilateral monopoly, (*b*) division of labor, (*c*) social circles, and (*d*) stratification. Each of these network forms is discussed below.

Unilateral Monopoly. In the network outlined below, actor A is a source of valuable resources for actors B_1, B_2, and B_3. Actors B_1, B_2, and B_3 provide rewards for A, but since A has multiple sources for rewards, and the Bs only have A as a source for their rewards, the situation is a unilateral monopoly.

Such a structure often typifies interpersonal as well as intercorporate units. For example, A could be a particularly desirable male date for three different women, B_1, B_2 and B_3. Or A could be a corporation which is the sole supplier of raw resources for three other manufacturing corporations, B_1, B_2, and B_3. Or A could be a governmental body and Bs dependent agencies. Thus, it is immediately evident that by focusing on the structure of exchange relationship, many of the micro versus macro problems of exchange analysis, as well as of sociological theory in general, are reduced.

Another important feature of the unilateral monopoly presented above is that, in terms of Emerson's definitions, it is imbalanced and thus its structure will be subject to change. Previous propositions and corollaries listed in Table 13–1 provide an initial clue as to what might occur. Corollary 1.3 argues that A will use its power advantage and increase costs for each B. Corollary 1.1 would indicate that with each increment in costs for the Bs, their behaviors will vary and they will seek alternatives for rewards in A_2, A_3 . . . A_n. If another A can be found, then the structure of the network would change.

Emerson develops additional corollaries and theorems to account for the various ways this unilateral monopoly can become balanced. For instance, if no A_2, A_3 . . . A_n exist and Bs cannot communicate with each other, the following corollary would apply (termed by Emerson, "Exploitation Type I"):

> Corollary 1.3.1:   The more an exchange relation between A and multiple Bs approximates a unilateral monopoly, the more additional resources each B will introduce into the exchange relation, with A's resource utilization remaining constant or decreasing.

Emerson sees this adaptation as short-lived, since the network is even more unbalanced. Assuming that Bs can survive as an entity without resources from A, then theorem 8 applies (termed by Emerson, "Exploitation Type II"):[11]

---

[11] I have omitted Emerson's theorems 6 and 7, because they are not directly relevant to the discussion.

Theorem 8: The more an exchange relation between A and multiple Bs approximates a unilateral monopoly, the less valuable to Bs the resources provided by A across continuing transactions. (From corollary 1.3, theorem 4 and corollary 4.1).

This theorem thus predicts that balancing operation 1—a decrease in the value of the reward for those at a power disadvantage—will operate to balance a unilateral monopoly where no alternative sources of rewards exist and where Bs cannot effectively communicate.

Other balancing operations are possible, if other conditions exist. If Bs can communicate, they might form a coalition (balancing operation 4) and require A to balance exchanges with a united coalition of Bs. If one B can provide a resource not possessed by the other Bs, then a division of labor among Bs (operations 3 and 4) would emerge. Or if another source of resources, A_2, can be found (operation 2), then the power advantage of A_1 is decreased. Each of these possible changes will occur under varying conditions, but corollary 1.3.1 and theorem 8 provide a "reason" for the initiation of changes—a "reason" which has been derived from basic operant principles.

Division of Labor. The emergence of a division of labor is one of many ways to balance exchange relations. If each of the Bs can provide for A different resources, then they are likely to use these in the exchange with A and to specialize in providing A with these resources. This decreases the power of A and establishes a new type of network. For example, in the schematic below the unilateral monopoly at the left is transformed to the division of labor form at the right, with B_1 becoming a new type of actor, C, with its own resources; with B_2 also specializing and becoming a new actor, D; and with B_3 doing the same and becoming actor E.

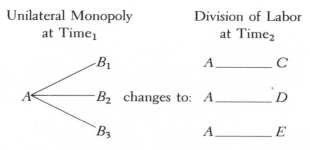

Emerson develops an additional theorem to describe this kind of change, where each B has its own unique resources:

Theoreom 9: The more resources are distributed *non*uniformly across Bs in a unilateral monopoly with A, the more likely each B to specialize and establish a separate exchange relation with A. (From theorems not discussed here and corollaries 1.1 and 1.3.1).

Several points should be emphasized. First, the units in this transformation can be individual or collective actors. Second, the change in the structure or form of the network is described in terms of a theorem systematically derived from operant principles, corollaries, and other theorems. The theorem can thus apply to a wide variety of micro and macro contexts. For example, the theorem could apply to workers in an office who specialize and provide A with resources not available from others. It could apply to a division in a corporation which seeks to balance its relations with the central authority by reorganizing itself in ways that distinguish it, and the services it can provide, from other divisions. Or, it could apply to relations between a colonial power (A) and its colonized nations (B_1, B_2, B_3) who specialize (becoming C, D, and E) in their predominant economic activities in order to establish a less dependent relationship with A.

Social Circles. Emerson emphasizes that some exchanges are inter-category and others intra-category. An inter-category exchange is one where one type of resource is exchanged for another type—money for goods, advice for esteem, tobacco for steel knives, and so on. The networks discussed thus far have involved *inter*-category exchanges between actors with different resources (A, B, C, D, E). An intra-category is one where the same resources are being exchanged—affection for affection, advice for advice, goods for goods, and so on. As was indicated earlier, such exchanges are symbolized by using the same letter—A_1, A_2, A_3, and so forth—to represent actors with similar resources. Emerson then develops another theorem to describe what will occur in these *intra*-category of exchanges:

> *Theorem 10:* The more an exchange approximates an *intra*-category exchange, the more likely are exchange relations to become closed (From theorem 5, corollaries 1.3 and 1.1).

Emerson defines "closed" as either a "circle" of relations diagrammed on the left in the schematic below, or as a balanced network where all actors exchange with each other (diagrammed on the right below).

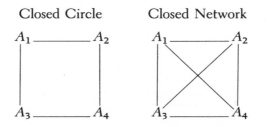

Closed Circle   Closed Network

Emerson offers the example of tennis networks to illustrate this balancing process. If two tennis players of equal ability, A_1 and A_2, play together regularly, this is a balanced intra-category exchange—tennis for tennis. However, if A_3 enters and plays with A_2, then A_2 now enjoys a power advantage, as is diagrammed below:

This is a unilateral monopoly, but unlike those discussed earlier, it is an intra-category monopoly. A_1 and A_3 are dependent upon A_2 for tennis. This relation is unbalanced and sets into motion processes of balance. A_4 may be found, creating either the circle or balanced network diagrammed above. Once this kind of closed and balanced network is achieved, it resists entry by others, A_5, A_6, A_7 . . . A_n, because as each additional actor enters, the network becomes unbalanced. Such a network, of course, is not confined to individuals; it can apply to nations forming a military alliance or common market, or to cartels of corporations, and other collective units.

Stratified Networks. The discussion on how intra-category exchanges often achieve balance through closure can help understand processes of stratification. If, for example, tennis players A_1, A_2, A_3 and A_4 are unequal in ability, with A_1 and A_2 having more ability than A_3 and A_4, an initial circle may form among A_1, A_2, A_3 and A_4, but over time, A_1 and A_2 will find more gratification in playing each other and A_3 and A_4 may have to incur too many costs in initiating invitations to A_1 and A_2. For an A_1 and A_3 tennis match is unbalanced; A_2 will have to provide additional resources—the tennis balls, praise, esteem, self-deprecation. The result will be for two classes to develop, as is diagrammed below:

Upper social class A_1 _____ A_2

Lower social class A_3 _____ A_4

Moreover, A_1 and A_2 may enter into new exchanges with A_5 and A_6 at their ability level, forming a new social circle or network. Similarly, A_3 and A_4 may form new tennis relations with A_7 and A_8, creating social circles and networks with players at their ability level. The result is for stratification to reveal the following pattern:

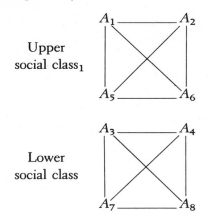

Upper
social class$_1$

Lower
social class

Emerson's discussion of stratification processes is tentative, but he seeks to develop a theorem to describe these stratifying tendencies:

Theorem 11: The more resources are equally valued and the more resources are unequally distributed across a number of actors, the more likely is the network to stratify in terms of resource magnitudes and the more likely are actors with a given level of resources to form closed exchange networks (From theorem 5, propositions 1 and 4).

Again, this theorem can apply to corporate units as well as individuals. Nations become stratified and form social circles, such as is the case with the distinctions between the "developed" and "underdeveloped" nations and the alliances among countries within these two "classes." Or, it can apply to traditional sociological definitions of class, since friendship, recreational, and other closed networks tend to form among members within, rather than across, social classes.

EXCHANGE NETWORK ANALYSIS: PROSPECTS FOR THE FUTURE

Much of the complexity of Emerson's approach has been eliminated in an effort to present the essentials of the exchange network approach. As has been emphasized, this approach offers at least one solution to problems encountered by exchange theory, especially that of Homans and Blau:

1. Emerson's approach evidences considerably more deductive rigor than Homans' scheme. Emerson has used operant principles to build a theoretical scheme that executes Homans' assertions about what theory should be. But in contrast to Homans' efforts, the scheme does not

define as givens what is of most interest to sociologists: patterns of social structure. Emerson's scheme has thus used the principles of operant psychology in a way that allows for *sociological* theorizing, while ignoring the issue of reductionism and avoiding the ad hoc and ex post facto flavor of Homans' polemics.

2. Emerson's network approach has retained and expanded upon Blau's, and more recently Homans', concern with the dynamics of power. Emerson has abandoned, however, the ideologically loaded concept of dialectics, and instead has sought to derive theorems which describe how dependence, use of power, and balancing operations operate as sources of change in social structures. Moreover, this analysis is free from the polemics of conflict theorizing, while providing a set of principles for explaining why imbalance in exchange relations sets into motion processes of change.

3. Emerson's approach also removes much of the vagueness surrounding Homans' and Blau's conceptualizations of social structures as "institutional piles" and "organized collectivities." Social structure in network analysis has a more precise definition as patterns of connections among actors in networks of exchange relations. Furthermore, using diagraph notation and concepts opens the possibility that social structures can be more precisely defined in the language of mathematics.

4. By concentrating on the forms of relations, analysis of the nature of individual actors is forfeited. Yet, this emphasis allows for theories that are distinctly sociological and that avoid the issue of whether or not they are micro or macro. Much exchange theory, and sociological theory in general, evidences considerable discontinuity between processes and structures among individuals and those among collective units. Network analysis is less prone to such discontinuity, since it focuses on the form of the relationship among units.[12]

5. Finally, network analysis bypasses the problem of tautology by taking as a given the existence of actors seeking gratification or reinforcement in social situations. This unit is a fact of social life and its existence is not the end point of analysis—as is the case in operant psychology—but the beginning of analysis. Sociological theory begins with an exchange relation and then seeks to understand variations and changes in its form in terms of *the properties of the relation* rather than the attributes of the actors.

These are the strong points of Emerson's network approach. To a

---

[12] This is, of course, the theoretical tactic first pursued by Georg Simmel. Unfortunately, Simmel's lead was not followed for many decades.

great extent the future of exchange theory hinges on how well these apparent advantages obviate the long-standing logical problem of tautology and substantive problems of vagueness and micro-macro discontinuity. It is difficult to know at this point just whether or not elaboration of Emerson's approach can resolve these problems. Yet it does present an alternative to Homans' and Blau's perspective which draws upon their insights, while offering at least the possibility for resolving the logical and substantive problems associated with Homans' and Blau's work in particular, and exchange theory in general.

PART IV

Interactionist Theorizing

14

THE EMERGENCE OF INTERACTIONISM

Some of the most intriguing questions of social theory concern the relationships between society and the individual. In what ways does one mirror the other? How does society shape individuals, or how do individuals create, and maintain, and change society? In what ways do society and the personality of individuals represent interrelated, and yet separate, emergent phenomena?

It is to these questions that sociological theory turned near the close of the 19th century, as the grand analytical schemes of Marx, Durkheim, Spencer, and other Europeans were supplemented by a concern for the specific processes that linked individuals to one another and to society. Instead of focusing on macro structures and processes, such as evolution, class conflict, and the nature of the "body social," attention shifted to the study of processes of social interaction and their consequences for the individual and society.

INTERACTIONIST CURRENTS IN EUROPE

Georg Simmel and "Sociation"

Georg Simmel was perhaps the first European sociologist to begin the serious exploration of interaction, or "sociability" as he called it. In so doing, he elevated the study of interaction from the taken-for-granted.[1] For Simmel, as for the first generation of American sociologists, the macro structures and processes studied by functional and some conflict theories—class, the state, family, religion, evolution—were ultimately reflections of the specific interactions among people. While these interactions had resulted in emergent social phenomena, considerable insight into the latter could be attained by understanding the basic interactive processes that first gave and then sustained their existence.

In Chapter 6, Simmel's analysis of the forms of conflict was explored. But Simmel's study of interaction extended beyond just the analysis of conflict. He was concerned with understanding the forms and consequences of many diverse types of interactions. Some of his most important insights, which were to influence American interactionists, concerned the relationship between the individual and society. In his famous essay on "the web of group affiliations,"[2] for example, Simmel emphasized that human personality emerges from, and is shaped by, the particular configuration of a person's group affiliations. What people are—that is, how they think of themselves and are prepared to act—is circumscribed by their group memberships. As he emphasized, "the genesis of the personality [is] the point of intersection for innumerable social influences, as the end-product of heritages derived from the most diverse groups and periods of adjustment."[3]

While Simmel was not to analyze in great detail the emergence of human personality, his "formal sociology" did break away from the macro concerns of early German, French, and British sociologists. He began in Europe a mode of analysis which was to become the prime concern of the first generation of American sociologists. Simmel thus could be considered one of the first European "interactionists."

Max Weber and "Social Action"

Another German sociologist, Max Weber, was also concerned with the micro social world, although his most important insights were in the area of macro and historical sociology. Yet Weber's definition of sociology was highly compatible with the flourishing American school of interactionism. For Weber, sociology was "that science which aims

---

[1] Georg Simmel, "Sociability," in *The Sociology of Georg Simmel,* ed. Kurt H. Wolff (New York: Free Press, 1950), pp. 40–57. For an excellent secondary account of Simmel's significance for interactionism, see Randall Collins and Michael Makowsky, *The Discovery of Society* (New York: Random House, 1972), pp. 138–42.

[2] *Conflict and The Web of Group Affiliations,* translated by Reinhard Bendix (Glencoe, Ill.: Free Press, 1955; originally published in 1922).

[3] Ibid., p. 141.

at the interpretative understanding of social behavior in order to gain an explanation of its causes, its course, and its effects."[4] Moreover, the behavior to be studied by sociology was seen by Weber as "social action" which includes:

> All human behavior when and insofar as the acting individual attaches a subjective meaning to it. Action in this sense may be overt, purely inward, or subjective; it may consist of positive intervention in a situation, of deliberately refraining from such intervention, or passively acquiescing in the situation. Action is social insofar as by virtue of the subjective meaning attached to it by the acting individual (or individuals), it takes account of the behavior of others and is thereby oriented in its course.[5]

Thus, Weber recognized that the reality behind the macro structures of society—classes, the state, institutions, and nations—are the meaningful and symbolic interactions among actual people. Moreover, Weber's methodology stressed the need for understanding macro structures and processes "at the level of meaning." For in the real world, actors interpret and give meaning to the reality around them and act in terms of these meanings. And yet, despite this key insight, Weber's actual analysis of social structures—class, status, party, change, religion, bureaucracy, and the like—rarely follows his own methodological prescriptions. As with other European thinkers, he tended to focus on social and cultural *structures* and the impact of these structures upon each other. The interacting and interpreting person is often lost amid Weber's elaborate taxonomies of structures and analyses of historical events.

Émile Durkheim's Metamorphosis

In his *Division of Labor in Society*, Durkheim portrayed social reality as an emergent phenomena, *sui generis*, and as not reducible to the psychic states of individuals. And yet, in his later works, such as *The Elementary Forms of Religious Life*,[6] Durkheim began to ask: How does society rule the individual? How is it that society "gets inside" individuals and guides them from within? Why do people share common orientations and perspectives? Durkheim never answered these questions effectively, for his earlier emphasis on social structures prevented him

---

[4] Max Weber, *Basic Concepts in Sociology* (New York: The Citadel Press, 1964), p. 29.

[5] Max Weber, *The Theory of Social and Economic Organization* (New York: Free Press, 1947; originally published after Weber's death), p. 88.

[6] Émile Durkheim, *The Elementary Forms of Religious Life* (New York: The Free Press, 1954).

from seeing the micro reality of interactions among individuals implicated in macro social structures. But it is significant that the most forceful advocate of the sociologistic position became intrigued with the relationship between the individual and society.

Thus, the giants of European sociology had, by the turn of the century, become interested in the very questions which are the hallmark of the interactionist perspective. Their inquiry was limited and their insights sparse in comparison to the explosion of concepts and frameworks in American sociology in the late 1800s and early 1900s, but the sociological imagination about the relationship between society and individuals had been stimulated on both sides of the Atlantic. And outside the confines of the European tradition, American social thinkers were to make the great intellectual breakthroughs and to unravel some of the mysteries about the relations among individuals, interaction, and society.

EARLY AMERICAN INSIGHTS

Modern interactionism draws its inspiration from a number of prominent thinkers, all of whom wrote between 1880 and 1920. Yet, interactionism stands in debt to the genius of one man, George Herbert Mead. Much like Darwin's great synthesis of the theory of evolution out of his own studies and the speculations of others, so interactionist ideas were codified by George Herbert Mead. Mead borrowed ideas from others, and combined them with his own insights, to produce a synthesis that still stands as the base for modern interactionism.

To appreciate Mead's feat, it is necessary to review the contributions of three thinkers who most influenced Mead: William James, John Dewey, and Charles Horton Cooley. Each of these scholars provided a key concept that was to form the basis of Mead's synthesis.

William James and the Concept of "Self"

The Harvard psychologist, William James, was perhaps the first social scientist to develop a clear concept of "self." James recognized that humans have the capacity to view themselves as objects and to develop self-feelings and attitudes toward themselves. Just as humans can (a) denote symbolically other people and aspects of the world around them, (b) develop attitudes and feelings toward these objects, and (c) construct typical responses toward objects, so they can denote themselves, develop self-feelings and attitudes, and construct responses toward themselves.

James called these capacities "self" and recognized their importance in shaping the way people respond in the world.

James developed a typology of selves that people have: the "material self," which includes those physical objects that humans view as "part of their being" and as crucial to their identity; the "social self" which involves the self-feelings that individuals derive from associations with other people; and the "spiritual self" which embraces the general cognitive style and capacities typifying an individual.[7] While this typology was never adopted by subsequent interactionists, James' notion of the "social self" was to become a part of all interactionists' formulations.

James' concept of the social self recognizes that people's feelings about themselves arise out of interaction with others. As he noted, "a man has as many social selves as there are individuals who recognize him."[8] Yet James did not carry this initial insight very far. He was, after all, a psychologist who was more concerned with internal psychological functioning of individuals than with the social processes out of which the capacities of individuals arise.

Self and Social Process: Charles Horton Cooley

Charles Horton Cooley made two significant breakthroughs in the study of self. First, he refined the concept of self. Self was seen by Cooley as the process by which individuals see themselves as objects, along with other objects, in their social environment. Second, he recognized that self emerges out of communication with others. As individuals interact with each other, they interpret each other's gestures and thus are able to see themselves from the viewpoint of others. They imagine how others evaluate them and they derive images of themselves or self-feelings and attitudes. Cooley termed this process "the looking glass self": The gestures of others serve as mirrors in which people see and evaluate themselves, just as they see and evaluate other objects in their social environment.

Cooley also recognized that self arises out of interaction in group contexts. He developed the concept of "primary group" to emphasize that participation in front of the looking glass of some groups is more important in the genesis and maintenance of self than participation in other groups. Those small groups where personal and intimate ties exist

---

[7] William James, *The Principles of Psychology* (Dover Publications, 1890), pp. 292–299 of Volume I.

[8] Ibid., p. 294.

are the most important in shaping people's self-feelings and attitudes.

Cooley thus refined and narrowed James' notion of self and forced the recognition that it arises out of symbolic communication with others in group contexts. These insights were to profoundly influence the thought of George Herbert Mead.

Pragmatism and Thinking: The Contribution of John Dewey

John Dewey was, for a brief period, a colleague of Cooley. But more important was Dewey's enduring association with George Herbert Mead. As the chief exponent of a school of thought known as "pragmatism," he stressed the process of human adjustment to the world. Humans constantly seek to master the conditions of their environment. And thus the unique characteristics of humans arise out of the process of adjusting to their life conditions.

What is unique to humans, Dewey argued, is their capacity for thinking. Mind is not a structure but a process that emerges out of efforts by humans to adjust to their environment. Moreover, mind is the unique capacity that allows humans to deal with conditions around them.

Dewey thus devoted considerable effort to understanding human consciousness. His basic questions were: How does mind work? And how does it facilitate adaptation to the environment? Mind for Dewey is the process of denoting objects in the environment, ascertaining potential lines of conduct, imagining the consequences of pursuing each line, inhibiting inappropriate responses, and then, selecting a line of conduct that will facilitate adjustment. Mind is thus the process of thinking, and thinking involves deliberation:

> . . . deliberation is a dramatic rehearsal (in imagination) of various competing possible lines of action. . . . Deliberation is an experiment in finding out what the various lines of possible action are really like. It is an experiment in making various combinations of selected elements . . . to see what the resultant action would be like if it were entered upon.[9]

Through conversations with Mead, Dewey's conception of mind as a process of adjustment, rather than as a "thing" or "entity," was to be critical in shaping Mead's thought. For, much as Cooley had done for the concept of self, Dewey had demonstrated that mind emerges and is sustained through interactions in the social world. This line of

---

[9] John Dewey, *Human Nature and Human Conduct* (New York: Henry Holt, 1922), p. 190. For an earlier statement of these ideas, see John Dewey, *Psychology* (New York: Harper Brothers, 1886).

thought from both Cooley and Dewey was to prove decisive as Mead's great synthesis unfolded.

Main Currents of Thought in America: Pragmatism, Darwinism, and Behaviorism

At the time that Mead began to formulate his synthesis, a particular convergence of ideas was occurring in America. This convergence appears to have influenced the direction of Mead's thought. Mead considered himself a behaviorist, but not of the mechanical stimulus-response type. In fact, many of his ideas were intended as a refutation of such prominent behaviorists as Watson. Mead accepted the basic premise of behaviorism—that is, the view that reinforcement guides and directs action. He was, however, to use this principle in a novel way. Moreover, he rejected as untenable the methodological presumption of early behaviorism that it was inappropriate to study the internal dynamics of the human mind. James', Cooley's, and Dewey's influence assured that Mead would rework the principle of reinforcement in ways that allowed for the consideration of mind and self.

Another strain of thought that shaped Mead's synthesis is pragmatism, as it was learned through exposure with Dewey. Pragmatism, as already stated, sees organisms as practical creatures who come to terms with the actual conditions of the world. Coupled with behaviorism, pragmatism offered a new way of viewing human life: Human beings seek to cope with their actual conditions, but learn those behavioral patterns that provide gratification, with the most important type of gratification being adjustment.

This line of argument was buttressed in Mead's synthesis by yet another related intellectual tradition, Darwinism. Mead recognized that humans were organisms who sought to find a niche in which they could adapt. This was true of humans as a species and, more important, it was true of individual humans as they discover a niche in the social world. Mead's commitment to behaviorism and pragmatism thus allowed him to apply the basic principle of Darwinian theory to each individual human: that which facilitates survival of the organism will be retained.

In this way, reinforcement, pragmatist, and Darwinian principles became merged into an image of humans as attempting to adjust to the world around them and as retaining those characteristics—particularly mind and self—which would enable them to adapt to their surroundings. Hence, mind, self, and other unique features of humans "evolve" out of efforts to "survive" in their social environment. They are thus capacities that arise from the processes of coping, adjusting, adapting, and achieving the ultimate gratification or reinforcement, survival. So it is for each newborn organism, and much of Mead's analysis focused on how it is that the infant organism acquires mind and self as an adaptation to society. But Mead did much more; he showed how society could only survive from the capacities for mind and self among individuals. Thus, mind, self, and society were intimately connected in life- and society-sustaining processes.

GEORGE HERBERT MEAD'S SYNTHESIS: MIND, SELF, AND SOCIETY

While the names of William James, Charles Horton Cooley, and John Dewey figure prominently in the development of interactionism, it was left to George Herbert Mead to bring their related concepts together into a coherent theoretical perspective that linked the emergence of the human mind, the social self, and the structure of society to the process of social interaction.[10] As has been emphasized, Mead appears to have begun his synthesis with two basic assumptions: (1) The biological frailty of human organisms force their cooperation with each other in group contexts in order to survive; and (2) those actions within and among human organisms that facilitated their cooperation, and hence their survival or adjustment, would be retained. Starting from these assumptions, Mead was able to reorganize the concepts of others so that they denoted how mind, the social self, and society arose and were sustained through interaction.

Mind

Following Dewey's lead, Mead recognized that the unique feature of the human mind is its capacity to (1) use symbols to designate objects in the environment, (2) to rehearse covertly alternative lines of action

---

[10] Mead wrote very little, and thus most of his seminal ideas can only be found in the published lecture notes of his students. His most important exposition of interactionism is found in his *Mind, Self, and Society*, ed. Charles W. Morris (Chicago: University of Chicago Press, 1934). Other useful sources include George Herbert Mead, *Selected Writings* (Indianapolis: Bobbs-Merrill Co., 1964); and Anselm Strauss, ed., *George Herbert Mead on Social Psychology* (Chicago: University of Chicago Press, 1964). For excellent secondary sources on the thought of Mead, see Tamotsu Shibutani, *Society and Personality: An Interactionist Approach* (Englewood Cliffs, N.J.: Prentice Hall, Inc., 1962); Anselm Strauss, *Mirrors and Masks: The Search for Identity* (Glencoe, Ill.: Free Press, 1959); and Bernard N. Meltzer, "Mead's Social Psychology," in *The Social Psychology of George Herbert Mead* (Ann Arbor, Mich.: Center for Sociological Research, 1964), pp. 10–31.

toward these objects, and (3) to inhibit inappropriate lines of action and select a proper course of overt action. Mead termed this process of using symbols or language covertly "imaginative rehearsal," revealing his conception of mind as a *process* rather than a structure. Further, as will be developed more fully later, the existence and persistence of society, or cooperation in organized groups, was viewed by Mead as dependent upon this capacity of humans to "imaginatively rehearse" lines of action toward each other and thereby select those behaviors that could facilitate cooperation, adjustment, and survival.

Much of Mead's analysis focused not so much on the mind of mature organisms, but on how this capacity first evolves in humans. Unless infants develop mind, neither society nor self can exist. In accordance with principles of behaviorism, Darwinism, and pragmatism, Mead stressed that mind arises out of a selective process in which the initially wide repertoire of random gestures emitted by an infant are narrowed as some gestures bring favorable reactions from those upon whom the infant is dependent for survival. Such selection of gestures facilitating adjustment can occur either through trial and error or through conscious coaching by those with whom the infant must cooperate. Eventually, through either of these processes, gestures come to have "common meanings" for both the infant and those in its environment. With this development, gestures now denote the same objects and carry similar dispositions for all the parties to an interaction. When gestures have such common meanings, Mead terms them "conventional gestures." These conventional gestures have increased efficiency for interaction among individuals because they allow for more precise communication of desires and wants as well as intended courses of action—thereby increasing the capacity of organisms to adjust to one another.

The ability to use and to interpret conventional gestures with common meanings represents a significant step in the development of mind, self, and society. By perceiving and interpreting gestures, humans reveal the capacity to "take the role of the other," since they can now assume the perspective (dispositions, needs, wants, and propensities to act) of those with whom they must cooperate for survival. By reading and then interpreting covertly conventional gestures, individuals are able to imaginatively rehearse alternative lines of action that will facilitate adjustment to others. Thus, by being able to put oneself in another's place, or to "take the role of the other" to use Mead's concept, the covert rehearsal of action can take on a new level of efficiency, since actors can better gauge the consequences of their actions for others and thereby increase the probability of cooperative interaction.

Thus, when an organism develops the capacity (1) to understand conventional gestures, (2) to employ these gestures to take the role of others, and (3) to imaginatively rehearse alternative lines of action, Mead believes such an organism to possess *mind*.

Self

Drawing from James and Cooley, Mead stressed that just as humans can designate symbolically other actors in the environment, so they can symbolically represent themselves as an object. The interpretation of gestures, then, can not only facilitate human cooperation, it can also serve as the basis for self-assessment and evaluation. This capacity to derive images of oneself as an object of evaluation in interaction is dependent upon the processes of mind. What Mead saw as significant about this process is that, as organisms mature, the transitory "self-images" derived from specific others in each interactive situation eventually become crystallized into a more or less stabilized "self-conception" of oneself as a certain type of object. With the emergence of these self-conceptions, actions of individuals were seen by Mead to take on consistency, since they are now mediated through a coherent and stable set of attitudes, dispositions, or meanings about oneself as a certain type of person.

Mead chose to highlight three stages in the development of self, each stage marking not only a change in the kinds of transitory self-images an individual could derive from role-taking, but also an increasing crystallization of a more stabilized self-conception. The initial stage of role-taking in which self-images could be derived was termed by Mead as "play." In play, infant organisms are capable of assuming the perspective of only a limited number of others, at first only one or two. Later, by virtue of biological maturation and practice at role-taking, the maturing organism becomes capable of taking the role of several others engaged in organized activity. Mead termed this stage the "game," because it designates the capacity of individuals to derive multiple self-images from, and to cooperate with, a group of individuals engaged in some coordinated activity. (Mead typically illustrates this stage by giving the example of a baseball game in which all individuals must symbolically assume the role of all others on the team in order to participate effectively.) The final stage in the development of self occurs when an individual can take the role of the "generalized other" or "community of attitudes" evident in a society. At this stage, individuals were visualized by Mead as capable of assuming the over-all perspective of a community, or the general beliefs, values, and norms of an individual's various spheres of interaction. This means that humans can both (1) increase the appropriateness of their responses to others with whom they must interact and (2) expand their evaluative self-images from the expectations of specific others to those of the broader community. Thus, it is this ever-increasing capacity to take roles with an ever-expanding body of "others" which marks the stages in the development of self.

Society

For Mead, *society,* or "institutions" as he often phrased the matter, represent the organized and patterned interactions among diverse individuals. Such organization of interactions is dependent upon mind. Without the capacities of mind to take roles and imaginatively rehearse alternative lines of activity, individuals could not coordinate their activities. Mead emphasized:

> The immediate effect of such role-taking lies in the control which the individual is able to exercise over his own response. The control of the action of the individual in a co-operative process can take place in the conduct of the individual himself if he can take the role of the other. It is this control of the response of the individual himself through taking the role of the other that leads to the value of this type of communication from the point of view of the organization of the conduct in the group.[11]

Society is also dependent upon the capacities of self, especially the process of evaluating oneself from the perspective of the "generalized other." Without the ability to see and evaluate oneself as an object from this "community of attitudes," social control would rest solely on self-evaluations derived from role-taking with specific and immediately present others—thus making coordination of diverse activities among larger groups extremely difficult.[12]

While Mead was vitally concerned with how society and its institutions are maintained and perpetuated by the capacities of mind and self, these concepts also allowed him to view society as constantly in flux and rife with potential change. The fact that role-taking and imaginative rehearsal are ongoing processes among the participants in any interaction situation reveals the potential these processes give individuals for adjusting and readjusting their responses. Furthermore, the insertion of self as an object into the interactive process underscores the fact that the outcome of interaction will be affected by the ways in which self-conceptions

---

[11] Mead, *Mind, Self, and Society,* p. 254.
[12] Ibid., pp. 256–57.

alter the initial reading of gestures and the subsequent rehearsal of alternative lines of behavior. Such a perspective thus emphasizes that society and various patterns of social organization are both perpetuated and altered through the adjustive capacities of mind and the mediating impact of self:

> Thus the institutions of society are organized forms of group or social activity—forms so organized that the individual members of society can act adequately and socially by taking the attitudes of others toward these activities. . . . [But] there is no necessary or inevitable reason why social institutions should be oppressive or rigidly conservative, or why they should not rather be, as many are, flexible and progressive, fostering individuality rather than discouraging it.[13]

In this passage is a clue to Mead's abiding distaste for rigid and oppressive patterns of social organization. He viewed society as a *constructed* phenomenon that arises out of the adjustive interactions among individuals; as such, society can be altered or reconstructed through the processes denoted by the concepts of mind and self. However, Mead frequently appeared to have gone one step further to stress that not only is change likely, but also that it is frequently unpredictable, even by those emitting the change-inducing behavior. To account for this indeterminacy of action, Mead used two concepts first developed by William James, the "I" and the "me."[14] For Mead, the "I" points to the impulsive tendencies of individuals, while the "me" represents the self-image of the behavior in question after it has been emitted. With these concepts Mead emphasized that the "I," or impulsive behavior, cannot be predicted, because the individual can only "know in experience" (the "me") what has actually transpired and what the consequences of the "I" for the interaction are to be.

In sum, then, society for Mead represented those constructed patterns of coordinated activity that are maintained by, and changed through, symbolic interaction among and within actors. Both the maintenance and change of society, therefore, occur through the processes of mind and self. While many of the interactions causing both stability and change in groups were viewed by Mead as predictable, the possibility for spontaneous and unpredictable actions that could alter existing patterns of interaction is also likely.

This conceptual legacy had a profound impact on a generation of American sociologists prior to the posthumous publication in 1934 of Mead's lectures. However, by that time it was becoming evident that,

---

13 Ibid., pp. 261–62.
14 See James' *Principles of Psychology*, pp. 135–76.

despite the suggestiveness of Mead's concepts, they failed to address some important theoretical issues.

The most important of these issues concerned the vagueness of his concepts in denoting the nature of social organization or "society" and the precise points of articulation between society and the individual. Mead viewed society as organized activity, regulated by the generalized other, in which individuals made adjustments and cooperated with one another. Such adjustments and the cooperation they ensured were then seen as possible by virtue of the capacities of "mind" and "self." While mind and self emerged out of existent patterns of social organization, the maintenance or change of such organization was seen by Mead as a reflection of the processes of mind and self. Although these and related concepts of the Meadian scheme pointed to the mutual interaction of society and the individual, and although the concepts of mind and self denoted crucial processes through which this dependency was maintained, they did not allow for the analysis of variations in patterns of social organization and in the various ways individuals were implicated in these patterns. To note that "society" was coordinated activity and that such activity was maintained and changed through the role-taking and the self-assessment processes of individuals offered only a broad conceptual portrait of the linkages between the individual and society. Indeed, Mead's picture of society did not indicate how variable types of social organization reciprocally interacted with variable properties of self and mind. Thus, in the end, Mead's concepts appeared to emphasize that society shaped mind and self and that mind and self affected society—a simple but profound observation for the times, but one that needed supplementation.

The difficult task of filling in the details of this broad portrait began only four decades ago, as researchers and theorists began to encounter the vague and circular nature of Mead's conceptual perspective. The initial efforts at documenting more precisely and less tautologously the points of articulation between society and the individual led to attempts at formulating a series of concepts that could expose the basic units from which society was constructed. It was felt that in this way the linkages between society and the individual could be more adequately conceptualized.

ROLE, STATUS, AND THE INDIVIDUAL

While Mead's synthesis provided the initial conceptual breakthrough, it did not satisfactorily resolve the problem of how participation in the *structure* of society shaped individual conduct, and vice versa. In an effort to resolve this vagueness, sociological inquiry began to focus on the concept of "role." Individuals were seen as playing roles associated with positions in larger networks of positions. And with this vision, efforts to understand more about social structures and how individuals are implicated in them intensified during the 1920s and 1930s. This line of inquiry was to become known as "role theory."

Robert Park and Role Theory

Robert Park, who came to the University of Chicago near the end of Mead's career, was one of the first to extend Mead's ideas through an emphasis on roles. As he observed, "everybody is always and everywhere, more or less consciously, playing a role."[15] But Park stressed that roles are linked to structural positions in society and that self was intimately linked to playing roles within the confines of the positions of social structure.[16]

> The conceptions which men form of themselves seem to depend upon their vocations, and in general upon the role they seek to play in communities and social groups in which they live, as well as upon the recognition and status which society accords them in these roles. It is status, i.e., recognition by the community, that confers upon the individual the character of a person, since a person is an individual who has status, not necessarily legal, but social.

Much as the German sociologist Georg Simmel had emphasized,[17] Park's analysis stressed the fact that self emerges from the multiple roles that people play. In turn roles are connected to positions in social structures. This kind of analysis shifted attention to the nature of society and how its structure influenced the processes outlined in Mead's great synthesis.

Jacob Moreno and Role Theory

Inspired in part by Mead's concept of role-taking and by his own studies in Europe, Jacob Moreno was one of the first to develop the

---

15 Robert E. Park, "Behind Our Masks," *Survey Graphic* 56 (May 1926): 135. For a convenient summary of the thrust of early research efforts in role theory, see: Ralph H. Turner, "Social Roles: Sociological Aspects," *International Encyclopaedia of the Social Sciences*, 1968.

16 Robert E. Park, *Society* (New York: Free Press, 1955), pp. 285–86.

17 Indeed, Park studied briefly with Simmel in Berlin and apparently acquired insight into Simmel's study of the individual and the web of group affiliations. Coupled with his exposure to William James at Harvard, who also stressed the multiple sources of self, it is clear that Mead's legacy was supplemented by Simmel and James through the work of Robert Park.

concept of role-playing. In *Who Shall Survive* and in many publications in the journals he founded in America, Moreno began to view social organization as a network of roles that constrained and channeled behavior.[18] In his early works, Moreno began to distinguish different types of roles: (*a*) "psychosomatic roles," in which behavior was related to basic biological needs, as conditioned by culture, and in which role enactment was typically unconscious; (*b*) "psychodramatic roles," in which individuals behaved in accordance with the specific expectations of a particular social context; and (*c*) "social roles," in which individuals conformed to the more general expectations of various conventional social categories (for example, worker, Christian, mother, father, and so forth).

Despite the suggestiveness of these distinctions, their importance came not so much from their substantive content, but from their intent: to conceptualize social structures as organized networks of expectations that required varying types of role enactments by individuals. In this way, analysis was able to move beyond the vague Meadian conceptualization of society as coordinated activity, regulated by the "generalized other," to a more sophisticated conceptualization of social organization as various *types* of interrelated role enactments regulated by varying *types* of expectations.

Ralph Linton and Role Theory

Shortly after Moreno's publication of *Who Shall Survive*, the anthropologist Ralph Linton further conceptualized the nature of social organization, and the individual's imbeddedness in it, by distinguishing the concepts of role, status, and individuals from one another:

> A status, as distinct from the individual who may occupy it, is simply a collection of rights and duties. . . . A *role* represents the dynamic aspect of status. The individual is socially assigned to a status and occupies it with relation to other statuses. When he puts the rights and duties which constitute the status into effect, he is performing a role.[19]

In this passage are a number of important conceptual distinctions. Now, social structure is perceived to reveal several distinct analytical elements: (*a*) a network of positions, (*b*) a corresponding system of expectations, and (*c*) patterns of behavior which are enacted with regard to the expectations of particular networks of interrelated positions. While,

---

[18] Jacob Moreno, *Who Shall Survive*, Nervous and Mental Disease Publication (Washington, D.C., 1934); rev. ed. (New York: Beacon House, 1953).

[19] Ralph Linton, *The Study of Man* (Copyright © 1936 by D. Appleton-Century Company, Inc.).

in retrospect, these distinctions may appear self-evident and trivial, they made possible the subsequent elaboration of many interactionist concepts:

1. Linton's distinctions allowed for the conceptualization of society in terms of clear-cut variables: the nature and kind of interrelations among positions and the types of expectations attending these positions.
2. The variables Mead denoted by the concepts of *mind* and *self* could be analytically distinguished from both social structure (positions and expectations) and behavior (role enactment).
3. By conceptually separating the processes of role-taking and imaginative rehearsal from both social structure and behavior, the points of articulation between society and the individual could be more clearly marked, since role-taking would pertain to covert interpretations of the expectations attending networks of statuses, and role would denote the enactment of these expectations as mediated by self.

Thus, by offering more conceptual insight into the nature of social organization, Park, Moreno, and Linton provided a needed supplement to Mead's suggestive concepts. For now it would be possible to understand more precisely the nature of, and the interrelations among, mind, self, and society.

MODERN INTERACTIONISM: A REVIEW

The Meadian legacy has inspired a theoretical perspective that can best be termed "symbolic interactionism." This perspective—to be discussed in the next chapter—focuses on how the symbolic processes of role-taking, imaginative rehearsal, and self-evaluation by individuals attempting to adjust to one another lay the basis for the understanding of how social structure is constructed, maintained, and changed. While accepting the analytical importance of these symbolic processes, a more recent theoretical tradition has placed more conceptual emphasis on the vision of social structure connoted by Park's, Moreno's, and Linton's concepts. Although not as clearly codified or as unified as the symbolic interactionist position, this theoretical perspective—the subject of Chapter 16—can be labeled "role theory," because it focuses primary analytical attention on the *structure of status networks and attendant expectations* as they circumscribe the internal symbolic processes of individuals and the eventual enactment of roles.

In some respects, the distinction between symbolic interactionism and role theory may initially appear arbitrary, since each perspective relies heavily on the thought of George Herbert Mead and since both are concerned with the relationship between the individual and society. Yet, despite the fact that each represents a variant of interactionism, there are great differences in emphasis between symbolic interactionism and role theory. These will be emphasized in the next two chapters. In a final chapter on the future of interactionism, however, a brief discussion of major issues will be followed by an overview of Ralph H. Turner's attempt to unite symbolic interactionism and role theory into a unified interactionist perspective. For the future of interactionism resides in the unification of the diverse theoretical traditions inspired by Mead's synthesis.

15

SYMBOLIC INTERACTIONISM: HERBERT BLUMER versus MANFORD KUHN

THE CHICAGO AND IOWA SCHOOLS

George Herbert Mead's synthesis still provides the inspiration for a school of thought known as "symbolic interactionism." As with most theoretical perspectives, however, there is a diversity of opinion on how to use Mead's insights to develop sociological theory. Nowhere is this divergence better illustrated than in the approaches of two symbolic interactionists, Herbert Blumer and the late Manford Kuhn.[1]

Herbert Blumer was Mead's student at the University of Chicago and took over his courses upon Mead's death. Blumer's use of Mead's concepts is thus known as the "Chicago School" of symbolic interactionism. Manford Kuhn was not trained by Mead and was exposed to a more positivistic, data-oriented group of mentors. Since Kuhn formulated a variant of Mead's thought while at the State University of Iowa, those who follow Kuhn's lead are a part of the "Iowa School" of symbolic interactionism. In many respects, this distinction between "schools" of interactionism is somewhat artificial. There is considerable overlap, since both schools follow Mead's lead. Yet, the work of Blumer and Kuhn represent the polar extremes of symbolic interactionism. Most interactionists fall somewhere between these extremes, but most lean toward one pole or the other.

---

[1] I am following, but greatly expanding upon, B. N. Meltzer's and J. W. Petras' interesting article, "The Chicago and Iowa Schools of Symbolic Interactionism" in T. Shibutani, ed., *Human Nature and Collective Behavior* (Englewood Cliffs, N.J.: Prentice-Hall, 1970).

Thus, in order to appreciate the scope and diversity of the symbolic interactionist approach, this chapter will examine the points of divergence between Blumer's and Kuhn's thought. In this way, it will be possible to visualize the full impact of Mead's thought on contemporary symbolic interactionist theory.

SYMBOLIC INTERACTIONISM: POINTS OF CONVERGENCE

Before stressing the points of divergence between the Iowa and Chicago Schools, however, their common legacy of assumptions from Mead's thought should be emphasized. These points of convergence are what make symbolic interactionism a distinctive theoretical perspective.[2]

Humans as Symbol-Users

Symbolic interactionists, as their name implies, place enormous emphasis on the capacity of humans to create and use symbols. In contrast to other animals, whose symbolic capacities are limited or nonexistent, the very essence of humans and the world that they create flows from their ability to symbolically represent each other, objects, ideas, and virtually any phase of their experience. Without the capacity to create symbols and to use them in human affairs, patterns of social organization among humans could not be created, maintained, or changed. Humans have become, to a very great degree, liberated from instinctual and biological programming and thus must rely on their symbol-using powers to adapt and survive in the world.

Symbolic Communication

Humans use symbols to communicate with each other. By virtue of their capacity to agree upon the meaning of vocal and bodily gestures,

---

[2] There are a number of excellent reference works on symbolic interactionism, including: Jerome G. Manis and Bernard N. Meltzer, eds., *Symbolic Interaction: A Reader in Social Psychology* (Boston: Allyn and Bacon, 1972); J. Cardwell, *Social Psychology: A Symbolic Interactionist Approach* (Philadelphia: Davis, 1971); Alfred Lindesmith and Anslem Strauss, *Social Psychology* (New York: Holt, Rinehart, 1968); Arnold Rose, ed., *Human Behavior and Social Process* (Boston: Houghton-Mifflin, 1962); Tamotsu Shibutani, *Society and Personality* (Englewood Cliffs, N.J.: Prentice-Hall, 1961); C. K. Warriner, *The Emergence of Society* (Homewood, Ill.: The Dorsey Press, 1970); Gregory Stone and H. Farberman, eds., *Symbolic Interaction: A Reader in Social Psychology* (Walthum, Mass.: Xerox, 1970); John P. Hewitt, *Self and Society: A Symbolic Interactionist Social Psychology* (Boston: Allyn & Bacon, 1976; Robert H. Laver and Warren H. Handel, *Social Psychology: The Theory and Application of Symbolic Interactionism* (Boston: Houghton Mifflin, 1977).

people can effectively communicate. Symbolic communication is, of course, extremely complex, since humans use more than word or language symbols in communication. They also use facial gestures, voice tones, body countenance, and other symbolic gestures over which there is common meaning and understanding.

Interaction and Role-Taking

As Mead emphasized, by "reading" and "interpreting" the gestures of others—that is, the symbols that they emit—humans communicate and interact. They become able to mutually "read" each other, to "anticipate" each other's responses, and to adjust to each other. Mead termed this basic capacity "role-taking"—the ability to see the other's attitudes and dispositions to act. Interactionists still emphasize the process of role-taking as the basic mechanism by which interaction occurs. For example, the late Arnold Rose, who was one of the leaders of contemporary interactionism, indicated that role-taking ". . . means that the individual communicator imagines—evokes within himself—how the recipient understands that communication."[3] Or, as another modern interactionist, Sheldon Stryker, emphasizes, role-taking is ". . . anticipating the responses of others with one in some social act."[4] And as Alfred Lindesmith and Anslem Strauss emphasize, role-taking is "imaginatively assuming the position or point of view of another person."[5]

Without the ability to read gestures and to use these gestures as a basis for putting oneself in the position of others, then, interaction could not occur. And without interaction the development of humans and patterns of social organization would be impossible.

Interaction, Humans, and Society

Just as Mead emphasized that mind, self, and society were intimately connected to each other, so contemporary interactionists emphasize the relation between the genesis of "humanness" and patterns of interaction. What makes humans unique as a species and what enables each individual person to possess distinctive characteristics is the result of interaction in society. Conversely, what makes society possible is the capacities that humans acquire as they grow and mature in society.

---

[3] Rose, *Human Behavior*, p. 8.

[4] Sheldon Stryker, "Symbolic Interaction as an Approach to Family Research," *Marriage and Family Living* 2 (May 1959): 111–19. See also his "Role-Taking Accuracy and Adjustment," *Sociometry* 20 (December 1957): 286–96.

[5] Lindesmith and Strauss, *Social Psychology*, p. 282.

Current symbolic interactionists tend to emphasize the same human capacities as Mead: the genesis of mind and self. Mind is the capacity to think: to symbolically denote, weigh, assess, anticipate, map, and construct courses of action. While Mead's term, "mind," is rarely used today, the processes that this term denotes are given great emphasis. As Rose indicates:

> Thinking is the process by which possible symbolic solutions and other future courses of action are examined, assessed for their relative advantages and disadvantages in terms of the values of the individual, and one of them chosen for action.[6]

Moreover, the concept of "mind" has been reformulated to embrace what W. I. Thomas termed "the definition of the situation."[7] With the capacities of mind, actors can name, categorize, and orient themselves to constellations of objects—including themselves as an object—in all situations. In this way they can assess, weigh, and sort out appropriate lines of conduct.[8]

As the concept of the "definition of the situation" underscores, self is still a key concept in the interactionist literature. Present emphasis in the interactionist orientation is on (a) the emergence of self-conceptions—or relatively stable and enduring conceptions that people have about themselves—and (b) the ability to derive self-images—or pictures of oneself as an object in social situations. Self is thus a major object that people inject into their definitions of situations. It shapes much of what they see, feel, and do in the world around them.

Society, or relatively stable patterns of interaction, is seen by interactionists as only possible by virtue of people's capacities to define situations and, most particularly, to view themselves as objects in situations. Society is thus created, maintained, and changed by human capacities for thinking and defining as well as for self-reflection and evaluation.

In sum, these points of emphasis constitute the core of the interactionist approach. Humans create and use symbols. They communicate with symbols. They interact through role-taking, which involves the reading of symbols emitted by others. What makes them unique as a species— the existence of mind and self—arises out of interaction, while conversely,

---

[6] Rose, *Human Behavior*, p. 12.

[7] W. I. Thomas, "The Definition of the Situation" in Manis and Meltzer, *Symbolic Interaction*, pp. 331–36.

[8] For clear statements on the concept of "definition of the situation" as it is currently used in interactionist theory, see: Lindesmith and Strauss, *Social Psychology*, pp. 280–83.

the emergence of these capacities allows for the interactions that form the basis of society.

AREAS OF DISAGREEMENT AND CONTROVERSY

From this initial starting point, Blumer and Kuhn often diverge, as do their followers in either the Chicago or Iowa Schools.[9] The major areas of disagreement revolve around the following issues: (1) What is the nature of the individual? (2) What is the nature of interaction? (3) What is the nature of social organization? (4) What is the most appropriate method for studying humans and society? And (5) What is the best form of sociological theorizing? Each of these points of controversy is discussed in this section.

The Nature of Humans

Both Blumer and Kuhn have emphasized the ability of humans to use symbols and to develop capacities for thinking, defining, and self-reflection. However, there is considerable disagreement over the degree of structure and stability in human personality. Blumer emphasizes that humans have the capacity to view themselves as objects and to insert any object into an interaction situation. Therefore, human actors are not pushed and pulled around by social and psychological forces, but are *active creators* of the world to which they respond. Interaction and emergent patterns of social organization can thus only be understood by focusing on the capacities of individuals to create symbolically the world of objects to which they respond. These assumptions emphasize the potential for spontaneity and indeterminacy in human behavior. If humans can invoke any object into a situation, they can radically alter their definitions of that situation, and hence, their behaviors. Self is

---

[9] The following comparison draws heavily from Meltzer and Petras, "The Chicago and Iowa Schools," but extends their analysis by drawing from the following works of Blumer and Kuhn. For Blumer, *Symbolic Interactionism: Perspective and Method* (Englewood Cliffs, N.J.: Prentice-Hall, 1969); "Comment on 'Parsons as a Symbolic Interactionist,'" *Sociological Inquiry* 45 (Winter 1975): 59–62. For Kuhn, "Major Trends in Symbolic Interaction Theory in the Past Twenty-Five Years," *Sociological Quarterly* 5 (Winter 1964): 61–84; "The Reference Group Reconsidered," *Sociological Quarterly* 5 (Winter 1964): 6–21; "Factors in Personality: Socio-Cultural Determinants As Seen Through the Amish," in Francis L. Kittsu, ed., *Aspects of Culture and Personality* (New York: Abelard-Schuman, 1954); "Self-attitudes by Age, Sex, and Professional Training" in Stone and Farberman, *Symbolic Interaction*, pp. 424–36; with T. S. McPartland, "An Empirical Investigation of Self-Attitude," *American Sociological Review* 19 (February 1954): 68–76; "Family Impact on Personality" in J. E. Hulett and R. Stagner, eds., *Problems in Social Psychology* (Urbana: University of Illinois, 1953); with C. Addison Hickman, *Individuals, Groups, and Economic Behavior* (New York: Dryden Press, 1956).

but one of many objects to be seen in a situation; other objects from the past, present, or anticipated future can also be evoked and provide a basis for action.

In contrast, Kuhn emphasized the importance of people's "core self" as an object. Through socialization, humans acquire a relatively stable set of meanings and attitudes toward themselves. The core self will shape and constrain the way people will define situations by circumscribing the cues that will be seen and the objects that will be injected into social situations. Human personality is thus structured and comparatively stable, giving people's actions a continuity and predictability. And if it is possible to know the expectations of those groups which have shaped a person's core self, and which provide a basis for its validation, then human behavior could, in principle, be highly predictable.[10] As Kuhn and Hickman noted:

> As self theory views the individual, he derives his plans of action from the roles he plays and the statuses he occupies in the groups with which he feels identified—his reference groups. His attitudes toward himself as an object are the best indexes to these plans of action, and hence to the action itself, in that they are the anchoring points from which self-evaluations and other-evaluations are made.[11]

The Nature of Interaction

Both Blumer and Kuhn have stressed the process of role-taking in which humans mutually emit and interpret each other's gestures. From the information gained through this interpretation of gestures, actors are able to rehearse covertly various lines of activity and then emit those behaviors that can allow cooperative and organized activity. As might be expected, however, Blumer and Kuhn disagree over the degree to which interactions are actively constructed. Blumer's scheme, and that of most in the Chicago School, emphasizes the following points:

1. In addition to viewing each other as objects in an interaction situation, actors select out and designate symbolically additional objects in any interaction. (a) One of the most important of these objects is the self. On the one hand, self can represent the transitory images that an actor derives from interpreting the gestures of others; on the other,

---

[10] For an interesting methodological critique of Kuhn's "self-theory," see Charles W. Tucker, "Some Methodological Problems of Kuhn's Self Theory," *Sociological Quarterly* 7 (Winter 1966): 345–58.

[11] Hickman and Kuhn, *Individuals, Groups, and Economic Behavior*, pp. 224–25.

self can denote the more enduring conceptions of one as an object that an actor brings to and interjects into the interaction. (b) Another important class of objects are the varying types of expectation structures—for example, norms and values—that may exist to guide interaction. (c) Finally, because of the human organism's capacity to manipulate symbols, almost any other "object"—whether another person, a set of standards, or a dimension of self—may be inserted into the interaction.

2. It is toward the objects in interaction situations that actors have various dispositions to act. Thus, in order to understand the potentials for action among groups of individuals, it is necessary to understand the world of objects that they have symbolically designated.

3. In terms of the particular cluster of objects and of the dispositions to act that they imply, each actor arrives at a definition of the situation. Such a definition serves as a general frame of reference within which the consequences of specific lines of conduct are assessed. This process is termed mapping.

4. The selection of a particular line of behavior involves complex symbolic processes. At a minimum, actors typically evaluate: (a) the demands of others immediately present; (b) the self-images they derive from role taking, not only with others in the situation, but also with those not actually present; (c) the normative expectations they perceive to exist in the situation; and (d) the dispositions to act toward any additional objects they may inject symbolically into the interaction.

5. Once behavior is emitted, redefinition of the situation and perhaps remapping of action may occur as the reactions of others are interpreted and as new objects are injected into, and old ones discarded from, the interaction.

Thus, by emphasizing the interpreting, evaluating, defining, and mapping processes, Blumer stresses the creative, constructed, and changeable nature of interaction. Rather than constituting the mere vehicle through which preexisting psychological, social, and cultural structures inexorably shape behavior, the symbolic nature of interaction assures that social, cultural, and psychological structures will be altered and changed through shifting the definitions and behaviors of humans.

In contrast to Blumer's scheme, Kuhn has stressed the power of the "core self" and the group context to constrain interaction. Much interaction is "released" rather than constructed, as interacting individuals follow the dictates of the self-attitudes and the expectations of their respective roles. While Kuhn would certainly not have denied the potential for constructing and reconstructing interactions, he tended to view individuals as highly constrained in their behaviors by virtue of their "core self" and the requirements of their mutual situation.

The Nature of Social Organization

Symbolic interactionism tends to concentrate on the interactive *processes* by which humans form social relationships rather than the *end products* of interactions. Moreover, both Blumer and Kuhn, as well as other interactionists, have tended to concentrate on micro processes among individuals within small group contexts. Blumer has consistently advocated a view of social organization as temporary and constantly changing, while Kuhn typically focused on the more structured aspects of social situations. Additionally, Blumer argues for a view of social structure as merely one of many objects that actors employ in their definition of a situation.

As Blumer has emphasized:

1. Since behavior is a reflection of the interpretive, evaluational, definitional, and mapping processes of individuals in various interaction contexts, social organization represents an active fitting together of action by those in interaction. Social organization must therefore be viewed as more of a process than a structure.

2. While social structure is an emergent phenomenon that is not reducible to the constituent actions of individuals, it is difficult to understand patterns of social organization without recognizing that they represent an interlacing of the separate behaviors among individuals.

3. While much interaction is repetitive, and structured by clear-cut expectations and common definitions of the situation, its symbolic nature reveals the potential for new objects to be inserted or old ones altered and abandoned in a situation, with the result that reinterpretation, reevaluation, redefinition, and remapping of behaviors can always occur. Social structure must therefore be viewed as rife with potential for alteration and change.

4. Thus, patterns of social organization represent emergent phenomena that can serve as "objects" that define situations for actors. However, the very symbolic processes that give rise and sustain these patterns can also operate to change and alter them.

In contrast to this emphasis, Kuhn usually sought to isolate the more structured features of situations. In conformity with what will be termed "role theory" in the next chapter, Kuhn saw social situations as constituting relatively stable networks of positions with attendant expectations or norms. Interactions often create such networks, but once created, people conform to the expectations of those positions in which they have anchored their self-attitudes.

In reviewing different assumptions of Blumer and Kuhn, or the Chicago and Iowa schools, over the nature of individuals, interaction, and social organization, it is clear that Chicago School interactionists view individuals as potentially spontaneous, interaction as constantly in the process of change, and social organization as fluid and tenuous.[12] Iowa School interactionists are more prone to see individual personality and social organization as structured, with interactions being constrained by these structures.[13] These differences in assumptions have resulted in, or perhaps have been a reflection of, varying conceptions of how to investigate the social world and how to build theory.

The Nature of Methods

E. L. Quarantelli and Joseph Cooper have observed that Mead's ideas provide for contemporary interactionists a "frame of reference within which an observer can look at behavior rather than a specific set of hypotheses to be tested."[14] There can be little doubt that this statement is true. Yet there is a large literature attempting to test some of the implications of Mead's ideas, especially those about self, with standard research protocols. This diversity in methodological approaches is underscored by the contrasting methodologies of Blumer and Kuhn. Indeed, the many students of these two figures tend to use Mead's ideas as either a sensitizing framework or as an inspiration for narrow research hypotheses.

Methodological approaches to studying the social world follow from thinkers' assumptions about what they can, or will, discover. The divergence between Blumer's and Kuhn's methodologies thus reflects their varying assumptions about the operation of symbolic processes. Ultimately, their differences boil down to the question of causality. Whether

---

[12] Prominent thinkers leaning toward Blumer's position include Anslem Strauss, Alfred Lindesmith, Tamotsu Shibutani, and Ralph Turner.

[13] Prominent Iowa School interactionists include Frank Miyamoto, Sanford Dornbusch, Simon Dinitz, Harry Dick, Sheldon Stryker, and Theodore Sarbin. For a list of studies by Kuhn's students, see Harold A. Mulford and Winfield W. Salisbury II, "Self-Conceptions in a General Population," *Sociological Quarterly* 5 (Winter 1964): 35–46. Again, these individuals and those in note 12 would resist this classification, since none advocate as extreme position as Kuhn or Blumer. Yet, the tendency to follow either Kuhn's or Blumer's assumptions is evident in their work, and in that of many others.

[14] E. L. Quarantelli and Joseph Cooper, "Self-conceptions and Others: A Further Test of Meadian Hypotheses," *Sociological Quarterly* 7 (Summer 1966): 281–97.

or not events are viewed as the result of deterministic causes will influence the methodologies that are employed. Thus, to appreciate why Blumer and Kuhn diverge in their methodological approaches, it is necessary to see how their assumptions about individual interaction and social organization have become translated into a set of causal images that dictates different methodological approaches.

Diverging Assumptions about Causality. For Blumer, the Meadian legacy challenges the utility of theoretical perspectives that underemphasize the internal symbolic processes of actors attempting to "fit together" their respective behaviors into an organized pattern.[15] Rather than being the result of system forces, societal needs, and structural mechanisms, social organization is the result of the mutual interpretations, evaluations, definitions, and mappings of individual actors. Thus, the symbolic processes of individuals cannot be viewed as a neutral medium through which social forces operate, but instead these processes must be viewed as shaping the ways social patterns are formed, sustained, and changed.

Similarly, as has been emphasized, Blumer's approach questions the utility of theoretical perspectives that view behavior as the mere releasing of propensities built into a structured personality. Just as patterns of social organization must be conceptualized as in a continual state of potential flux through the processes of interpretation, evaluation, definition, and mapping, so the human personality must also be viewed as a constantly unfolding process rather than a rigid structure from which behavior is mechanically released. By virtue of the fact that humans can make varying and changing symbolic indications to themselves, they are capable of altering and shifting behavior, with the result that behavior is not so much "released" as "constructed" by actors making successive indications to themselves.

Social structures and the expectations they embody are seen as "objects" which must be interpreted and then used to define a situation and map out the prospective behaviors that ultimately go to make up social structures. Typically, overt behavior at one point in time is considered to result in "self-images" that serve as objects to be used by individuals in symbolically mapping subsequent actions at another point in time, while existing personality traits, such as self-conceptions, self-esteem, and internalized needs, are viewed as mediating each successive phase

---

[15] See particularly Blumer's "Society as Symbolic Interaction" in Rose, ed., *Human Behavior and Social Process*, 179–92 (reprinted in Blumer's *Symbolic Interactionism*); "Sociological Implications of the Thought of George Herbert Mead" in *Symbolic Interactionism;* and "The Methodological Position of Symbolic Interactionism" in *Symbolic Interactionism.*

of interpretation of gestures, evaluation of self-images, definition of the situation, and mapping of diverse behaviors.

In such a scheme, causality is difficult to discern. Social structures do not "cause" behavior since they are only one class of "objects" inserted into an actor's seemingly unpredictable symbolic thinking. Similarly, self is only another object inserted into the definitional process. Action is thus "created" out of the potentially large number of objects that actors can insert into situations. Action, under this vision of the social world, does not reveal clear causes. Indeed, the variables influencing an individual's definition of the situation and action are of the actor's "own choosing" and apparently not subject to clear causal analysis.

In contrast to this seemingly *in*deterministic view of causality, Kuhn argued tht the social world is deterministic. The apparent spontaneity and indeterminacy of human behavior is simply the result of insufficient knowledge of the variables influencing people's definitions and actions. Kuhn thus argued that if the social experiences of individuals can be discerned, it is possible to know what caused the emergence of the "core self" of an individual. With knowledge of the "core self," the expectations that have become "internalized" as a result of people's experiences, and the particular expectations of a given situation, people's definitions of situations and their conduct can be understood. Naturally, this level of understanding is currently impossible with current methodological techniques, but insight into deterministic causes of behavior, and emergent patterns of social organization, is possible *in principle*. Methodological strategies should therefore be directed at seeking the causes of behaviors.

Diverging Methodological Protocols. These differing assumptions about causality have shaped divergent methodological approaches within symbolic interactionism. The extremes of these diverging approaches are personified in Blumer's and Kuhn's protocols.

Blumer has mounted a consistent and persistent line of attack on sociological theory and research.[16] This criticism questions the utility of current research procedures for unearthing the symbolic processes from which social structures and personality are built and sustained. Rather than letting the nature of the empirical world dictate the kinds of research strategies used in its study, Blumer and others have argued that present practices allow research strategies to determine what is to be studied:

---

[16] See, in particular, Blumer's "The Methodological Position of Symbolic Interactionism."

Instead of going to the empirical social world in the first and last instances, resort is made instead to a priori theoretical schemes, to sets of unverified concepts, and to canonized protocols of research procedure. These come to be the governing agents in dealing with the empirical social world, forcing research to serve their character and bending the empirical world to their premises.[17]

Too often, then, the fads of research protocol serve to blind investigators and theorists to the "real character" of the social world. Such research and theoretical protocols force analysis away from the direct examination of the empirical world in favor of preconceived notions of what is "true" and how these "truths" should be studied. In contrast, the processes of symbolic interaction dictate that research methodologies should respect the character of empirical reality and adopt methodological procedures that encourage its direct and unbiased examination.[18]

To achieve this end, the research act itself must be viewed as a process of symbolic interaction in which researchers "take the role" of those individuals whom they are studying. To do such "role taking" effectively, researchers must come to the study of interaction with a set of concepts that, rather than prematurely structuring the social world for investigators, "sensitize" them to interactive processes. This approach would enable investigators to maintain the distinction between the concepts of science and those of the interacting individuals under study. In this way, the interpretive and definitional processes of actors adjusting to one another in concrete situations would guide the refinement and eventual incorporation of the concepts of science into theoretical statements on the interactive processes that go to make up society.

Blumer has advocated a twofold process of research, involving, first of all, "exploration" in which researchers approach concrete situations prepared to observe and then revise their observations as new impressions of the situation arise. Second, Blumer emphasizes that exploration must be followed by a process of "inspection," whereby researchers use their observations to dictate how scientific concepts are to be refined and incorporated into more abstract and generic statements of relationships among concepts. In this dual research process, investigators must understand each actor's definition of the situation, the relationship of this definition to the objects perceived by actors in this situation, and the

---

[17] Ibid., p. 33.

[18] For an interesting discussion of the contrasts between these research strategies, see Llewellyn Gross, "Theory Construction in Sociology: A Methodological Inquiry," in *Symposium on Sociological Theory*, ed. L. Gross (New York: Harper & Row, 1959), pp. 531–63.

relationship of objects to specific others, groups, and expectations in both the actor's immediate and remote social worlds.[19] In this way, the research used to build the abstract concepts and propositions of sociological theory would be connected to the empirical world of actors interpreting, evaluating, defining, and mapping the behaviors that create, maintain, or change patterns of social organization.

A major area of controversy over the methodological position advocated by Blumer concerns the issue of operationalization of concepts. How is it possible to operationalize concepts, such as self and definition of the situation, so that different investigators at different times and in different contexts can study the same phenomena? Blumer has typically chosen to define away the problem of how the interpretative, evaluational, definitional, and mapping processes are to be studied in terms of clear-cut operational definitions, for such questions "show a profound misunderstanding of both scientific inquiry and symbolic interactionism."[20] For Blumer, the concepts and propositions of symbolic interactionism allow for the direct examination of the empirical world; therefore, "their value and their validity are to be determined in that examination and not in seeing how they fare when subjected to the alien criteria of an irrelevant methodology." According to Blumer, these "alien criteria" embrace a false set of assumptions about just how concepts should be attached to events in the empirical world. In general, these "false" assumptions posit that for each abstract concept a set of operational definitions should guide researchers, who then examine the empirical cases denoted by the operational definition.

Blumer has consistently emphasized current deficiencies in the attachment of sociological concepts to actual events in the empirical world.

> This ambiguous nature of concepts is the basic deficiency in social theory. It hinders us in coming to close grips with our empirical world, for we are not sure of what to grip. Our uncertainty as to what we are referring obstructs us from asking pertinent questions and setting relevant problems for research.[21]

---

[19] For an eloquent and reasoned argument in support of Blumer's position, see Norman K. Denzin, *The Research Act: A Theoretical Introduction to Sociological Methods* (Chicago: Aldine Publishing Co., 1970), pp. 185–218; and Norman K. Denzin, "Symbolic Interactionism and Ethnomethodology," in *Understanding Everyday Life: Toward a Reconstruction of Sociological Knowledge*, ed. Jack D. Douglas (Chicago: Aldine Publishing Co., 1970), pp. 259–84.

[20] Blumer, "Methodological Position," p. 49.

[21] Herbert Blumer, "What Is Wrong with Social Theory?" *American Sociological Review* 19 (August 1954): 146–58.

Blumer argues that it is only through the methodological processes of exploration and inspection that concepts can be attached to the empirical. Rather than seeking a false sense of scientific security through rigid operational definitions, sociological theory must accept the fact that the attachment of abstract concepts to the empirical world must be an *ongoing process* of investigators exploring and inspecting events in the empirical world.

In sum, then, Blumer's presentation of the methodological position of symbolic interactionism questions the current research protocols and advocates as an alternate (*a*) the more frequent use of the exploration-inspection process, whereby researchers seek to understand the symbolic processes that shape interaction; and (*b*) the recognition that only through these research activities can concepts remain attached to the fluid interaction processes of the empirical world. In turn, this methodological position has profound implications for the construction of theory in sociology.

In contrast to Blumer's position, Kuhn's vision of a deterministic world led him to emphasize the commonality of methods in all the sciences. The key task of methodology is to provide operational definitions of concepts so that their implications can be tested against the actual facts of social life. Most of Kuhn's career was thus devoted to taking the suggestive but vague concepts of Mead's framework and developing measures of them. He sought to find replicable measures of such concepts as self, social act, social object, and reference group.[22] His most famous measuring instrument—the Twenty Statements Test (TST)—can serve to illustrate his strategy. He sought to measure "core self," or the more enduring and basic attitudes that people have about themselves, by assessing answers that people give to the question, "What kind of person are you?"[23] For example, the most common variant of the TST reads as follows:

> In the spaces below, please give twenty different answers to the question, "Who Am I?" Give these as if you were giving them to yourself, not to somebody else. Write fairly rapidly, for the time is limited.

Answers to such questions can be coded and scaled so that variations in self-conceptions of people can be linked to either prior social experiences or behaviors. Thus, Kuhn sought to find empirical indicators of key concepts. These indicators would allow for viewing recorded varia-

---

[22] Meltzer and Petras, "The Chicago and Iowa Schools."

[23] For an important critique of this methodology, see Tucker, "Some Methodological Problems."

tions in one concept, such as self, to be linked to variations in other measurable concepts. In this way, Mead's legacy could be tested and used to build a theory of symbolic interactionism.

The Nature and Possibilities of Sociological Theory

Blumer's and Kuhn's assumptions about the nature of the individual, interaction, social organization, causality, and methodology are reflected in their different visions of what theory is, should, and can be. Again, Blumer and Kuhn stand at opposite poles, with most interactionists standing between these extremes, and yet leaning toward one pole or the other.

Blumer's Theory-Building Strategy.   Blumer's assumptions, image of causal processes, and methodological position have all come to dictate a particular conception of sociological theory. The recognition that sociological concepts do not come to grips with the empirical world is seen by Blumer as the result not only of inattention to actual events in the empirical world, but also of the kind of world it is. While the use of more "definitive concepts" referring to classes of precisely defined events is perhaps desirable in theory building, it may be impossible, given the nature of the empirical world. Since this world is composed of constantly shifting processes of symbolic interaction among actors in various contextual situations, the use of concepts that rip from this context only some of the actual ongoing events will fail to capture the contextual nature of the social world. More important, the fact that social reality is ultimately "constructed" from the symbolic processes among individuals assures that the actual instances denoted by concepts will shift and vary and thereby defy easy classification through rigid operational definitions.

These facts, Blumer argues, require the use of "sensitizing concepts," which, while lacking the precise specification of attributes and events of definitive concepts, do provide clues and suggestions about where to look for certain classes of phenomena. As such, sensitizing concepts offer a general sense of what is relevant and thereby allow investigators to approach flexibly a shifting empirical world and "feel out" and "pick one's way in an unknown terrain." The use of this kind of concept does not necessarily reflect a lack of rigor in sociological theory, but rather a recognition that if "our empirical world presents itself in the form of distinctive and unique happenings or situations and if we seek through the direct study of this world to establish classes of objects and relations between classes, we are . . . forced to work with sensitizing concepts."

While the nature of the empirical world may preclude the development of definitive concepts, sensitizing concepts can be improved and refined. By approaching flexibly empirical situations denoted by sensitizing concepts and then by assessing how actual events stack up against the concepts, it is possible to refine and revise concepts. Although the lack of fixed bench marks and definitions makes this task more difficult for sensitizing concepts than for definitive ones, the progressive refinement of sensitizing concepts is possible through "careful and imaginative study of the stubborn world to which such concepts are addressed."[24] Furthermore, sensitizing concepts formulated in this way can be communicated and used to build sociological theory; and although formal definitions and rigid classifications are not appropriate, sensitizing concepts can be explicitly communicated through descriptions and illustrations of the events to which they pertain.

In sum, the ongoing refinement, formulation, and communication of sensitizing concepts must inevitably be the building block of sociological theory. With careful formulation, they can be incorporated into provisional theoretical statements that specify the conditions under which various types of interaction are likely to occur. In this way, the concepts of theory will recognize the shifting nature of the social world and thereby provide a more accurate set of statements about the conditions under which patterns of social organization emerge, persist, change, and break down.

The nature of the social world and the type of theory it dictates have profound implications for just how such theoretical statements are to be constructed and organized into theoretical formats. Blumer's emphasis on the constructed nature of reality and the types of concepts this fact necessitates has led him to emphasize inductive theory construction. In inductive theory, generic propositions are abstracted from observations of concrete interaction situations. This emphasis on induction is considered desirable, since current attempts at deductive theorizing in sociology usually do not involve rigorous derivations of propositions from each other, nor a scrupulous search for the negative empirical cases that would refute propositions.[25] These failings, Blumer contends, assure that deductive sociological theory will remain unconnected to the events of the empirical world and, hence, unable to correct for errors in its theoretical statements. Coupled with the tendency for fads of research protocol to dictate research problems, and methods used to investigate them, it appears unlikely that deductive theory and the

---

[24] Blumer, "What's Wrong with Social Theory," p. 150.

[25] Blumer, "Methodological Position."

research it inspires can unearth those processes that would confirm or refute its generic statements. In the wake of this theoretical impasse, then, it is crucial that sociological theorizing refamiliarize itself with the actual events of the empirical world: "No theorizing, however ingenious, and no observance of scientific protocol, however meticulous, are substitutes for developing familiarity with what is actually going on in the sphere of life under study."[26] Without such inductive familiarity, sociological theory will remain a self-fulfilling set of theoretical prophecies bearing little relationship to the phenomena it is supposed to explain.

Kuhn's Theory-Building Strategy. Kuhn advocated a more deductive format for sociological theorizing than Blumer. While his own work does not reveal great deductive rigor, he holds that subsumption of lower order propositions under more general principles is the most appropriate way to build theory. He visualized his own "self-theory" as one step in the building of theory. By developing general statements on how self-attitudes emerge and shape social action, it would be possible to understand and predict human behavior. Moreover, less general propositions about aspects of self could be subsumed under general propositions about processes of symbolic interaction.

While Kuhn recognized that symbolic interaction theory had become partitioned into many suborientations, including his own self-theory, he held a vision of a unified body of theoretical principles. As he concluded in an assessment of interactionist theory:

> I would see in the next 25 years of symbolic interaction theory an accelerated development of research techniques, on the one hand, and a coalescing of most of the separate subtheories. . . .[27]

Thus, the ultimate goal of theory is consolidation or "coalescing" of testable lower-order theories under a general set of symbolic interactionist principles. Self-theory, as developed by Kuhn, would be but one set of derivations from a more general system of interactionist principles. In contrast to Blumer, then, theory for Kuhn was ultimately to form a unified system from which specific propositions about different aspect or phases of symbolic interactionism could be derived.

The Chicago and Iowa Schools: An Overview

In Table 15–1, an overview of the preceding discussion is presented. The table explores a number of issues over which there is disagreement

---

[26] Ibid., p. 39.

[27] Kuhn, "Major Trends in Symbolic Interaction Theory in the Past Twenty-Five Years," p. 80.

among interactionists. These disagreements, however, must be placed within the context of the points where symbolic interactionists agree. And, thus, the first column in Table 15–1 highlights the features that make symbolic interactionism a distinctive feature.

It should be emphasized again that distinctions between a Chicago and Iowa School are hazardous when examining the work of a particular symbolic interactionist. The disinction only denotes *tendencies* to view humans, interaction, social organization, methods, and theory in a particular way. Few symbolic interactionists follow literally either Blumer's or Kuhn's positions. These positions merely represent the boundaries within which symbolic interactionists work.

SYMBOLIC INTERACTIONISM: A CONCLUDING COMMENT

Blumer's vision of symbolic interactionism advocates a clear-cut strategy for building sociological theory. The emphasis on the interpretive, evaluative, definitional, and mapping processes of actors has come to dictate that it is only through induction from these processes that sociological theory can be built. Further, the ever-shifting nature of these symbolic processes necessitates that the concepts of sociological theory be "sensitizing" rather than "definitive," with the result that deductive theorizing should be replaced by an inductive approach. Thus, whether as a preferred strategy or as a logical "necessity," the Blumer interactionist strategy is to induce generic statements, employing sensitizing concepts, from the ongoing symbolic processes of indviduals in concrete interaction situations.

Such a strategy is likely to keep theorizing attuned to the processual nature of the social world. However, this approach, and to a lesser extent, Kuhn's approach, has not been able to link conceptually the processes of symbolic interaction to the formation of different patterns of social organization. Furthermore, the utility of induction from the symbolic exchanges among individuals for the analysis of interaction among more macro, collective social units has yet to be demonstrated. Unless these problems can be resolved, it does not seem wise to follow exclusively the strategy of Blumer and others of his persuasion. Until symbolic interactionists of all persuasions demonstrate in a more compelling manner than is currently the case that the inductive approach, utilizing sensitizing concepts, can account for more complex forms of social organization, pursuit of its strategy will preclude theorizing about much of the social world.

TABLE 15–1
Convergence and Divergence in the Chicago and Iowa Schools of Symbolic Interactionism

Theoretical Issues	Convergence of Schools
The nature of humans	Humans create and use symbols to denote aspects of the world around them.
	What makes humans unique are their symbolic capacities.
	Humans are capable of symbolically denoting and invoking objects which can then serve to shape their definitions of social situations, and hence, their actions.
	Humans are capable of self-reflection and evaluation. They see themselves as objects in most social situations.
The nature of interaction	Interaction is dependent upon people's capacities to emit and interpret gestures.
	Role-taking is the key mechanism of interaction, for it enables actors to view the other's perspective, as well as that of others and groups not physically present.
	Role-taking and mind operate together by allowing actors to use the perspectives of others and groups as a basis for their deliberations, or definitions of situations, before acting. In this way, people can adjust their responses to each other and to social situations.
The nature of social organization	Social structure is created, maintained, and changed by processes of symbolic interaction.
	It is not possible to understand patterns of social organization—even the most elaborate—without knowledge of the symbolic processes among individuals who ultimately make up this pattern.
The nature of sociological methods	Sociological methods must focus on the processes by which people define situations and select courses of action.
	Methods must focus on individual persons.
The nature of sociological theory	Theory must be about processes of interaction and seek to isolate out the conditions under which general types of behaviors and interactions are likely to occur.

Chicago School	Iowa School
Humans with minds can introject any object into a situation.	Humans with minds can define situations, but there tends to be consistency in terms of the objects that they introject into situations.
While self is an important object, it is not the only object.	Self is the most important object in the definition of a situation.
Humans weigh, assess, and map courses of action before action, but humans can potentially alter their definitions and actions.	Humans weigh, assess, and map courses of action, but they do so through the prism of their core self and the groups in which this self is anchored.
Interaction is a constant process of role-taking with others, and groups.	Interaction is dependent upon the process of role-taking.
Others and groups thus become objects that are involved in people's definitions of situations.	The expectations of others and norms of the situation are important considerations in arriving at definitions of situations.
Self is another important object that enters into people's definitions.	People's core self is the most important consideration and constraint on interaction.
People's definitions of situations involve weighing and assessing objects and then mapping courses of action.	
Interaction involves constantly shifting definitions and changing patterns of action and interaction.	Interaction most often involves actions that conform to situational expectations as mitigated by the requirements of the "core self."
Social structure is constructed by actors adjusting their responses to each other.	Social structures are composed of networks of positions with attendant expectations or norms.
Social structure is one of many objects that actors introject into their definitions of situations.	While symbolic interactions create and change structures, once these structures are created they operate to constrain interaction.
Social structure is subject to constant realignments as actors' definitions and behaviors change, forcing new adjustments from others.	Social structures are thus relatively stable, especially when people's "core self" is invested in particular networks of positions.
Sociological methods must seek to penetrate the actors' mental world and see how they construct courses of action.	Sociological methods must seek to measure with reliable instruments actors' symbolic processes.
Researchers must be attuned to the multiple, varied, ever-shifting, and often indeterminate influences on definitions of situations and actions.	Research should be directed toward defining and measuring those variables that causally influence behaviors.
Research must therefore use observational, biographical, and unstructured interview techniques if it is to penetrate people's definitional processes and take account of changes in these processes.	Research must therefore use structured measuring instruments, such as questionnaires, to get reliable and valid measures of key variables.
Only "sensitizing concepts" are possible in sociology.	Sociology can develop precisely defined concepts, with clear empirical measures.
Deductive theory is thus not possible in sociology.	Theory can thus be deductive, with a limited number of general propositions subsuming lower-order propositions and empirical generalizations on specific phases of symbolic interaction.
At best, theory can offer general, and tentative, descriptions and interpretations of behaviors and patterns of interaction.	Theory can offer abstract explanations that can allow for predictions of behavior and interaction.

Both Blumer's and Kuhn's strategy calls attention to some important substantive and theoretical issues that are often ignored. First, it is necessary that sociological theorizing be more willing to undertake the difficult task of linking conceptually structural categories to classes of social processes that underlie these categories. For this task, symbolic interactionism has provided a wealth of suggestive concepts. Second, macro sociological theorizing has traditionally remained detached from the processes of the social world it attempts to decribe. Much of the detachment stems from a failure to define concepts clearly and provide operational clues about what processes in the empirical world they denote. To the extent that symbolic interactionist concepts can supplement such theorizing, they will potentially provide a bridge to actual empirical processes and thereby help attach sociological theory to the events it purports to explain.

Symbolic interactionism has great potential for correcting the past inadequacies of sociological theory, but it has yet to demonstrate exactly *how* this corrective influence is to be exerted. At present symbolic interactionism seems capable of analyzing micro social patterns and their impact on personality, particularly self. While interactionism has provided important insights in the study of socialization, deviance, and micro social processes, it has yet to demonstrate any great potential for analyzing complex, macro social patterns. At best, it can provide in its present form a supplement to macro analysis by giving researchers a framework, and a measuring instrument, to analyze micro processes within macro social events.

Much of symbolic interaction, especially Blumer's advocacy, consists of gallant assertions that "society is symbolic interaction," without indicating what types of emergent structures are created, sustained, and changed by what types of interaction in what types of contexts. Much like the critics' allegations about Parsons' "social system," Dahrendorf's "imperatively coordinated association," Homans' "institutional piles," or Blau's "organized collectivities," social structural phenomena emerge somewhat mysteriously and are then sustained or changed by vague references to interactive processes. The vagueness of the links between the interaction process and its social structural products leaves symbolic interactionism with a legacy of assertions, but little in the way of carefully documented statements about how, when, where, and with what probability interaction processes operate to create, sustain, and change varying patterns of social organization. It is to this goal that interactionist theory must redirect its efforts.

16

ROLE THEORY:
IN SEARCH OF
CONCEPTUAL UNITY

The differences between role theory and symbolic interactionism become clearly evident when human interaction is viewed as varying along a continuum.[1] At one pole of this continuum, individuals are seen as players in the "theater," while, at the other end, players are considered to be participants in a "game." When human action is seen as occurring in a theater, interaction is likely to be viewed as highly structured by the script, directors, other actors, and the audience. When conceptualized as a game, however, interaction is more likely to be seen as less structured and as influenced by the wide range of tactics available to participants.

As was emphasized in the last chapter, however, interactionists such as Manford Kuhn viewed symbolic interactions as occurring within structured contexts. The structure of self was viewed by Kuhn as the most important force, but he was also concerned with social structures—that is, networks of statuses, norms, values, and groups—as crucial determinants of human action. Kuhn's work can be seen as the boundary between symbolic interactionism on the one hand, and what has become defined as "role theory" on the other.

The broad interactionist tradition encompassing both symbolic interactionism and role theory can thus be viewed as a continuum, moving

---

[1] Bernard Farber, "A Research Model: Family Crisis and Games Strategy" in *Kinship and Family Organization*, ed. Bernard Farber (New York: John Wiley & Sons, 1966), pp. 430–34. Walter Wallace (*Sociological Theory* [Chicago: Aldine Publishing Co., 1969], pp. 34–35) has more recently chosen this same analogy to describe symbolic interactionism.

from Herbert Blumer's brand of symbolic interactionism at one extreme, through Kuhn's form of symbolic interaction, and then to Talcott Parsons' functional approach, emphasizing highly structured image of status-roles within institutionalized social systems, at the other extreme. Role theory is thus an extremely eclectic theoretical tradition, with few dominant figures who have provided an over-arching framework.[2] It represents a series of narrow research findings and theoretical insights which have yet to become organized into a well-articulated theoretical perspective. And yet, "role theories" and "role analyses" abound in the sociological literature, and hence, it is necessary to examine this large literature. For indeed, it is through role analysis that many of George Herbert Mead's important insights have been used to analyze and understand patterns of social organization.

THE GENERAL THRUST OF ROLE THEORY

The thrust of the role perspective, as it flowed from a mixture of Park's, Simmel's, Moreno's, Linton's, and G. H. Mead's insights, has often been captured by quoting a famous passage from Shakespeare's *As You Like It* (act 2, scene 1):

> All the world's a stage
> And all the men and women merely players:
> They have their exits and their entrances;
> And one man in his time plays many parts.

The analogy is then drawn between the players on the stage and the actors of society.[3] Just as players have a clearly defined part to play, so actors in society occupy clear positions; just as players must follow a written script, so actors in society must follow norms; just as players must obey the orders of a director, so actors in society must conform to the dictates of those with power or those of importance; just as players must react to each other's performance on the stage, so members of society must mutually adjust their responses to one another; just as players respond to the audience, so actors in society take the role of various audiences or "generalized others"; and just as players with varying abilities

---

[2] For the first early analytical statements, see Jacob Moreno, *Who Shall Survive*, rev. ed. (New York: Beacon House, 1953) (original ed., 1934); and Ralph Linton, *The Study of Man* (New York: Appleton-Century, 1936).

[3] For an example of this form of analogizing, see Bruce J. Biddle and Edwin Thomas, *Role Theory: Concepts and Research* (New York: John Wiley & Sons, 1966), pp. 3–4. For the best-known "dramaturgical" model, see Erving Goffman, *The Presentation of Self in Everyday Life* (New York: Doubleday & Co., 1959).

and capacities bring to each role their own unique interpretation, so actors with varying self-conceptions and role-playing skills have their own styles of interaction.

Despite its simplicity, the analogy is appropriate. As this chapter unfolds, it will become evident that the role-theoretic perspective supports the thrust of Shakespeare's passage. However, at the outset it should be noted that, despite its pervasiveness in sociology, role analysis is far from being a well-articulated and unified theoretical perspective. In fact, the very task of reviewing the many diverse substantive and theoretical works on role theory requires a tentative theoretical synthesis.[4]

IMAGES OF SOCIETY AND THE INDIVIDUAL

Shakespeare's passage provides the general outline of what role theorists assume about the social world. In the "stage" are assumptions about the nature of social organization; in the concept of "players" are implicit assumptions about the nature of the individual; and in the vision of men and women as "merely players" who have "their exits and their entrances" are a series of assumptions about the relationship of individuals to patterns of social organization.

The Nature of Social Organization

For role theorists, the social world is viewed as a network of variously interrelated *positions*, or statuses, within which individuals enact roles.[5] For each position, as well as for groups and classes of positions, various kinds of *expectations* about how incumbents are to behave can be discerned.[6] Thus, social organization is ultimately composed of various networks of statuses and expectations.

Statuses are typically analyzed in terms of how they are interrelated

---

[4] For some recent attempts to bring together role-theoretic concepts, see Biddle and Thomas, Role Theory, pp. 1–64; Morton Deutsch and Robert M. Krauss, Theories in Social Psychology (New York: Basic Books, 1965), pp. 173–211; and Marvin E. Shaw and Philip R. Costanzo, Theories of Social Psychology (New York: McGraw-Hill Book Co., 1970), pp. 326–46.

[5] For an early analysis of this viewpoint, see Kingsley Davis, Human Society (New York: Macmillan Co., 1949); Linton, Study of Man; Moreno, Who Shall Survive; Emile Benoit, "Status, Status Types, and Status Interrelations," American Sociological Review 9 (April 1944): 151–61; George P. Murdock, Social Structure (New York: Macmillan Co., 1949); and Robert K. Merton, Social Theory and Social Structure (New York: Free Press, 1951), pp. 368–79.

[6] Mead's concept of the "other" pointed to the impact of perceived expectations upon the way individuals enacted roles. However, it was not until after World War II that the systematic analysis of types of expectations was undertaken.

to one another to form various types of social units. In terms of variables such as size, degree of differentiation, and complexity of interrelatedness, status networks are classified into forms, ranging from various types of groups to larger forms of collective organization. While there has been some analysis on their formal properties, status networks are rarely analyzed independently of the types of expectations attendant upon them.[7] Part of the reason for this close relation between form and content is that the types of expectations that typify particular networks of positions represent one of their defining characteristics. It is usually assumed that the behavior emitted by incumbents is not an exclusive function of the structure of positions, per se, but also of the kinds of expectations that inhere in these positions.

The range of expectations denoted by role-theoretic concepts is diverse. Pursuing the dramaturgical analogy to a play, three general classes of expectations appear to typify role theory's vision of the world: (a) expectations from the "script"; (b) expectations from other "players"; and (c) expectations from the "audience."

Expectations from the "Script." Much of social reality can be considered to read like a script in that for many positions there are *norms* specifying just how an individual ought to behave. The degree to which activity is regulated by norms varies under different conditions; thus, one of the theoretical questions to be resolved by role theory concerns the conditions under which norms vary in terms of such variables as scope, power, efficacy, specificity, clarity, and degree of conflict with each other.[8]

Expectations from Other "Players." In addition to the normative structuring of behavior and social relations, role theory also focuses on the demands emitted by the "other players" in an interaction situation. Such demands, interpreted through role taking of other's gestures, constitute one of the most important forces shaping human conduct.

---

[7] See, for example, Jacob L. Moreno, "Contributions of Sociometry to Research Methodology in Sociology," *American Sociological Review* 12 (June 1947): 287–92; and J. L. Moreno, ed., *The Sociometry Reader* (Glencoe, Ill.: Free Press, 1960); Oscar A. Oeser and Frank Harary, "Role Structures: A Description in Terms of Graph Theory," *Human Relations* 15 (May 1962): 89–109; and Darwin Cartwright and Frank Harary, "Structural Balance: A Generalization of Heider's Theory," *Psychological Review* 63 (September 1956): 277–93.

[8] For early analysis of normative phenomena, see Davis, *Human Society;* Samuel Stauffer, "An Analysis of Conflicting Social Norms," *American Sociological Review* 14 (December 1949): 707–17; Robin M. Williams, Jr., *American Society: A Sociological Interpretation*, 2d ed. (New York: Alfred Knopf, 1960), pp. 25–38; and George C. Homans, *The Human Group* (New York: Harcourt, Brace & World, 1950). For a diversity of more recent citations, see Biddle and Thomas, *Role Theory;* pp. 23–63.

Expectations from the "Audience." A final source of expectations comes from the "audiences" of individuals occupying statuses. These audiences can be real or imagined, constitute an actual group or a social category, involve membership or simply a desire to be a member. It is only necessary that the expectations imputed by individuals to such variously conceived audiences be used to guide conduct. As such, the audiences comprise a frame of reference, or reference group,[9] that circumscribes the behavior of actors in various statuses.

In sum, then, much of the social world is assumed by role theory to be structured in terms of expectations from a variety of sources, whether the script, other players, or various audiences. Just which types of expectations are attendant upon a given status, or network of positions, is one of the important empirical questions that follows from this assumption.

Although role theory implicitly assumes that virtually the entire social spectrum is structured in terms of statuses and expectations, rarely is this whole spectrum studied. In fact, role analysis usually concentrates on restricted status networks, such as groups and small organizations, and the types of expectations evident in these more micro social units. Such an emphasis can be seen as representing a strategy for analytically coping with the incredible complexity of the entire status network and attendant expectations of a society or of some of its larger units. In this delimitation of the field of inquiry, however, there is an implicit assumption that the social order is structured only by certain basic kinds of micro groups and organizations. Larger analytical phenomena, such as social classes or nation-states and relations among them, are less relevant, because there is a presumption that these phenomena can be understood in terms of their constituent groups and organizations.

This emphasis on the micro structures of society is perhaps inevitable in light of the fact that role theory ultimately attempts to account for types of role performances by individuals. While macro patterns of social organization are viewed as providing much of the "order" to these per-

---

[9] Mead's concept of the "generalized other" anticipated this analytical concern with reference groups. For some of the important conceptual distinctions in the "theory" of reference group behavior, see Robert K. Merton, "Continuities in the Theory of Reference Groups and Social Structure," pp. 225–80; Tamotsu Shibutani, "Reference Groups as Perspectives," *American Journal of Sociology* 60 (May 1955): 562–69; Harold H. Kelley, "Two Functions of Reference Groups," in *Readings in Social Psychology*, ed. G. E. Swanson, et al. (New York: Henry Holt Co., 1958); Ralph H. Turner, "Role-taking, Role Standpoint, and Reference Group Behavior," *American Journal of Sociology* 61 (January 1956): 316–28; and Herbert Hyman and Eleanor Singer, eds., *Readings in Reference Group Behavior* (New York: Free Press, 1968).

formances, society cannot be conceptualized independently of its individual incumbents and their performances.

The Nature of the Individual

Individuals occupying positions and playing roles are typically conceptualized by role theory as revealing two interrelated attributes: (a) self-related characteristics, and (b) role-playing skills and capacities. The self-related concepts of role theory are diverse, but they tend to cluster around an analytical concern for the impact of self-conceptions on the interpretation of various types of expectations that guide conduct in a particular status. Role-playing skills denote those capacities of individuals to perceive various types of expectations and then, with varying degrees of competence and with different role-playing styles, to follow a selected set of expectations. These two attributes—self and role-playing skills—are perceived to be highly interrelated, since self-conceptions will mediate the perception of expectations and the way roles are enacted, while role-playing skills will determine the kinds of self-images, to use Mead's concept, which are derived from an interaction situation and which go into the construction of a stable self-conception.

This conceptualization of the individual roughly parallels Mead's portrayal of mind and self. For both Mead and contemporary role theorists, it is the capacity to take roles and mediate self-images through a stable self-conception that distinguishes the human organism. Although this conceptualization of self and role-playing capacities offers the potential for visualizing unique interpretations of expectations and for analyzing spontaneous forms of role playing, the opposite set of assumptions are more often connoted in role theory. That is, concern appears to be with the way individuals conform to what is expected of them by virtue of occupying a particular status. The degree and form of conformity are usually seen as the result of a variety of internal processes operating on individuals. Depending upon the interactive situation, these internal processes are conceptualized in terms of variables such as (1) the degree to which expectations have been internalized as a part of individual's need structure,[10] (2) the extent to which negative or positive sanctions are perceived by individuals to accompany a particular set of expectations,[11] (3) the degree to which expectations are used as a yardstick

---

[10] For example, Talcott Parsons, *The Social System* (New York: Free Press, 1951), pp. 1–94; and William J. Goode, "Norm Commitment and Conformity to Role-Status Obligations," *American Journal of Sociology* 66 (November 1960): 246–58.

[11] For example, B. F. Skinner, *Science and Human Behavior* (New York: Macmillan Co., 1953), pp. 313–55, 403–19; Biddle and Thomas, *Role Theory*, pp. 27–28; Shaw and Costanzo, *Theories of Social Psychology*, pp. 332–33.

for self-evaluation,[12] and (4) the extent to which expectations represent either interpretations of others' actual responses or merely anticipations of their potential responses.[13] Just which combination of these internal processes operates in a particular interaction situation depends upon the nature of the statuses and attendant expectations. While this complex interactive process has yet to be comprehended with even an incipient inventory of theoretical statements, it remains one of the principal goals of role theory.

From this conceptualization, the individual is assumed to be not so much a creative role entrepreneur who tries to change and alter social structure through varied and unique responses, but rather a pragmatic performer who attempts to cope with and adjust to the variety of expectations inhering in social structure. These implicit assumptions about the nature of the individual are consistent with Mead's concern with the adaptation and adjustment of the human organism to society, but they clearly underemphasize the creative consequences of mind and self for the construction and reconstruction of society. Thus, role theory has tended to expand conceptually upon only part of the Meadian legacy. While this tendency assures some degree of assumptive one-sidedness, it is understandable in light of the role theorists' concern for sorting out only certain types of dynamic interrelationships between society and the individual.

The Articulation between the Individual and Society

The point of articulation between society and the individual is denoted by the concept of "role" and involves individuals who are incumbent in statuses employing self and role-playing capacities to adjust to various types of expectations. Despite agreement over these general features of role, current conceptualizations differ.[14] Depending upon which component of role is emphasized, three basic conceptualizations are evident.[15]

---

[12] Biddle and Thomas, *Role Theory*, p. 27; Kelley, "Two Functions of Reference Groups"; Turner, Role-taking, Role Standpoint"; and Ralph H. Turner, "Self and Other in Moral Judgement," *American Sociological Review* 19 (June 1954): 254–63.

[13] Turner, "Role-taking, Role Standpoint"; Biddle and Thomas, *Role Theory*.

[14] For summaries of the various uses of the concept, see Lionel J. Neiman and James W. Hughes, "The Problem of the Concept of Role—A Re-survey of the Literature," *Social Forces* 30 (December): 141–49; Ragnar Rommetveit, *Social Norms and Roles: Explorations in the Psychology of Enduring Social Pressures* (Minneapolis: University of Minnesota Press, 1955); Biddle and Thomas, *Role Theory;* Shaw and Costanzo, *Theories of Social Psychology*, pp. 334–38; and Deutsch and Krauss, *Theories in Social Psychology*, pp. 173–77.

[15] Deutsch and Krauss, *Theories in Social Psychology*, p. 175; Daniel J. Levinson, "Role, Personality, and Social Structure in the Organizational Setting," *Journal of Abnormal and Social Psychology* 58 (March 1959): 170–80.

Prescribed Roles. When conceptual emphasis is placed upon the expectations of individuals in statuses, then the social world is assumed to be composed of relatively clear-cut prescriptions. The individual's self and role-playing skills are then seen as operating to meet such prescriptions, with the result that analytical emphasis is drawn to the degree of conformity to the demands of a particular status.

Subjective Roles. Since all expectations are mediated through the prism of self, they are subject to interpretations by individuals in statuses. When conceptual emphasis falls upon the perceptions and interpretations of expectations, then the social world is conceived to be structured in terms of individuals' subjective assessments of the interaction situation. Thus, conceptual emphasis is placed upon the interpersonal style of individuals who interpret and then adjust to expectations.

Enacted Role. Ultimately, expectations and the subjective assessment by individuals of these expectations are revealed in behavior. When conceptual priority is given to overt behavior, then the social world is viewed as a network of interrelated behaviors. The more conceptual emphasis is placed upon overt role enactment, the less analytical attention to the analysis of either expectations or individual interpretations of them.

Obviously, when viewed separately from each other, these three conceptual notions are inadequate. Indeed, overt human behavior involves a subjective assessment of various types of expectations. In fact, in reviewing the research and theoretical literature on role theory, it is evident that, although the prescriptive, subjective, or enacted component of role may receive particular emphasis, theoretical efforts usually deal with the complex causal relationships among these components.

Perhaps more than any conceptual perspective, role theory portrays images of causality rather than an explicit set of causal linkages. Part of the reason for this vagueness stems from the fact that the label "role theory" embraces a wide number of specific perspectives in a variety of substantive areas. Despite these qualifications, however, role theorists have tended to develop concepts that denote specific interaction processes without revealing the precise ways these concepts are causally interrelated.

To the extent that role theory's causal images can be brought into focus, they appear to emphasize the deterministic consequences of social structure on interaction. However, rarely are larger, more inclusive units of culture and structure included in this causal analysis. Rather, concern tends to be with the impact of specific norms, others, and reference groups associated with particular clusters of status positions on (a) self-interpretations and evaluations, (b) role-playing capacities, or (c) overt role behavior. While considerable variability is evident in the role-theoretic literature, self-interpretations and evaluations are usually viewed as having a deterministic impact on role-playing capacities, with role-playing capacities then circumscribing overt role behavior. Despite the fact that particular concern with prescribed roles, subjective roles, or role enactment will influence which causal nexus is emphasized, the general causal imagery still tends to portray this sequence, as is delineated in the top portion of Figure 16–1.

FIGURE 16–1
The Causal Imagery of Role Theory

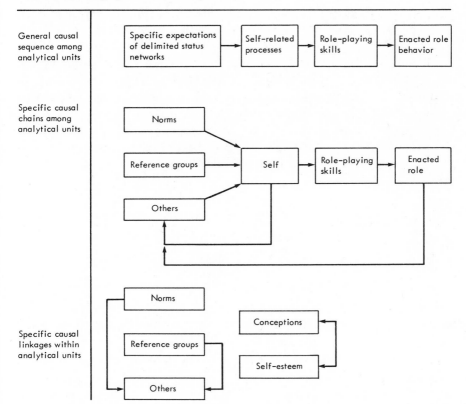

As the middle section of Figure 16–1 reveals, the specific causal images evident in the literature are more complex than the general portrayal at the top of the figure. While expectations are still viewed as determinative, role theorists have frequently emphasized the reciprocal nature of causal processes. That is, certain stages in the causal sequence are seen as "feeding back" and affecting the subsequent causal relations among the analytical units in the middle section of Figure 16–1. Although there are numerous logical interconnections among these units, role theory has emphasized only a few of these causal linkages, as is designated by the solid arrows in the figure. Furthermore, to the extent that specific units of analysis are conceptualized for expectations, self-variables, role-playing skills, and overt behavior, only some of the causal interconnections among these units are explored, as is revealed at the bottom of Figure 16–1.

With respect to the interrelations among expectations, self, role-playing skills, and overt behavior, role theory appears to be concerned primarily with conceptualizing how different types of expectations emanating from different sources—norms, others, and reference groups—are mediated by self-interpretations and evaluations and then circumscribed by role-playing skills in a way that a given style of role performance is evident. This style is then typically analyzed in terms of its degree of conformity to expectations.[16] However, at each stage in this sequence, certain "feedback" processes are also emphasized so that the degree of "significance" of norms, others, or reference groups for the maintenance of self-conceptions of individuals is considered critical in influencing which expectations are most likely to receive the most attention. Emphasis in this causal nexus is on the degree of imbeddedness of self in certain groups,[17] the degree of intimacy with specific others,[18] and the degree of commitment to, or internalization of, certain norms.[19] Another prominent feedback process that has received considerable attention is

---

[16] The study of deviance, socialization, and role playing in complex organizations and small groups has profited from this form of analysis.

[17] For example, see Norman Denzin, "Symbolic Interactionism and Ethnomethodology" in *Understanding Everyday Life: Toward a Reconstruction of Sociological Knowledge*, ed. Jack D. Douglas (Chicago: Aldine Publishing Co., 1970), pp. 259–84. For the most thorough set of such studies in this area, see Sarbin's examinations of the intensity of self-involvement and role-playing behavior: Theodore R. Sarbin, "Role Theory" in *Handbook of Social Psychology*, G. Lindzey, vol. 1 (Reading, Mass.: Addison-Wesley Publishing Co., (1954), pp. 223–58; Theodore R. Sarbin and Norman L. Farberow, "Contributions to Role-taking Theory: A Clinical Study of Self and Role," *Journal of Abnormal and Social Psychology* 47 (January 1952): 117–25; and Theodore R. Sarbin and Bernard G. Rosenberg, "Contributions to Role-taking Theory," *Journal of Social Psychology* 42 (August 1955): 71–81.

[18] See, for example, Tamotsu Shibutani, *Society and Personality* (Englewood Cliffs, N.J.: Prentice-Hall, Inc., 1961), pp. 367–403.

[19] John Finley Scott, *Internalization of Norms: A Sociological Theory of Moral Commitment* (Englewood Cliffs, N.J.: Prentice-Hall, Inc., 1971), pp. 127–215; William Goode, "Norm Commitment and Conformity"; B. F. Skinner, *Science and Human Behavior.*

the impact of overt behavior at one point in time on the expectations of others as they shape the individual's self-conception and subsequent role behavior at another point in time. In this context, the childhood and adult socialization of the individual and the emergence of self have been extensively studied,[20] as has the analysis of the emergence of deviant behavior.[21]

With respect to interrelations within the analytical units of the overall causal sequence, the arrows at the bottom of Figure 16–1 portray the current theoretical emphasis of the literature. In regard to the interrelations among types of expectations, analytical attention appears to be on how specific "others" personify group norms or the standards of reference groups. In turn, these "significant" others are often viewed as deterministically linking the self-interpretations and evaluations of an individual to either the norms of a group or the standards of a reference group.[22] With respect to the relations among the components of self, analysis appears to have followed the lead of William James by focusing on the connections between the "self-esteem" and the self-conception of an individual.[23,24] In turn, the interaction between self-esteem and other components of self is viewed as the result of reactions from various others who affect the self-images of the individual. Finally, all these components interact in complex ways to shape the overt behavior of the individual.

Thus, looking back at Figure 16–1, it is evident that of the many possible causal interrelations, only a few have been extensively conceptualized in the role-theoretic literature. While studies can be found which draw attention to each possible causal nexus, little theoretical attention has been paid to the following connections: (a) broader social and cultural structure and specific patterns of interaction, (b) enacted role behaviors and their effect on role-playing capacities, (c) these role-playing capacities and self, and (d) enacted roles and the self assessments that occur

---

[20] For example, see Anselm Strauss, *Mirrors and Masks* (Glencoe, Ill.: Free Press, 1959), pp. 100–118; Shibutani, *Society and Personality*, pp. 471–596; Orville G. Brim and Stanton Wheeler, *Socialization after Childhood* (New York: John Wiley & Sons, 1966).

[21] See Edwin Lemert, *Social Pathology* (New York: McGraw-Hill Book Co., 1951); Thomas Scheff, "The Role of the Mentally Ill and the Dynamics of Mental Disorder: A Research Framework," *Sociometry* 26 (December 1963): 436–53; Howard Becker, *Outsiders: Studies in the Sociology of Deviance* (New York: Free Press, 1963).

[22] Turner, "Role-taking, Role Standpoint"; Shibutani, *Society and Personality*, pp. 249–80.

[23] William James, *Principles of Psychology*, 2 vols. (New York: Henry Holt, 1890).

[24] See Shibutani, *Society and Personality*, pp. 433–46.

independently of role taking with specific others or groups.[25] Rather, concern has been on the relations between self and expectations as they affect, and are affected by, enacted roles.

PROBLEMS AND ISSUES IN BUILDING ROLE "THEORY"

Constructing Propositions

To this point, role-theoretic concepts provide a means for categorizing and classifying expectations, self, role-playing capacities, role enactment, and relationships among these analytical units. The use of concepts is confined primarily to classification of different phenomena, whether attention is drawn to the forms of status networks,[26] types and sources of expectations,[27] relations of self to expectations,[28] or the enactment of roles.[29] In the future, as they begin the difficult task of building interrelated inventories of propositions, role theorists confront several theoretical problems. First, it will be necessary to fill in the gaps in their causal imagery. To continue emphasizing only some causal links at the expense of ignoring others is to invite an incomplete and inaccurate set of theoretical statements. Particularly crucial in this context will be the development of propositions that specify the linkages between concepts denoting more inclusive social and cultural variables, on the one

[25] There is a large experimental literature on the impact of various types of "contrived" role playing on attitudes and other psychological attributes of individuals; as yet, the findings of these studies have not been incorporated into the role-theoretic framework. For some examples of these studies, see Bert T. King and Irving L. Janis, "Comparison of the Effectiveness of Improvised versus Non-improvised Role-playing in Producing Opinion Changes," *Human Relations* 9 (May 1956): 177–86; Irving C. Janis and Bert T. King, "The Influence of Role Playing on Opinion Change," *Journal of Abnormal and Social Psychology* 49 (April 1954): 211–18; Paul E. Breer and Edwin A. Locke, *Task Experience as a Source of Attitudes* (Homewood, Ill.: Dorsey Press, 1955); Theodore Sarbin and V. L. Allen, "Role Enactment, Audience Feedback, and Attitude Change," *Sociometry* 27 (June 1964): 183–94.

[26] For example, see Davis, *Human Society;* Merton, *Social Theory and Social Structure;* Benoit, "Status, Status Types"; and Biddle and Thomas, *Role Theory,* pp. 23–41.

[27] Davis, *Human Society;* Richard T. Morris, "A Typology of Norms," *American Sociological Review* 21 (October 1956): 610–13; Alan R. Anderson and Omar K. Moore, "The Formal Analysis of Normative Concepts," *American Sociological Review* 22 (February 1957): 9–16; Williams, *American Society.*

[28] Turner, "Role Taking, Role Standpoint"; and Sarbin and Allen, "Role Enactment, Audience Feedback."

[29] Goffman, *Presentation of Self;* Sarbin, "Role Theory"; John H. Mann and Carola H. Mann, "The Effect of Role-playing Experience on Role-playing Ability," *Sociometry* 22 (March 1959): 69–74; and William J. Goode, "A Theory of Role Strain," *American Sociological Review* 25 (August 1960): 483–96.

hand, and concepts pointing to specific interaction variables, on the other.

Second, the current "propositions" that do exist in the role-theoretic literature will have to be reformulated so that conditional statements specifying when certain processes are likely to occur will be more explicit. For example, in the "theory" of reference-group behavior, propositions take the form of asserting that the use of a particular group as a frame of reference is likely to occur when: (a) contact with members of a reference group are likely, (b) dissatisfaction with alternative group memberships exists, (c) perception of potential rewards from a group is likely, (d) the perception of that group's standards is possible, and (e) perception of the availability of significant others in the group is possible.[30] Although these propositions are suggestive, they offer few clues as to what forms of contact, what levels of dissatisfaction, what types of rewards and costs, which group standards, and what type of significant others serve as conditions for use as a frame of reference by an individual. Furthermore, many relevant variables are not included in these propositions. For instance, in order to improve the "theory" of reference-group behavior, it would be minimally necessary to incorporate theoretical statements on the intensity of self-involvement, the capacity to assume roles in a group, the nature of group standards and their compatibility with various facets of an individual's self-conception.

These are the problems that a theoretical perspective attempting to link social structural and individual personality variables will inevitably encounter. When psychological variables, such as self-concept, self-esteem, and role-playing capacities, are seen as interacting with cultural and structural variables, such as status, norm, reference group, and "others," the resulting inventory of theoretical statements will become complex. Such an inventory must not only delve into the internal states of individuals, but must also cut across several levels of emergent phenomena—at a minimum, the individual, the immediate interaction situation, and the more inclusive structural and cultural contexts within which the interaction occurs.

Methodological Implications

The potential utility of role theory derives from its concern with the complex interrelations among the expectations derived from social structure, the mediation of these expectations through self- and role-

---

[30] Example drawn from summary in Alvin Boskoff, *The Mosaic of Sociological Theory* (New York: Thomas Y. Crowell Co., 1972), pp. 49–51.

playing capacities of actors in statuses, and the resulting enactment of role behaviors. Measurement of role enactment does not pose a major methodological obstacle, since it is the most observable of the phenomena studied by role theorists. However, to the extent that such overt behavior is considered to reflect the impact of expectations and self-related variables, several methodological problems become evident. The complexity of the interrelations between role behavior, on the one hand, and self and expectations, on the other, as well as the difficulty of finding indicators of these interrelations, poses a series of methodological problems that will continue to make it difficult to construct bodies of theoretical statements on the relation between society and the individual.

Since one of the assumed links between society and the individual revolves around the expectations that confront individuals, it is theoretically crucial that various types of expectations, and the ways they affect individuals, be measurable. To the degree that these concepts cannot be measured, the utility of the role-theoretic perspective for building sociological theory can be questioned. One method that has been employed in the measurement of expectations is to infer from observed behavior the kinds of expectations that guided its unfolding. The most obvious and important problem with such a method is that expectations can only be known after the fact of the behavior they are supposed to circumscribe. Therefore, the concept of expectations as inferred from behavior has little theoretical utility, since it cannot be measured independently of behavior. Hence, role behavior cannot be predicted from the content of expectations and their relationship to self. An alternative method involves (a) the accumulation of verbal accounts of individuals[31] prior to a particular interaction sequence, (b) the inference of what types of expectations are guiding conduct, and (c) the prediction of how role behavior will unfold in terms of these expectations. This method has the advantage of making predictions about the impact of expectations, but it suffers from the fact that, much like inferences drawn from role enactment, expectations are not measurable independently of the individual who is to be guided by them.[32] The end result of these methodological dilemmas is for expectations to represent analytical inferences that are

---

[31] There are many ways to accumulate such accounts, ranging from informal observations and unstructured interviews with subjects to highly structured interviews and questionnaires. All of these have been employed by role theorists, whether in natural settings or the small-group laboratory.

[32] This dilemma anticipates the discussion of ethnomethodology to be undertaken in a later chapter, for, as the ethnomethodologist would argue, these verbal accounts are the "reality" that guides conduct. From this perspective, the assumption of a "really real" world, independent of an actor's mental construction of it, is considered to be unfounded.

difficult to discern independently of the behavior—whether verbal accounts or role enactment—that they are supposed to guide.

A final alternative to this methodological problem is for researchers to become active participants in social settings, and from this participation to derive some "intuitive sense" of the kinds of expectations that are operating on actors. From this "intuitive sense" it is then presumed that more formal conceptual representation of different types of expectations, and of their varying impact on selves and behavior, can be made. The principal drawback to such an approach is that one researcher's "intuitive sense" is not another's, with the result that *the* expectation structure observed by different researchers in the same situation might well be a "negotiated" product as researchers attempt to achieve consensus as to exactly what this structure is to be. However, to the extent that such a negotiated conceptualization has predictive value, it would represent an indicator of the expectation structure that is, in part at least, derived independently of the verbal statements and behavior of those whose conduct it is supposed to guide.

In sum, then, studying expectations is a difficult enterprise. Since most bodies of sociological theory assume the existence of an expectation structure, it is crucial that these methodological problems be exposed, because they have profound implications for theory building. The most important of these implications concerns the possibility of building theory with concepts that are not measurable, even in principle. Examining either role behavior or verbal statements and then inferring the existence of expectations tends to make specific propositions tautologous, since variation in behavior is explained by variation in phenomena inferred from such behavior. The use of participant or observational techniques overcomes this problem, but presents the equally perplexing issue of how different researchers are to replicate, and hence potentially refute, each other's findings. If conceptualization of the expectation structure is a "negotiated" product, the subsequent investigation of similar phenomena by different investigators would require "renegotiation." When the nature of phenomena that are incorporated into theoretical statements is not explicitly defined and classified in terms of independently verifiable, clear-cut, and agreed-upon standards, but is rather the product of "negotiation," then the statements are not refutable, even in principle. As products of negotiation they have little utility for building a scientific body of knowledge. Ultimately, the severity of these problems is a matter of subjective assessment, since for some they would appear to be fundamental, while for others they stem from the inadequacies of current research techniques.

Whether problems with conceptualizing expectations are seen as either fundamental or technical, they are compounded by the methodological problems of measuring self-related variables. How is it possible to derive operational indicators of self-conceptions, self-esteem, and intrapsychic assessments of the situation? As the discussion of Blumer and Kuhn in the last chapter stressed, verbal accounts and observational techniques have typically been used to tap these dimensions of interaction. While they are "technically" inadequate in that their accuracy can be questioned, they do not raise the same fundamental questions as do expectations, since they do seem measurable in principle. The problems arise only when attempts are made to link these self-related variables to expectations that are presumed to have an independent existence that guides the creation and subsequent operation of self-related processes. While the independent existence of norms, others, reference groups, and the like is intuitively pleasing, just how these phenomena are to be conceptualized and measured separately from the self-related processes they are assumed to circumscribe remains a central problem of role theory, in particular, and all forms of interactionism in general.

Substantive Implications

The substantive criticisms of the role-theoretic perspective focus on the overly structured and circumscribed vision of human behavior, and presumably of social organization, that it connotes. Although it can be argued that current role theory is too diverse to be vulnerable to this line of criticism, its prominent theoretical schemes, as well as the cumulative impact of its empirical studies, reveal a highly structured conceptualization of social reality.

Role theory assumes the social world to be structured in terms of status networks, and corresponding clusterings of expectations, within which individuals with selves and various capacities enact roles. Despite the fact that expectations are viewed as mediated by self- and role-playing capacities (subjective role), the main analytical thrust is on how individuals adjust and adapt to the demands of the "script," other "actors," and the "audiences" of the "play." Undoubtedly, much social action is structured in this way, but the connotative impact of the concepts loads analysis in the direction of assuming too much structure and order in the social world.

The conspicuous conceptualization of "role conflicts"[33] (conflicts

---

[33] For example, see John W. Getzels and E. C. Guba, "Role, Role Conflict, and Effectiveness," *American Sociological Review* 19 (February 1954): 164–75; Talcott Parsons, *Social System*, pp. 280–93; Merton, *Social Theory and Social Structure*, pp. 369–79; and Robert L. Kahn, et al., *Organizational Stress: Studies in Role Conflict and Ambiguity* (New York: John Wiley & Sons).

among expectations), "role strain"[34] (the impossibility of meeting all expectations), and "anomie"[35] (the lack of clear-cut expectations) in role theory would seemingly balance this overly structured conception of reality. Yet frequently, strain, conflict, and anomie are viewed as "deviant" situations that represent "exceptions" to the structure of the "normal" social order. What is critical, then, is that these concepts be elaborated upon and inserted into current theoretical statements. In this way, they can serve to specify the conditions under which the social world is less circumscribed by social structure.

The causal imagery of role theory also contributes to an overly structured vision of social reality. Figure 16–1 emphasizes that the causal thrust of the role theory is on the way expectations, as mediated by selves and role-playing capacities, circumscribe role enactment. Although attention is drawn to the feedback consequences of role enactment for expectations, this analysis usually concerns how behaviors of individuals alter the reactions of others in such a way that self-conceptions are reinforced or changed.

What is ignored are the determinative consequences of role enactments for changes and alterations in social structure. In focusing primarily on how changes of behavior affect self-conceptions, role theory has underemphasized the fact that behavior can also force changes in the organization of status networks, norms, reference groups, the responses of others, and other features of social structure. Until the causal imagery of role theory stresses the consequences of role enactment, not only for self-related variables but also for social structural variables, it will continue to conceptualize the social world as excessively circumscribed by the expectation structure.

Some of the logical problems of role-theoretic analysis further contribute to this conception of the social world. The vagueness of just how and under what conditions social structure affects self and role enactment leaves much of role analysis with the empty assertion that society shapes individual conduct. If role-theoretic assumptions are to have theoretical significance, it is essential to specify just when, where, how, and through what processes this circumscription of role behavior occurs. In fact, in the absence of theoretical specificity, a subtle form of imperativism is connoted: The needs of social structure and the individual require that behavior be circumscribed. This imperativism is further sustained by the classificatory nature of role-theoretic concepts. In denoting the types of interrelations among society, self, and behavior without indicating

---

[34] Goode, "Theory of Role Strain."
[35] Merton, Social Theory and Social Structure, pp. 121–51.

the conditions under which these relationships are likely to exist, these concepts appear to denote what processes must occur without indicating when, where, and how they are to occur.[36]

Finally, the methodological problems of measuring expectations separately from the very individual processes that they are supposed to circumscribe makes even more "mysterious" just how and in what ways social structure affects individual conduct. Again, the inability to measure this crucial causal nexus leaves the role theorist with the uninteresting assertion, loaded with imperativist connotations, that society shapes and guides individual conduct.

REDIRECTING ROLE THEORY: SOME CONCLUDING REMARKS

Since the concept of role represents the point of articulation between the individual and society, its examination is necessary for theoretical understanding of why different patterns of social organization emerge, persist, change, and break down. At present, the main thrust of the role-theoretic strategy has been to focus on how specific social contexts determine variations in individual conduct, and to give comparatively little attention to how such conduct, as mediated by self and role-playing capacities, affects these social contexts as well as more general patterns of social organization. While this strategy has provided considerable insight into individual and group processes, role theory has yet to explore the utility of its concepts for understanding more macro social structures and processes.

Until this analytical effort is undertaken, it is difficult to determine the place of the role perspective in sociological theory. Clearly, it has enormous utility for the study of organizations, groups, and individual conduct, but at what point do its concepts, and their incorporation into theoretical propositions, cease being theoretically useful? Role theorists typically presume that the concepts developed by their perspective have wide theoretical applicability. However, except in the most cursory way, they have not incorporated these concepts into propositions that would account for a variety of patterns of social organization. Rather,

---

[36] Although most role theorists would vehemently deny it, they have followed Parsons' strategy for building theory, except on a more micro level. In developing concepts to classify and order role-related phenomena, without also developing clear-cut propositions, they have created a conceptual order without indicating when and how the order denoted by concepts is maintained (or broken down or reconstructed).

role theory has been content to assert that, since complex social patterns are ultimately built from the specific role behaviors of individuals with selves and various role-playing capacities, the concepts of role theory will be critical in the development of sociological theory. To assert that such is the case appears to have done little to stimulate the development of generic propositions that would demonstrate the role theorist's case.

In order to realize the full potential of role theory, a shift in strategy is necessary. First, it is critical that role theory begin developing propositions that incorporate its rapidly multiplying body of classificatory concepts. To continue the proliferation of systems of concepts in lieu of developing systems of propositions will prevent role theory from realizing its full potential for developing sociological theory. Second, these propositions must begin to consider not only the implications of self-related processes and role-playing capacities on behavior, but also the consequences of such circumscribed behavior on a variety of patterns of social organization. Third, the accumulation of these latter types of propositions should begin to reveal the power of role-theoretic concepts in providing both prediction and a sense of understanding of social events for different levels of social organization. Should it become evident that role theory does not have theoretical utility for certain emergent social phenomena, then the limitations of role-theoretic concepts will be more evident than is currently the case. In sum, then, it is to the demonstration of its limitations that role-theoretic strategy should now address itself.

17

THE FUTURE OF INTERACTIONISM: RALPH H. TURNER'S SYNTHESIS

In contrast to other theoretical perspectives, interactionism focuses almost exclusively upon the relationship between the individual and society. How do individual actions shape the profile of society? And, conversely, how does society constrain and circumscribe the individual?

As is evident, interactionists approach these questions with different viewpoints. Symbolic interactionists, such as Herbert Blumer, emphasize the process of interaction as actors construct, and reconstruct, lines of joint conduct. Others, like Manford Kuhn and his followers, stress the structure of personality and social settings as individuals act in terms of their core self-attitudes and the expectations of situations. And role theorists, operating in many different research contexts, emphasize the expectations of social structures as these interact with self- and role-playing skills to produce role enactments.

Thus, there is considerable diversity in the orientations of theorists who work within the interactionist perspective. Emerging out of this diversity, however, are a number of key substantive, methodological, and theory-building issues. The future of interactionist theory hinges upon resolution of these issues.

KEY ISSUES IN INTERACTIONISM

Substantive Issues

Substantive issues concern the image of social organization that a perspective communicates. While interactionist theories all rely upon

366

the concepts of person, interaction, other, self, role, situation, and society, they reveal marked differences in emphasis. The future of interactionism resides in the resolution of three related substantive issues: (1) the range of phenomena to which interactionist theory is relevant; (2) the degree of fluidity or structure in human relations which the theory must assume; and (3) the degree to which the social world is seen as governed by deterministic processes. Each of these questions is briefly explored below:

   The Range of Interactionist Theory.   Is interactionism only useful when examining the micro world? Or, does it have wider applicability to macro social relations among collective or corporate units? Currently, interactionism appears most amenable to the analysis of relatively small numbers of individuals. Yet such advocates as Herbert Blumer claim that symbolic interactionism is *the* basic, and the only, process among all types of social units. Role theorists tend to be somewhat more restrained, arguing that individual behaviors are circumscribed by their roles and that social organization is ultimately a network of role relations. Thus, a key issue in interactionist theory is: Are the concepts and propositions of the perspective tied to the analysis of individuals? Can interactionist theory inform social theory when it seeks to understand the full complexity of patterns of human organization?

   The Degree of Fluidity of Structure.   Blumer's version of symbolic interactionism stresses the degree to which the social world is in flux.[1] Emphasis is placed upon the *process* of constructing, and reconstructing, transitory social arrangements. Social structure is merely one of many "objects" introjected into actors' symbolic calculations. In contrast, Kuhn and most role theorists emphasize the constraints that social structure places upon actors' options.[2] Another critical substantive issue in interactionism thus revolves around the question: Can the concepts and propositions of this perspective capture varying degrees of structure and fluidity? Can the same concepts and propositions explain both processes that operate to create and change relations as well as those that function to maintain patterns of social organization?

   Indeterminacy versus Determinacy.   Mead's original work contains concepts, such as the "I," which argue for a more indeterminate vision of the world.[3] Individuals reveal the potential for spontaneous acts as

---

[1] Herbert Blumer, "Society as Symbolic Interaction," in A. Rose, ed., *Human Behavior and Social Processes* (Boston: Houghton Mifflin, 1962).

[2] Manford H. Kuhn, "Major Trends in Symbolic Interaction Theory in the Past Twenty-Five Years," *Sociological Quarterly* 5 (Winter 1964): 61–84.

[3] George Herbert Mead, *Mind, Self, and Society* (Chicago: Chicago University Press, 1933).

they construct lines of conduct. Kuhn, in contrast, stressed the determinate nature of human action: If it is possible to know people's past experiences, self-attitudes, and current group affiliations, then it is possible to predict their behaviors. Thus, a third substantive issue, which has enormous consequences for the nature of social theory, is: To what degree are events in the world the result of determinate causes? Are human acts so random and unique that their causes are unknowable?

In sum, then, interactionist theory must come to grips with these questions. Concepts and propositions will need to specify the range of phenomena to which they apply; they will have to help explain both structured and unstructured situations; and they will have to take a stand on the issue of cause and effect.

Methodological Issues

Mead's penetrating criticism of the extreme behaviorism of his day stressed the fact that humans are symbol-using cognitive organisms.[4] They have mind and self, with these processes profoundly influencing their actions. Mead recognized that social theory must therefore enter the "black box" of human cognition. All current interactionist orientations stress that the mental processes of actors must be understood if theories of human behavior and patterns of social organization are to be complete.

The dispute among interactionists occurs over *how* to measure people's self-conceptions and other cognitive processes that go to make up their "definition of the situation." Blumer's position argues for the importance of investigators sympathetically penetrating the mental world of the actor through nondirective and inobtrusive techniques.[5] Kuhn, and most role theorists, argue for the operationalization of key concepts through structured measuring instruments.[6] The key issue thus becomes: How are social scientists to measure the concepts and test the theories of the interactionist perspective?

The future of interactionism rests on its capacity to generate testable theory. Presently, much of the interactionist research literature consists of narrow studies—from unstructured observations to highly controlled experiments—on a wide variety of topics: deviation, conformity, commu-

---

[4] Ibid.

[5] Herbert Blumer, "The Methodological Position of Symbolic Interactionism" in his *Symbolic Interactionism: Perspective and Method* (Englewood Cliffs, N.J.: Prentice-Hall, 1969).

[6] Manford H. Kuhn and Thomas S. McPartland, "An Empirical Investigation of Self-Attitude," *American Sociological Review* 19 (February 1954): 68–76.

nication, role conflict, role strain, marital harmony, and the like. One reason for the scattered profile of the current research is that interactionism has yet to develop a broad theoretical base. While there are specific propositions on particular topics, there is no over-arching body of theoretical propositions toward which studies could be directed. This fact raises the question of the status of interactionism *as theory*.

Theory-Building Issues

Blumer has argued that sociological theorizing can, at best, consist of a body of sensitizing concepts that will allow for some degree of understanding of social events.[7] Prediction will always be difficult and, under the most favorable of circumstances, probabilistic. Blumer's vision of interactionism thus emphasizes the sensitizing and orienting functions of theory. In contrast to this view is one that sees interactionist theory as like all other theory and as embracing clearly defined concepts grouped into abstract propositions that can explain why events occur. But as long as interactionism remains a general orientation, it cannot be tested except in the vague sense that its concepts "help" social interpreters perceive that "they understand." To become theory, interactionism will need to move toward formulating abstract propositions that can subsume the empirical generalizations of the large research literature and that can direct research toward theory-testing. Implied in such an effort is the assumption that the processes of the world are determinitive and that it is possible, at least in principle, to measure with some precision these processes. Without these assumptions, the construction of theory would be an empty exercise.

These substantive, methodological, and theoretical issues are placed in bold relief in the context of assessing interactionist theory. They are, of course, relevant to the other theoretical perspectives examined in Parts II, III, and IV of this book. And yet, because interactionism seeks to understand behavior and social organization by entering the mysterious world of the human personality and by trying to understand the relations between personality and society, these issues become especially prominent. Interactionism, if it is to be a *theoretical* orientation, will need to develop theory that is testable, in principle, and that can capture both the fluid and processual nature of human conduct and organization as well as the structured nature of personality and social organization. Such theory will continue to draw upon Mead's great syn-

---

[7] Herbert Blumer, "Sociological Analysis and the 'Variable'," *American Sociological Review* 21 (December 1956): 683–90; and "Sociological Implications of the Thought of George Herbert Mead," *Symbolic Interactionism*.

thesis, while incorporating the insights of Park, Moreno, and Linton, and the large research literature.

One accumulating line of theory-building within the interactionist tradition has attempted to pursue this strategy. This is the "role theory" of Ralph H. Turner.[8] And before closing this assessment of the future of interactionism, Turner's strategy and theory-building efforts should be explored.

AN ALTERNATIVE FORM OF INTERACTIONISM: THE "ROLE THEORY" OF RALPH H. TURNER

Over the course of two decades, Ralph H. Turner has mounted a consistent line of criticism against role theory.[9] This criticism incorporates several lines of attack: (1) Role theory presents an overly structured vision of the social world, with its emphasis upon norms, status positions, and the enactment of normative expectations. (2) Role theory tends to concentrate an inordinate amount of research and theory-building effort on "abnormal" social processes, such as role conflict and role strain, thereby ignoring the normal processes of human interaction. (3) Role theory is not theory, but rather, a series of disjointed and unconnected propositions. (4) Role theory has not utilized, to the degree required, Mead's concept of "role-taking" as its central concept.

To correct for these deficiencies, Turner proposes that interactionist theory concentrate its efforts on developing abstract theory which incorporates Mead's key insights and which focuses on normal social processes. In this way, processes like role conflict can be deduced from the same abstract propositions as more typical processes. Moreover, by developing *abstract* propositions about key *social processes*, role theory will be able to explain both highly structured and fluid patterns of interaction. These are the goals of Turner's role theory, and in recent years, he has advocated a specific strategy for their implementation.[10] To appreciate this strategy,

---

[8] I am often asked if I am related to Ralph H. Turner. To avoid charges of familial favoritism, let me emphasize that we are not related to, nor personally well acquainted with, each other.

[9] See, for example, Ralph H. Turner, "Role-Taking: Process Versus Conformity," in A. Rose, ed., *Human Behavior and Social Processes.*

[10] Professor Turner has graciously provided me with a number of working papers which, along with various published works, have guided the following discussion. These unpublished works, as of this writing, include: "A Strategy for Developing an Integrated Role Theory"; "Role Theory as Theory"; "The Role and the Person"; and "Role-Taking as Process." Particularly influential published works include "Social Roles: Sociological Aspects," *International Encyclopedia of the Social Sciences* (New York: Macmillan, 1968), which was written as an unpublished working paper; "Role Theory: A Series of Proposi-

it is necessary to understand (1) Turner's basic assumptions about the nature of interaction, (2) his specific theory construction guidelines, and (3) his efforts to construct theoretical propositions.

TURNER'S BASIC ASSUMPTIONS ABOUT THE NATURE OF INTERACTION

In a number of places, Turner has commented upon the lack of consensus over the definition of the concept, *role*.[11] For example, role has been variously defined as: (*a*) the overt behavior of people, (*b*) the conceptions that people have of expected behaviors, (*c*) the norms attached to status positions, and (*d*) the part that a person learns to play in a situation. Turner often notes that role theory, following Ralph Linton's early lead (see Chapter 14), has tended to present a "conformity model" of role in which actors in a given status position (*a*) perceive the normative expectations of their status, (*b*) enact conforming behavior, (*c*) and receive social approval for their conforming behavior.[12] Turner argues that, while not incorrect, such a model accounts for only certain empirical situations. Much action and interaction does not involve simple conformity, but active construction of reciprocal lines of conduct among actors who seek to come to terms with each other in less structured situations. Role theory, Turner stresses, must recognize this fact and incorporate all the varying definitions of role into a unified conception of role that can capture the interactive processes underlying the creation, maintenance, and change of patterns of social organization. In developing this conception of role, Turner makes a number of assumptions about the nature of the social world.

The Role-Making Process

Turner utilizes and extends Mead's concept of "role-taking" in attempting to describe the nature of social action. Turner assumes that "it is the tendency to shape the phenomenal world into roles which is the key to the role-taking as the core process in interaction."[13] Like Mead and Blumer, Turner stresses the fact that actors emit "gestures"

---

tions," 1965; "Rule Learning as Role Learning," *International Journal of Critical Sociology* 1 (September 1974); "Ambiguity and Interchangeability in Role Attribution," *American Sociological Review* 41 (December 1976) with Norma Shosid; "The Normative Coherence of Folk Concepts," *Research Studies of State College of Washington* 25 (June 1957).

[11] See "Role-Taking as Process" and "Social Roles: Sociological Aspects."

[12] See, in particular, "Role-Taking: Process vs. Conformity."

[13] Ibid., p. 22.

or "cues"—words, bodily countenance, voice inflections, dress, facial expressions, and other gestures—as they interact. Actors use these gestures to "put themselves in the other's role" and to adjust their lines of conduct in ways that can facilitate cooperation. This is essentially Mead's definition of "taking the role of the other" or "role-taking."[14]

Turner then extends Mead's concept. He first argues that cultural definitions of roles are often vague and even contradictory. At best, they provide a general framework within which actors must construct a line of conduct. Thus, actors must *make* their roles and communicate to others *what* role they are playing. Turner then argues that humans act *as if* all others in their environment are playing *identifiable roles*.[15] Humans assume others to be playing a role and this assumption is what gives interaction a common basis. Operating with this "folk assumption," people then read gestures and cues in an effort to determine what role others are playing.[16] This effort is facilitated by the fact that these others must often create and assert their role, with the result that they actively emit cues as to what role they are attempting to play.

For Turner, then, role-taking is also "role-making." Humans "make roles" in three senses: (1) They are often faced with only a loose cultural framework in which they must "make" a role to play. (2) They assume others are playing *a role* and thus "make" an effort to discover the underlying role behind a people's acts. (3) Humans seek to "make" a role for themselves in all social situations by emitting cues to others that give them claim on a particular role. This role-taking process as it becomes transformed into a *role-making process* is the underlying basis for all human interaction. It is what ultimately allows people to interact and cooperate with each other.

The "Folk Norm of Consistency"

As people interact with each other, Turner argues, they assess behavior not in terms of its "conformity" to imputed norms, but rather, in regard to its *consistency*.[17] Humans seek to group each other's behavior into coherent wholes or units, and by doing so, they can "make sense" of each other's actions, anticipate each other's responses, and adjust their responses to each other. If an other's responses are inconsistent and not capable of being seen as part of an underlying role, then interaction with that other will prove difficult. Thus, Turner asserts, there is an

---

14 Mead, *Mind, Self, and Society.*
15 "Role-Taking and Process," and "Role-Taking as Process."
16 Ibid. and "The Normative Coherence of Folk Concepts."
17 "Role-Taking as Process," and "Role-Taking and Process."

implicit "norm of consistency" in people's interactions with each other. Humans attempt to assess consistency of others' actions to discern the underlying role that is being played.

With the concepts of role-making and the norm of consistency, Turner shifts the analysis of roles toward a position that symbolic interactionists such as Blumer might appreciate. This shift is underscored by a third major assumption with which Turner approaches the analysis of roles: Interaction is always a tentative process.

The Tentative Nature of Interaction

Turner echos Blumer's position when he states that "interaction is always a *tentative* process, a process of continuously testing the conception one has of the role of the other."[18] Humans are constantly interpreting additional cues emitted by others, and using these new cues to see if they are consistent with those previously emitted and with the imputed roles of others. If they are consistent, then the actor will continue to adjust responses in accordance with the imputed role of the other. But as soon as inconsistent cues are emitted, the identification of other's role will undergo revision. Thus, a given imputation of a particular role to an other will only persist as long as it provides a stable framework for interaction. The tentative nature of the role-making process points to another facet of roles: the process of role verification.

The Process of Role Verification

Actors seek to verify that behaviors and other cues emitted by people in a situation do indeed constitute a role. Turner argues that such efforts at "verification" or "validation" are achieved by the application of "external" and "internal" criteria. The most often used "internal criterion" is the degree to which an actor perceives the imputation of a role to an other as facilitating interaction. External criteria can vary, but in general, they involve an actor's assessment as to whether or not a role imputed to alter (an other) is likely to be judged as such by important people, relevant groups, or commonly agreed upon standards. When an imputed role is "validated" or "verified" in this way, then it can serve as a stable basis for continued interaction among actors.

Self-Conceptions and Role

All humans reveal self-conceptions of themselves as certain kinds of objects. Humans develop self-attitudes and feelings out of their interac-

---

[18] "Role-Taking: Process vs. Conformity," p. 23.

tions with others, but as Turner and all role theorists emphasize, actors attempt to present themselves in ways that will reinforce their self-conception.[19] Since alters seek to determine an actor's role, it becomes necessary for an actor to inform alter, through cues and gestures, about the degree to which self is anchored in a role. Thus, actors will consistently inform each other about their self-identity and the extent to which their role is consistent with their self-conception. For example, roles which are not consistent with a person's self-conception will likely be played with considerable distance and disdain, while those which an individual considers central to self-definitions will be played much differently.[20]

These assumptions emphasize the processual nature of roles. Turner argues that these assumptions incorporate all of the various definitions of role, since none of the points of emphasis of any definition is precluded. For example, the emphasis on behavioral aspect of role is retained, since it is through behavioral cues that actors impute roles. The notion that roles are conceptions of expected behaviors is preserved, for the assignment of a role to a person invokes an expectation that a certain type and range of responses will ensue. The view that roles are the norms attendant on status positions is not ignored, since norms and positions are often the basis for assigning and verifying roles. And the conception of roles as parts that people learn to play is preserved, for people are able to denote each other's roles by virtue of their prior socialization into a common role repertoire.

Not only do these assumptions embrace the major points of emphasis in prominent definitions, they also help reconcile the differences between symbolic interactionism and role theory. Turner's assumptions employ the key concepts of Mead's synthesis, while taking cognizance of Blumer's emphasis on the processes that underlay patterns of joint action. These assumptions also point to the normal processes of interaction, but are sufficiently general to embrace the possibility of conflictual and stressful interactions. And these assumptions about the role-making process do not preclude the analysis of structured interaction, since formal norms and status positions are often the major cues for ascertaining the roles of people, while being principal sources of verification for imputed roles.

Turner's assumptions, however, are only as good as the theory that they can generate. Significantly, Turner has sought to delineate an explicit

---

19 "Role and the Person"; "Social Roles: Sociological Aspects."
20 Ibid.

strategy for translating these assumptions into theoretical propositions. It may be that the execution of this strategy will help interactionism bridge the gap between suggestive assumptions and concepts on the one hand and the current plethora of narrow empirical propositions on the other. It is thus critical that this strategy for building role theory be examined.

TURNER'S STRATEGY FOR BUILDING ROLE THEORY

While Turner appears to accept much of the process orientation of Blumer, he is committed to developing interactionism into "something akin to axiomatic theory."[21] He recognizes that, in its present state, role theory is segmented into a series of narrow propositions and hypotheses and that role theorists have been reluctant "to find unifying themes to link various role processes."[22]

Turner's strategy is to use the wide variety of propositions of the large number of research studies to build more formal and abstract theoretical statements. The goal of his strategy is thus to maintain a productive dialog between specific empirical propositions and more abstract theoretical statements. His approach is somewhat distinctive and in need of amplification.

The Concepts of Role Theory

Turner argues against rigid definitions of concepts when beginning the theory-building process. It is more useful, he contends, to begin with loosely defined concepts such as *actor, role, other, situation,* and the like. The concepts will take on greater clarity as propositions incorporating these concepts are developed. Moreover, early attention to concept formation "turns our attention from empirical to definitional concerns, from dynamic to static questions, and many a theory-building enterprise becomes hopelessly diverted into creating an elegant system that neither suggests nor generates new empirical propositions."[23]

Turner thus initially adopts Blumer's position that theorists must begin with "sensitizing concepts." As will become evident, however, he is to use these concepts in ways that will allow for more precise definitions and for more formal theoretical propositions.

---

[21] "A Strategy for Developing an Integrated Role Theory," and "Role Theory as Theory."

[22] "A Strategy," p. 2.

[23] Ibid., p. 3.

Sorting Out Tendencies

Without definitive concepts and with a large body of segmented propositions, an alternative way of linking sensitizing concepts to observed empirical regularities is necessary. Turner advocates the use of what he terms "main tendency" propositions to link concepts to empirical regularities and to consolidate the thrust of these empirical regularities.[24] What Turner seeks is a series of statements which highlight what *tends to occur in the normal operation of systems of interaction*. These statements are not true propositions because they are not of the form: Under C_1, C_2, C_3 . . . C_n, x varies with y. Rather, they are statements of the form: In most normal situations, event x tends to occur. These are not statements of co-variance, but statements of what is presumed to typically transpire in the course of interaction.

Turner has provided a long list of main tendency propositions with respect to a number of issues: (*a*) the emergence and character of roles, (*b*) role as an interactive framework, (*c*) roles in relation to actors, (*d*) role in organizational setting, (*e*) role in societal setting, and (*f*) role and the person. These headings provide a way of grouping tendency propositions. Each group of propositions is summarized below under these headings:

Emergence and Character of Roles. In these propositions Turner presents a series of observations about the nature of the social world as a series of empirical tendencies. It should be emphasized, however, that such tendencies are observed through the heavy prism of Turner's assumptions.

1. In any interactive situation, behavior, sentiments, and motives tend to be differentiated into units which can be termed roles; once differentiated, elements of behavior, sentiment, and motives which appear in the same situation tend to be assigned to existing roles. (Tendencies for role differentiation and accretion.)

2. In any interactive situation, the meaning of individual actions for ego (the actor) and for any alters is assigned on the basis of the imputed role. (Tendencies for meaningfulness.)

3. In connection with every role, there is a tendency for certain attributes of actors, aspects of behavior and features of situations to become salient cues for the identification of roles. (Tendencies for role cues.)

4. The character of a role—that is, its definition—will tend to change if there are persistent changes in either the behaviors of those

---

[24] "Social Roles: Sociological Aspects"; "Role Theory: A Series of Propositions."

presumed to be playing the role or the contexts in which the role is played. (Tendencies for behavioral correspondence.)

5. Every role tends to acquire an evaluation in terms of rank and social desirability. (Tendencies for evaluation.)

These propositions both reassert Turner's assumptions about the social world and provide several points of elaboration. People are seen as viewing the world in terms of roles; they are seen as employing a "folk norm" to seek consistency of behaviors and to assign behavioral elements to an imputed role (role differentiation and accretion). Actors are viewed as interpreting situations by virtue of imputing roles to each other (meaningfulness tendency). Humans are observed to use cues of other actor's attributes and behaviors, as well as the situation, to identify roles (role cues). When role behaviors or situations are permanently altered, the definition of role will also undergo change (behavioral correspondence). And humans tend to evaluate roles by ranking them in terms of power, prestige, and esteem, while assessing them with regard to their degree of social desirability and worth (tendency for evaluation).

Role as an Interactive Framework. In these tendency propositions, Turner elaborates his assumption that interaction cannot proceed without the identification and assignment of roles. These propositions specify the ways in which roles provide a way and means for interaction to occur.

6. The establishment and persistence of interaction tends to depend upon the emergence and identification of ego and alter roles. (Tendency for interaction in terms of roles.)

7. Each role tends to form as a comprehensive way of coping with one or more relevant alter roles. (Tendency for role complementarity.)

8. There is a tendency for stabilized roles to be assigned the character of legitimate expectations. (Tendency for legitimate expectations.)

In these propositions, Turner indicates that interaction is dependent upon the identification of roles. Moreover, roles tend to be complements of other roles—as is the case with wife-husband, parent-child, boss-employee roles—and thus operate to regularize interaction among complementary roles. Finally, roles which prove useful and which allow for stable and fruitful interaction are translated into expectations that future transactions will and should occur as in the past.

Role in Relation to Actor. These propositions concern the relationship between actors and the roles that provide the framework for interaction.

9. Once stabilized, the role structure tends to persist, regardless of changes in actors. (Tendency for role persistence.)

10. There is a tendency to identify a given individual with a given role, and a complementary tendency for an individual to adopt a given role, for the duration of the interaction. (Tendency in role allocation.)

11. To the extent to which ego's role is an adaptation to alter's role, it incorporates some conception of alter's role. (Tendency for role-taking.)

12. Role behavior tends to be judged as adequate or inadequate by comparison with a conception of the role in question. (Tendency to assess role adequacy.)

13. The degree of adequacy in role performance of an actor determines the extent to which others will respond and reciprocate an actor's role performance. (Tendency for role reciprocity.)

In these propositions, Turner stresses that once actors identify and assign each other to roles, the roles persist and new actors to a situation will tend to be assigned to those roles that already exist in a situation. Humans also tend to adopt roles for the duration of an interaction, while having knowledge of the roles that others are playing. Additionally, actors carry with them general conceptions of what a role entails and what constitutes adequate performance. Finally, the adequacy of a person's role performance greatly influences the extent to which the role, and the rights, privileges, and complementary behaviors that it deserves, will be acknowledged.

Role in Organizational Settings. Turner recognizes that many roles are enacted in structured contexts. This fact, he argues, necessitates a listing of additional tendencies in the role-making processes.

14. To the extent to which roles are incorporated into an organizational setting, organizational goals tend to become crucial criteria for role differentiation, evaluation, complementarity, legitimacy or expectation, consensus, allocation, and judgements of adequacy. (Tendency for organization goal dominance.)

15. To the extent to which roles are incorporated into an organizational setting, the right to define the legitimate character of roles, to set the evaluations on roles, to allocate roles, and to judge role adequacy tend to be lodged in particular roles. (Tendency for legitimate role definers.)

16. To the extent to which roles are incorporated into an organization

setting, differentiation tends to link roles to statuses in the organization. (Tendency for status.)

17.   To the extent to which roles are incorporated into an organizational setting, each role tends to develop as a pattern of adaptation to multiple alter roles. (Tendency for role sets.)

18.   To the extent to which roles are incorporated into an organizational setting, the persistence or roles is intensified through tradition and formalization. (Tendency for formalization.)

In these propositions, Turner stresses that the goals of organizations and key personnel become important in the role-making process in structured situations. Moreover, it is within organizations that status and role become merged. In this way, Turner incorporates Linton's insight that status and role *can* become highly related, but he does not abandon Mead's and Blumer's emphasis that much interaction occurs in constructed contexts where roles are not circumscribed by networks of clearly defined status positions. Turner also recognizes that roles in structured situations develop as ways of adapting to a number of other roles which are typically assigned by role definers or required by organizational goals. Finally, roles within organizations tend to become formalized in that written agreements and tradition come to have the power to maintain a given role system and to shape normative expectations.

Role in Societal Setting.

19.   Similar roles in different contexts tend to become merged, so as to be identified as a single role recurring in different relationships. (Tendency for economy or roles.)

20.   To the extent to which roles are referred to a social context, differentiation tends to link roles to social values. (Tendency for value anchorage.)

21.   The individual in society tends to be assigned and to assume roles which are consistent with each other. (Tendency for allocation consistency.)

In these propositions, Turner recognizes that many roles are identified, assumed, and imputed in relation to a broader societal context. Turner first argues that people tend to group behaviors in different social contexts into as few unifying roles as is possible. Thus, people will identify a "mother role," or "male role," or "female role" as a way of "making sense" of disparate behaviors in different contexts. At the societal level, values are the equivalent for goals in organizational settings for identifying, differentiating, allocating, evaluating, and legitimating roles. Finally, all people tend to assume multiple roles in society, but they tend to assume roles that are consistent with each other.

   Role and the Person.   The "person" is a concept employed by Turner to denote "the distinctive repertoire of roles" that an individual enacts in relevant social settings. The concept of person is his means for summarizing the way in which individuals cope with their roles.

22.   Actors tend to act so as to alleviate role strain arising out of role contradiction, role conflict, and role inadequacy, and to heighten the gratifications of high role adequacy. (Tendency to resolve role strain.)

23.   Individuals in society tend to adopt as a framework for their own behavior and as a perspective for interpretation of the behavior of others a repertoire of role relationships. (Tendency to be socialized into common culture.)

24.   Individuals tend to form self-conceptions by selective identification of certain roles from their repertoires as more characteristically "themselves" than other roles. (Tendency to anchor self-conception.)

25.   The self-conception tends to stress those roles which supply the basis for effective adaptation to relevant alters. (Adaptivity of self-conception tendency.)

26.   To the extent to which roles that must be played in situations contradict the self-conception, those roles will be assigned role distance and mechanisms of demonstrating lack of personal involvement employed. (Tendency for role distance.)

   In these propositions, Turner stresses that people seek to resolve tensions among roles and to avoid contradictions between self-conceptions and roles. These propositions are, to a very great extent, elaborations of Turner's assumptions about the relationship between self-conceptions and role.

   These 26 propositions represent the first step in Turner's theoretical strategy. These tendencies incorporate the loosely defined concepts of interactionism, but they link these concepts to actual events which are presumed to occur in the social world. Naturally, more tendencies might be discerned and recorded. The list of 26 is sufficient, however, to illustrate what Turner views as the "next step" in developing a more integrated interactionist theory.

Generating and Organizing Empirical Propositions

   The tendency propositions, as has been emphasized, are not true propositions. They do not reveal relations of co-variance among variables.

However, Turner believes that the tendency propositions can help generate true empirical propositions of the form: x varies with y. This is done by attempting to determine the empirical conditions that shape the degree or rate of variation in a tendency proposition. For example, tendency proposition 22—"the actor tends to act so as to alleviate role strain"—becomes the dependent variable in a search for independent variables that can specify the conditions under which actors "tend to act to alleviate role strain." The tendency proposition thus provides an initial set of guidelines for developing true propositions about relationships among variables.

Furthermore, since the tendency propositions tend to be grouped together, as was done in the various sections above, the true empirical propositions will be organized around related tendencies. As such, the propositions are less scattered and disparate than would be the case if the search for propositions had not begun with the delineation of certain normal tendencies.

Turner has not used his tendency propositions to generate and organize true empirical propositions, except in one area: the relationship between role and the person (the last section in the above tendency propositions).[25] Even here, however, the transition from the tendency propositions to the true empirical propositions is often vague. But Turner's inventory of propositions about the person and role can illustrate the potential utility of his theory-building strategy.

As has been noted, Turner views "the person" as the repertoire of roles that an individual plays. And while Turner recognizes that "people are normally quite different actors in different roles, and even have senses of 'who they are,' "[26] humans also use roles as a means for self-identification and self-validation. Some roles are thus more important to individuals and resist compartmentalization, or separation, from a person's self-concept. Roles which arouse strong self-feelings, which people appear to play across situations, which they refuse to abandon, and which they embellish with associated attitudes are likely to involve considerable merger of the individual's self with the role.

Turner's discussion of "person and the role" thus addresses the following question: Under what conditions do individuals become identified with roles, using the role for purposes of self-identification and validation? This question can be viewed as an attempt to use tendency propositions 24 and 26 as dependent variables that can organize a search for the conditions under which individuals tend "to form self-conceptions by

---

[25] "Role and the Person."
[26] Ibid., p. 2.

selective identification of certain roles from their repertoire as more characteristically themselves than other roles" and to show "role distance" and "a lack of personal involvement" in situations which "contradict the self-conception." For all the other tendency propositions listed, a similar search should be initiated in an effort to discover the empirical conditions that influence their rate, degree, and extent of occurrence.

Turner divides his discussion of person and role into two general lines of analysis: (1) How do others in the situation discover a merger of role and person; and (2) how do the individuals themselves come to lodge their self in certain roles? Each of these questions organizes the propositions listed, respectively, in Tables 17–1 and 17–2.

In Table 17–1, Turner examines the simplest situation where an actor's interaction with others is confined to one situation. When so confined, others in that situation will identify the role as integral to the person's self-identification, and the person will accept this identification by others under the conditions listed in each of the eleven propositions. For example, if there is little flexibility in assuming a role (proposition 1), then merger of person and role is increased. In proposition 2, the more clearly defined and distinguishable the role, the greater the tendency for person-role merger. In proposition 3, the more that roles among person and others are in conflict, the greater the role-person merger. And so on for the remaining propositions. What is critical in these and other propositions in Tables 17–1, 17–2, and 17–3 is that they reveal co-variance between variables, and thus constitute true propositions.

Turner recognizes that social settings of actors often overlap. People see each other in different settings, but as they interact, they seek to discover which role is part of a person's self-identification. The five propositions in Table 17–2 are examples of some of the considerations that Turner views as operating in multiple social settings to influence role-person merger. People in multiple settings will be likely to identify the role with person, and the person will likely accept this identification, when: the role cuts across many social settings (no. 1), the role influences the other roles that a person can play and/or how they are played (no. 2), the role is highly conspicuous (no. 3), the role exemplifies, or personifies, the nature of the social unit in which it is lodged (no. 4). Proposition 5 is an example of a condition under which roles will not merge with the person. When a role is short-lived and inconsistent with other roles played by a person, then the individual will not identify with the role.

The propositions in Tables 17–1 and 17–2 have addressed the question of how others in situations discover a person-role merger. However, people are rarely passive, accepting the labels of others. People actively seek

Table 17–1
Others and Role Merger in One Situation

1. The more inflexible the allocation of actors to a role, the greater the tendency for members of the social circle to identify the role with the person and the stronger the tendency for the actors to accept that identification for themselves.

2. The more comprehensively and strictly differentiated the role, the greater the tendency for members of the social circle to identify the role with person and the stronger the tendency for the actors to accept that identification for themselves.

3. The more conflictual the relationship between roles, the greater the tendency for members of the social circle to identify the role with the person, and the stronger the tendency for the actors to accept that identification for themselves.

4. The higher and more consistent the judgments of role adequacy, the greater the tendency for members of the social circle to identify with the role with the person, and the stronger the tendency for the actors to accept that identification for themselves.

5. The more difficult the role is thought to be, the greater the tendency for members of the social circle to identify the role with the person, and the stronger the tendency for actors to accept that identification for themselves.

6. The more polar the evaluation of a role as favorable or unfavorable, the greater the tendency for members of the social circle to identify the role with the person, and the stronger the tendency for the actors to accept that identification for themselves.

7. The more polar the social rank of a role as high or low, the greater the tendency for members of the social circle to identify the role with the person and the stronger the tendency for the actors to accept that identification for themselves.

8. The greater the potential power vested in a role, the greater the tendency for members of the social circle to identify the role with the person and the stronger the tendency for the actors to accept that identification for themselves.

9. The greater the discretion vested in a role, the greater the tendency for members of the social circle to identify the role with the person and the stronger the tendency for the actors to accept that identification for themselves.

10. The greater the extent to which members of a social circle are bonded to role incumbents by ties of identification, the greater the tendency for them to identify the role with the person and the stronger the tendency for the actors to accept that identification for themselves.

11. The more intimate the role relationship between actors, social circle, and alter roles, the greater the tendency for them to identify the role with the person and the stronger the tendency for the actors to accept that identification for themselves.

to determine and influence the merger of self and a role. Turner recognizes this fact with his concept of role-making, thus requiring still more propositions on self and role merger.

Turner expands upon Mead's insight that the emergence of self-conceptions in individuals facilitates interaction and the functioning of society. Self provides individuals with a way to discriminate among roles and to partition them in terms of their importance and significance. If individuals could not do this, they would emotionally exhaust themselves. They could disrupt the flow of society by trying to play all roles equally well and with the same degree of intensity. Additionally, self allows

TABLE 17–2
Others, Person, and Role in Multiple Settings

1. The broader the setting in which a role is lodged, the greater the tendency for others to identify the role with the person and the stronger the tendency for the actors to accept that identification for themselves.

2. The greater the extent to which a role in one setting determines allocation and performance of roles in other settings, the greater the tendency for others to identify the role with the person and the stronger the tendency for the actors to accept that identification for themselves.

3. The more conspicuous and widely recognizable the role cues, the greater the tendency for others to identify the role with the person and the stronger the tendency for the actors to accept that identification for themselves.

4. The more a role exemplifies the goals and nature of the group or organization in which it is lodged, the greater the tendency for others to identify the role with the person and the stronger the tendency for the actors to accept that identification for themselves.

5. The more that allocation to a role is understood to be temporary, and the role discontinuous in content with respect to preceding and succeeding roles, the greater the tendency for community members not to identify the role with the person, and the stronger the tendency for the actors not to identify role with self.

actors to maintain an identity across roles and to resist sanctions that would force them to act in contradictory ways. And, finally, self gives action consistency and coherence across roles which allows others to anticipate that an actor will behave in a given way, thereby enabling others to adjust their response to the actor.

Turner then presents the propositions in Table 17–3. People are likely to locate their self in roles that are highly evaluated, that they can perform well, that are both highly evaluated *and* played well (actors will, by implication, avoid roles of high evaluation which they cannot play well), that are visible and more readily subject to evaluation by others, that are comprehensive and cut across social contexts, that provide personal and subjectively defined benefits, that involve the expenditure of time and effort, that involve sacrifice in reaching, that are publicly played and in need of public justification, and that involve prolonged role strain and effort to eliminate strain.

These propositions of "the person and role" listed in Tables 17–1, 17–2, and 17–3 are only tentative. They are, however, highly suggestive and testable. Moreover, they have been developed in the context of a larger theoretical strategy: to develop true empirical propositions that specify relations of co-variance among concepts, and that cohere around observed tendencies in human interaction. As has been noted, similar empirical propositions need to be developed for Turner's other tendency statements.

TABLE 17–3
Individual Efforts at Role Merger

1. The more highly evaluated a role, the greater the tendency to locate self in that role.

2. The more adequately a role can be performed, the greater the tendency to locate self in that role.

3. The higher the evaluation of roles among a repertoire of roles that can be played adequately, the greater the tendency to locate self in the roles of highest evaluation.

4. The more visible and readily appraisable role performance, the greater tendency to locate self in highly evaluated roles will be modified by the tendency to locate self in roles that can be played with high degrees of adequacy.

5. The more the scope of an individual's social world exceeds the boundaries of the social circle of a given role, the greater the tendency to use evaluations of the larger community rather than those of a specific social circle to locate self in a role.

6. The more intrinsic (as opposed to extrinsic) the benefits derived from enacting a role, the greater the tendency to locate self in that role.

7. The greater the investment of time and effort in gaining or maintaining the opportunity to claim a role, or in learning to play a role, the greater the tendency to locate self in that role.

8. The greater the sacrifice made in gaining or maintaining the opportunity to claim a role, or in learning to play a role, the greater the tendency to locate self in that role.

9. The more publicly a role is played and the more actors must explain and justify a role, the greater the tendency to locate self in that role.

10. The more unresolved role strain encountered in a role has been prolonged, the greater the tendency to locate self in that role.

Turner recognizes, however, that the empirical propositions represent only crude groupings of statements around tendencies. Such propositions are the result of "speculation" and they can, no doubt, suggest additional propositions. But these propositions are not organized *deductively*—that is, in a way that would allow empirical propositions to be deduced from a small number of abstract propositions or axioms. The next step in Turner's strategy, therefore, involves an effort to generate explanatory propositions.

Developing Explanatory Propositions

Turner has applied a number of different labels to what are termed here "explanatory" propositions.[27] Turner's avowed strategy is to ask the questions: Why should a series of empirical propositions cohere around a main tendency? Is there some common principle which would explain why the tendency should occur and why the empirical propositions with the tendency as the dependent variable should hold true?

---

[27] "A Strategy," and "Role Theory As Theory."

Once a number of potential explanatory propositions have been discovered, Turner suggests that efforts be made to determine if some have more explanatory power than others and if those with less power can be seen as derivatives of the more powerful propositions. In this way, explanatory propositions are consolidated into a small number of abstract statements from which lower-level explanatory propositions, empirical propositions, and main tendency propositions can be deduced.

Turner has only partially followed his avowed strategy. He tends to move rather quickly in his search for explanatory propositions to just two: (1) a proposition about *functionality* and (2) another proposition about *viability*.[28] His statement of these two propositions is not precise, and thus, it is necessary to explore each one briefly.

The Functionality "Proposition." Turner usually discusses this explanatory proposition in the context of the tendency for roles to become differentiated (tendency proposition 1), to use role cues (tendency 3), and to be assigned or allocated for the duration of an interaction (tendency 10). However, he views this proposition as a potential explanation of many more tendencies. He concentrates on these tendencies because he considers them to be the most important.

What is the functionality proposition? Turner never states it in propositional form, but rather as an assumption: "Shared or separate aims govern interaction, and activities are partitioned to serve the aims."[29] What Turner has in mind is the process of using roles "to get a job done." Functionality is thus *the processes whereby roles are used to achieve ends or goals in an effective and efficient manner.* As can be seen, however, Turner has not stated these functionality considerations as true propositions with at least two variables; it is simply a statement of fact: people often use roles as a way to efficiently and effectively reach goals and this fact will "explain" many tendency and empirical propositions.

Applying this functionality "proposition" to the tendency for role differentiation yields the following "deductive explanation": "The nature and degree of role differentiation tend to vary according to functional requirements of effectiveness and efficiency." For Turner, such an application "explains" role differentiation in a "deductive sense."

The Viability "Proposition." The viability proposition is also not stated as a true proposition, but rather as an assumption: "We speak of a role as viable when the conditions surrounding performance of

---

[28] Ibid.

[29] "A Strategy," p. 9.

that role make it possible to play it with some personal reward."[30] Thus, people must receive reinforcement, whether this be confirmation of self, bolstering of self-esteem, an equitable ratio of rights to duties, or some other consideration. Applying this "explanatory proposition" to the tendency for role differentiation results in the following "deductive explanation": "The nature and degree of role differentiation vary according to the requirements of role viability."

Turner's search for explanatory propositions does not end here, however. He then asks: When are functionality or viability considerations more likely to prevail? In his exploration for these conditions, Turner develops a series of true propositions:

1. The more goal-oriented interaction among individuals, the more operative are considerations of functionality and the less operative considerations of viability.
2. The more individuals bring to an interaction external power and other salient attributes, the more operative are considerations of viability and the less operative are considerations of functionality.

Each of these two propositions now possess at least two variables and thus can serve as more powerful explanatory propositions. Considerations of viability and functionality are now dependent variables that vary under the impact, respectively, of the external attributes of actors, such as power, and the degree of instrumentality of interaction.

Returning to the tendency proposition of role differentiation, Turner's explanation can be reconstructed in a more precise deductive format:

1. The more goal-oriented interaction among individuals, the more operative considerations of functionality and the less operative considerations of viability.
2. Plurality of actors, A, in situations, S, are seeking to reach specific goal, G.
3. Therefore, the more A interacts in S in pursuit of G, the more considerations of functionality, and the less considerations of viability, operate in the differentiation of roles among A in S.

In this way, the form of deductive theory is achieved, with a specific prediction about what should occur being deduced from a true abstract proposition.

Thus far, Turner's explanatory propositions have been applied only

---

[30] Ibid., p. 10.

to tendency propositions. Turner also intends that explanatory propositions be applied to empirical propositions. Turner's empirical propositions on "the person and role," summarized in Tables 17–1, 17–2, and 17–3, cannot all be examined here, and thus, only one will be explored with an eye to assessing the usefulness of Turner's explanatory propositions. What is said about the utility of Turner's strategy for this one proposition also applies to the others. What do Turner's explanatory propositions offer to the following empirical proposition?

> The greater the investment of time and effort in gaining or maintaining the opportunity to claim a role, the greater the tendency to locate self in that role.

This empirical proposition should, in principle, be deducible from Turner's two explanatory propositions. A crude deductive explanation can be developed, as in outlined below:

1. The more goal-oriented interaction among individuals, the more operative considerations of functionality and the less operative considerations of viability.
2. The more individuals bring to interaction external power and other salient attributes, the more operative are considerations of viability and the less operative considerations of functionality.
3. Investment of time and effort in claiming and maintaining a role usually means that an actor will bring to that role special attributes.
4. Therefore, by 2 above, the more individuals bring salient attributes to a role, the more operative are considerations of viability, and hence, the greater the tendency to locate self in that role.

Is this a precise deductive system? And, does it deductively "explain?" Clearly, it does not and cannot. But the attempt to deduce the empirical propositions does yield considerable insight into *why* people are willing to locate their self in a role. By working hard to claim and maintain a role, actors set up expectations that they should receive rewards proportionate to their investments. In other words, viability considerations become important. And when viability considerations become more important than functionality considerations, people are more willing to locate their self in—that is, to identify with—a role.

The insertion of the concept of viability also provides, as Turner intended, an explanation for *why* the independent variables in the other "person and role" propositions should increase the likelihood of self-location in roles. For example, to the extent that "role adequacy," "role evaluation," "role visibility," "scope of social world," "intrinsic benefits," and the other independent variables of Turner's empirical propositions on "individual efforts at role merger" (see earlier listings in table 17–3) can be seen as specific types or forms of the viability principle, then Turner has provided a common explanation of *why* people should locate self in a role. The "adequacy" of this common principle is suspect, since the subsumption of all these variables under the viability proposition could prove difficult.

Yet what Turner has done is attempt to unite role theory and research into propositions,.and most important, to explain deductively regularities and patterns in these propositions. He has chosen to be alone in this kind of effort and he has gone further than any other role theorist in this direction. His efforts must therefore be seen as first steps in the direction of unifying role theory and of bridging the gap between symbolic interactionism and role theory. Turner's accomplishments, and his strategy's future potential, must therefore be assessed in this light before closing this chapter on the future of role theory.

TURNER'S STRATEGY: A BRIEF ASSESSMENT

In assessing Turner's strategy, it is best to return to the issues of substance, method, and theory that have plagued interactionism. With regard to substantive issues, Turner's assumptions emphasize the fluid nature of interactive processes, but unlike Blumer he appears to hold a deterministic view of causality. Moreover, unlike Blumer, Turner does not make exaggerated claims about the range and scope of his theoretical efforts. His theoretical concerns are with individuals and the micro processes by which they come to terms with each other in varying types of social contexts. There is thus no claim that all social events can be understood by his "role theory"; but rather, to the extent that attention to the interactive processes of individuals is considered important, then Turner seems to argue that his approach is the most appropriate.

With respect to method, Turner's own empirical work on a variety of topics would attest to his recognition that operationalization of concepts is critical.[31] While observation techniques are an important research

---

[31] For representative examples of the variety of empirical research conducted by Turner, see "The Navy Disbursing Officer as a Bureaucrat," *American Sociological Review* 12 (June 1947):342–48; "Moral Judgement: A Study in Roles," *American Sociological Review* 17 (January 1952):70–77; "Occupational Patterns of Inequality," *American Journal of Sociology* 50 (March 1954):437–47; "Zoot-suiters and Mexicans: Symbols in Crowd Behavior" (with S. J. Surace), *American Journal of Sociology* 62 (July 1956):14–20; "The Changing Ideology of Success: A Study of Aspirations of High School Men in Los Angeles," *Transactions of the Third World Congress of Sociology* 5 (1956):35–

tool, survey and experimental techniques, utilizing structured measuring instruments, are also deemed appropriate.

Finally, Turner has been concerned with building theory. He has recognized that it is necessary to move beyond sensitizing frameworks to propositions, and that interactionism must begin to explore strategies for developing deductive relations among propositions. While his "functionality" and "viability" propositions may prove less useful than he contends, he has at least developed a strategy that can perhaps yield more powerful propositions.

In sum, then, Turner's "role theory" represents an effort to incorporate all varieties of symbolic interactionism and role theory into a conceptual framework and strategy that stresses theory building and theory-testing. The general direction and thrust of his approach will need to be emulated if interactionism is to become a more viable theoretical perspective.

44; "An Experiment in Modification of Role Conceptions," *Yearbook of the American Philosophical Society* (1959):329–32; "Some Family Determinists of Ambition," *Sociology and Social Research* 46 (July 1962):397–411; *The Social Context of Ambition* (San Francisco: Chandler, 1964); and "Ambiguity and Interchangeability in Role Attribution."

PART V:

Phenomenological and Ethnomethodological Theorizing

18

THE EMERGENCE OF PHENOMENOLOGY

THE PHENOMENOLOGICAL ALTERNATIVE

Most theoretical perspectives in sociology operate under a number of assumptions: (1) Reality exists external to individuals; once individuals come into interaction, they form social structures which constrain their subsequent interactions. Sociology must therefore inquire into the properties of social structure, as well as the processes that create, maintain, and change these structures. (2) Through the development of abstract theory, the nature of the social world can be understood. (3) In trying to understand the social world, the contaminating influence of human senses and intellectual biases can be suspended by the application of the scientific method.

Symbolic interactionists of the Chicago tradition might temper these assumptions by emphasizing the problems involved in employing structured measuring instruments and definitive concepts to understand a fluid social world mediated by mental and symbolic processes. Phenomenologists take the symbolic interactionist's concerns one step further: The subjective world of actors is a reality in itself. Theory should not be about what is "outside" consciousness, but it should be about how, and in what ways, the subjective states of actors are created, maintained, or changed.

In this chapter, attention will be focused on how the phenomenological position first emerged.[1] Particular emphasis will be given to the work of Edmund Husserl and Alfred Schutz, the titular founders of this theoretical orientation. It should be emphasized, however, that this analysis will be selective; the work of these two scholars will be assessed with regard to how it helped lay the groundwork for the topic of the next chapter, ethnomethodology.

EARLY PHENOMENOLOGY: EDMUND HUSSERL
(1859–1938)

The German philosopher, Edmund Husserl, is often credited with being the "father of phenomenology." There can be little doubt that his thought has profoundly influenced contemporary social science. Yet, as will become evident, his ideas have been transformed. Indeed, he would be upset at what is now attributed to his genius. As Z. Bauman notes: "It took guile, utterly illegitimate as viewed from the Husserlian perspective, to devise a social science which would claim to be the brainchild, or logical consequence of the phenomenological project."[2]

Husserl's ideas, then, have been selectively borrowed and used, in ways that he would not condone, to develop modern phenomenology. In reviewing Husserl's contribution, therefore, it is necessary to focus more on what was borrowed than on the details of his complete philosophical scheme. In reviewing Husserl's contribution, several features of his work will be highlighted:[3] (1) the basic philosophical dilemma, (2) the

---

[1] For some readable, general references on phenomenology, see George Psathas, ed., *Phenomenological Sociology* (New York: Wiley, 1973); Richard M. Zaner, *The Way of Phenomenology: Criticism as a Philosophical Discipline* (New York: Pegasus, 1970); Peter L. Berger and Thomas Luckman, *The Social Construction of Reality* (Garden City, N.Y.: Doubleday, 1966); Herbert Spiegelberg, *The Phenomenological Movement*, vols. I and II, 2d ed. (The Hague: Martinus Nijhoff, 1969); Hans P. Neisser, "The Phenomenological Approach in Social Science," *Philosophy and Phenomenology* 20 (1959): 198–212; Stephen Strasser, *Phenomenology and the Human Sciences* (Pittsburgh: Duquesne University Press, 1963); and Maurice Natonson, ed., *Phenomenology and the Social Sciences* (Evanston, Ill.: Northwestern University Press, 1973); Quentin Lauer, *Phenomenology: Its Genesis and Prospect* (New York: Harper Torchbooks, 1965).

[2] Bauman, "On the Philosophical Status of Ethnomethodology," *The Sociological Review* 21 (February 1973): 6.

[3] Husserl's basic ideas are contained in the following: *Phenomenology and the Crisis of Western Philosophy* (New York: Harper & Row, 1965, originally published 1936); *Ideas: General Introduction to Pure Phenomenology* (London: Collier-Macmillan, 1969, originally published in 1913); "Phenomenology" in *The Encyclopedia Britannica*, 14th ed., vol. 17, col. 699–702, 1929. For excellent secondary analyses, see: Helmut R. Wagner, "The Scope of Phenomenological Sociology" in Psathas, *Phenomenological Sociology*, pp. 61–86 and "Husserl and Historicism," *Social Research* 39 (Winter 1972): 696–719; Aron Gurwitsch, "The Common-Sense World as Social Reality," *Social Research* 29 (Spring, 1962): 50–72; Robert J. Antonio, "Phenomenological Sociology" in George Ritzer, *Sociology: A Multiple Paradigm Science* (Boston: Allyn & Bacon, 1975), pp. 109–112; Robert Welsh Jordan, "Husserl's Phenomenology as an 'Historical Science'," *Social Research* 1 (Spring 1966): 243–259.

properties of consciousness, (3) the critique of naturalistic empiricism, and (4) the philosophical alternative to social science.

The Basic Philosophical Problem

Basic questions confronting all inquiry are: What is real? What actually exists in the world? How is it possible to know what exists? As a philosopher, these were central questions for Husserl. They required attention. Husserl reasoned that humans know about the world only through experience. All notions of an external world, "out there," are mediated through the senses and can only be known through mental consciousness. The existence of other people, values, or norms, and physical objects is always mediated by experiences as they register on people's conscious awareness. One does not directly have contact with reality; contact is always indirect and mediated through the processes of the human mind.

Since the process of consciousness is so important and central to knowledge, philosophic inquiry must attempt to understand how this process operates and how it influences human affairs. It is this concern with the process of consciousness—of how experience creates a sense of an external reality—that was to become the central concern of phenomenology.

The Properties of Consciousness

Husserl initially made reference to the "world of the natural attitude." Later, he was to use the phrase "life world." In either case, with these concepts he emphasized that humans operate in a taken-for-granted world that permeates their mental life. It is the world that humans sense to exist. It is composed of the objects, peoples, places, ideas, and other things that people "see" and "perceive" as "out there" in the external world and as setting the parameters for their existence, for their activities, and for their pursuits.

This "life world" or "world of the natural attitude" *is* reality for humans. Two features of Husserl's conception of "natural attitude" were to become the foundations of modern phenomenology and should be emphasized:

1. The "life world" is taken for granted. It is rarely the topic of reflective thought; and yet, it structures and shapes the way people act and think.
2. Humans operate on the presumption that they experience the same world. Since each person experiences only their own consciousness, the individual has little capacity to directly determine if this presump-

tion is correct. Yet people act *as if* they experienced a common world.

Human activity, then, is conducted in a life world that is taken for granted and that is presumed to be experienced collectively. This fact brought Husserl back to his original problem: How do humans break out of their life world and ascertain what is real? If people's life-world structures their consciousness and their actions, how is an objective science of human behavior and organization possible? These questions led Husserl to criticize what he termed, "naturalistic-science," or what is now labeled, "positivism."

The Critique of Science

Science assumes that a factual world exists "out there," independent of, and external to, human senses and consciousness. Through the scientific method, this factual world can be directly known. With successive efforts at its measurement, increasing understanding of its properties can be ascertained. But Husserl challenged this vision of science: If one can only know through consciousness and if consciousness is structured by an implicit "life world," then how can objective measurement of some "external" and "real" world be possible? How is science able to "measure" objectively an external world when the only world that individuals experience is the "life world" of their consciousness?

Husserl's Radical Solution

Husserl's solution to this problem is a philosophical one. He advocated what he termed the search for the "essence" of consciousness. To understand social events, the basic process through which these events are mediated—that is, consciousness—must be comprehended. The substantive *content* of consciousness, or the life world, is not what is important, but the abstract processes of consciousness, per se, are to be the topic of philosophic inquiry.

Husserl advocated what he termed the "radical abstraction" of the individual from interpersonal experience. Investigators must suspend their natural attitude and seek to understand the fundamental processes of consciousness, per se. One must discover, in Husserl's words, "Pure Mind." To do this it is necessary to perform "epoch,"—that is, to see if the substance of one's life world can be suspended. Only when divorced of the substance of the life world can the fundamental and abstract properties of consciousness be exposed and understood. And with understanding of these properties, then real insight into the nature of reality would be possible. For if all that humans know is presented through consciousness, it is necessary to understand the nature of consciousness in abstraction from the specific substance or content of the "life world" or "natural attitude" that is created by the fundamental processes of consciousness.

It should be cautioned that Husserl was not advocating Max Weber's method of *verstehen*, or sympathetic introspection into an investigator's own mind. Nor was he suggesting the unstructured and intuitive search for people's definitions of situations. These methods would, he argued, only produce data on the substance of the life world and would be no different than the structured measuring instruments of positivism. Rather, Husserl's goal was to create an abstract theory of consciousness that bracketed out, or suspended, any presumption of an external social world "out there."

Husserl's Contribution to Phenomenology

Husserl's philosophical doctrine failed. He never succeeded in developing an abstract theory of consciousness, radically abstracted from the life world. But his ideas set into motion a new line of thought which was to become the basis for modern phenomenology and for its elaboration into ethnomethodology.

Husserl's basic ideas which now serve modern phenomenology can be summarized as follows:

1. The emphasis on the abstract process of consciousness stimulated thinkers to inquire into how the basic mental processes of individuals shape the nature of the social world. Rather than viewing the world as imposed upon consciousness, concern shifted to how it is created out of the subjective processes of the human mind.
2. The concern with the creation of a "life world" led scholars to question how humans create a *sense* of reality and how this sense of reality, as opposed to some "really real," external world, can be the main ingredient in resolving the problem of order.
3. The critique of social science has served others in phenomenology who suggest that an objective science of humans may not be possible, or at the very least, will not be the same as the science of the physical world.
4. The failure of Husserl's radical solution appears to have convinced phenomenologists that understanding of human consciousness and social reality can only occur by examining individuals in actual interaction (not in bracketed, radical abstraction).

Today, the term "phenomenology" denotes a variety of intellectual approaches. As Natanson notes, phenomenology is "a generic term to include all the positions that stress the primacy of consciousness and subjective meaning in the interpretation of social action."[4] The transformation of Husserl's radical phenomenology into this general rubric occurred through the efforts of another social philosopher, Alfred Schutz.

THE PHENOMENOLOGY OF ALFRED SCHUTZ
(1899–1959)

Alfred Schutz migrated to the United States in 1939 from Austria, after spending a year in Paris. With his interaction in American intellectual circles, and the translation of his early works into English over the last decades, Schutz's contribution to sociological theorizing is becoming increasingly recognized.[5] As will be emphasized, his contribution resides in his ability to blend Husserl's radical phenomenology with Max Weber's action theory and American interactionism. This blend was, in turn, to stimulate the further development of phenomenology and the emergence of ethnomethodology.

Schutz's Analysis of Max Weber

As was emphasized in Chapter 14 on the emergence of interactionism, the German sociologist Max Weber employed the concept of "social action" in his many and varied inquiries. Social action occurs when actors are consciously aware of each other and attribute meanings to their common situation. For Weber, then, a science of society must seek to understand social reality "at the level of meaning." Sociological inquiry must penetrate people's consciousness and discover how they view, define, and see the world. Weber advocated the method of "verstehen," or "sympathetic introspection." Investigators must become sufficiently involved in situations to be able to get inside the subjective world of actors. Causal and statistical analysis of complex social structures would be incomplete and inaccurate without such verstehen analysis.

Schutz's first major work addressed Weber's conception of action.[6]

---

[4] Maurice Natanson, "Philosophy and Social Science," in Literature, Philosophy and Social Science (The Hague: Nijhoff, 1968), p. 157.

[5] For basic ideas of Alfred Schutz, see his The Phenomenology of the Social World (Evanston, Ill.: Northwestern University Press, 1967; originally published in 1932); Collected Papers, vols. 1, 2, 3 (The Hague: Martinus Nijhoff, 1964, 1970, and 1971, respectively). For excellent secondary analyses, see Maurice Natanson, "Alfred Schutz on Social Reality and Social Science," Social Research 1 (Spring 1966): 217–44.

[6] The Phenomenology of the Social World, 1932.

His analysis is critical and detailed, but turns on Weber's failure to use his *verstehen* method and to explore *why*, and through what processes, actors come to share common meanings. In Schutz's eye, Weber simply assumes that actors share subjective meanings, leading Schutz to ask: Why and how do actors come to acquire common subjective states in a situation? How do they create a common view of the world? This is the problem of *intersubjectivity* and it is central to Schutz's intellectual scheme. As Richard D. Zaner summarizes:

> How is it possible that although I cannot live in your seeing of things, cannot feel your love and hatred, cannot have an immediate and direct perception of your mental life as it is for you—how is it that I can nevertheless share your thoughts, feelings, and attitudes? For Schutz the "problem" of intersubjectivity is here encountered in its full force.[7]

Schutz's Departure from Husserl

Schutz was profoundly influenced by Husserl's phenomenology. And yet he departs immediately from Husserl's strategy of holding the individual in "radical abstraction" and of searching for "Pure Mind" or the abstract laws of consciousness. He accepts Husserl's notion that humans hold a "natural attitude" and "life world" that is taken-for-granted and that shapes who they are and what they will do. He also accepts Husserl's notion that people perceive that they share the same life world and act *as if* they lived in a common world of experiences and sensations. Moreover, Schutz acknowledges the power of Husserl's argument that social scientists cannot know about an external social world "out there" independently of their own life world.

Having accepted these lines of thought from Husserl, however, Schutz advocates Weber's strategy of sympathetic introspection into people's consciousness. Only by observing people in interaction, rather than in radical abstraction, can the processes whereby actors come to share the same world be discovered. Social science cannot come to understand how and why actors create a common subjective world independently of watching them do so. This abandonment of Husserl's phenomenological project liberated phenomenology from philosophy and allowed sociologists to study empirically what Schutz considered the most important social reality: the creation and maintenance of intersubjectivity—that is, a common subjective world among pluralities of interacting individuals.

---

[7] Richard M. Zaner, "Theory of Intersubjectivity: Alfred Schutz," *Social Research* (Spring 1961), p. 76.

Contact with Early Symbolic Interactionists

With his immigration to the United States, Schutz's phenomenology came under the influence of early symbolic interactionists, particularly G. H. Mead and W. I. Thomas. While he devotes some attention to symbolic interactionism,[8] the influence of this orientation on Schutz may have been subtle, if not subliminal. The early symbolic interactionist's concern with the process of constructing shared meanings was, of course, similar to Schutz's desire to understand intersubjectivity. Schutz thus found immediate affinity with W. I. Thomas' concept of "definition of the situation," since this concept emphasizes that actors construct orientations to, and dispositions to act in, situations. Moreover, Thomas' recognition that definitions of situations are learned from past experiences while being altered in present interactions appears to have influenced his conceptualization of the process of intersubjectivity.

George Herbert Mead, as was emphasized in Chapter 14, was concerned with how mind, self, and society are interrelated and interdependent. Mead's recognition that mind is a social process, arising out of interaction, and yet facilitating interaction, probably had considerable appeal for Schutz. A more important influence on Schutz, however, is Mead's concept of role-taking by which actors assume the attitude of others through the interpretation of gestures. For, indeed, Schutz became vitally concerned with the process whereby actors come to know each other's role and to typify each other as likely to behave in certain ways. Additionally, Mead's concept of the "generalized other" may have influenced Schutz in that actors are seen with this concept as sharing a "community of attitudes"—or, in other words, common subjective states. Yet, while there is considerable affinity, and perhaps some cross-fertilization, between early symbolic interactionist's conceptualizations and Schutz's phenomenology, Schutz was to inspire a line of sociological inquiry that leads away from interactionism.

Having reviewed some of the intellectual influences on Schutz, it is now possible to summarize his scheme and its implications for sociological theorizing. Unfortunately, Schutz died just as he was beginning a systematic synthesis of his ideas, and thus only a somewhat fragmented, but suggestive framework, is evident in Schutz's collective work. But his analysis of Weber, Husserl, and interactionism led him to become concerned with a number of key issues: (1) How do actors create a common subjective world? (2) What implications does this creation have for how social order is maintained?

---

[8] See his *Collected Papers* for references to interactionists.

Schutz's Phenomenological Orientation

All humans, Schutz asserts, carry in their minds rules, social recipes, conceptions of appropriate conduct, and other information that allows them to act in their social world. Extending Husserl's concept of "life world," Schutz views the sum total of these rules, recipes, conceptions, and information as the individual's "stock knowledge at hand." Such "stock knowledge" gives people a frame of reference or orientation with which they can interpret events as they pragmatically act on the world around them.

Several features of this "stock knowledge at hand" are given particular emphasis by Schutz:

1. People's reality *is* their stock knowledge. For the members of a society, their stock knowledge constitutes a "paramount reality"— a sense of an absolute reality that shapes and guides all social events. Actors use this stock knowledge and sense of reality as they pragmatically seek to deal with others in their environment.

2. The existence of stock knowledge which bestows a sense of reality on events gives the social world, as Schutz argued along with Husserl, a taken-for-granted character. The stock knowledge is rarely the object of conscious reflection but rather an implicit set of assumptions and procedures which are silently used by individuals as they interact.

3. Stock knowledge is learned. It is acquired through socialization within a common social and cultural world, but it becomes *the* reality for actors in this world.

4. People operate under a number of assumptions which allows them to create a sense of a "reciprocity of perspectives": (*a*) Others with whom an actor must deal are considered to share an actor's stock knowledge at hand. (*b*) Others may have unique components in their stock knowledge because of their particular biographies, but these can be ignored by an actor when dealing with others.

5. The existence of stock knowledge, its acquisition through socialization, and the assumptions that give actors a reciprocity of perspectives all operate to give actors in a situation a *sense* or *presumption* that the world is the same for all and that it reveals identical properties for all. What often "holds society together" is this presumption of a common world.

6. The presumption of a common world allows actors to engage in the process of "typification." Action in most situations, except the most personal and intimate, can proceed through mutual typification as actors use their stock knowledge to categorize each other and

to adjust their responses to these typifications.[9] With typification, actors can effectively deal with their world, since every nuance and characteristic of their situation does not have to be examined. Moreover, typification facilitates entrance into the world; it simplifies adjustment because it allows for humans to treat each other as categories, or as "typical" objects of a particular kind.

These points of emphasis in Schutz's thought represent, as was noted earlier, a blending of ideas from European phenomenology and American interactionism. The emphasis on "stock knowledge" is clearly borrowed from Husserl, but it is highly compatible with Mead's notion of the "generalized other." The concern with the taken-for-granted character of the world as it is shaped by stock knowledge is also borrowed from Husserl, but similar to early interactionists' discussions of habit and routine behaviors. The emphasis on the acquired nature of stock knowledge coincides with early interactionists' discussions of the socialization process. The concern with the reciprocity of perspectives and with the process of typification owes much to Husserl and Weber, but more to Mead's notion of role-taking by which actors read each other's role and perspective. But the major departure from interactionism should also be emphasized: Actors operate on an unverified *presumption* that they share a common world; and this *sense* of a common world, and the practices that produce this sense, may be more important in maintaining social order than the content or substance of a common world. Social order, in other words, may be possible not so much by stock knowledge, reciprocity of perspectives, or successful typification, but by actors' presumption that they share intersubjective states. Schutz did not carry this line of inquiry far, but it was to inspire new avenues of phenomenological inquiry.

Schutz's Contribution

Schutz is primarily responsible for liberating Husserl's concern with the basic properties and processes of consciousness from radical abstraction. Schutz brought Husserl's vision of a "life world" back into the process of interaction. In so doing, he began to ask how actors come to share, or presume that they share, intersubjective states. He borrowed from interactionists' concern with socialization and role-taking as well as from their concern with pragmatic actors seeking to cope with their world, but he gave these concerns a new twist: Humans act *as if* they

---

[9] Ralph H. Turner's emphasis on role differentiation and accretion is an example of how these ideas have been extended by role theorists. See Chapter 17.

see the world in similar ways and they deal with each other *as if* others could be typified and categorized. If these presumptions allow for adjustment, social order is maintained not so much by real and external rules, codes, communities of attitudes, and the like, but by the practices that produce the illusion that there is a common world. As will become evident in the next chapter, this point of emphasis was to become the basis of ethnomethodology.

THE STATE OF CURRENT PHENOMENOLOGY: A CONCLUDING COMMENT

Phenomenologists vary in their willingness to acknowledge an external social world independent of people's subjective states of consciousness. Some argue for a bracketing of assumptions about an external world— suggesting much like Husserl that a prior concern must be processes of consciousness that create this world. Others argue that the exploration of human consciousness must be systematically linked to events in the external world. What is clear, however, is that current phenomenology, to the degree that it is to be distinguished from Chicago School symbolic interactionism, has yet to become a unified or coherent theoretical perspective.[10] It represents, at present, a series of criticisms of current theorizing and a set of assertions about the primacy of studying the processes of human consciousness.

In American sociology, the concerns of phenomenologists have been extended by ethnomethodologists. While ethnomethodologists often disagree, the legacy of Husserl and Schutz has been extended into an alternative theoretical paradigm—one that challenges the assumptions of most sociological theory.

---

[10] For a sampling of opinions and evaluations of phenomenology, see Robert J. Antonio, "Phenomenological Sociology"; Maurice Natanson, "Philosophy and Social Science"; Peter K. Manning, "Existential Sociology," *The Sociological Quarterly* 14 (Spring 1973): 200–225; James L. Heap and Phillip A. Roth, "On Phenomenological Sociology," *American Sociological Review* 38 (June 1973): 354–67; Edward A. Tiryakian, "Existential Phenomenology," *American Sociological Review* 30 (October 1965): 674–88.

19

ETHNOMETHODOLOGY

THE ETHNOMETHODOLOGICAL CHALLENGE

Common to all the dominant efforts among mainstream sociologists to understand society is the presumption that patterns of social organization are *real and external entities,* which can be described and studied through the use of various theoretical constructs and methodologies. Not at issue in the jurisdictional disputes and quibbles among proponents of the various conceptual perspectives in sociology is the presumption that society is "out there" waiting to be studied. What is at issue are the concepts, theory-building strategies, and methodologies that will best capture the essence of "society."

All this perhaps seems so obvious and self-evident to most sociologists that it is rarely discussed. Recently, however, just this issue has been debated. Drawing their inspiration from phenomenology, and to some extent, from interactionism, some scholars are now asking a fundamental and disturbing question: What should sociologists study? This is not a mere jurisdictional dispute over whether sociologists should develop theories of micro and macro processes; whether society should be viewed in terms of action, symbolic interaction, or exchange; and whether conflict-consensus and stability-change dominate the social scene. Rather, the question concerns whether sociological theory should continue to operate under the presumption that society is amenable to study by current theoretical perspectives. This challenge raises an alternative theoretical question: How do sociologists and other groups of humans create and sustain for each other the *presumption* that the social world has a real character. A "more real" phenomenon for those who propose this question revolves around the complex ways people (laypersons and sociologists alike) go about consciously and unconsciously constructing, maintaining, and altering their "sense" of an external social reality. In fact, the cement that holds society together may not be the values, norms, common definitions, exchange payoffs, role bargains, interest coalitions, and the like of current social theory, but people's explicit and implicit "methods" for creating the presumption of a social order.

Such is the challenge of the relatively recent sociological perspective, ethnomethodology. For the ethnomethodologist, what is directly observable are people's efforts to create a common sense of social reality. The substance of this reality is viewed as less interesting than the *methods* used by groups of persons, whether sociologists or laypersons, to construct, reaffirm, and alter a vision and image of what exists "out there." It is perhaps appropriate, therefore, that a book on sociological theory should close with a perspective which challenges the appropriateness of its contents.

THE EMERGENCE OF ETHNOMETHODOLOGY

Ethnomethodology borrows and extends ideas from both symbolic interactionism and phenomenology. In extending the ideas of these schools of thought, however, ethnomethodology begins to posit a different view of the world—thus making it an alternative paradigm in sociology. To appreciate just how this alternative paradigm differs from more traditional forms of sociological theory, it should be assessed in relation to those perspectives with which it is often confused, but from which it still has drawn considerable inspiration.

Blumer's Interactionism and Ethnomethodology

As was emphasized in Chapter 15, Herbert Blumer's interactionism emphasized the constructed and fluid nature of interaction. Because actors possess extensive symbolic capacities, they are capable of: (*a*) introjecting new objects into situations, (*b*) redefining situations, and (*c*) realigning their joint-actions. As Blumer emphasizes, "it would be wise to recognize that any given [act] is mediated by acting units interpreting the situations with which they are confronted."[1] While these situations

---

[1] Herbert Blumer, "Society as Symbolic Interaction" in A. Rose, ed., *Human Behavior and Social Process* (Boston: Houghton Mifflin, 1962).

consist of norms, values, roles, beliefs, and social structures, these are merely types of many "objects" that can be symbolically introjected and reshuffled to produce new definitions of situations.

These ideas advocate a concern with how meanings, or definitions, are created by actors interacting in situations. The emphasis is on the *process* of interaction and on how actors create common meanings in dealing with each other. This line of inquiry is also pursued by ethnomethodologists. The ethnomethodologist also focuses on interaction and on the creation of meanings in situations. But there is an important shift in emphasis: In what ways do people create a *sense* that they share a common view of the world? And how do people arrive at the *presumption* that there is an objective, external world? Blumer's interactionism stresses the process of creating meaning, but it acknowledges the existence of an external social order. Ethnomethodology suspends, or "brackets" in Husserl's terms, the issue of whether or not there is an external world of norms, roles, values, and beliefs. Instead, it concentrates on how interaction creates among actors a *sense* of a factual world "out there."

Goffman's Dramaturgical Analysis and Ethnomethodology

Paul Attewell has argued that the work of the symbolic interactionist, Erving Goffman, represents a significant source of inspiration for ethnomethodology.[2] Goffman's work has often been termed the "dramaturgical school" of interactionism because it focuses upon the ways that actors manipulate gestures to create an impression in a particular social scene. Goffman tends to emphasize the process of impression management, per se, and not the purposes or goals toward which action is directed. Much of Goffman's analysis thus concentrates on the form of interaction itself rather than on the structures it creates, sustains, or changes.[3] For example, Goffman has insightfully analyzed how actors validate self-conceptions, how they justify their actions through gestures, how they demonstrate their membership in groups, how they display social distance, how they adjust to physical stigmas, and how they interpersonally manipulate many other situations.

---

[2] Paul Attewell, "Ethnomethodology Since Garfinkel," *Theory and Society* 1 (1974): 179–210.

[3] This is not always true, especially in some of his more institutional works, such as *Asylums* (Garden City, New York: Anchor Books, 1961). Other representative works by Goffman include *The Presentation of Self in Everyday Life* (Garden City, New York: Doubleday, 1959); *Interaction Ritual* (Garden City, New York: Anchor, 1967); *Encounters* (Indianapolis: Bobbs-Merrill, 1961); *Stigma* (Englewood Cliffs, N.J.: Prentice-Hall, 1963).

This concern with the management of social scenes is also prominent in ethnomethodological analysis. Ethnomethodologists share Goffman's concern with the techniques by which actors create impressions in social situations, but their interest is not with individuals' impression-management, but with how actors create a *sense* of a common reality. Ethnomethodologists thus concentrate on interactional techniques, but they ask a somewhat different question than Goffman. That is: How do such interpersonal techniques sustain a sense of social reality?

Phenomenology and Ethnomethodology

Schutz's phenomenology, as was noted in the last chapter, liberated phenomenology from Husserl's philosophical project.[4] It asserted the importance of studying how interaction creates and maintains a "paramount reality." It placed particular emphasis on how actors achieve reciprocity of perspectives and how they construct a taken-for-granted world that gives order to social life.

This emphasis on the taken-for-granted nature of the world and the importance of this "life world" for maintaining actor's sense of reality becomes a prime concern of ethnomethodologists. Indeed, many ethnomethodological concepts are borrowed or adapted from Husserl's and Schutz's phenomenology. Yet ethnomethodologists adapt phenomenological analysis to the issue of how social order is maintained by the practices that actors use to create a sense that they share the same "life world."

In sum, then, ethnomethodology draws from and extends the concerns of interactionists such as Blumer and Goffman and the phenomenological projects of Husserl and Schutz. It emphasizes the process of interaction, the use of interpersonal techniques to create situational impressions, and the importance of perceived consensus among actors over the nature of the world in maintaining social order. In extending interactionism and phenomenology, ethnomethodology begins to posit a different vision of the social world and an alternative orientation for understanding the Hobbesian problem of how social organization is created, maintained, and changed. But as Hugh Mehan and Houston Wood note, the Hobbesian problem of order is rephrased:

> [Hobbes] was led to ask how order is possible. Contemporary theorists reject Hobbes' answer, but retain his question. [We] have chosen to ask

---

[4] See, in particular, the works of Schutz: Alfred Schutz, *Collected Papers I: The Problem of Social Reality*, ed. Maurice Natanson (The Hague: Martinus Nijhoff, 1962); Alfred Schutz, *Collected Papers II: Studies in Social Theory*, ed. Arvid Broderson (The Hague: Martinus Nijhoff, 1964); and Alfred Schutz, *Collected Papers III: Studies in Phenomenological Philosophy* (The Hague: Martinus Nijhoff, 1966).

not how order is possible, but rather to ask *how a sense of order is possible* [emphasis added].[5]

ETHNOMETAPHYSICS OR ETHNOMETHODOLOGY?

Ethnomethodology has often been misunderstood by sociologists. Part of the reason for this misunderstanding stems from the vagueness of the prose of some ethnomethodologists,[6] but perhaps a more fundamental reason derives from the fact that sociologists who have been steeped in the theoretical traditions outlined in Chapters 1 through 17 have had difficulty recognizing a radical alternative to these traditions. Indeed, even with clear and readable sources now available, most sociologists would profess not to understand the ethnomethodological position— perhaps indicating that their commitment to existing modes of theorizing operates as a set of intellectual blinders. In addition, even when authors assume to understand ethnomethodology, misinterpretations still abound.

One form of such misinterpretation asserts that ethnomethodology represents a "corrective" to current sociological theorizing by pointing to sources of bias among scientific investigators. From this position, it is assumed that ethnomethodology can serve to "check" the reliability and validity of investigators' observations by exposing not only their biases, but those of the scientific community accepting their observations. While ethnomethodology might be used for this purpose, if one were so inclined, those who advocate this use have failed to grasp the main thrust of the ethnomethodological position. For the ethnomethodologist, emphasis is not upon questions about the reliability and validity of investigators' observations, but upon the methods used by "scientific" investigators and laypersons alike to construct, maintain, and perhaps alter what each considers and believes to be a "valid" and "reliable" set of statements about order in the world. The "methodology" in the ethnomethodological

---

[5] Hugh Mehan and Houston Wood, *The Reality of Ethnomethodology* (New York: Wiley, 1975), p. 190. This is an excellent statement of the ethnomethodological perspective.

[6] See, for example, Garfinkel, *Studies in Ethnomethodology* (Englewood Cliffs, N.J.: Prentice-Hall, 1967). However, recent portrayals of the ethnomethodological position have done much to clarify this initial vagueness. See, for example: Mehan and Wood, *The Reality of Ethnomethodology;* D. Lawrence Wieder, *Language and Social Reality* (The Hague: Mouton, 1973); Don H. Zimmerman and Melvin Pollner, "The Everyday World as Phenomenon" in J. D. Douglas, ed., *Understanding Everyday Life* (Chicago: Aldine, 1970), pp. 80–103; Don H. Zimmerman and D. Lawrence Wieder, "Ethnomethodology and the Problem of Order: Comment on Denzin" in *Understanding Everyday Life*, pp. 285–95; Randall Collins and Michael Makowsky, *The Discovery of Society* (New York: Random House, 1972), pp. 209–13; George Psathas, "Ethnomethods and Phenomenology," *Social Research* 35 (September 1968): 500–520; and Roy Turner, ed., *Ethnomethodology* (Baltimore: Penguin, 1974).

perspective does not address questions about the "proper," "unbiased," or "truly scientific" search for knowledge; rather, ethnomethodology is concerned with the common methods people employ—whether scientists, housewives, insurance salespersons, or laborers—to create a sense of order about the situations in which they interact. The best clue to this conceptual emphasis can be found in the word, "ethnomethodology"—*ology*, "study of"; *method*, "the methods [used by]"; and *ethno*, "folk or people."

Another related source of misunderstanding in commentaries on ethnomethodology comes from those who assume that this perspective simply seeks to use "soft" research methods, such as participant observation, to uncover some of the taken-for-granted rules, assumptions, and rituals of members in groups.[7] This interpretation would appear to transform ethnomethodology into a research-oriented variant of the symbolic interactionist perspective.[8] Such a variant of ethnomethods would now represent a more conscientious effort to "get at" actors' interpretative processes and the resulting "definitions of the situation." By employing various techniques for observation of, and participation in, the symbolic world of those interacting individuals under study, a more accurate reading of how situations are defined, how norms emerge, and how social action is controlled could be achieved. While ethnomethodologists do employ observation and participant methods to study interacting individuals, their concerns are not the same as those of symbolic interactionists. Like all dominant forms of sociological theorizing, interactionists operate under the presumption that common definitions, values, and norms emerge from interaction and serve to regulate how people perceive the world and interact with each other. For the interactionist, concern is with the conditions under which various types of explicit and implicit definitions, norms, and values emerge and thereby resolve the problem of how social organization is possible. In contrast, ethnomethodologists are interested in *how* members come to agree upon an *impression* that there are such things as rules, definitions, and values. Just what types of rules and definitions emerge is not a central concern of the ethnomethodologist, since there are more fundamental questions: Through *what types of methods* do people go about seeing, describing, and asserting that rules and definitions exist? How do people use their beliefs that definitions and rules exist to describe for each other the "social order"?

---

[7] For example, see Norman K. Denzin, "Symbolic Interactionism and Ethnomethodology," *American Sociological Review* 34 (December 1969): 922–34.

[8] For another example of this interpretation, see Walter L. Wallace, *Sociological Theory* (Chicago: Aldine Publishing Co., 1969), pp. 34–36.

Thus, again, the "methods" of ethnomethodology do not refer to a new and improved technique on the part of scientific sociology for deriving a more accurate picture of peoples' definitions of the situation and of the norms of social structure (as is the case with interactionists). For the ethnomethodologist, emphasis is on the *methods employed by those under study* in creating, maintaining, and altering their presumption that a social order, forcing certain kinds of behavior, actually exists "out there" in the "real" world.

CONCEPTS AND PRINCIPLES OF ETHNOMETHODOLOGY

Alfred Schutz postulated one basic reality—the paramount—in which peoples' conduct of their everyday affairs occurs.[9] Most contemporary ethnomethodologists, however, are less interested in whether or not there is one or multiple "realities," "life-worlds," or "natural attitudes." Far more important in ethnomethodological analysis is the development of concepts and principles that can help explain how peoples' sense of reality is constructed, maintained, and changed. While ethnomethodology has yet to develop a unified body of concepts or propositions, it is possible to visualize the broad outlines of a conceptual core to the ethnomethodological perspective. This core consists of two key concepts: (1) reflexivity, (2) indexicality, as well as an emerging series of propositions. This conceptual core is explored below.

Reflexive Action and Interaction[10]

Much interaction operates to sustain a particular vision of reality. For example, ritual activity directed toward the gods sustains the belief that gods influence everyday affairs. Such ritual activity is an example of reflexive action; it operates to maintain a certain vision of reality. Even when the "facts" would seem to contradict a belief, human interaction upholds the contradicted belief. For instance, should intense prayer and ritual activity not bring forth the desired intervention from the gods, rather than reject beliefs in the gods the devout proclaim that "they did not pray hard enough," that "their cause was not just," or that "the gods in their wisdom have a greater plan." Such behavior is

---

[9] See Chapter 18.

[10] For an early discussion of this phenomenon, see: Garfinkel, *Studies in Ethnomethodology*. A more readable discussion can be found in Mehan and Wood, *The Reality of Ethnomethodology*, pp. 137–78.

reflexive; it upholds or reinforces a belief, even in the face of evidence that the belief may be incorrect.

Much human interaction is reflexive. Humans interpret cues, gestures, words, and other information from each other in a way that sustains a particular vision of reality. Even contradictory evidence is reflexively interpreted to maintain a body of belief and knowledge. The concept of reflexivity thus focuses attention on how people in interaction go about maintaining the presumption that they are guided by a particular reality. Much of ethnomethodological inquiry will address the question of how reflexive interaction occurs. That is, what concepts and principles can be developed to explain the conditions under which different reflexive actions among interacting parties are likely to occur.

The Indexicality of Meaning

The gestures, cues, words, and other information sent and received by interacting parties have meaning in a *particular context*. Without some knowledge of the context—the biographies of the interacting parties, their avowed purpose, their past interactive experiences, and so forth—it would easily be possible to misinterpret the symbolic communication among interacting individuals. The fact of interactive life is denoted by the concept of indexicality.[11] To say that an expression is indexical is to emphasize that the meaning of that expression is tied to a particular context.

This phenomenon of indexicality draws attention to the problem of how actors in a context construct a vision of reality in that context. They develop expressions that invoke their common vision about "what is real" in their situation. The concept of indexicality thus directs an investigator's attention to actual interactive contexts in order to see how actors go about creating indexical expressions—words, facial and body gestures, and other cues—to create and sustain the presumption that a particular reality governs their affairs.

With these two key concepts—reflexivity and indexicality—interactionists' concern with the process of symbolic communication is retained, while much of the phenomenological legacy of Schutz is rejuvenated. Concern is with how actors use gestures to create and sustain a "life world," "body of knowledge," or "natural attitude" about what is real. The emphasis is not on the context of the "life world," but on the

[11] Garfinkel, *Studies in Ethnomethodology;* Garfinkel and Sacks, "The Formal Properties of Practical Actions" in J. C. McKinney and E. A. Tiryakian, eds., *Theoretical Sociology* (New York: Appleton-Century-Crofts, 1970).

methods or techniques that actors use to create, maintain, or even alter a vision of reality. As Mehan and Wood note, "the ethnomethodological theory of the reality constructor is about the *procedures* that accomplish reality. It is not about any specific reality."[12] This emphasis has led to the isolation by ethnomethodologists of general types of methods employed by interacting actors.

Some General Interactive Methods

When analytical attention focuses on the methods that people use to construct their reality, the task of the theorist is to isolate the general types of interpersonal techniques that people employ in interaction. Aaron Cicourel, for example, has summarized a number of such techniques or methods isolated by ethnomethodologists: (1) searching for the normal form, (2) doing reciprocity of perspectives, and (3) using the et cetera principle.[13]

Searching for the Normal Form. If interacting parties sense that ambiguity exists over what is real and that their interaction is thus difficult, they will emit gestures to tell each other to return to what is "normal" in their contextual situation. Actors are presumed to hold a vision of a "normal" form for situations, or to be motivated to create one; and hence much of their action is designed to reach this form.

Doing a Reciprocity of Perspectives. Borrowing from Schutz's formulation, ethnomethodologists have emphasized that actors operate under the presumption, and actively seek to communicate the fact, that they would have the same experiences were they to switch places and that until so informed by specific gestures, they can each ignore differences in perspectives which might arise from their unique biographies. Thus, much interaction will be consumed with gestures that seek to assure others that a reciprocity of perspectives does indeed exist.

Using the Et Cetera Principle. In examining an actual interaction, much is left "unsaid." Actors must constantly "fill in" or "wait for" information necessary to "make sense" of another's words or deeds. When actors fill in or wait for needed information, they are using the "et cetera principle." They are agreeing not to disrupt the interaction by asking for the needed information; they are willing to wait or to fill in. For example, the common phrase, "you know," which usually appears

---

[12] Mehan and Wood, *The Reality of Ethnomethodology*, p. 114.

[13] Aaron V. Cicourel, *Cognitive Sociology* (London: Macmillan, 1973), pp. 85–88. It should be noted that these principles are implicit in Garfinkel's *Studies in Ethnomethodology*.

after an utterance, is often an assertion by one actor to another invoking the et cetera principle. The other is thus informed not to disrupt the interaction and the reality of the situation with a counter utterance, such as: "No, I do not know."

These three general types of "folk methods" are but examples of what ethnomethodologists seek to discover. There are certainly more folk methods; and the ultimate goal of ethnomethodological theory is to determine the conditions under which these and other interpersonal techniques will be used to construct, maintain, or change a reality. Few such propositions, however, can be found in the ethnomethodological literature. Yet the nature of propositions, should they ever be developed, should briefly be explored.

Two General Ethnomethodological Propositions

Ethnomethodological propositions will tend to follow from several assumptions: (1) Social order is maintained by the use of techniques that give actors a sense that they share a common reality. (2) The substance of the common reality is less important in resolving the problem of order than the acceptance by actors of a common set of techniques. With these assumptions, two examples of ethnomethodological propositions can be offered to illustrate what ethnomethodological theory may become:

1. The more actors fail to agree on the use of interactive techniques, such as the et cetera principle, the search for the normal form, and the doing reciprocity of perspectives, the more likely is interaction to be disrupted, and hence, the less likely is social order to be maintained.
2. The more interaction proceeds on the basis of different, taken-for-granted visions of reality, the more likely is interaction to be disrupted, and hence, the less likely is social order to be maintained.

These propositions can perhaps be visualized as general axioms from which more specific propositions on how actors go about constructing, maintaining, or changing their sense of reality. What is needed in ethnomethodology is to discover the *specific conditions* under which particular folk techniques are likely to be used to create a sense of a common world among interacting individuals. It is to this "filling in" of such general propositions that ethnomethodological theory and research must be directed if it is to pose a serious challenge and alternative to the currently dominant perspectives in sociology.

VARIETIES OF ETHNOMETHODOLOGICAL INQUIRY

Garfinkel's Pioneering Inquiries

Harold Garfinkel's *Studies in Ethnomethodology* firmly established ethnomethodology as a distinctive theoretical perspective.[14] While the book is not a formal theoretical statement, the studies reported and the surrounding commentary established the domain of ethnomethodological inquiry. Subsequent ethnomethodological research and theory begins with Garfinkel's insights and takes them in a variety of directions.

Garfinkel's work establishes ethnomethodology as a field of inquiry which seeks to understand the methods employed by people to make sense out of their world. He places considerable emphasis on language as the vehicle by which this reality construction is done. Indeed, for Garfinkel, interacting individuals' efforts to account for their actions— that is, to represent them verbally to others—is the primary method by which the world is constructed. In Garfinkel's terms, "to do interaction is to tell interaction"; or in other words, the primary folk technique used by actors is verbal description. In this way, people use their accounts to construct a sense of reality.

Garfinkel places enormous emphasis on indexicality—that is, on the fact that member's accounts are tied to particular contexts and situations. An utterance, Garfinkel notes, indexes much more than it actually says; it also evokes connotations that can only be understood in the context of a situation. Garfinkel's work was thus the first to stress the indexical nature of interpersonal cues and to emphasize that individuals seek to use accounts to create a sense of reality.

In addition to laying much of the groundwork for current ethnomethodology, Garfinkel and his associates conducted a number of interesting empirical studies in an effort to document the validity of their assumptions about "what is real." One line of empirical inquiry is known as the "breeching experiment" in which the normal course of interaction is deliberately interrupted. For example, Garfinkel reports a series of conversations in which student experimenters challenged every statement of selected subjects. The end result was a series of conversations revealing the following pattern:[15]

> **Subject:** I had a flat tire.
>
> **Experimenter:** What do you mean, you had a flat tire?

---

[14] Garfinkel, *Studies in Ethnomethodology.*
[15] Ibid., p. 42.

Subject (appears momentarily stunned and then replies in a hostile manner): What do you mean, "What do you mean?" A flat tire is a flat tire. That is what I meant. Nothing special. What a crazy question!

In this situation, the experimenter was apparently violating an implicit rule for this type of interaction situation and thereby aroused not only the hostility of the subject but also a negative sanction, "What a crazy question!" Seemingly, in any interaction there are certain background features which "everyone should understand," and which "should not be questioned" in order that all parties to the situation be able to "conduct their common conversational affairs without interference."[16] Such implicit methods appear to guide a considerable amount of everyday affairs and are critical for the construction of at least the perception among interacting humans that an external social order exists. In this conversation, for example, the "et cetera principle" and the "search for the normal form" are being invoked by the subject. Through breeching, Garfinkel hoped to discover implicit ethnomethods by forcing actors to *actively* engage in the process of reality reconstruction after the situation had been disrupted.

Other research strategies also yielded insights into the methods used by parties to an interaction for constructing a sense of reality. Garfinkel and his associates summarized the "decision rules" jurors employed in reaching a verdict.[17] By examining a group such as a jury, which must—by the nature of its task—develop an interpretation of "what really happened," the ethnomethodologist might achieve some insight into the generic properties of the processes of constructing a sense of "social reality." From the investigators' observations of jurors, it appeared that "a person is 95 percent juror before he comes near the court," indicating that through their participation in other social settings and through instructions from the court they had come to accept the "official" rules for reaching a verdict. However, these rules were altered somewhat as participants came together in an actual jury setting and began the "work of assembling the 'corpus' which serves as grounds for inferring the correctness of a verdict."[18] Because the inevitable ambiguities of the cases before them made difficult strict conformity to the "official rules" of jury deliberation, new decision rules were invoked in order to allow jurors to achieve a "correct" view of "what actually happened." But in their retrospective reporting to interviewers of how they reached their

---

[16] Ibid.
[17] Ibid., pp. 104–15.
[18] Ibid., p. 110.

decision, jurors typically invoked the "official line" to justify the correctness of their decisions. When interviewers drew attention to discrepancies between the jurors' ideal accounts and actual practices, jurors became anxious, indicating that somewhat different rules had been used to construct the corpus of "what really happened."

In sum, these two examples of Garfinkel's research strategy illustrate the general intent of much ethnomethodological research: to penetrate natural social settings or create social settings in which the investigator can observe humans attempting to assert, create, maintain, or change the rules for constructing the appearance of consensus over the structure of the "real world." By focusing on the process or methods for constructing "a reality," rather than on the substance or content of the reality itself, research from the ethnomethodological point of view can potentially provide a more interesting and relevant answer to the question of "how and why society is possible." Garfinkel's studies have stimulated a variety of research and theoretical strategies. Several of the most prominent strategies are briefly discussed below.

Harvey Sacks' Linguistic Analysis

Until his untimely death in 1976, Harvey Sacks exerted considerable influence within ethnomethodology. While his work is not well known outside ethnomethodological circles, it represents an attempt to extend Garfinkel's concern with verbal accounts, while at the same time to eliminate some of the problems posed by the fact of indexicality.

Sacks was one of the first ethnomethodologists to articulate the phenomenological critique of sociology and to use this critique to build an alternative form of theorizing.[19] The basic thrust of Sacks' critique can be stated as follows: Sociologists assume that language is a resource used in generating concepts and theories of the social world. In point of fact, however, sociologists are confusing resource and topic. In using language, sociologists are creating a reality; their words are not a neutral vehicle but *the* topic of inquiry for true sociological analysis.[20]

Sacks' solution to this problem in sociology is typical of phenomenologists. If the pure properties of language can be understood, then it would be possible to have an objective social science without confusing resource with subject matter. Sacks' own research tended to concentrate on the

---

[19] Harvey Sacks, "Sociological Description," *Berkeley Journal of Sociology* 8 (1963): 1–17.

[20] Harvey Sacks, "An Initial Investigation of the Usability of Conversational Data for Doing Sociology" in David Sundow, ed., *Studies in Interaction* (New York: Free Press, 1972).

formal properties of language in use. Typically, Sacks would take verbatim transcripts of actors in interaction and seek to understand the formal properties of the conversation, ignoring its substance. Such a tactic "resolved" the problem of indexicality, since Sacks simply ignored the substance and context of conversation and focused on its form. For example, "sequences of talk" among actors might occupy his attention.[21]

Sacks thus began to take ethnomethodology into formal linguistics. More importantly, he sought to discover universal forms of interaction— that is, abstracted patterns of "talk"—that might apply to all conversations. In this way, he began to search for the laws of reality construction among interacting individuals.

Aaron Cicourel's Cognitive Approach

In his *Method and Measurement in Sociology*,[22] Aaron Cicourel, launched a line of attack on sociology similar to that of Sacks'. The use of mathematics, he argued, will not remove the problems associated with language, because mathematics is a language which does not necessarily correspond to the phenomena that it is used to describe:[23] "[It] . . . distorts and obliterates, acts as a filter or grid for that which will pass as knowledge in a given era." The use of statistics similarly distorts: Events cannot be counted, averaged, and otherwise manipulated. Such statistical manipulations soon make sociological descriptions inaccurate and mold sociological analysis to the dictates of statistical logic.

In a less severe tone, Cicourel also questions Garfinkel's assertion that interaction and accounts are the same process.[24] He notes that humans see, sense, and feel much that they cannot communicate with words. Humans use "multiple-modalities" for communicating in situations. Verbal accounts represent crude and incomplete translations of what is actually communicated in interaction. This recognition has led Cicourel to rename his brand of ethnomethodology "cognitive sociology."

The details of his analysis are less important than the general intent of his effort to transform sociological research and theory. Basically, he has sought to uncover the universal "interpretive procedures" by which

---

[21] His best-known study, for example, is the co-authored article (with Emmanuel Schegloff and Gail Jefferson), "A Simplest Systematics for the Analysis of Turn Taking in Conversation," *Language* 50 (1974): 696–735.

[22] Aaron V. Cicourel, *Method and Measurement in Sociology* (New York: Free Press, 1964).

[23] Ibid., p. 35.

[24] "Cross Modal Communication" in R. Shuy, ed., *Linguistics and Language Science, Monograph 25* (Washington, D.C.: Gerogetown University Press, 1973).

humans organize their cognitions and give meaning to situations.[25] It is through these interpretive procedures that people develop a "sense of social structure" and are able to organize their actions. These interpretive procedures are universal and invariant in humans; and their discovery would allow for understanding of how humans create a "sense of social structure" in the world around them.

Zimmerman's, Pollner's, and Wieder's Situational Approach

Sacks and Cicourel have focused on the universal properties, respectively, of language-use and cognitive perception/representation. This concern with invariance, or universal "folk methods," has become increasingly prominent in ethnomethodological inquiry. Don Zimmerman, D. Lawrence Wieder, and Melvin Pollner have, in a number of essays,[26] similarly developed an approach that seeks to uncover the universal procedures employed by people to construct a sense of reality. Their position is perhaps the most clearly stated, drawing inspiration from Garfinkel, but extending his ideas. Their basic approach can be stated as follows:

1. In all interaction situations humans attempt to construct the appearance of consensus over relevant features of the interaction setting.
2. These setting features can include attitudes, opinions, beliefs, and other cognitions about the nature of the social setting in which they interact.
3. Humans engage in a variety of explicit and implicit interpersonal practices and methods to construct, maintain, and perhaps alter *the appearance* of consensus over these setting features.
4. Such interpersonal practices and methods result in the assembling and disassembling of what can be termed an "occasioned corpus"— that is, the *perception* by interacting humans that the current setting has an orderly and understandable structure.
5. This appearance of consensus is not only the result of agreement on the substance and content of the occasioned corpus, but also a reflection of each participant's compliance with the "rules" and "procedures" for assemblage and disassemblage of this consensus. In communicating, in however subtle a manner, that parties accept

---

[25] See, for example, his *Cognitive Sociology;* "Basic and Normative Rules in the Negotiation of Status and Role" in H. D. Dreitzel, ed., *Recent Sociology No. 2* (New York: Macmillan, 1970).

[26] See, for example: Zimmerman and Pollner, "The World as a Phenomenon"; Zimmerman and Wieder, "Ethnomethodology and the Problem of Order"; Wieder, *Language and Social Reality.*

the implicit rules for constructing an occasioned corpus, they go a long way to establishing consensus over what is "out there" in the interaction setting.

6. In each interaction situation, the rules for constructing the occasioned corpus will be unique in some respects and hence not completely generalizable to other settings—thus requiring that humans in each and every interaction situation use interpersonal methods in search for agreement on the implicit rules for the assemblage of an occasioned corpus.

7. Thus, by constructing, reaffirming, or altering the rules for constructing an occasioned corpus, members in a setting are able to offer to each other the appearance of an orderly and connected world "out there" which "compels" certain perceptions and actions on their part.

It is from these kinds of assumptions about human interaction that Zimmerman's, Pollner's, and Wieder's ethnomethodology takes its subject matter. Rather than focusing on the actual content and substance of the occasioned corpus and on the ways members believe it to force certain perceptions and actions, attention is drawn primarily to the *methods humans use to construct, maintain, and change* the appearance of an orderly and connected social world. These methods are directly observable and constitute a major portion of people's actions in everyday life. In contrast, the actual substance and content of the occasioned corpus is not directly observable and can only be inferred. Furthermore, in concentrating on the *process* of creating, sustaining, and changing the occasioned corpus, the ethnomethodologist can ask: Is not a more fundamental answer to the Hobbesian problem of order being provided? Indeed, is not the process of creating for each other the appearance of a stable social order more critical to understanding how society is possible than the actual substance and content of the occasioned corpus? Is there anything more to "society" than members' beliefs that it is "out there" forcing them to do and see certain things? If this fact is true, "order" is not the result of the particular structure of the corpus, but of the human capacity to continually assemble and disassemble the corpus in each and every interaction situation. These facts suggest to the ethnomethodologist that theoretical attention should therefore be placed upon the ongoing process of assembling and disassembling the appearance of "social order" and to the particular methods people employ in doing so.

This concern with the processes of assembling and disassembling the occasioned corpus represents a radical departure from traditional modes of sociological theorizing. Most theoretical perspectives, and certainly each of those covered in Chapters 2 through 17 conceptualize the occasioned corpus itself rather than the processes of its creation, maintenance, and alteration.

In contemporary sociological theorizing, analytical attention focuses on the norms, values, perceived exchange payoffs, definitions of the situation, and other features of interaction settings created by actors. In fact, from the ethnomethodological perspective, sociological formulations themselves represent a particular vision of reality among the members of a community called professional sociology. Each of the theoretical perspectives covered in Parts 1 through 4 of this volume can, from an ethnomethodological point of view, be analyzed as assertions about the nature of what is "out there" in the "real" world, with the result that the methods employed by sociologists to create, sustain, and change these assertions could be a fertile field of study for the ethnomethodologist.

ETHNOMETHODOLOGY AND THE PROBLEM OF ORDER: A CONCLUDING COMMENT

In Chapter 1 the task of sociological theorizing was viewed as that of providing a "solution" to the Hobbesian "problem of order." This solution was visualized as documenting with verified abstract statements the conditions under which various patterns of social organization were created, maintained, changed, and broken down. The succeeding chapters have focused on the concepts, propositions, theoretical formats, and strategies of the functional, conflict, interactionist, and exchange perspectives. Each of these perspectives was seen to hold to the assumption that there is a "natural order out there" existing independently of peoples' perceptions.[27] In fact, such perceptions and other forms of human cognition are in part structured by the real social order. Theory building and research are thus directed to discerning the regularities in the operation of this social order—thereby offering a scientific solution to how and why society is possible.

In contrast with these assumptions and theory-building strategies are the views of ethnomethodologists, which call into question the relevance

---

[27] For an interesting discussion of this assumption that challenges the ethnomethodological perspective, see Bill Harrell, "Symbols, Perception, and Meaning," in *Sociological Theory: Inquiries and Paradigms*, ed. Llewellyn Gross (New York: Harper & Row, 1967), pp. 104–27.

of this pursuit. What is most readily observable, and hence real, are the attempts by interacting humans to persuade each other that there is an order to specific social settings and to a broader "society." What is "really real," then, are the methods people employ in constructing, maintaining, and altering for each other a sense of order—regardless of the content and substance of their formulations. While not all ethnomethodologists would go this far, it is a reasonable conclusion that "order" is not maintained by some society "out there," but by *peoples' capacity to convince each other* that society is out there. Furthermore, the substance and content of their visions of society are perhaps not as important in maintaining order as the continually ongoing *processes* of constructing, maintaining, and altering some kind of vision, whatever it may be. The ethnomethodological solution to the Hobbesian problem of order is thus radically different from that proposed by current theoretical strategies, since for the ethnomethodologist, efforts should be directed toward developing a body of abstract and verified theoretical statements on the generic properties of how actors go about invoking and using rules for constructing a "sense of social order." The "sense of order" is not what makes society possible, but the capacity of humans to *actively and continually* create and use methods for persuading each other that there is a real world.

From an ethnomethodological point of view, the pages of this volume—including those of this last chapter—constitute a phenomenon for study. For, indeed, the author has attempted throughout to persuade the reader that there are preferable ways of conceptualizing the social world. Some of the methods that have been invoked to accomplish this task remain hidden, enabling the author to offer this book as data for study by ethnomethodologists.

Indexes

NAME INDEX

SUBJECT INDEX

431

This book has been set in 10 and 9 point Avanta, leaded 3 points. Part numbers are 32 point Compano and part titles are 22 point Compano. Chapter numbers are 72 point Caslon and chapter titles are 18 point Compano. The size of the type page is 27 by 46 picas.